CW01511081

Musical Instrument Makers of New York

A Directory of Eighteenth-and Nineteenth-Century
Urban Craftsmen

The first permanent factory and warerooms of Steinway & Sons, at 82-88 Walker Street c. 1858. The firm's entire staff have assembled on the sidewalk for the picture.

MUSICAL INSTRUMENT MAKERS OF NEW YORK

A Directory of Eighteenth-and Nineteenth-Century Urban Craftsmen

by
Nancy Groce

ANNOTATED REFERENCE TOOLS IN MUSIC No. 4

PENDRAGON PRESS
STUYVESANT, NY

Additional Titles in the Annotated Reference Tools In Music Series:

1. *Heinrich Schenker: Index to Analysis* by Larry Laskowski (1978) ISBN 0-918728-06-1

2. *Padre Martini's Collection of Letters in the Civico Museo Bibliografico Musicale in Bologna: An annotated index* by Anne Schnoebelen (1979) ISBN 0-918728-11-8

3. *Pleyel as Music Publisher* by Rita Benton (1990) ISBN 0-918728-61-4

Library of Congress Cataloging-in-Publication Data

Groce, Nancy
    Musical instrument makers of New York: a directory of eighteenth- and nineteenth-century urban craftsmen / by Nancy Groce.
      p. cm. -- (Annotated reference tools in music ; no. 4)
      Includes bibliographic references.
      ISBN 0-918728-97-5 : $64.00
      1. Musical instrument makers--New York (N.Y.)--Biography--Dictionaries.
    I. Title. II. Series
      ML404.G76 1991
      784.19'092'27471--dc20   91-37076
      [B]   CIP
                               MN

CONTENTS

LIST OF ILLUSTRATIONS

PREFACE

The present volume documents the careers of hundreds of musical instrument makers who were active in the City of New York before 1890. From its humble eighteenth-century beginnings, instrument making grew to be one of the city's largest and most important trades. By the 1840s, the city was the largest producer of instruments in the Western Hemisphere, and, in the decades that followed, designs and innovations pioneered by New York artisans influenced and inspired instrument makers throughout the world.

Today, little remains to remind us of this craft which sought to combine industry with art. Due to the lack of readily accessible information, modern researchers have tended to overlook New York's significant contributions to the history of organology. I decided to undertake research on the New York instrument trade after working with the collections of several large American museums. In their storerooms, I found scores of New York-made instruments, but it was difficult, and sometimes impossible, to locate information about their makers. My hope is that the research herein will help remedy this situation.

Prior to 1890, New York City included only the present borough of Manhattan; makers who worked in the greater metropolitan area await future study. Information on organ builders has not been included, since this topic was recently documented in John Ogasapian's *Organ Building in New York City: 1700-1900* (1977); nor does space permit the identification of the thousands of music store owners and sheet music dealers who worked in the industry. However, this directory does list all other *master-craftsmen* known to be active in the trade during this period.

Although it is not possible to include the names of all the scholars throughout the United States and Europe who generously assisted me with my research, before proceeding I would like to acknowledge the special contributions of several individuals and organizations. Initial research on this topic was made possible by an Andrew W. Mellon Fellowship to the Department of Musical Instruments, Metropolitan Museum of Art. Special thanks to Laurence Libin, the Metropolitan's Curator of Musical Instruments, for his help and advice; and to Dr. Richard Crawford, of the University of Michigan, who assisted me with the initial presentation of this research as a dissertation. I am indebted to Drs. Robert Berkhofer, Marion Marzolf, and Yvonne Lockwood of Ann Arbor, Michigan, for their advice; and to Eric Selch, John Ogasapian, and Robert Sheldon for information on specific makers. Dr. Robert Eliason and Vera Brodsky Lawrence earned my deepest gratitude for unselfishly sharing their unpublished research with me in order that this study would be more complete. My personal thanks to Deborah Autorino, who assisted me in the preparation of this manuscript, to Dr. Martin Burke for his suggestions, and to Raymond and Marian Groce for their support and encouragement. I would also like to express my appreciation to the staffs of the New York Public Library, the New York Genealogical and Biographical Society, the Thomas C. Watson Library at the Metropolitan Museum, and the New-York Historical Society's Library, who were unfailingly helpful and cooperative during my prolonged visits to their institutions; and to the Program in American Culture at the University of Michigan for intellectual and financial support. Finally, I wish to thank Robert Kessler and Pendragon Press for their assistance in the preparation of this manuscript for publication.

A fashionably-dressed young lady plays a Firth, Hall & Pond upright piano in this advertising lithograph c. 1843.

INTRODUCTION

The history of any skilled urban trade is ultimately tied to the growth and development of the city in which it is located. In New York, the musical instrument-making trade did not secure a firm foothold until the middle of the eighteenth century, when the wealth and population of the city had grown large enough to support the manufacture of luxury goods.

The present City of New York was founded as the colony of New Amsterdam by representatives of the Dutch West India Company in 1624. European music was performed, at least on an amateur level, by the first settlers, who had musical instruments imported for their use. The earliest known record of musical instruments in New Amsterdam is contained in a letter dated 1659, sent by the Directors of the Dutch West India Company in Holland to the colonists with a shipment of supplies, in which they mentioned including the "drums requested for the train-band . . . also some drumskins, snares and strings, to be used when necessary." (**Stokes** 1915: I: 70)

The British, who wrested control of the colony from the Dutch in 1664, brought about little change in the prevailing liberal attitudes towards music and musical entertainment in New York. During the eighteenth century, New Yorkers enjoyed theatrical performances and concerts of both sacred and secular music. Choral societies and music teachers flourished as New York's worldly and prosperous merchant population supported music in their homes, churches, and theatres.

The earliest professional musical instrument maker in New York seems to have been a colorful, if somewhat obscure craftsman named Geoffrey Stafford. Stafford, a London-born luthier and part-time criminal, was deported to Massachusetts in 1691. Once there, he continued his career as an instrument maker for only a short time before finding a more exciting calling as an Indian fighter on the Albany frontier. His success in Albany prompted Benjamin Fletcher, then Royal Governor of New York, to offer him a regular military commission in the city. During his stay in New York, Stafford reportedly built several lutes and violins, but soon managed to incur the Governor's displeasure when he "ran Fletcher's favorite body-servant through with the governor's sword." (**Spillane** 1890: 74-75) Very shortly thereafter, Stafford left the city, apparently moving to the Hudson River Valley where he was reportedly hanged for attempted robbery.

There is no record of another musical instrument maker in New York until 1739. On June 1st of that year, the vestry of Trinity Church at Broadway and Wall Street, voted that John Clemm (or Klemm), an organ builder from Philadelphia, "be forthwith employed to make an organ." (**Ogasapian** 1977:3) Clemm's church organ was completed in 1741 and served the parish until 1762, when it was replaced with a larger instrument imported from England.

Many of the earliest records pertaining to instrument building in New York concern church organs. This does not mean that other types of instruments were not being made, imported, or played, only that the records documenting smaller instruments were less likely to be preserved in official archives. Among the instruments popular in eighteenth-century New York were flutes, oboes, bassoons, horns, trumpets, violins, viols, lutes, guitars, citterns, fifes, harpsichords, dulcimers, kitts, drums, harps, and bagpipes.

After 1750, newspaper advertisements began to more frequently announce the work and wares of city-based instrument makers. The first instrument maker to advertise seems to have been Gilbert Ash, who on March 15, 1756, gave notice in the *New York Mercury* that:

> For the Benefit of a Poor Widow, on Thursday the 18th Instant, will be open'd at the City-Hall, in the City of New York, A NEW ORGAN, made by Gilbert Ash . . . who continues the Business of Organ building, by who Gentlemen and Ladies, may be furnished with that noble Instrument, in a convenient Times after it is bespoken.

Ash later advertised himself as a maker of soap, candles, and furniture, so it is possible that the public's response to his advertisement was not overwhelming.

During the following decades, the arrival of several more professionally trained instrument makers firmly established the craft in New York. Many of these newly arrived makers found it expedient to combine the manufacture of new instruments with the sale of imported instruments and sheet music, and the repair of older instruments. In 1761, for example, David Wolhaupter, "living at the Sign of the Musical instrument-Maker," advertised that "he continues to make and mend, all Sorts of Musical Instruments, such as German Flutes, Hautboys, Clareonets, Bassoons, Fifes; and also Silver Tea-Pot Handles." (*New York Gazette*, Nov. 16, 1761)

Wolhaupter's versatility was not unusual. The age of specialization was yet to dawn, and most New York makers advertised their ability to make, or at least mend, any type of musical instrument. Specialists like Samuel Brouwer, who made only drums at his King George Street shop in 1787, were very much the exception. For some craftsmen, instrument making was only one of the ways to earn a living. It entailed many of the same woodworking skills needed for the construction of furniture, and quite a few instrument makers were cabinetmakers at some point in their careers. Likewise, the turning of wood and ivory on hand-powered lathes was a specialized craft, and during the eighteenth century, umbrella makers, whose vocation also involved the use of lathes, sometimes advertised their ability to make turned woodwind instruments such as flutes and oboes.

A wonderful example of the industry and versatility of New York's early instrument makers was Joseph Adams Fleming, who in 1785 advertised:

> Joseph Adams Fleming who for many years carried on the HARPSICHORD making, CABINET UPHOLSTERY AND TRUNK WORK in Europe, begs leave to offer himself to the Gentry & Public in general, for their Patronage and Protection. He has taken the House No. 27 Crown Street, where he intends carrying on the above branches, vis: Harpsichords made, sold, bought, exchanged or lent at quarterly payments . . . desks, tallboys shaving tables, soffas, wardrobes, clock cases . . . state and canopy beds . . . parlour and fire screens, Venetian blinds, bed and window curtains, window cornishes in wood or paper mache, moulding gilt and plain, paper hung on shortest notice, feather beds, mattrasses with sacking bottoms, and umbrellas made and repaired: Trunk work in all its branches, vis. camp, couch, and portmanuta trunks . . . fiddle and guitar cases . . . canteens and valeeses, furr caps and band boxes . . . the best varnishes in oyl and spirits, gold lacker, fat oil . . . a few chests of toys . . . and a Bird Organ with twenty tunes on two barrels.[1]

Advertisements by city instrument makers decreased during the Revolutionary War; probably due to a drop in the number of newspapers being published rather than to a decline in the trade. After the withdrawal of American troops from New York in November 1776, the city became the center of British military operations in North America until the signing of the Treaty of Paris in February 1783. During those eight years, thousands of British officers and soldiers were stationed in New York. Their presence, and that of their camp followers and loyalist refugees, swelled the city's population to a new high of perhaps 33,000 persons. Far from the front lines, and faced with long periods of calm between military operations, the residents of New York had both the time and the money for

---

[1]See Joseph Adams Fleming, p.53.

leisure activities. An increased number of theatrical performances, concerts and social functions during the war helped stimulate demand for musical instruments. In addition, New York instrument makers benefited from a widespread boycott of British-made goods by members of the American public. When the boycott was discontinued after the war, local instrument makers suffered from renewed competition as great numbers of British-made instruments were again imported.

During the post-war years, a new wave of immigrant instrument makers arrived in the city. Why these craftsmen, some of whom were well-established in Europe, chose to emigrate to New York is not always clear. A few probably came to escape restrictive guild regulations, others with the hope of financial success, or to improve their social status. Typical of many of these post-war immigrants was the guitar maker Christian Claus, who moved from Germany to London sometime before 1783. Claus was apparently quite successful in England, but in 1789 he decided to immigrate to New York, where he set up shop, first on Partition Street and later on Dover Street. In 1791, Claus joined another recent immigrant, the key-board maker Thomas Dodds, to establish the partnership Dodds & Claus, which claimed to make "every kind of musical instrument . . . finished according to the present taste, and with the latest improvements." (**Diary; or Loudon's Register**, [N.Y.] Sept. 19, 1792)

CRAFTSMEN AND WORKING CONDITIONS

Like most eighteenth-century artisans, musical instrument makers usually worked in small shops under the direct supervision of a mastercraftsman. The typical New York craftsman of the late-eighteenth or early-nineteenth centuries lived in a small two- or three-storied house. His workshop was usually located on the ground floor, which left the basement, kitchen, and upper stories of the house free for use as his family's living quarters. Heavy woodworking tasks, such as sawing, planing, and sanding were done in barn-like buildings located in the rear of the craftsman's property. The front room, which opened onto the street, served as a showroom for the artisan's finished products, and was managed by the craftsman, his wife, or another member of his family.

In early nineteenth-century New York, a variety of terms were used to describe skilled craftsmen: mastercraftsman, mechanic, artisan, artificer, and journeyman were all used interchangeably. By the 1820s, however, the term *mastercraftsman* was increasingly applied to the owner of a workshop. The master, in turn, employed two main types of labor: the *journeyman* and the *apprentice.*

As in other cities, New York apprentices were young workers still involved in learning their trade. Apprentices working in New York shops, however, had somewhat more social freedom and economic leverage than did their European counterparts. Skilled craftsmen were in great demand throughout America, and there was little incentive for a young man to spend years apprenticing, when with a minimum of training apprentices could, and often did, establish shops of their own. This reality was reflected by the repeated liberalization of New York's apprenticeship laws during the seventeenth and eighteenth centuries. By the late eighteenth century, it was common for masters to pay their apprentices a small amount in wages, and for the young men to board outside their master's house.

If a master required more skilled help than an apprentice could provide, he often hired a *journeyman.* Journeymen—or, as they were commonly called, mechanics—were free-lance workers who were hired for the completion of a specific task: for example, the making of a piano case, or the carving of a violin scroll. Journeymen usually owned their own tools, and in most cases were paid for their work "by the piece" rather than receiving daily wages. The piece-work system was so deeply rooted in the New York instrument trade that it continued to be the standard method of compensation even after large factories had replaced smaller workshops.

By 1810, the successful mastercraftsman might expect to accumulate a moderate worth of $2,000 in house, land, and property. Journeymen usually earned enough to live on, but seldom owned more than $150 worth of personal property, and, unlike their employers, almost never owned a house or land. There is no record of any early nineteenth-century New York instrument maker accumulating a substantial amount of money, and some, like pianomaker Archibald Whaites, died in straitened circumstances. Later in the century, however, the owners of some of the larger piano firms—such as William Steinway and Albert Weber—would make sizeable fortunes in the trade.

An examination of the careers of nineteenth-century New York instrument makers suggests that few successful artisans continued to work as journeymen past their early twenties. Many journeymen were content to spend the rest of their careers working for a mastercraftsmen, but for the ambitious, several avenues of advancement were open. Journeymen, especially those working in small shops, might eventually be asked to join the firm as partners. In such cases, the journeyman's name would be added to the firm's title, usually after the names of the older and more experienced "senior" partners. Other journeymen, especially those working in large shops where the likelihood of being asked to join the partnership was remote, often left to form their own shops. They frequently went into partnership with one or two other young journeymen. Many failed, yet, even with their often limited skills, equipment, and capital, a fair number succeeded.

Because skilled craftsmen were at a premium, partnerships provided a way for journeymen to enjoy the prestige of being mastercraftsmen, while at the same time pooling their skills and resources and dividing the work. Partnerships had a rapid turnover rate. Many lasted only two or three years, and it was a rare craftsman who did not enter into several partnerships during the course of his career. The musical instrument trade was a closely knit one. During the eighteenth and nineteenth centuries, the swapping of partners, business locations, workshops, and inventories on the commercial side, mirrored in-group social interactions as makers and their relatives intermarried, named children for one another, and apprenticed relatives in each other's shops.

Many instrument makers were active in the trade for only a few years. These craftsmen usually came from allied crafts such as carpentry or cabinet making, and worked as instrument makers for only a few years before moving on or returning to another trade. A few were musicians who built an occasional instrument for extra income or for the use of their students. The names of many instrument makers appear in New York records for only one or two years before suddenly disappearing, leaving no trace of their subsequent activities.

NINETEENTH-CENTURY EXPANSION

During the 1790s, twenty-one instrument-making firms were active in New York: fifteen general "musical instruments" makers, two organ builders, one drummaker, one bell founder, and two manufacturers of that newly fashionable instrument, the piano. Pianos were introduced in New York during the 1770s, and in the years that followed they quickly replaced harpsichords as the standard keyboard instrument. The enormous popularity of the piano during the first half of the nineteenth century led to the rapid expansion of New York's instrument-making trade. By the late 1820s, instrument making rivaled shipbuilding, sugar refining, metal working, and furniture making as one of the largest industries in the city.

(**Ernst** 1949:17) During the following decade, led by the continued growth of the city's piano manufacturers, New York surpassed Philadelphia as the leading center of instrument making in North America.

Early New York pianos were usually of the square variety and most were modeled on British-made instruments. By the 1820s, however, a recognizable local style had evolved. New York pianos tended to be quite heavy in weight and form. Many were made with massive wooden bottom planks up to five inches in thickness. Despite the use of this heavy interior bracing, New York artisans were often able to make instruments into elegant pieces of furniture. Solid rectangular outer cases were frequently supported by four or six gracefully carved legs, sometimes ending in the "hairy paw" foot found on other pieces of early nineteenth-century New York furniture. Pianos cases often rested on separately constructed trestle tables, fitted with shallow drawers for the storage of sheet music. New York pianos tended to be liberally decorated with inlays of expensive woods, elaborately carved fretwork, painted and stenciled decorations, and often featured on their fallboards the elegantly scripted names and addresses of their makers.

The most distinctive part of New York pianos, however, was not their external decorations but their innovative internal designs. As pianists began to demand greater volume, range and tone from their instruments, piano makers throughout the world experimented with various methods of enlarging their instruments. Many New York makers turned away from the use of massive internal bracing for these larger instruments, experimenting first with hollow metal bars, known as "compensating tubes," and then with molded cast-iron frames. A major improvement in cast-iron frames was patented in the 1850s by the New York firm of Steinway & Sons, and the widespread acclaim this firm achieved after winning a gold medal at the 1862 London's World Fair directed serious international attention to other innovations being made in city workshops.

In order to manufacture these larger and more complex pianos, New York's master-craftsmen required larger workshops and a greater investment in stock and equipment. Whereas the average late eighteen-shop century rarely employed more than one master-craftsman and his assistants, shops of the 1830s and 1840s began to employ greater numbers of workers. The increasing size of instrument-making shops also brought about a change in socio-economic terminology. As shops added extra journeymen and semi-skilled workers—who were still referred to as apprentices even though they were now fully paid for their services—the mastercraftsman's shop became a *manufactory,* and he, in turn, became a *manufacturer.* These terms, however, must be viewed in their proper mid-nineteenth-century contexts. Although some piano firms, such as Steinway & Sons, did build larger and larger workshops, a *manufactory* or *factory* did not necessarily refer to a giant highly mechanized operation, but rather to an establishment "where raw materials can be converted into finished goods by consecutive, harmonious processes carried along by a central power." (**Kirkland** 1961: 171)

Despite the increased size of some of New York's more successful instrument factories, what took place within them was usually just an expanded version of the eighteenth-century workshop. Deeply held beliefs about the importance of individual work and the value of hand-craftsmanship mitigated against change. The mechanization of the instrument trade seems to have been resisted by both mastercraftsmen and workers. Until the middle of the twentieth century, journeymen, even in the largest New York instrument factories, often worked with their own tools, on their own benches, and at their own pace under the personal supervision of the shop-owning mastercraftsman.[2]

In addition to the expansion of instrument shops, the mid-nineteenth century also saw a shift in the immigration patterns of instrument

---

[2]See **Groce,** *Manufacturing Harmony* (Pendragon Press 1992 [in press]).

makers. In the 1820s, economic difficulties in Great Britain had caused the displacement of many skilled British craftsmen: William and Robert Nunns, John Stodart, Morgan Davis, and John Kearsing were among the well-known craftsmen who migrated to New York during that period. During the 1830s and 1840s, however, instrument makers began to arrive in significant numbers from Germany and central Europe. These German-speaking workers initially entered the trade as journeymen, but many quickly rose to the rank of shop supervisor, and some eventually established shops of their own. The 1855 New York Census found that 553 of the 836 instrument makers then living in New York were immigrants, and of these, 58% were German. In fact, German participation in the trade was so pronounced that when the city's piano makers first met to organize a union in 1860, the meeting was conducted in German.

During the eighteenth century, the instrument trade was located primarily on the east side of Manhattan. As New York's commercial district gradually moved uptown during the early nineteenth century, the instrument shops followed; many moving to the newly fashionable area around the recently constructed City Hall at Broadway and Chambers Street. The retail music business then moved progressively northward: first establishing itself along the Bowery near Cooper Square in the 1850s, then moving to 14th Street during the 1870s and 1880s. The movement uptown also answered the need of some shops, especially piano shops, for more work space. By the end of the century, an increase in shop size, combined with skyrocketing land values, made it economically unfeasible for instrument makers to remain in Manhattan. Many firms moved their factories to the undeveloped farm lands of the outer boroughs, keeping only a small salesroom in the city.

DECLINE OF THE TRADE

In 1861 it was claimed that "the capital invested in the manufacture of pianofortes alone in the United States is fully equal to that employed in the manufacture of cotton goods." (*American Musical Directory* 1861: xiv) The expansion of the trade was noted with pride by government officials who saw in the growth of this art-related industry a reflection of America's bright future. "Our advancement and refinement," one wrote in 1862, "is attested to by the rapid increase in the manufacture of pianofortes and other Musical Instruments." (**U.S. Office of the Census,** *Preliminary Report* 1862: 69) Another noted that "the extent and perfection to which the manufacture of music is carried at the present day may be safely received as an index of the general progress of mankind in civilization and social comfort." (**U.S. Office of the Census,** *Eighth Census* 1865: cxlvi) The expansion of the New York musical instrument trade continued unabated until the 1890s. According the 1890 Federal Census, 131 instrument-making firms were then located in the city. These firms employed 5,958 craftsmen

who that year produced $12,824,451 worth of musical instruments; 41% of the national total for the industry. (**U.S. Office of the Census,** *Report on Manufacturers* 1895: 2: 402, 645)

The 1890s was the zenith of the instrument-making trade in New York. Soon thereafter, a succession of technological innovations and socio-economic changes reversed the fortunes of the industry. The former began with the introduction of the automated "player piano." With player pianos, it was no longer necessary to make music oneself: the average American could now be an observer rather than a participant in home music making. Initially, the trade benefited from huge sales of player pianos, but this boon was more than offset during the following decades as the concept of automation was extended, first to the phonograph and then the radio. By the 1930s, home-ownership of instruments was no longer essential for family musical entertainment.

Paralleling these technological changes were periods of economic uncertainty, beginning with the depression of the 1890s and extending through the Great Depression of the 1930s, which dampened musical instrument sales, and forced many instrument-making firms into bankruptcy. The hard-hit trade also suffered during the Second World War, when many of the larger piano factories were requisitioned by the War Department for the production of goods necessary to the war effort. Very few of the larger pianos factories were able to reopen after the war.

Today, many small ateliers making high-quality musical instruments are still found in New York, but the instrument-making trade no longer plays the major role it once did in the city's economic life. This directory documents the hundreds of craftsmen and firms that established New York as a major producer of musical instruments and their significant contributions to American musical history.

USING THE DIRECTORY

In this directory the term *mastercraftsman* is used to designate those artisans who owned their own workshops, and who were personally involved in the manufacturing of instruments. Most of these artisans were *practical* makers who spent long years learning their craft. Some, however, were shop owners and importers who merely bought and sold instruments. These "non-practical" businessmen often stamped or "stencilled" their names on instruments made by others, making it difficult in some cases to differentiate between actual makers and dealers.

The directory is organized alphabetically, and entries on individual craftsmen are followed by entries on their business partnerships. Partners and partnerships are listed under the name of the artisan whose name appears first in a firm's title. Where evidence suggests that a member of a partnership was not a practical craftsman, but a dealer, importer, shop owner, or family member who was only tangentially involved in the trade, his activities are discussed only in relation to his more prominent partner.

The names of craftsmen with separate entries are italicized; e.g., *Thomas Kearsing*. Unless otherwise indicated, all dates and addresses have been obtained from the *New York City Directory*. To keep the directory to a reasonable size without omitting ready access to documentation, the Harvard system of citation has been used. Each quotation or statement requiring documentation is followed by parentheses containing an author's surname, the year of publication, and the page(s) cited; e.g. (**Langwill** 1980:17). If the source of information is clear from the text, only the year of publication and page number(s) will be contained in the parentheses. A bibliography of all reference materials will be found on page 188.

For expediency, frequently cited references have been abbreviated: a list of these abbreviations will be found on page xx. This study ends with the year 1890; however, all craftsmen and firms which continued in operation past that date are indicated with the notation "1890+."

SOURCES

Among the primary sources used in this study were city, regional, and trade directories, census reports, catalogs of fairs, autobiographical memoirs, newspapers, periodicals, and extant instruments. Secondary sources included books, articles, biographical dictionaries, local histories, genealogical records, museum catalogs, interviews, and personal correspondence. For those unfamiliar with New York documents, a brief overview might be helpful.

PRIMARY SOURCES

Local Directories

Much of the information in this study comes from city directories. In New York, city directories were published by private printers almost every year from 1786 through 1890. Very much like present day "yellow pages," the directories contained names and addresses, but usually also included residents' occupations. Not all New Yorkers were listed in the directories; those listed tended to be the more prosperous property owners, while the names of many less-wealthy craftsmen were omitted.

Traditionally, moving day in New York was May 1st, and the city directories bore titles that reflected this; for example, *"Trow's New York City Directory for the Year Ending May 1, 1865."* In lieu of full citations, which are cumbersome, as well as confusing, directories are referred to solely by their year of publication. Thus, the preceding example will be referred to as the 1864 *New York City Directory*, or, when cited in abbreviated form, as the 1864 *NYCD*.

In addition to residential city directories, a *New York City Business Directory* was also published during the 1840s, 1850s, and 1860s, in which the names of craftsmen and firms were listed under general trade headings: e.g. as "keyboard," "brass," or "string" instrument makers. There was usually a great deal of overlap between the city and business directories.

Another frequently cited source of information is the *New York City Commercial Register*, "Containing the Cards of the Principal Merchants, Manufacturers, & c., in the City and Vicinity Classified According to the Business forming a Business Directory of Reliable Parties in all the Various Branches." (1864 *CmRg*) This compilation first appeared in 1856 as an addendum to the *New York City Directory*. Later, with the rise of cheap lithography, advertisements in the *Commercial Register* became quite elaborate. Not all manufacturers advertised in the *Commercial Register*; the names of smaller concerns are notably absent. Finally, the irregularly-published *New York City Co-Partnership Directory*, which first appeared in 1849, is also cited.

Regional and Trade Directories

Two national listings of workers in the music industry proved extremely valuable in identifying craftsmen. The earlier of the two, the *American Musical Directory, 1861*, contained a relatively complete listing of city instrument makers, and also helpfully differentiated between mastercraftsmen and journeymen. The *American Musical Directory of the United States and Provinces 1885*, was also a useful source; however, its publication was delayed for several years hence some of its entries were out-dated when it finally appeared in 1885.

Census Reports

Although the first federal census of manufacturers was conducted in 1810, the five subsequent censuses contained little relevant information. The "Schedule of Manufacturers" from the Ninth U.S. Census (1870), now located in the Office of the County Clerk for New York County in Manhattan, was the first to extensively record the activities of New York's instrument shops.

The State of New York conducted its own census every ten years from 1825 to 1875. Although compiled returns from each census were published, all city schedules, with the exception of the 1855 "Manufacturers Schedule," have been lost or destroyed. The latter may also be examined at the Office of the County Clerk for New York County.

Exhibitions and Fairs

Exhibitions and commercial fairs were extremely popular in the nineteenth century, and documents from these events provided useful information on city instrument makers. The papers of the American Institute of the City of New York, now at the New-York Historical Society, were particularly helpful. This organization, modeled on the earlier Franklin Institute of Philadelphia, was incorporated in 1828, "for the purpose of encouraging and promoting domestic industry." (**Wile** 1928: v.) To this end, the Institute organized annual fairs where American-made products were publicly exhibited, judged by a committee of selected experts, and awarded prizes. The first American Institute Fair was held in 1828 at the Masonic Hall on Broadway, with an opening address delivered by Edward Everett of Boston. Eventually, makers from all parts of the country competed at the American Institute fairs.

For city instrument makers, these fairs represented an opportunity to view the latest and best of their competitors' wares. From the start, musical instruments were exhibited and judged as a separate category. Winners received gold and silver medals or diplomas of merit, and many instrument makers mentioned their American Institute medals in later advertisements, or on the labels of their instruments. Most New York makers, even those with very small shops or those still working as journey-

men, entered samples in at least one American Institute fair.

The success of the American Institute led to the founding of a similar society known as the Mechanics' Institute of the City of New York, which was incorporated in 1833. It also held competitive exhibitions; but the records of the Mechanics' Society have not been located.

Extant Instruments and Museum Catalogs

Information about makers can often be obtained from the instruments they produced, and many New York-made instruments survive in museums and private collections. No attempt has been made to give locations of individual instruments, although references to secondary sources containing such information is included. Instrument labels were particularly useful in locating small-scale and semi-professional makers who did little advertising and were rarely listed in other sources.

Other Primary Sources

Some information on instrument makers was found in the *Minutes of the Common Council of the City of New York* (*MCC*), which contain information on property ownership, appointments to local offices—e.g., election supervisors, ward captains, and other posts frequented by craftsmen; as well as memberships in the volunteer fire engine companies, which seem to have been popular pastimes with apprentice instrument makers. Wills, birth certificates, partnership agreements, and other official documents were also consulted.

A number of other sources also contained valuable information, such as the Landauer Collection of the New-York Historical Society which has an outstanding collection of business cards, advertising flyers, and ephemera from the instrument trade. Also located at the New-York Historical Society are the manuscript records of the St. Andrews Society, various churchyard records, and diaries and letters from members of the trade. Correspondence and interviews with descendants of several instrument-making families also led to important information.

SECONDARY SOURCES

Histories written by members of the trade provided useful, if not always completely accurate, information. Daniel Spillane's *History of the American Pianoforte* (1890), and Alfred Dolge's *Pianos and Their Makers* (1911), are extremely informative about the piano trade. *George Gemunder's Progress in Violin Making* (1881), by the slightly eccentric luthier of the same name, discusses many stringed-instrument makers and dealers in great detail; and Morris Steinert's *Reminiscences* (1900), is a good source of period information on the American musical trade.

Although most general references on organology lack extensive information on New York makers, Langwill's *Index of Wind-Instrument Makers* (1980), Henley's *Universal Diction-ary of Violin and Bow Makers* (1959), Roda's *Bows for Musical Instruments of the Violin Family* (1959), and the *New Grove Dictionary* (1980) were helpful. Pierce's wildly uneven *Piano Atlas* (1965), and Ayar's *Contributions to the Art of Music in America by the Music Industries of Boston* (1937) were also occasionally useful.

Additional information about New York City instrument makers was obtained through the generosity of individual scholars. Data obtained from personal correspondence is noted by the abbreviation "PC" followed by the name of the source; for example, information contributed by Dr. Robert Eliason is noted in the Directory as (PC: Eliason).

ABBREVIATIONS USED IN THE DIRECTORY

In addition to standard abbreviations for streets, avenues, directions, cities, states, nations, etc., the following abbreviations and symbols are used in the Directory.

c.	circa
CmRg	*Commercial Register*
DAB	*Dictionary of American Biography*
DMC	*Dayton Miller Collection Catalogue* (Library of Congress)
h.	house (in *NYCD* for home address)
HFM	Henry Ford Museum (Dearborn, Michigan)
manuf	manufacturer
MCC	*Minutes of the Common Council of the City of New York*
MCMA	Massachusetts Charitable Mechanics' Association
mkr	maker
MMA	Metropolitan Museum of Art, NYC
mus instr mkr	musical instrument maker
n.	near
NCAB	*National Cyclopedia of American Biography*
NYBD	*New York Business Directory*
NYCD	*New York City Directory*
NY Co-Part	*New York Co-Partnership Directory*
NYHS	New-York Historical Society
PC	personal correspondence
SI	Smithsonian Institution
supt.	superintendent (i.e. shop manager)
V. & A.	Victoria & Albert Museum, London
1831 AAD	*American Advertising Directory* (1831)

1855 New York Census	Manufacturing Schedules of the 1855 New York State Census, Office of the County Clerk (MS)
1861 AMD	*American Musical Directory (1861)*
1870 U.S. Census	Manufacturing Schedules of the 1870 U.S. Federal Census
1885 AMD	*American Musical Directory of the United States and Provinces* (1885)
+	Used after a date to indicate that the firm continued in operation.
------	Symbol used in *NYCD* when an address/occupation was omitted.
Ackerly / Ackley	Used to indicate alternate spellings; most frequently used spelling appears first.
Child(s)	Name appeared both with and without letter(s) in parentheses.
"	Entry identical to that of the preceding year.

A

ABBOTT, John

1835	piano mkr	Walker
1836	"	Bowery
1837	"	325 Bowery
1838	"	Anthony
1839-40	"	385 Broadway
1841-42	"	83 Anthony

Abbott was born in 1815 in London. (**Kaufman** 1976:22) He and his brothers, James, Abiel and *William*, were involved in the manufacture of pianos. As a young man, Abbott immigrated to New York where he was trained in the shop of *R. & W. Nunns*. (**Spillane** 1890:159-60). Abbott's first shop was located at 66 Walker Street in 1835, and at that year's American Institute Fair, one of his pianos, said to be "possessed of great brilliancy of tone, pleasant touch, and made in a superior manner," was awarded a silver medal. At the 1836 Fair, the maker was awarded another silver medal "for the second best specimen of a horizontal grand action pianoforte. " (*American Institute Records*)

Spillane (1890:160) wrote that Abbott "went out of the trade in the course of a few years," but **Kaufman** (1976:22-24) found evidence that Abbott was working in New Jersey c. 1844. At one time, Abbott owned a hotel in Hackensack, New Jersey, and was involved with the piano-action-making firm Abbott & Sons of Fort Lee, New Jersey, which was owned by his brother James. John Abbott was still alive in 1890 when **Spillane** wrote his monograph on the piano trade.

ABBOTT, Nathaniel B.

1839	piano mkr	44 20th
1840	not listed	
1841	piano mkr	99 Eleventh
1842	"	9 Ave. 3
1843	pianos	20th c. Ave. 3
1844	"	E. 21st n. Broad-way
1845-46	not listed	
1847	pianos	Ave. 6 c. W. 26th
1848	"	Broadway c. W. 27th
1849	not listed	
1850+	policeman	E. 30th n. Ave. 3

Possibly a brother of *John Abbott* and *William Abbott*, Nathaniel left the piano trade to become a policeman. Later in the 1850s, he was listed as a carpenter in the *NYCD*.

ABBOTT, William

1834	piano mkr	9 Amity la.

A brother of *John Abbott*, William was born in 1816 in England. He worked in New York for only a short time before moving to New Jersey, where he was later involved with the piano-action-making firm Abbott & Sons owned by his brother James. William Abbott died in New Jersey during 1889. (**Kaufman** 1976:22-24; **Spillane** 1890:159-60)

ACKERLY / ACKLEY, Henry S.

1833-34	cabinet mkr	59 Norfolk
1835	"	47 Delancey
1836-44	"	30 Chrystie
1845	pianoforte mkr	E. 28th n. Ave. 3
1846	not listed	
1847	pianoforte mkr	50 E. 28th
1848	pianos	"
1849	"	E. 27th n. Ave. 1
1850-53	piano mkr	170 E. 27th
1854	"	231 Ave. 3
1856	"	170 E. 27th
1860-61	pianos	h. 361 Second

Ackerly, who was occasionally listed as Ackley, was a small scale piano manufacturer. **Spillane** (1890:197) referred to his firm as "Ackley & Company," but no record of this title is found in primary sources. Ackerly was awarded a diploma for a piano he exhibited at the 1848 American Institute Fair. (*American Institute Records*) After leaving the trade as a manufacturer, he reappeared briefly as a piano dealer from 1860-61.

ADAMS, Nathan

1824	mus instr mkr	112 Chambers

Born August 21, 1783, in Dunstable, New Hampshire, Adams was an important designer of brass instruments. He worked as an instrument maker in New York for only a short time before enlisting in the Navy during September 1824. Stationed on board the U. S. S. Constitution, Adams served as a Navy bandmaster from 1824-28, and was later listed as an instrument maker in Lowell, Massachusetts from 1828-35. He was also listed as a machinist in Boston during 1834, and in Provincetown, Massachusetts from 1849-50 and 1856. Adams is sometimes credited with the invention of rotary valves on brass instruments, and although this has yet to be proved, he certainly played an important role in the early development of rotary valves. Adams died in Milford, New Hampshire on March 16, 1864. For further information, see **Eliason** (1970:86-91); *New Grove* (1980:I:100).

ADLER, Albert C.

1854	accordions	h. 81 Delancey
1855	"	430 Houston
1856	"	45 Dey

Adler was also listed as a "musical instrument maker" in the *NYBD*s of 1854-56. In 1855 the firm *Adler & Company* was listed at 430 Houston Street.

ADLER & COMPANY

1855	mus instr mkrs	430 Houston

See above Albert Adler.

AHLERS, William

1874-75	accordeons	88 Forsyth
1876-77	mus instrs	77 Forsyth
1878-81	accordeons	"
1882-84	mus instrs	85 Ave. A

Ahlers might have been an importer as well as an instrument maker. Although he was not listed past 1884 in the *NYCD*, he was included in the *1885 AMD* (p. 200) as an accordion manufacturer at 77 Forsyth Street.

ALATHE, Ernst

See below *Ernst Aleithe*.

ALBERT, Charles Francis

A violin maker born at Freiburg, Baden, Germany in 1842, Albert was the son of *John Albert*. Charles Francis was active in New York c. 1865, although he was not listed in that year's *NYCD*. He later moved to Philadelphia, where he worked as an instrument maker until his death in 1908. (**Henley** 1960:I:16) See below *John Albert*.

ALBERT, John

John Albert was born in Baden, Germany and trained as a lawyer. Instrument making, which began as his hobby, became his profession after he immigrated to New York in 1848. According to **Henley** (1960:I:16), Albert quickly established a reputation as an excellent violin maker, however, neither he nor his son *Charles Francis Albert*, were ever listed as

instrument makers in the *NYCD*. Albert moved to Philadelphia where he was listed as a violin maker at 612 Callowhill Street in 1861. (*1861 AMD* p. 185) His son was listed at the same Philadelphia address, but might have returned to New York c. 1865 to open a short-lived branch store. **Gerson** (1970:136, 139) notes that Albert exhibited a case of string instruments at the 1876 Centennial Exhibition at Philadelphia.

ALBRECHT, John B.

1855-56	mus instrs	r. 42 Delancey
1857	"	67 Chrystie
1858	"	175 Chrystie
1859-60	"	142 Mott
1861	musician	"

From 1856-58, Albrecht and *Christian R. Stark* were partners in the instrument-making firm *Stark & Albrecht*. Albrecht apparently specialized in the making of woodwinds, and in the *1861 AMD* (p. 91), he was listed as a "Flute & Clarionet Manufacturer." A 9-key flute made by Albrecht was noted by **Langwill** (1980: 2), but the maker might have also been involved in the stencilling of imported instruments. His relation to the Philadelphia piano maker Charles Albrecht is not known. See below *Christian R. Stark*; *Stark & Albrecht*.

ALBRO, William

1834	carpenter	76 Attorney
1835-37	piano mkr	172 Spring
1838	------	"

A person of the same name was listed in the *NYCD* as a painter from 1824-30, and as the owner of a "fancygoods" shop from 1839-49, however the relationship of this artisan to the piano maker is not known.

ALEITHE / ALATHE, Ernst

1854	mus instr mkr	206 W. 37th

In the 1854 *NYBD* Aleithe was listed as a partner of *August Luedo[l]ff* in the instrument-making firm *Aleithe & Luedoff*. Their partnership was short-lived, and the following year Aleithe & Company, "manufacturers of piano keys," was listed at the 206 W. 37th Street address. Since both Aleithe and Luedolff were later active as piano makers, it is likely that their early instrument-making venture specialized in pianos. See *August Luedolff*.

ALEITHE & LUEDOFF

1854	mus instr mkrs	206 W. 37th

See *Ernst Aleithe*.

ALLEN, Joseph Lathrop

1862	mus instrs	224 Broome
1863	manuf	250 Canal
1864	mus instrs	62 Centre
1865-67	"	2ll Grand
1868	mus instr mkr	"
1869	mus instrs	6 Astor pl.
1870-71	------	h. 5ll Third
1872	alarms	204 E. 29th
1873-79	not listed/not traceable	
1880-81	supt.	114 E. 14th
1886	machinist	"
1891	inspector	25 Anne
1897	stereopticons	219 Center

An accomplished maker of brass instruments, Allen was born in Holland, Massachusetts on September 24, 1815. Allen worked at Sturbridge, Connecticut (c. 1838-41), Boston (1842-45 and 1852-61), and Norwich, Connecticut (1846-49), before establishing a shop in New York in 1862.

In New York, Allen headed the firm *Allen & Company* from 1865-68 and at some point also had some business dealings with the *Dodworth* family. Allen is best remembered for the improvements he made in rotary valves. After 1869, Allen left the instrument-making trade and was subsequently involved in a number of other professions before his death c. 1905. For further information see **Eliason** (1970: 93-94;1976;1979:15-22); *New Grove* (1980: I:281).

ALLEN & COMPANY

1865-68	mus instrs	2ll Grand

Allen had been involved in several partnerships before coming to New York, but no information on who the "& Company" was has been found. See *Joseph Allen*.

ALLOVON, Jean D.

1849	pianoforte mkr	113 Elm

In the 1849 *NYBD*, Allovon advertised himself as a maker of "new piccolo pianofortes." **Pierce** (1965: 10) lists a maker of the same name who worked in San Francisco in 1856, but the relationship of the East and West Coast piano makers has not been established.

ALTENBURGH, Frederick E.

1865-66	piano mkr	h. 78 Ave. A
1867-68	pianos	27 E. Houston
1869	piano mkr	43 Ave. A
1870-71	pianos	59 First

Pierce (1965:11) writes that Altenburgh began his career in Germany during the 1840s. By 1865 he was in New York, and in 1868 he was involved in a short-lived partnership with an Edward Ehrlich. Their firm, *F. E. Altenburgh & Ehrlich*, manufactured "upright pianos" for about a year. Nothing more is known about Ehrlich, who was probably an instrument dealer. Altenburgh continued to manufacture pianos on his own, possibly assisted by his relative *Otto Altenburgh*, who shared his 43 Avenue A address in 1869.

ALTENBURGH, Otto

1869	pianos	185 Bowery h. 43 Ave. A
1870	not listed	
1871	piano mkr	h. 165 Essex

A relative of *Frederick Altenburgh*, with whom he shared an address at 43 Avenue A in 1869, Altenburgh advertised that he manufactured upright and square pianos. (*CmRg* 1869:111) **Pierce** (1965: 11) claims that Otto Altenburgh later ran a piano store in Elizabeth, New Jersey.

ALTENBURGH, F. E. & EHRLICH

1867-68	upright pianos	27 E. Houston

See *Frederick Altenburgh*.

AMBLER, Samuel M.

1855-57	pianos	83 Spring
1858-59	"	358 Bowery
1860-62	"	88 Walker
1863	"	" & 46 Thompson
1864-65	"	455 Broome & 40 Thompson
1866	"	49 Mercer
1867-68	not listed	
1869-70	pianos	r. 40 Thompson
1871	"	151 Wooster

Spillane (1890:252) included *Ambler & Company* "among the other piano-making firms that had attained some note toward 1870 as makers of instruments for the masses." Actually, Samuel Ambler was listed as the head of Ambler & Company only from 1856-58, although it is likely that the firm was in business at least until 1870 when it was listed in that year's U. S. Census.

According to the *1870 U. S. Census*, Ambler & Company owned $3,000 of real capital, and had $1,140 worth of raw materials in stock. During that year, the firm employed 14 men for 11 months and paid them a total of $3,000 in wages. In 1870, Ambler & Company manufactured 140 pianos worth $8,000.

AMBLER & COMPANY

1856-58	pianos	358 Bowery

See above *Samuel Ambler*.

ANDERBERG, Pehr A.

Guitar maker Pehr Anderberg was born in Malmo, Sweden and immigrated to New York about the time of the Civil War. In New York, Anderberg worked for *Charles Bruno* until about 1870 when he moved a few miles north of Manhattan to Mt. Vernon, New York and went into business for himself. In 1880 he moved again, this time to Boston where he established a successful shop. Anderberg manufactured guitars for John C. Haynes & Company of Boston, and after 1890 also produced guitars and mandolins for *Pollman & Sons* of New York. In later years, Anderberg specialized in making "Tilton" guitars, a innovation that had been developed and patented by New Yorker *William Tilton*. (**Ayars** 1937:306)

Anderberg is typical of many artisans who are known to have lived and worked in New York even though their names do not appear in the city directories, possibly because like Anderberg they worked on a small scale or labored in another craftsman's shop.

ANDERSON, Andrew

1842	pianos	2 Hancock
1843-45	piano mkr	4 Hancock
1846-47	"	204 Bleecker
1848-49	pianos	"
1850	piano mkr	E. 10th n. Ave. 3
1851-54	"	204 Bleecker
1855-64	pianos	"
1865	"	81 Greenwich
1866-72	"	204 Bleecker
1873-85	"	208 Bleecker

Anderson advertised regularly as a "piano manufacturer" in the *NYBD*s, and was also listed as a piano maker in the *1861 AMD* and *1885 AMD*. It is possible, however, that Anderson was actually a dealer who stenciled rather than manufactured his instruments.

ANDREWS, John

1854	jewsharps	496 Greenwich
1855	jewsharp-maker	72 King
1856-57	not listed/not traceable	
1858	harps	h. 86 Vandam
1859-61	not listed	
1862	jewsharps	86 Vandam
1863-66	toys	"
1867	mus instrs	h. 71 Ninth Ave.
1868	jewsharps	"
1869-70	harps	"
1871-72	jewsharps	r. 83 Ninth
1873-75	harps	"
1876	jews harps	"
1877	mus instrs	"
1878-79	harps	"
1880	"	123 Greenwich
1881-83	jewsharps	"
1884	harps	"
1885	jewsharps	"
1886-87	mus instrs	"

According to the *1861 AMD* (p. 200), Andrews was indeed a "Manufacturer of Jews-harps." Unfortunately, nothing more is presently known about his operation.

ARION PIANO-FORTE COMPANY

1870	Arion Piano Forte, Manner's patent, warerooms at Covell & Co.	544 Broadway
1871	" / Manufactory C. H. Covell, Pres. J. B. Simpson, Sec.	" & 187 & 189 Bowery
1872	" / "	554 Broadway & 92 Crosby manuf. 149th
1873	" / "	5 E. 149th
1874-75	" / "	" & 150 n. St. Ann's
1875	See *Simpson & Company*	

Spillane (1890:283) wrote that "among the pianofortes that became known as reputable instruments towards 1876 . . . may be mentioned the 'Arion' piano. This instrument subsequently became extinct." The Arion Company grew out of *George Manner*'s piano firm. Around 1870, Manner, who had been active in the trade since 1854, sold his shop, patents and manufacturing rights to C. H. Covell, head of Covell & Company. This firm had been in existence since 1866, and by 1870 was involved in various enterprises including "gas fixtures, French china & cutglass, bronzes and fancy goods, wareroom of the patent Arion Piano Forte. " (1870 *NYCD*) George Manner continued to work for the firm as a "superintendent" until 1874 when he was listed as a mere "workman" in the uptown factory.

In 1875, *John Simpson*, who had served as secretary of Arion since 1871, took over control and changed the firm's name to *Simpson & Company*. William Simpson, John Simpson, Jr. and *Robert Proddow* served as board members. According to the firm's 1875 catalog, "six years ago there were none of our piano-fortes in existence, and to-day there are over 7,500 in use. " (**Arion**: np) Simpson & Company

continued to use the Arion stencil on some of their pianos for many years, and when the firm was sold again to Estey, the latter continued to manufacture some of their pianos under the Arion label well into the 1920s. See *George Manner*; *John Simpson*.

AVERELL, W. H. & E. D.

| 1857 | mus instr mkrs | 86 Bleecker |

The Averells were listed as musical instrument makers only in 1857. In 1858, they were joined by a third relative, E. W. Averell, and their newly-formed firm, Averell & Brothers, turned to the selling of sheet music. It is probable that the Averells were instruments dealers rather than manufacturers.

B

BAACK, Edward / Heinrich Eduard

1837-38	mus instrs	r. 28 Cherry
1839-40	"	55 Gold
1841	"	" & 258 Grand
1842-43	"	55 Gold
1844	"	" & 72 1/2 Chatham
1845-46	mus instrs, bronze powder, ultramarine blue, Dutch metal, Florence leaf gold	81 Fulton & 72 1/2 Chatham
1847-49	mus instrs	" & "
1850-52	"	87 Fulton & "
1853-70	"	87 Fulton h. Fordham
1871	"	147 Fulton

Baack was born Heinrich Eduard Baack at Hamburg in 1809. He is thought to have absented himself without permission from the Elector of Hamburg's army and run away to America. Baack was first listed in the 1837 *NYCD* as a member of the firm *Baack & Paulus*. His partner, *William Paulus*, who might have been a member of the German-based wind instrument-making family, disappeared from the records the following year, but Baack went on to an extremely successful career as an instrument manufacturer, importer and dealer.

In 1840, "Henry E. Baack" became a naturalized American citizen, and c. 1850 he returned to Hamburg to buy his release from the Elector's army, as well as an honorary captaincy. Thereafter, the prosperous merchant often styled himself "Capt. Edward H. Baack. "

Baack was probably more active as an importer and dealer than as a maker of instruments. Early in his career, he advertised himself as a "Manufacturer and Importer of Musical Instruments of every description" who had "constantly on hand a large assortment of musical merchandise. " (1841 *NYBD*) In 1844, Baack claimed to manufacture flutes, guitars, and violins (*NYBD* 1844:184), and by 1846 had added brass instruments and "clarionets" to his inventory. (1846 *NYBD*) In 1853, "Edward Baack, importer" entered a "fine violin by August Glass of Germany" in the New York Crystal Palace Exhibition. Following the Civil War, Baack, who it was rumored had grown rich selling bugles to the Confederate Army, established a country seat called "Belmont" in the Fordham section of the Bronx. [The author is indebted to Prof. George E. Valley, Jr. of Concord, Massachusetts for information about Baack's personal life. PC:10/19/85.]

BAACK & PAULUS

| 1837 | mus instrs | r. 28 Cherry |

The firm was headed by *Edward Baack* and *William Paulus*.

BACH, Jacques

Piano maker Jacques Bach was born in Alsace in 1833. He immigrated to New York in 1852 and worked for many years in the piano industry. Bach was trained in the shop of *Adam Stodart* and later helped found the *New York Pianoforte Company* and *Kranich & Bach*. The maker died on October 30, 1894. (*New York Sun,* October 30,1894) See *Kranich & Bach*.

BACON, Francis

The son of *George Bacon,* see below, Francis took over his father's interest in the firm *Bacon & Raven* after the elder Bacon died c. 1855. His partner, *Richard Raven*, was a respected artisan and quite a bit older than Francis, a fact which probably explains why the firm's name was initially changed to *Raven, Bacon & Company* (1856-61), and later to *Raven & Bacon* (1862-72). Although this partnership was listed until 1872, it probably ended in 1871 when Bacon formed a partnership with William H. Karr. Karr, later the superintendent of the *Freeborn G. Smith* piano factory, left *Bacon & Karr* c. 1879, and Bacon continued to manufacture pianos on his own for many years. His firm, *Francis Bacon*, "Successors to Bacon & Karr," was listed from 1880-90 + at 473 Broadway. For further information see *NCAB* (1893:2:447); **Spillane** (1890:190, 224).

BACON, George

1825-26	------	1 Mercer
1827	------	149 Broadway
1828-33	------	167 Broadway
1834-35	music store	"
1836-37	music	"
1838-40	"	285 Broadway
1841-42	"	164 Centre
1843-47	piano manuf	"
1848-49	"	162 Centre
1850	pianos	160 Centre
1851-52	piano manuf	162 Centre
1853-54	pianos	"
1855	"	135 Grand

Bacon came from Philadelphia where he was affiliated with and probably related to the music publisher Allyn Bacon c. 1815-24. George, who might have worked as an engraver for Allyn Bacon, published a few pieces of music under his own name during 1823-24 before moving to New York c. 1825. (**Wolfe** 1980:49; **Dichter** 1977:168)

Bacon began his career as a New York piano manufacturer with partner *William Dubois*, an importer and music dealer. Their firm, *Dubois & Bacon*, active 1835-38, was successor to the music dealership founded in 1789 by John Jacob Astor and owned for many years by the Paff Brothers. In 1836, a third partner, *Thomas Chambers*, was admitted and the firm's name changed to *Dubois, Bacon & Chambers*.

In 1841, Bacon left and entered into a new partnership with piano maker *Richard Raven*. Their firm, *Bacon & Raven*, lasted until the Bacon's death c. 1855, and thereafter continued as *Raven & Bacon* when George's son *Francis Bacon* was admitted into partnership. Bacon & Raven was a large and successful piano manufacturer. According to the *1855 New York Census*, the firm owned $44,000 of real capital and $5,000 of tools. It kept in stock 17,000 feet of wood, as well as leather and hardware worth $40,000. That year, the firm employed 125 men, who were paid $4,800 in monthly wages to produce 500 pianos worth $120,000. See **Spillane** (1890: 108-9,224); *Dubois & Bacon*; *Dubois, Bacon & Chambers*.

BACON & KARR

1871-79	pianos	255 Greene

This firm was headed by *Francis Bacon* and William H. Karr. The latter had been active as a music dealer since 1861, and had shared a work address with Bacon since 1864, which suggests that Karr had been Bacon's employee before he was admitted into full partnership.

BACON & RAVEN

1841-54	pianos	160-164 Centre
1855	"	135 Grand

Founded in 1841 by George Bacon and *Richard Raven*, the firm's name was changed to *Raven, Bacon & Company* when Bacon's son *Francis Bacon* succeeded his father in 1856. In 1862, the firm became *Raven & Bacon* and it continued to manufacture pianos under this title until 1872. See *George Bacon*; *Francis Bacon*.

BADGER, Alfred G.

1848-64	flutes	181 Broadway
1865-80	mus instrs	179 Broadway
1881-90+	flutes	"

Born in 1815, Badger worked as a musical instrument maker for Ball & Douglas in Utica, New York (1834, 1837); for the music store Nickels & Badger in Buffalo (1839-41); and as a flute manufacturer in Newark, New Jersey (1844-47), before moving to New York in 1846. (**Kaufman** 1976:26; PC: Eliason)

Badger was noted as a fine flute maker, and his instruments won awards at American Institute Fairs in 1846, 1847, 1848, 1852, 1853 and 1856. He was among the first in America to encourage the use of Boehm-system flutes, and exhibited one of his own making at the 1853 New York Crystal Palace. (*Official Catalogue* 1853: 95) In his booklet, *An Illustrated History of the Flute & Sketch of the Successive Improvements Made in the Flute,* Badger wrote "My mechanical education and long experience as a Flute-maker, I feel confident, had prepared me to occupy this position [i. e. as spokesman for the Boehm-system flute], having been bred in all branches of the profession. " (**Boehm** 1853:iiv) In the late 1850s, Badger constructed several experimental flutes of the new material "ebonite" for Charles Goodyear, and in 1859 he wrote an article praising its merits for the *Scientific American.* (**Libin** 1985:72)

Badger generally worked alone, however, from 1860-65, he headed the firm *Badger & Company.* The *DMC* also has a flute made c. 1858 labeled "Badger & Monzani. " Although no record of this partnership had been found, a *Theobald F. Monzani* was listed as a New York flute maker from 1835-48 and might have been employed in Badger's shop during the 1850s. Perhaps Monzani formed part of the "Company" in Badger & Company. The piano maker *William Robertson* is listed as sharing Badger's 181 Broadway address in 1854, but the relationship between these two makers is unknown.

According to the *1855 New York Census,* Badger owned no "real capital," and had only $500 worth of tools. His shop employed 2 men and one boy at monthly wages of $65. That year, using $200 of wood and $800 of silver, Badger produced $3,000 worth of flutes.

Badger died in Brooklyn on November 8, 1892. Examples of his work are found in many instrument collections. See **Langwill** (1980:7); *DMC*; **Simpson** (1982); *New Grove* (1984: I:96).

BADGER & COMPANY

| 1860-63 | flutes | 181 Broadway |

See *Alfred Badger.*

BADGER & MONZANI

See *Alfred Badger.*

BAIRD, Lyman

| 1830 | piano-forte mkr | 534 Pearl |

1831	"	79 1/2 Bowery
1832	"	103 Bowery
1833-34	piano mkr	"
1835	"	72 Bowery

No further information is presently known about this maker.

BAKER, Samuel

1844-49	cabinet mkr	various addresses
1850	pianoforte mkr	43 Greene
1851-53	pianos	548 Broadway
1854	"	183 Wooster
1855-58	"	120 MacDougal
1859	"	422 Hudson

Although Baker occasionally advertised himself as a "maker" in the *NYBD*, it is possible that he was a journeyman rather than a mastercraftsman.

BALDWIN

See *Goodman & Baldwin.*

BALL, Sheldon X.

1871	clerk	h. 177 E. 29th
1872	pianos	"
1873-76	"	15 E. 14th
1877	"	11 E. 14th
1878	not listed	
1879-85 +	pianist	25 E. 14th

It is unclear whether Ball was an instrument maker himself, or merely a dealer, however his firm, *S. X. Ball & Company,* in business from 1873-77, advertised as "Manufacturers & Dealers in Grand, Square, and Upright Pianos & Organs for sale on Installments and for Rent. " (*CmRg* 1874:102)

BALL, S. X. & COMPANY

1873	pianos	15 E. 14th
1874-76	pianos & organs	"
1877	"	11 E. 14th

See *Sheldon Ball.*

BALL, William H.

1826-27	see *Hooper & Ball*	
1829	mus instr mkr	11th n. Ave. 3
1830	"	8th c. Ave. 3
1831	"	96 Walker c. Elm
1832	"	42 Allen

Almost certainly the same craftsman who headed the firm *Hooper & Ball* from 1826-27, Ball joined *John Overin* in 1831 in the instrument-making partnership *Ball & Overin*. In 1833, Ball moved to Utica, New York, and with partners G. W. Bingham and J. D. Douglas, specialized in

Mus. , Military & Jewelry.

The flute maker *Alfred Badger* was employed by this Utica firm. (PC:Eliason) Ball was primarily a woodwind maker, and a 1-key flute of his manufacture is extant. (**Langwill** 1980:8) See *Hooper & Ball*.

BALL & OVERIN

1831	mus instr mkrs	96 Walker c. Elm

Headed by *William H. Ball* and *John Overin*. See above.

BARBER, Thomas

1855	mus instr mkr	149 Hester

Barber was listed only in the 1855 *NYBD* (p. 280). The 1853-54 *NYCD*s listed two persons of the same name, both musicians, but their relation to this instrument maker has not been established.

BARBERIE, Andrew V. T.

1858	key maker	38 White
1859	pianos	157 Baxter
1860-64	"	173 Grand
1865	piano mkr	h. 17 N. 3rd, Brooklyn

From 1858-63, Barberie and *Edward Bloomfield* were owners of the piano-manufacturing firm *Barberie & Bloomfield*. The partners began as makers of piano keys and subsequently turned to the making of pianos. One of their instruments was awarded a premium at the 1859 American Institute Fair. (*1861 AMD* p. 45) The partnership apparently ended after 1863 when Bloomfield is listed on his own at 173 Grand Street. Barberie listed only his home address in 1865, suggesting the likelihood that he was employed as a journeyman.

BARBERIE & BLOOMFIELD

1858	key makers	38 White
1859	pianos	157 Baxter
1860-63	"	173 Grand

The firm consisted of *Edward Bloomfield* and *Andrew V. T. Barberie*. See above.

BARMORE, Garrit/Garrett

1836-41	pianos	120 Barrow
1842-48	"	301 Bleecker
1849-54	"	348 Bleecker
1855-56	"	87 Charles, 348 Bleecker & W. 13th n. 10th
1857-72	"	348 Bleecker & 278 W. 13th
1873-74	"	368 Bleecker
1875	Hester widow Garrett	h. 65 Perry

Barmore spent most of his career working with his brother *Harvey Barmore*. According to **Spillane** (1890:160), their company, *G. & H. Barmore*, founded in 1836, attained "some reputation as makers of popular-priced instruments." At the 1836 American Institute Fair, the brothers were awarded a diploma "for a piano-forte of a very fine touch" with a metal plate, French action, and a highly finished rosewood case valued at $475. (*American Institute Records*)

In 1861, the Barmores advertised themselves as manufacturers of improved over-strung pianos that had been "Pronounced unrivalled by the best judges & guaranteed for three years, at great bargains." (*CmRg* 1861:45) The *1870 U. S. Census* reported that the Barmores owned $10,000 of capital, and had in stock lumber, hardware, leather, varnish & c. worth another $9,500. They employed 12 men at annual wages of $7,500 who that year had constructed 100 pianos worth $20,000. After Garrett's death, c. 1875, Harvey continued on his own for several years, changing the firm's title to *H. Barmore & Company*.

BARMORE, Harvey

1836-41	pianos	120 Barrow
1842-48	"	301 Bleecker
1849-72	"	348 Bleecker
1873-83	"	368 Bleecker
1884	not listed	
1885	pianos	"

See *Garrit Barmore*.

BARMORE, G. & H.

1836-41	pianos	120 Barrow
1842-48	"	301 Bleecker
1849-55	"	348 Bleecker
1856-72	"	" & 278 W. 13th
1873-75	"	368 Bleecker

After the death of *Garrit Barmore* c. 1875, the firm continued under the leadership of *Harvey Barmore* as *H. Barmore & Company*. See above.

BARMORE, H. & COMPANY

1876-85	pianos	368 Bleecker

The successor to *G. & H. Barmore*, this firm was headed by *Harvey Barmore*. See above.

BARNES, J. C.

See below *Myron Decker*.

BASSFORD, Abraham

1820	turner	479 Pearl
1821	"	r. 476 Pearl
1822	"	r. 477 Pearl
1823-24	turner & porter-house	"
1825	musician	"
1826-27	not listed	
1828-33	ivory turner	477 Pearl & 218 Broadway
1834-37	"	547 Pearl & 218 Broadway
1838	"	4 Ann & 218 Broadway
1839	billards	4 Ann
1840	"	440 Broadway
1841-42	------	" & 165 Fourth
1843-52	foundry, billards, billard tables, & c.	" & "
1853	billard tables & pianos	63 Centre & 8 Ann
1854	piano manuf	" & ", 149 Fulton, 603 Broadway
1855	pianos & billards	149 Fulton
1856	pianos	"
1857-59	pianos & billards	"
1860	billards	"

In the middle of the nineteenth century, the legs and cases of pianos and billard tables were quite similar, and it is likely that Bassford initially became involved in the piano trade as a case maker. Although he was listed as a piano maker only from 1853-59, his 1824 listing as a musician indicates an early interest in the art. Bassford exhibited a piano at the 1853 New York Crystal Palace (**Rimbault** 1860:402), and according to the *1855 New York Census*, he owned no real capital and only $500 worth of tools. He did have in stock 12,000 feet of lumber worth $960, 50 sets of piano hardware worth $500, 50 sets of ivories worth $325, and $150 worth of leather. His shop employed 5 men and 1 boy at monthly wages of $220, and that

year produced 50 pianos worth $15,000. In addition to Abraham, a Julius and William K. Bassford were also active in the firm. (**Redway** 1941:59)

The maker's relation to the pianist S. W. Bassford, who appeared in a 1839 concert is not known, nor has any connection been established with the owner of Bassford's Rooms, a concert hall at 1 3/4 Ann Street that advertised "Invisible Musicians" in 1840. (**Lawrence** 1988: 52, 106)

BAUER, Frederick

See *Stultz & Bauer*.

BAUER, Julius

Bauer, an major instrument importer and dealer from Chicago, opened retail outlets in several American cities. In 1868, he opened a New York branch store which continued in operation past 1890. In is unlikely that Bauer, who was an uncle of *William Tonk*, was a maker himself, however, stencils bearing his name appeared on both pianos and woodwinds. The New York branch of Bauer & Company occupied several addresses: 544 Broadway c. 1873; 129 E. 129th Street c. 1885. See **Tonk** (1926:passim; **Spillane** (1890:133); **Kaufman** (1976:27); **Langwill** (1980:10).

BAUS, Augustus

1878-82	clerk	h. 308 E. 53rd
1883-84	pianos	26 W. 23 & 528 W. 43rd
1885-87	"	404 E. 30th
	president	58 W. 23 & 231 E. 33rd
1888-90+	"	553-555 W. 30th

According to **Spillane** (1890:304), "Augustus Baus & Company began to manufacture pianos in 1880, and enjoys a very excellent reputation as a courteous business house, and as makers of reputable and meritorious instruments. Up to a couple of years ago this firm was coming rapidly into notice . . . but they encountered some business reverses, which resulted from entirely honorable causes familiar to the commercial sphere. They maintained a . . . wareroom for several years in the metropolis, but were compelled . . . to give up their retail department temporarily, and devote themselves to the wholesale trade. Meanwhile the former standard of their pianos has been maintained, and they are fast regaining their old plane of popularity . . . Mr.

Baumeister is in charge of the practical department and is in every respect a qualified superintendent. He is, in addition, a member of Baus & Company. "

Baus seems to have been a businessman with no practical knowledge of piano making. His firm, *Baus & Company*, continued in operation until 1900, when, according to **Pierce** (1965), it was taken over by *Jacob Doll*. The company's motto, which appeared in an advertisement in the *Musical Trade Review* (1887:143) was "Excelsior!"

BAUS & COMPANY

1883-84	pianos	26 W. 23 & 538 W. 43rd
1885-87	"	404 E. 30 & 58 W. 23rd
1888-90+	"	553-555 W. 30th

See *Augustus Baus.*

BAUSCH, Ludwig

1860-61	violins	614 Broadway

Born in Dessau, Germany on November 10, 1829, Bausch was trained as a violin and bow maker by his father Ludwig C. A. Bausch, who was "ultimately sobriquetted as the German Tourte. " (**Henley** 1960:I:92) The younger Bausch worked in New York for several years and then returned to Leipzig c. 1855 to join his father in Bausch & Sons. While in New York, Bausch advertised himself as a "manufacturer & importer of stringed instruments & bows. " (*CmRg* 1861: 320) A less famous maker than his father, Bausch died at Leipzig on April 7, 1871. (**Baker** 1958)

BEAME, James F.

1858-68	piano tuner	various addresses
1869-70	pianos	117 W. 11th
1871	piano manuf	"
1872	not listed	
1873-79	pianos	208 8th Ave.
1880-81	"	209 E. 19th
1882	"	453 W. 36th
1883	piano mkr	h. 156 9th Ave.
1884	not listed	
1885-86	pianos	453 W. 36th
1887-89	"	796 10th Ave.

From 1869-80, Beames was a member of the small piano-manufacturing firm *Beames, Bent & Company*. The firm was taken over by *Richard Bent* c. 1880, however, Beames continued to be listed at the same address through 1869 even though he was apparently no longer Bent's partner. Beames' relationship to the earlier instrument maker *Jonathan Beames* is not known.

BEAMES, Jonathan

1818-26	umbrella mkr	various addresses
1827	not listed	
1828-41	mus instr mkr	18 Batavia
1842-43	machinist	"
1844	"	87 Walker
1845-47	not listed	
1848-52	machinist	88 Elizabeth
1853+	late machinist	140 1/2 Bowery

Beames was related to the music teacher and writer Clare W. Beames with whom he lived during the 1840s. Given his background as an umbrella maker, it is probable that Beames made woodwinds during his short career as an instrument maker. He is not traceable after 1853, and his relationship to the later piano manufacturer *James Beames* is not known.

BEAMES, BENT & COMPANY

1869-70	pianos	117 W. 11th
1871-72	piano manuf	"
1873-79	pianos	208 8th Ave.

The firm was headed by *James Beames* and *Richard Bent*. See above *James F. Beames.*

BECK, Gottlieb

1866 & before	piano tuner	various addresses
1867-69	pianos	203 W. 46th
1870-76	piano mkr/pianos	201 W. 46th
1885	dealer	"

The only evidence to suggest that Beck was more than a piano dealer and repairman appeared in the 1871 *CmRg* (p. 101) in which Beck listed himself as a "Manufacturer of Piano-Fortes. "

BEDELL, Joseph L.

1853-54	piano mkr	524 Hudson
1855-79	pianos	324 Spring

Bedell was probably a piano dealer, although he advertised himself as a maker in the *1861 AMD* (p. 169) and the *1861 CmRg* (p. 45). In later years, he apparently worked only as a dealer.

BEGGS, Joseph P.

See *Sonntag & Beggs*.

BEHNING, Henry

1864	piano case manuf	196 W. Houston
1865	cases	"
1866	pianos	" & 21 Minetta
1867-69	"	99 Bleecker
1870	"	" & 424 Broome
1871-74	"	445 W. 42nd
1875	"	Ave. 1 c. 124th
1876	"	401 E. 124th
1877	"	760 3rd & 2420 Ave. 1
1878	" & v. pres.	2422 Ave. 1 & 294 B'way
1879-80	pianos,keys & v. pres	" & 216 Centre
1881	manager	" & "
1882-85	pianos	", 1 W. 14th, E. 125th
1886-90+	pres. & pianos	1 W. 14th & 159 E. 128th

Born November 3, 1832 in Hanover, Germany, Behning was apprenticed in the piano-making shop of Julius Gerke, and later worked for Helmholtz. In 1856, he immigrated to New York where he found work in the shop of *Lighte, Newton & Bradbury*. Laid off during the depression of 1857, he left the city for Bridgeport, Connecticut, where he worked as a piano maker until joining the Union Army during the Civil War. Following his discharge, Behning returned to New York where, according to **Spillane** (1890:243-48), he established a shop at 196 Elm Street as early as 1861. (No record of a Behning shop has been found prior to the 1864 *NYCD* listing given above.)

In 1866, Behning and *Albrecht Klix* established the piano-manufacturing firm *Behning & Klix*, which continued in operation until 1873 when Klix sold his interest to *Justus Diehl*. The resulting partnership, *Behning & Diehl*, was said by **Spillane** to be the first to move their operations to Harlem, building a large factory there in June 1875.

Diehl withdrew from partnership in 1877 and Behning continued on his own for several years before admitting his son, Henry Behning, Jr. , and changing the firm's name to *Behning & Son*. During the 1890s, as more of his sons joined, the firm's name was changed again to *Behning & Sons*. Behning was the father-in-law of the Chicago instrument maker

William Tonk, who wrote of negotiating the dissolution of Behning & Diehl. (**Tonk** 1926:66-67) The senior Behning retired from the trade in 1894 and died on June 10, 1905. (Also see **Dolge** 1911:319.)

BEHNING & DIEHL

1874	pianos	445 W. 42nd
1875	pianos "Successors to Behning & Klix"	Ave. 1 c. 124th
1876	pianos	401 E. 124th
1877	"	760 3rd & 2420 Ave. 1

The firm consisted of *Justus Diehl* and *Henry Behning*. See above.

BEHNING & KLIX

1866	pianos	196 W. Houston & 21 Minetta
1867-70	"	99 Bleecker
1871-73	"	445 W. 42nd

Partners were *Albrecht Klix* and *Henry Behning*. See above.

BEHNING & SON(S)

1882-86	pianos	1 W. 14th & 129 E. 125th
1887-90+	"	159 E. 128th

Begun by Henry Behning and his son Henry Behning, Jr. , the firm's title changed to *Behning & Sons* in the 1890s as more of Behning's children were admitted into partnership. See above.

BEHR, Henry

1877	pianos	294 11th Ave.
1878-80	cases	"
1881-82	pianos	"
1883-84	"	" & 42 Union Square
1885-90+	"	15 E. 14th & 294 11th Ave.

Born 1848 in Hamburg, Germany, Behr immigrated to America as a youngster and entered the piano trade after serving in the Union Army. In 1877, Behr and a maker named Peck—who was probably the same person as *Leopold Peck*, later associated with *Hugh Hardman*—established the piano-manufacturing firm *Behr & Peck*. The firm lasted until 1879, and the following year Behr and his brother Edward founded *H. Behr & Brother*. The firm's name was changed to *Behr, Brother & Company* in 1884, but it was often referred to simply as "Behr Brothers. " Both brothers were practical makers and they were awarded several patents for their innovations. For further information see **Spillane** (1890:270-75).

BEHR, H. & BROTHER

1880	cases	294 Ave. 11
1881-82	pianos	"
1883	"	42 Union Square

See *Henry Behr.*

BEHR, BROTHER & COMPANY

1884	pianos	42 Union Square
1885-90+	"	15 E. 14th

See *Henry Behr.*

BEHR & PECK

1877	pianos	294 Ave. 11
1878-79	cases	"

See *Henry Behr.*

BENDER, John Joseph

1853	mus instr mkr & pianoforte mkr	Ave. 4 n. 40th
1854	piano mkr	176 W. 30th

Bender might have been a journeyman rather than a mastercraftsman. **Pierce** (1965:27) lists a piano maker named John Bender as active in San Francisco c. 1860, and there was also a John J. Bender, piano maker, working in Detroit in 1874. The relationship of either or both of these men to the New York maker has not been established.

BENJAMIN, Joel

1827	pianoforte mkr	26 Factory
1828	"	32 Factory
1829	"	26 Asylum
1830	"	27 Marion
1831-36	"	21 Minetta

Nothing further is presently known about this maker.

BENNET, Isaiah

1826	pianoforte mkr	Bedford c. Burton

Nothing further is presently known about this maker.

BENNETT

Several members of the Bennett family were active in piano manufacturing during the 1840s and 1850s. It is often difficult to determine which family member was involved in any given concern because of the frequency with which they traded addresses. Most prominent members of the Bennett family were:

Sullivan E. Bennett

1848-49	piano mkr	152 Fulton
1850-51	" & oils	" & 24 Old Slip
1852-53	pianos	361 Broadway
1854-55	"	" & 313 Rivington
1856	"	300 B'way & 3l3 Rivington

William W. Bennett

1844	pianos	152 Fulton
1845	late pianos	293 Third
1846	pianos	152 Fulton
1847-52	not listed	
1853-54	pianos	361 Broadway
1855-56	"	300 B'way & 313 Rivington
1857	"	434 Broome
1858	"	h. 49 Stanton

Also active during this period were relatives George A. Bennett (1851-54); Robert O. Bennett (1854-57); Sumner W. Bennett (1856); and Solomon A. Bennett (1854). There was also a piano maker named John L. Bennett, active 1846-47, and a musical instrument maker named Isaac M. Bennett, but the relationships of these individuals to the other Bennetts is not known.

From 1846-48, either William and/or Sullivan Bennett worked with *Abel Rogers* in the partnership *Bennett, Rogers & Company*. Their firm succeeded Rogers' previous concern, *Glen, Rogers & Company*, which had been located at the same 152 Fulton Street address from 1844-46.

In 1849, one of the Bennetts (Sullivan?) joined Benjamin B. Wilder to form the piano-manufacturing firm *Bennett & Wilder*, which was also located at the 152 Fulton Street address.

George A. Bennett and Sullivan E. Bennett headed *Bennett & Company* from 1850-56. A piano manufactured by this firm was exhibited at the 1853 New York Crystal Palace. (**Rimbault** 1860:42)

In 1857, Robert O. Bennett and William W. Bennett joined the piano maker *William Senior* in the partnership *Bennett, Senior & Company*. It is probable that many of the Bennetts were dealers rather than makers. Members of the family disappeared from the *NYCD* around 1858.

BENNETT & COMPANY

1850-51	pianos	152 Fulton
1852-53	"	361 Broadway
1854-55	"	" & 313 Rivington
1856	"	300 B'way & 313 Rivington

The firm was apparently headed by George A. Bennett and *Sullivan E. Bennett*. See *Bennett*.

BENNETT, ROGERS & COMPANY

1846-48	pianos	152 Fulton

Partners included *Abel Rogers* and *William* and/or *Sullivan Bennett*. See *Bennett*.

BENNETT, SENIOR & COMPANY

1857	pianos	434 Broome

This partnership was headed by *Robert O. Bennett*, *William W. Bennett* and *William Senior*. See above *Bennett*.

BENNETT & WILDER

1849	pianos	152 Fulton

Members of this firm were Benjamin B. Wilder and (Sullivan?) Bennett. See *Bennett*.

BENT, Richard M.

1869	see *Beames, Bent & Company*	
1870-72	pianos	117 W. 11th
1873-79	"	208 8th Ave.
1880-81	"	209 E. 19th
1882-86	"	453 W. 36th
1887-90+	"	767 10th Ave.

Bent and his partner *James Beames* headed the piano-manufacturing firm *Beames, Bent & Company* from 1869-80. Bent apparently gained control of the firm in 1880, and its name was changed to *R. M. Bent & Company*. Little is known about Bent, although he might have been the same person as the piano and organ dealer of the that name who had been active in Charleston, South Carolina c. 1861. (*1861 AMD* p. 200) His relationship to the later Chicago-based piano manufacturer George P. Bent is not known. See also *James Beames*.

BENT, R. M. & COMPANY

1880-81	pianos	209 E. 19th
1882-86	"	453 W. 36th
1887-90+	"	767 Ave. 10

See *Richard M. Bent*.

BERGE, Louis

1865	teacher	h. 178 Ave. 3
1866-69	grand, square & upright piano- fortes, organs & melodeons	97 Bleecker
1870	pianos	342 Ave. 2
1871	"	97 Bleecker
1872	"	18 E. 14th
1873-74	music & pianos	" & 30 E. 14th
1875-79	pianos	30 E. 14th
1880-84	variety	646 Ave. 8
1885+	music dealer	664 Ave. 8

A piano and music dealer, Berge briefly headed the small-time piano-manufacturing firm *Berge & Company* (1866-67), which advertised that it made "grand, square, and upright pianos, organs and melodeons. " (1867 *CmRg*) Berge continued to advertise as a piano manufacturer in the *1885 AMD* (p. 201), however, it is possible that throughout his career Berge was a dealer who stencilled rather than manufactured instruments.

BERGE & COMPANY

1866-67	grand, square, & upright pianofortes, organs & melodeons	97 Bleecker

See *Louis Berge*.

BERGIN, Rudolph

1860	pianofortes	263 W. 51st
1861	"	h. W. 51st n. 9th
1862-63	piano mkr	h. 263 W. 51st
1864-65	not listed	
1866	piano mkr	394 Hudson
1867-68	pianos	88 Walker
1869	"	342 Ave. 2
1870	"	409 W. 51st

Listed as a piano manufacturer in the *1861 AMD* (p. 169), Bergin's name also appeared as a trustee on the incorporation papers of the co-operatively owned *New York Piano-Forte Company* in 1864.

According to the *1870 U. S. Census,* Bergen [*sic*] owned $6,000 of capital and $3,000 of raw materials. He employed 6 men, at annual wages of $4,000, to produce $6,000 worth of pianos. It is possible that Adolph Bergin, a journeyman piano maker active during the 1870s, was related to this maker.

BERGMAN, John

See *Narvesen, Bergman & Haugaard.*

BERGQUIST, Gustave

1843	pianofortes	115 Franklin
1844		not listed
1845-46	pianofortes	1 St. John's la.
1847-49	"	Ave. 5 bet. 10th & 11th
1850-55	"	40 Ave. 5
1856-65	"	44 W. 15th
1866-72	"	484 Ave. 6
1873-78	"	120 W. 25th

From 1846-50, Bergquist and his partner, Peter Wennerstrom, headed the piano-manufacturing firm *Wennerstrom & Bergquist.* After their firm's dissolution, Bergquist continued on alone as a small-time piano maker for several years. Bergquist might have been related to a piano maker of the same surname who was active in Stockholm during this period. (**Pierce** 1965:28) See *Wennerstrom & Bergquist.*

BERNARD, Frederick

1879 & before	barber	various addresses
1880	mus instrs	h. 247 W. 27th
1881-83	not listed	
1884	watchmaker	339 W. 37th

Prior to 1880, Bernard was listed as a barber. His career as an instrument maker was short-lived, and although the *1885 AMD* (p. 201) listed Bernard as a "Repairer & Musical Instrument Manufacturer," he had probably already left the city by that date.

BERNDARDT, Louis

Berndardt, a "Musical Instrument Manufacturer" with a shop at 107 Elizabeth Street, was listed in the **1885 AMD** (p. 201). The *NYCD*s of that period list only a tailor of that name who was probably not the same person.

BERNHADT, Edward

1885	mus instrs	151 Ludlow
1886	"	166 E. 4th

Probably an instrument dealer, Bernhadt was listed as a manufacturer at 117 East 4 Street only in the *1885 AMD* (p. 201). His relationship to Hardman Bernhart, an organ maker active c. 1885, is not known.

BERTAU, Ferdinand/Frederick

1856	drum maker	h. 91 Walker
1857	"	139 W. Broadway
1858	"	155 W. Broadway
1859	mus instr mkr	4 Laurens
1860-65	drums	2 Laurens
1866-68	not listed	
1869-70	drum mkrs	h. 633 E. 9th
1871	mus instrs	"
1872	not listed	
1873-77	drums/drum mkr	"
1878	not listed	
1879-85	drums/drum mkr	"
1886	not listed	
1887	drums	"

Bertau and his relative Henry Bertau headed the drum manufacturing firm *F. & H. Bertau* in 1857. Henry Bertau left the trade in 1860, but Ferdinand continued to make drums until 1887.

BERTAU, Henry

1857	drums	139 W. Broadway
1860	frames	86 Bleecker

See *Ferdinand Bertau.*

BERTAU, F. & H.

1857	drums	139 W. Broadway

The firm consisted of *Ferdinand* and *Henry Bertau.* See above.

BERTELING, Theodore

1859-60	mus instrs	219 Centre
1861	not listed	
1862-63	mus instrs	189 Grand
1864-66	"	167 Bowery
1867	"	98 Bowery
1868	flutes	"
1869	not listed	
1870-74	mus instrs	"
1875-90+	mus instrs/flutes	177 Bowery

A prominent wind instrument maker, Berteling was born in 1821 in Prussia, and immigrated to Boston c. 1848. In Boston, Berteling worked with instrument makers E. G. Wright (1849), Graves & Company (1851-53), and *Joseph Allen* (1854), before coming to New York c. 1855.

In his later advertisements, Berteling implied that he first established a New York shop in 1857, however, no record of his shop has been found before 1859. Berteling was the maker of high quality woodwind instruments. In addition to flutes and clarinets he also made oboes and piccolos, and was awarded patents in 1868 (No. 79,389) and 1882 (No. 264,611) for mechanical improvements to Boehm-system woodwinds. His instruments were shown at various fairs, including the Massachusetts Charitable Mechanics' Association Exhibits of 1850 and 1856.

In 1875, Berteling founded *Berteling & Company*. Information about the firm appeared in their *1885 AMD* (p. 215) advertisement: "T. Berteling & Co. Est. 1848. 177 Bowery. Manufacturers of Superior Quality of Flutes, Clarionets, & other Wind Instruments . . . Ever since establishment of our business we have been manufacturing these Instruments exclusively for Musicians. One of our first customers was the well-known Clarionet Virtuoso JAMES K. KENDALL, for whom Mr. Berteling, our Senior Partner, (when in Boston), made a full set of Clarionets in the year 1849, which KENDALL used with the greatest satisfaction all his lifetime . . . In 1857 our business was removed to New York . . . To indicate their popularity it may be mentioned that in New York & Brooklyn alone there have been seventy (70) sets of our clarinets in use in the hands of Musicians. "

Berteling died in New York on September 4, 1889, however, his firm continued in operation until 1912, managed for a time by his widow Sophia (d. 1904). See *New Grove* (1980:2:635); **Libin** (1985:77-78).

BERTELING & COMPANY

1875-90+	mus instrs	177 Bowery

See Theodore Berteling.

BETTS, Charles J.

1861-70	pianos	4 Leroy pl.
1871-72	"	94 Bleecker
1873-76	"	788 Broadway
1877-84	"	8 Union Square

Betts was probably more active as an instrument dealer than manufacturer. He was listed as a music and piano dealer in the *1861 AMD* (p. 94), and as a maker of square and upright pianos in the *1885 AMD* (p. 201). His relationship to Edward Betts, a Philadelphia piano maker active c. 1837 (**Catalano** 1979:96), is not known.

BILLINGS, Andrew

1874-75	organs	14 E. 14th
1876	pianos	"
1877	"	21 E. 14th
1878-85	"	" & 124 W. 25th
1886	"	2 W. 14th

Billings was the senior partner in several large piano-manufacturing concerns. According to **Spillane** (1890:285-86), the first of these partnerships was with *William Tremaine,* and although no record of this firm is found in the **NYCD**, **Spillane** noted that this "well-known firm commanded a large wholesale business about 1875 as manufacturers of pianofortes . . . Mr. Tremaine separated from Billings about 1876, when Billings & Company appeared. " Despite their separation, the two men continued to be listed at the same business address for several years thereafter.

After leaving Tremaine, Billings formed a partnership with *William Wheelock*; their firm, *Billings & Wheelock*, was in business from 1874-76. (Interestingly, in 1874 Billings shared his 14 East 14th Street address with the large piano manufacturer *Lindeman & Sons*, raising the possibility that he might still have been employed as a journeyman at that date.) Billings then founded *Billings & Company*, active from 1877-85, and in 1884 was also listed as a partner in the piano dealership *Billings & Richmond*. The maker apparently left the trade c. 1886.

BILLINGS & COMPANY

1877	pianos	21 E. 14th & 421 E. 12th
1878-85	"	21 E. 14th & 124 W. 124th

See *Andrew Billings*.

BILLINGS & RICHMOND

1884	pianos	21 E. 14th

See *Andrew Billings*.

BILLINGS & TREMAINE

Partnership was headed by *William Tremaine* and *Andrew Billings*. See above.

BILLINGS & WHEELOCK

1874-75	organs	14 E. 14th
1876	pianos	"

Firm consisted of *William Wheelock* and *Andrew Billings*. See above.

BJUR, William L.

1887-88	pianos	342 E. 34th

Bjur became a well-known manufacturer after 1890 when he and his brother Warner built their firm, *Bjur Brothers*, into a successful concern. See **Dolge** (1911:462).

BJUR BROTHERS

1889	pianos	r. 342 E. 34th
1890+	"	301 E. 29th

See *William Bjur*.

BLACK, Frederick

1835	piano mkr	22 Fifth
1836-37	not listed	
1838	piano mkr	10 Fifth
1839	"	Ave. 3 n. 19th
1840-41	not listed	
1842	piano mkr	135 Ave. 3
1843	"	32 Troy
1844-45	"	47 Ave. 3
1846-47	"	217 Ave. 3
1848	"	208 Ave. 3

Nothing more is presently known about Black, and it is possible that he was a journeyman rather than a mastercraftsman.

BLOOMFIELD, Edward

1858	see *Barberie & Bloomfield*	
1859	pianos	157 Baxter
1860-63	"	173 Grand
1864	not listed	
1865-67	pianos	r. 29 King
1868	"	678 Broadway & r. 29 King
1869-70	"	199 Wooster
1871-78	"	209 E. 19th

Bloomfield and *Andrew Barberie* were partners in the piano-manufacturing firm *Barberie & Bloomfield* from 1858-63. After leaving Barberie, Bloomfield operated a shop of his own for several years before entering into another partnership with *Dwight Otis*. Their firm, *Bloomfield & Otis*, was in business until 1877 when Otis advertised himself as "Successor and Manufacturer of the Bloomfield & Otis Piano-Forte. " (*CmRg* 1877:52) Bloomfield had listed his home address as Indiana in 1876 and Illinois in 1878, and it is possible that he moved to the mid-west after he disappeared from city records in 1879. See *Barberie & Bloomfield*.

BLOOMFIELD & OTIS

1868	pianos	678 Broadway & r. 29 King
1869-70	"	199 Wooster
1871-77	"	209 E. 19th

This firm was headed by *Dwight Otis* and *Edward Bloomfield*. See above.

BLOUNT, George

1831-34	cabinet mkr	8 Batavia
1835-40	piano mkr	"

Blount might have been a journeyman rather than a mastercraftsman, but no further information about his career is presently known.

BOEDICKER, John Daniel

1858	pianos	84 E. 28th
1859	musician	"
1860	tuner	"
1861	carpenter	r. "
1863	piano mkr	h. "
1864-66	pianos	"
1867-68	pianos	r. 136 E. 28th
1869	not listed	
1870-75	pianos	r. 407 E. 24th
1876-90+	piano mkr	"

In 1877, Boedicker, a "manufacturer of all kinds of overstrung Piano Fortes," (*CmRg* 1866:111) was joined by his sons Henry W. and W. E. Boedicker in the firm *Boedicker & Sons*. The firm's factory moved to Brooklyn c. 1885, although its showroom remained at 407 East 24th Street past 1890.

BOEDICKER, J. D. & SONS

1877-90+	pianos	407 E. 24th

See *John Daniel Boedicker*.

BOGAN, John J.

1862-63	banjos	240 10th
1864	mus instrs	5 Ave. 2
1865	not listed	
1866	mus instrs	131 E. Houston
1867-68	banjoist	315 Bowery

1869	"	68 Bleecker
1870-80	mus instrs/banjos	100 E. Houston
1881	mus instrs	203 E. 22nd
1882-84	banjos	260 Bowery
1885	mus instrs	210 E. 34th
1886-90+	banjos/teacher	260 Bowery

The only evidence to indicate that Bogan was more than a banjo teacher and instrument dealer is found in the *1885 AMD* (p. 201) which lists him as a "Banjo Manuf. 10 Prince Street. "

BOGARDUS, Henry S.

1824	cabinet mkr	11 Thomas
1825	"	Bowery-hill
1826	not listed	
1827	pianoforte mkr	215 Mulberry
1828	"	29 First
1829	"	Sixth n. Ave. 3
1830-32	"	270 Elizabeth
1833	"	423 Bowery

Bogardus apparently began as a cabinet maker before turning to piano manufacturing in 1827. He might have been the same person as the music and instrument dealer H. S. Bogardus who was active in Savannah, Georgia c. 1861. (*1861 AMD* p. 30)

BOGERT / BOGART, David

1844	mus instrs	29 Clarkson
1845	not listed	
1846	mus instrs	120 Perry
1847-48	"	138 Perry
1849	"	148 Elm
1850	mus instr manuf	"
1851	mus instrs	"
1852	Susan widow of David	141 Charles

Bogert and *John Clearman* headed the instrument-making firm *Clearman & Bogert* from 1849-51. Little else is presently known about this maker. See *John Clearman*.

BOLEN, John

1794	oval & round turner & mus instr mkr	32 Fair
1795-1805	not listed	
1806-11	turner	76 Chatham
1812-14	not listed	
1815	------	30 Orange
1816	------	83 Mulberry

Nothing further is presently known about Bolen, however, his woodworking skills might have led to his short-lived career as an instrument maker.

BOLLERMANN BROTHERS

Charles, Edwin, and Richard Bollermann were listed as piano dealers, journeymen and tuners from the 1860s onwards. They were listed as piano manufacturers at 2192 Second Avenue only in the *1885 AMD* (p. 201). Although both **Dolge** (1911:462) and **Pierce** (1965) wrote that the Bollermanns established their firm in 1880, there is little to suggest they were active in a significant way before 1887. See below.

BOLLERMANN & SONS

1887-90+	pianos	208 E. 117th

Arthur, Arthur M., Charles A., Edwin and Richard Bollermann were partners in this family business. Bollermann & Sons was still active in 1910. See *Bollermann Brothers*.

BONNET, Carl

1883-90+	musician	various addresses

During the period of this study Bonnet was listed only as a musician. He later became a maker of woodwinds and mouthpieces, and was active in New York as late as 1913. A Bonnet piccolo is in the *DMC*. See **Langwill** (1980:16).

BORNHOEFT, John

1843-45	piano manuf	103 Walker
1846	pianos	"
1847-49	"	" & 45 Canal
1850-52	"	47 Canal
1853	"	31 Howard
1854	not listed	
1855	------	h. 11 E. 11th
1856-80+	mahogany/rosewood	176 Centre

Bornhoeft lived in Brooklyn before moving to New York c. 1843. In 1839, a piano built in his Brooklyn shop was awarded a diploma at the American Institute Fair. (*American Institute Records*) In addition to making pianos and pianos stools (*NYBD* 1846: 170), Bornhoeft turned briefly to the making of wood planes in 1850, (**Roberts** 1971:153), and later in his career, became a wood merchant. An elaborately carved square piano in a rosewood case made by this artisan is in the collection of the Smithsonian Institution. (*S. I. Checklist* 1975:Cat. No. 303,524)

BORST, Charles

See *Rogers & Company*.

BOSTON, Bartholomew

| 1812 | pianoforte mkr | 60 Broome |

Possibly the same person as James Boston, see below. Nothing further is presently known about this maker.

BOSTON, James B.

| 1831 | piano mkr | 64 Carmine |

Possibly the same person or a relative of the earlier piano maker *Bartholomew Boston*, see above.

BOWDEN, William H.

1852-53	piano mkr	105 W. 29th
1854	not listed	
1855-57	piano mkr	"
1858-66	pianos/piano mkr	"

Bowden might have been the same person as the cabinet maker of the name listed from 1849-50 in the *NYCD*. At the 1853 New York Crystal Palace, Bowden exhibited a "Miniature pianoforte, eighteen inches in length. " (*Official Catalogue* 1853:95)

BOYDE, George

| 1791 | mus instr mkr | 54 William |
| 1792 | cabinet & mus instr mkr | 17 Frankfort |

No further information is presently known about this maker.

BRADBURY, William Batchelder

1842-51	mus teacher/ prof of mus/ music	various addresses
1852-53	not listed	
1854-62	pianos	421 Broome & 120 Wooster
1863-64	"	427 Broome & 25 Howard
1865	"	425 & 427 Broome
1866-67	"	" & 65 & 116 Elizabeth

Bradbury was a music editor, conductor, organist and composer of hymns who provided financial backing and lent his prestigious name to several piano-manufacturing firms. Born October 6, 1816 at York, Maine, Bradbury studied with Lowell Mason and spent time in Leipzig before returning to establish himself as a respected musician in the United States. (**Baker** 1958:195) In 1854, Bradbury joined the piano-making firm *Lighte & Newton*, and the resulting concern, *Lighte, Newton & Bradbury*, continued in successful operation until 1858 when *Henry Newton* withdrew. The firm was then reorganized as *Lighte & Bradbury*, with the composer's brother, E. G. Bradbury, becoming involved.

After breaking with *Ferdinand Lighte* in 1864, Bradbury went on the establish his own firm and hired mastercraftsman *Freeborn G. Smith* to act as superintendent of the Bradbury piano company. In 1867, wrote **Spillane** (1890:248), "Mr. F. G. Smith succeeded to Mr. Bradbury's interest and goodwill in the business, and from that year upward has been the sole manufacturer of the instrument bearing that familiar old name. Bradbury died January 7, 1868 at Montclair, New Jersey. See **Jones** (1971:22); **Lawrence** (1988: 286-87, 608-610); *New Grove* (1980:3: 150). Also *Lighte, Newton & Bradbury*; *Lighte & Bradbury*; *Freeborn Smith*.

BRAINARD, James E.

1857-58	pianos	ft. of E. 24th
1859-62	"	73 E. 22nd
1863-66	"	143 E. 23rd
1867-68	"	219 E. 23rd
1869	melodeons	"
1870-76	pianos	"
1877	------	h. 217 E. 23rd
1878	piano mkr	h. 150 E. 52nd
1879	"	h. 236 E. 26th

Although Brainard advertised himself in 1857 as "Successor to A. E. [Alanson E.] Brooks, Manufacturer of Piano Fortes," (*CmRg* 1857:347), the *1861 AMD* (p. 167) listed him merely as a piano dealer. Whether or not Brainard actually made pianos himself, he did later serve as the head of several large piano companies.

After taking over *Alanson Brooks'* piano firm in 1857, Brainard and his partner, *Cornelius Ogden*, formed *Brainard & Ogden*. Their firm lasted until 1858, and the following year Brainard joined *Luman Wing* to establish *Brainard, Wing & Company*. In 1870, the firm became *Brainard & Wing*, and it continued in operation under this title until 1879. Brainard might have been related to the Cleveland music publisher and dealer Silas Brainard (1814-1871), but this has not been confirmed.

BRAINARD & OGDEN

| 1857-58 | pianos | ft. E. 24th |

Firm headed by *Cornelius Ogden* and *James Brainard*. See above.

BRAINARD, WING (& COMPANY)

| 1869 | organs | 219 E. 23rd |
| 1870 | pianos | " |

In 1870, the "& Company" was dropped from the firm's title. See above.

BRAMBACH, Stephen

1872	piano mkr	h. 29 S. Fifth
1873	not listed	
1874	piano mkr	h. Eagle Ave.
1875-77	not listed	
1878	pianos	5 E. 14th & 150th n. St. Ann's
1879	supt.	h. 101 E. 86th
1880-83	pianos	5 E. 14th, 40 Clinton, & 129 E. 129th
1884	"	127 E. 129th & 12 E. 17th
1885-90+	pianos/supt. /pres.	12 E. 17th, 12 & 230 E. 40th

For many years, Brambach was the superintendent of the Estey Piano Company. **Spillane** (1890:283) wrote:"Much of the technical and musical merit of these pianos is due to the competency and skill of Mr. Brambach, who is a gentleman of fine musical and mechanical sensibilities, the celebrated German composer of that name being his brother, while he himself is one of the best tuners in New York, in which capacity he originally held a leading place in the chief shops of the city. " Brambach was awarded several patents (**Spillane** 1890:366) and c. 1885 finally founded his own firm, *Brambach & Company*.

BRAMBACH & COMPANY

| 1885-90+ | pianos | 12 E. 17; 12 & 230 E. 40th; 125 E. 129th |

See above *Stephen Brambach*.

BRAND, John

| 1835 | piano mkr | r. 14 Spring |

Possibly related to *Thomas Brand*, see below, nothing more is presently known about this maker.

Elaborate 7-octave square piano in a rosewood case manufactured by John Bornhoeft c.1845-50.

BRAND/BRANT, Thomas

1816	mus inst mkr	120 Warren
1817-18	"	Washington n. Provost
1819	piano mkr	355 Washington
1820	not listed	
1821-22	piano mkr	"
1823	"	r. 25 Thomas
1824	"	113 Chambers
1825-28	"	17 Thomas
1829	"	23 Leonard
1830	not listed	
1831-32	piano mkr	1 Beach

Brand, occasionally listed as Brant, might have been related to *John Brand*, see above, but this has not been confirmed. Brand might have died c. 1835 since the *NYCD* of that year lists an "Elizabeth, widow of Thomas Brand. "

BRAUMULLER, Otto L.

1886	pianos	14 E. 14th
1887	"	553 W. 30th
1888-90+	"	542 W. 40th

First listed in 1890, the Braumuller Piano Company might have been established in the late 1880s. **Spillane** (1890:303-04) wrote:"The Braumueler [*sic*] Company has a recent origin. In connection with this concern, A. H. Hastings, superintendent . . . is in charge of the Braumueler factory. " It is likely that Braumuller was a dealer and businessman rather than a practical workman. See *A. H. Hastings*.

BRAUTIGAM, Adam

1858	pianos	h. 194 Third
1859	not listed	
1860-61	pianos	47 Amity
1862-70	"	21 Amity
1871-75	"	701 Broadway
1876-83	"	23 Union Square
1884-90+	"	8 E. 17th

Brautigam was first listed as a piano tuner in 1855. Although he advertised himself as a piano manufacturer from 1870 (*CmRg* 1870:130) through 1885 (*1885 AMD* p. 202), Brautigam was probably more active as a dealer. (See *1861 AMD* p. 167)

BRENNISON, William

1835	piano mkr	139 Amity
1836	"	178 Spring c. Sullivan
1837	"	144 Elm
1842	see *Peek & Brennison*	

Brennison was not listed under his own name after 1837, but was probably a partner in the piano-manufacturing firm *Peek & Brennison*, active at 197 Mercer Street in 1842.

BRIDGLAND, James M.

1832-33	piano mkr	451 Broadway
1834	"	449 Broadway
1835	"	465 Broadway
1836-37	"	459 Broadway

Bridgland and *John Jardine* headed the piano-manufacturing firm *Bridgland & Jardine* from 1833-37. Jardine was probably the practical partner, but both are credited with designing and making overstrung pianos as early as 1833. (**Spillane** 1890:158) In 1835, they shared their shop at 465 Broadway with *Torp & Company*, which advertised themselves as retail agents for the former. Jardine continued on his own after 1837, when Bridgland's name disappeared from city records.

BRIDGLAND & JARDINE

1833	piano mkrs	451 Broadway
1834	"	449 Broadway
1835	"	465 Broadway
1838-37	"	459 Broadway

See *James Bridgland.*

BRIGGS, Gilbert V.

1838	see *Corbett & Briggs*	
1839	pianos	143 Centre
1840	"	64 Gold
1841-42	"	430 Broadway
1843	piano manuf	"
1844	"	h. 18 Eldridge
1845	not listed	
1846	piano mkr	E. 15th n. Ave. 3
1847	"	238 11th
1848	not listed	
1849	pianoforte mkr	42 Ave. 4

Briggs first appeared in city records in 1838 as a member of the partnership *Corbett & Briggs*. He was, according to **Spillane** (1890:162), "a maker of some note," who had been trained in the shop of *Nunns & Clark*. Briggs was not related to the Boston piano maker C. C. Briggs, and his name disappeared from city records after 1849.

BRISTOW, George Frederick

1854	pianos	423 Broadway
1855-56	"	419 Broadway
1857-60+	music/teacher	"

Bristow (b. Dec. 19, 1825, Brooklyn, N. Y.) was a well-known composer of opera and symphonic music, a teacher, and the superintendent of music in New York public schools. From 1854-56, Bristow was briefly involved in piano manufacturing with partner E. L. Morse. Given his other activities, Bristow might well have lent his name rather than his time to their firm, *Bristow, Morse & Company*. See **Baker** (1958); **Jones** (1971:23-24); *New Grove* (1980:3:288).

BRISTOW, MORSE & COMPANY

| 1854-56 | pianos & melodeons | 423 Broadway |

See *George Bristow*.

BRITTON, Jacob

| 1832 | piano mkr | 27 Thompson |

Nothing further is presently known about this maker.

BROOKS, Alanson E.

1848-49	machinist	180 Ave. 3
1850	"	r. 67 Forsyth
1851-52	not listed	
1853	piano mkr	h. 128 E. 27th
1854	pianos	181 E. 26th & 75 E. 22nd
1856-58	piano legs	75 E. 22nd

During the 1850s, Brooks apparently specialized in the making of piano legs. According to the *1855 New York Census*, Brooks owned $12,000 of real capital and $1,000 worth of tools. He had in stock 500,000 feet of pine and rosewood worth $150,000, and employed 60 men and 1 boy at average monthly wages of $39. His firm that year produced 490,000 feet of piano legs and cases worth $300,000. In 1857, the firm *Brainard & Ogden* advertised themselves as "Successors to A. E. Brooks. "

BROUWER/BROWER, Samuel S.

1787	drum mkr	5 King George
1792	house carpenter	15 John
1794	drum mkr & composition fanlight mkr	74 Chatham
1795	house carpenter	"
1796	composition & fanlight mkr	"
1797-1800	carpenter	"
1801-02	drum mkr	"
1803-04	" & band-caster	10 Harman
1805	" & "	95 James
1806	not listed	
1807	------	r. 95 James
1808-10	grocer	16 Burlington Slip

Information about this maker is found in a *New-York Packet* advertisement of June 19, 1787:"The subscriber having previous to the late war, carried on the drum-making business in this city; he, by the advice of his friends, again undertakes the same. The gentlemen of the militia, can be supplied with Drums, on short notice and reasonable terms at applying at No. 5 King George-street, nearly opposite the German Lutheran Church. Drums repaired with care and expedition. "

Brouwer, whose name occasionally was listed as Brower, left woodworking to become a grocer in 1808. His activities prior to the Revolutionary War have not been documented.

BROWN, John W.

| 1835 | piano mkr | 220 Division |
| 1836 | " | 130 Division |

Possibly the same person as a printer of this name who was active in the city during this period.

BROWN, Thomas B.

| 1834-35 | piano mkr | 239 Greene |
| 1836 | " | Ave. 3 n. 9th |

A musician of the same name was frequently hired to provide music for official city functions from 1816 onwards. (See *MCC* 1917:passim) His relation to this maker is not known.

BROWNE, Edgar J.

1870-71	trunk mkr	h. 587 9th
1872-78	mus instrs	h. 110 W. Houston
1879	Mary widow of Edgar	h. 531 W. 45th

Probably a son of harp maker *John F. Browne,* see below, this maker took control of the latter's firm in 1872.

BROWNE, John Face

1843	harp manuf	385 Broadway
1844-45	"	" & r. 75 Chambers
1846-47	"	281 Broadway & "
1848-52	"	295 Broadway
1853	not listed	
1854-58	harp manuf	"
1859-66	harps	709 Broadway
1867-68	"	581 Broadway
1869-71	"	644 Broadway

Browne was born in London c. 1815 and trained at Erard's shop. He was granted a "Royal Letter of Patent" for his work, and apparently immigrated in the late 1830s. (*NYCD* 1846) Browne claimed to have established a shop in New York as early as 1841, however, no record of his firm has been found before 1843. In 1844, Browne apparently formed a partnership with the harpmaker J. Delveau, and their firm, Delveau & Browne, advertised themselves as, "Manufacturers of Improved Double-Action Harps . . . J. F. Browne respectfully informs his Friends in the Musical World, that he has established himself in New York, for the manufacture and importing of these very beautiful instruments. His arrangements are such as to enable him to transact business at European prices, thereby saving the purchasers the high duties imposed by Tariff on these Instruments . . . Particular care is taken to fit them for the extremes of climate in this country . . . Prices $500-$750. " (*NYHS*; **Landauer**, n. d.) No other record of this partnership has been found.

From 1846-56, Browne headed the firm *John F. Browne & Company.* At the 1856 American Institute Fair he was awarded a gold medal for the best "double action harp," and in 1857 received a "large silver medal" for a "very superior" harp. In 1853 a "Grand gothic double action harp, of 6 3/4 octaves" made by Browne was exhibited at the New York Crystal Palace. (*Official Catalogue* 1853:94)

Browne probably died c. 1871 when his firm was taken over by *Edgar J. Browne,* see above, probably a son, who had previously worked as a trunk maker. The latter later admitted *George Buckwell* to partnership, and their firm, *Browne & Buckwell,* remained in business until 1878. See also *New Grove* (1984:I:274).

BROWNE, JOHN F. & COMPANY

| 1846-47 | harp manuf | 281 Broadway & 73 Chambers |
| 1848-56 | " | 295 Broadway |

See above *John Browne.*

BROWNE & BUCKWELL

| 1872 | mus instrs | 110 W. Houston |
| 1873-78 | harp mkrs | " |

The "Successors to John F. Browne & Company," this partnership continued until the death of *Edgar Browne* in 1878 when the firm was taken over by *George Buckwell.* See above.

BROWNING, Thomas C., Sr.

1825	pianoforte mkr	47 Murray
1826	"	93 Anthony
1827	"	57 Elm & 167 Elizabeth
1828	"	167 Elizabeth
1829-30	"	142 Hammond
1831	not listed	
1832-37	piano mkr	"
1838-40	not listed	
1841-42	piano mkr	463 Fourth
1843	"	65 Cherry
1844-45	"	h. 72 Catherine
1846-47	"	h. 37 Chrystie
1848	not listed	
1849	pianos	r. 13 1/2 Perry
1850	piano mkr	55 Factory & r. 9 Perry

Browning was the father of *Thomas C. Browning,* see below, however, the two apparently did not share any working addresses during their careers. Three other members of the Browning family were also active in the piano trade during this period: Benjamin J. (1846,1849,1862,1864); George (1842,1864); and John G. (1842-46).

BROWNING, Thomas C., Jr.

1834	piano mkr	662 Greenwich
1835	"	60 Hammond
1836	"	215 20th
1837	not listed	
1838	piano mkr	Ave. 9 n. 18th
1839	"	60 Hammond
1840-42	"	Ave. 6 n. 21st
1843	"	105 W. 17th
1844	not listed	
1845	piano mkr	40 W. 14th
1846	not listed	
1847	piano mkr	24 Wooster
1848	not listed	
1849-51	piano mkr	177 Price

Browning might have worked only as a journeyman. See above *John C. Browning, Sr.*

BRUGGMANN, William

1882-84	musician	h. 112 E. 4th
1885-89	mus instrs	"

A "Manufacturer of Musical Instruments," (*1885 AMD* p. 202), nothing else is presently known about this maker, although he might have been a relative of the woodwind maker F. G. B. Bruggemann of Leyden, Germany.

BRUMLEY, Augustus

1835	piano tuner	31 Reade
1836	piano mkr	"
1837-38	pianos	411 Broadway

In 1836, Brumley joined the well-known piano maker *William Nunns* in the firm *Nunns & Brumley*. The following year, he joined James Smyth in the short-lived firm *Brumley & Smyth*. See *Nunns & Smyth*; *Brumley & Smyth*.

BRUMLEY & SMYTH

1837-38	late Nunns & Brumley, manuf. of grand action pianofortes	411 Broadway

See above *Augustus Brumley.*

BRUNO, Charles

1837	books	212 Fulton
1838-39	mus instrs	"
1840-48	not listed	
1849	merchant	92 E. 15th
1850	mus instrs	62 Liberty
1851-53	"	47 Maiden la.
1854	mus instrs mkr	2 Maiden la.
1855-63	importer mus instrs	"
1864-65	mus instrs	203 Broadway
1866-67	" & agent for C. F. Martin	581 Broadway
1868-81	mus instrs/merchant	4 Courtlandt
1882	mus instrs	10 Courtlandt
1883-90+	"	54 Maiden la. & 29 Liberty

An instrument importer and dealer, Bruno immigrated from Germany to Macon, Georgia in 1832. In 1834, Bruno moved to New York where he probably worked as a clerk or salesman for several years before being listed as a book seller in 1837. In 1838, Bruno formed the first of his many partnerships, this one with the famous guitar maker *Christian F. Martin*. His book shop on Fulton Street probably served as a retail outlet for Martin's guitars, and when *Bruno & Martin* dissolved in 1839, Bruno left the city for several years.

After his return to the city, Bruno first was a member of the partnership *Bruno & Cargill* from 1851-53, and then, with Herman W. Wiessenborn, a member of *Bruno, Wiessenborn & Company* from 1854-57. In 1860, Bruno and Richard M. Morris established the firm *Bruno & Morris*, which lasted until 1863. Bruno then spent several years heading his own concern before admitting his son, Charles Bruno, Jr., to form *Bruno & Son*. This last partnership was successful, and after Bruno's death in 1884, his son continued to run the business. Bruno & Son remains in business; however, it no longer deals in instruments. The firm's main office is located in San Antonio, Texas; its New York office, extant until 1982, specialized in refrigerators. When the latter closed, some of its old account books were donated to the Musical Instrument Department of the Metropolitan Museum of Art, New York.

Charles Bruno's 19th-century firms sold all types of instruments, but it is not known how many were actually manufactured rather than stenciled by the company. At one point, Bruno had an agreement with *William Steinway* that he would not carry pianos. (PC: Bruno & Sons.) See *Martin & Bruno.*

BRUNO & CARGILL

1850	mus instrs	62 Liberty
1851-53	"	47 Maiden la.

Bruno & Cargill, "manuf. & importers," exhibited guitars, fifes, accordeons, flutes and brass instruments at the New York Crystal Palace Exhibition. (*Official Catalogue* 1853:passim) See *Charles Bruno.*

BRUNO & MORRIS

1860-63	mus instrs	2 Maiden la.

Nothing more is presently known about Richard M. Morris. See above *Charles Bruno.*

BRUNO & SON

1868-81	mus instrs/mus merchant	4 Courtlandt
1882	mus instrs	10 Courtlandt
1883-90+	"	54 Maiden la.

During the 1870s, this firm claimed to be the "Proprietor and Manufacturer of the Tilton Patent

Banjo and American Guitars" (*CmRg* 1870:111). Guitar maker *Pehr Anderberg* is known to have worked as a subcontractor for Bruno & Son. See above *Charles Bruno*.

BRUNO, WEISSENBORN & COMPANY

1854-57	mus instr mkr	2 Maiden la.

See above *Charles Bruno*.

BUCHAN / BUCKIN / BUCKEN / BUCKING, James

1802	cabinet mkr	55 Church
1803	"	72 Murray
1804	"	28 Vesey
1805-06	"	48 Anthony
1807	not listed	
1808-09	mus instr mkr	8 Anthony
1810	"	upper end Chapel
1811	"	40 Thomas
1812	"	36 Anthony
1813-14	"	Anthony n. Hudson
1815	cabinet mkr	r. 7 Anthony
1816-17	organ builder	170 Grand
1818-21	not listed	
1822-23	cabinet mkr	221 Church
1824	"	Desbrosses n. Greenwich
1825	"	8 Lispenard

Buchan, who also spelled his name Buckin (1808-09), Bucking (1811-14), and Bucken (1817 and 1822), might have been an organ builder. (See **Ochse** 1975:168)

BUCKBEE, John H.

1881-82	mus instrs	Thomas c. E. 178th
1883	not listed	
1884-87	mus instrs	Webster Ave. c. E. 178th
1888-90+	"	1963 Webster

Although the *1885 AMD* (p. 202) listed Buckbee as a "Musical Instrument Manufacturer," he apparently specialized in making banjos, many of which were stencilled and sold through other firms. Banjo dealer *Henry C. Dobson* reportedly had many of "his" instruments manufactured by *J. H. Buckbee Company*, "which was the largest shop of its kind from 1860 to 1890. In 1897 that company was taken over by Rettburg & Lange. " (**Howard** 1959:46)

BUCKIN/BUCKING, James

See above *James Buchan*.

BUCKWELL, George H.

1867-71	harps / harp mkr	h. 138 Sullivan
1872	mus instrs	h. 110 West Houston
1873-78	harps	"
1879-82	"	h. 623 Ave. 6
1883-84	"	h. 217 E. 112th
1885-86	"	619 Sixth
1887-89	"	1266 Broadway

In 1872, Buckwell joined harp maker *Edgar J. Browne*, who had just taken over his father's firm *John F. Browne & Company*, and the two men formed *Browne & Buckwell*. Their partnership lasted until Browne's death c. 1877, after which Buckwell took control of the firm, appropriating some of the former's claims (e. g. "Est. 1810") as his own. A Joseph F. Buckwell, possibly George's son, became the firm's manager c. 1890.

BULL, Francis I.

1816	pianoforte manuf	Lispenard n. Mercer
1817	"	219 Church

No further information about this maker is presently available.

BUSCH, Frederick

1870-73	mus instrs	r. 255 Bowery
1874	not listed	
1875-79	mus instrs	251 Bowery
1880	"	r. 47 Lafayette Pl.
1881-90+	"	r. 255 Bowery

Busch probably came from Germany, and throughout his career was more active as an instrument dealer than a maker. First appearing in New York records in 1870, Busch and violin maker *August Glasel* formed the partnership *Busch & Glaesel* [sic], which lasted only a year. In 1871, Busch advertised himself as a "Manuf. and Dealer in all Kinds of BRASS & STRING MUSICAL INSTRUMENTS. The best French, German, and Italian Violin Strings constantly on hand. Also, ACCORDEONS & HARMONICAS of the best quality. " (*CmRg* 1871:125) See **Langwill** (1980:22).

BUSCH & GLAESEL

1870	mus instrs	255 Bowery

See above *Frederick Busch*.

BUTLER, John

1808	mus instr mkr	156 Broadway

According to **Lawrence** (1988: xxxi), on January 5, 1807, soon after his arrival, Butler advertised in the *Evening Post*, that his new Patented Flageolet had been "Patronized by the Royal Family and Nobility of Great Britain" where it was held in such high esteem "among Ladies of the first rank" that he had decided to introduce it in the United States, where it had already "met with a general approbation among Ladies of the first circles." Moreover, his flageolet possessed a fingering system "so easy that Ladies and Gentlemen not knowing music may in a few weeks acquire proficiency."

Wolfe (1980:56), writes that Butler was originally from London, and while in New York published several pieces of music, including the works of the redoubtable musician and teacher Dr. George K. Jackson, who seems to have been a close associate of the instrument maker.

BUTTIKOFER, John

1839	piano mkr	33 Warren
1840	"	36 White
1841	"	228 Church
1842	not listed	

1843	piano mkr	139 Centre
1844	"	32 Canal
1845	"	104 Walker
1846-56	"	102 Elm
1857	pianos	100 Elm
1858	"	58 Walker
1859-63	"	444 Broome
1864	"	62 E. 13th
1865-90+	"	52 E. 13th

A native of Switzerland, Buttikofer had worked for instrument makers Erard and Pape in Paris, as well as other shops in Brussels and London before coming to America in 1839. According to **Spillane** (1890:198), by 1851 Buttikofer "had built up quite a reputation among musicians in the metropolis . . . and is credited with having made excellent grands as early as 1845, which were the 'talk of the town' . . . Within more recent years he was known as a small manufacturer of very reputable pianos . . . [and] is at present in business in an unpretentious way in this city."

The *1855 New York Census* reported Buttikofer owned no real capital, but did have $500 worth of tools and 3,000 feet of wood. He employed 10 men, at wages of $40 per month, and in 1855 his shop produced $8,000 worth of pianos.

C

CABLE, Robert

1870-71	piano mkr	h. 454 W. 33rd
1872	pianos	470 Ave. 8
1873	not listed	
1874	pianos	107 W. 23rd
1875-76	"	" & 443 W. 19th
1877	"	" & 529 W. 24th
1878-79	"	" & 215 W. 36th
1880-81	"	217 Ave. 6
1882	piano mkr	h. 417 W. 30th
1883-90+	pianos/cases	506 W. 15th/79 Tenth

Cable was joined by his son Robert Jr. in 1873 and Thomas in 1874. In 1885, their firm, *Cable & Sons*, was listed as manufacturing piano cases at 79 Tenth Avenue. (*1885 AMD* p.202) The firm was in operation until 1964.

CABLE & SONS

1874-79	pianos	107 E. 23rd
1880-82	"	217 Sixth
1883-90+	" / cases	550 W. 38th / 506 W. 15th

See above *Robert Cable*.

CALENBERG, Henry S.

1860-63	pianos	13 Leroy
1864-68	"	101 Bleecker & 136 Ludlow
1869-84	"	333 W. 36th & 10 Union Sq.
1885-89	"	" & 440 Ave. 7
1890+	"	" & 200 W. 34th

In 1863, Calenberg established *H.S. Calenberg & Company*. The following year he admitted *Adam*

Vaupel as a partner. Their firm, *Calenberg & Vaupel*, was noted for making good, popularly-priced instruments, and by 1869 it was the nation's 23rd largest piano manufacturer with gross annual sales $57,387. In the *1885 AMD* (p.202) the firm was also listed as manufacturing of piano keys.

Spillane (1890:251) wrote: "Callenberg [*sic*] & Vaupel . . . were well known makers of good moderate-priced instruments as far back as 1864 . . . Both members composing this old concern are practical, and have enjoyed a large experience in the piano business." Calenberg was awarded a patent (No. 32,427) for piano actions on October 8, 1861. An instrument maker named *Henry Kallenberg* was also active during this period, but there is no evidence that they were related.

CALENBERG, H.S. & COMPANY

1863	pianos	13 Leroy

Calenberg & Company was the maker's first firm. Years later, in 1893, when he dissolved his long-time partnership with *Adam Vaupel*, he again used this title for his business. See above *Henry S. Calenberg*.

CALENBERG & VAUPEL

1864-68	pianos	101 Bleecker & 136 Ludlow
1869-84	"	333 & 335 W. 36th
1885-89	office & warerooms	S.W. c. of 34th & Ave. 7
	manufactory	333 & 335 W. 36th
1890+	pianos	400 W. Ave. 7 & 333 W. 36th

This partnership, which was occasionally listed as *Calenberg, Vaupel & Company*, was in operation until 1893. See above *Henry Calenberg*.

CALLAWAY, Thomas C.

1837-51	piano tuner/musician	various address
1852	piano tuner	59 Ave. 3
1853	tuner	"
1854-58	pianoforte mkr	"
1859-60	"	94 & 96 3rd
1861	piano dealer	"
1863-70s	machines	"

It is probable that Callaway worked as a journeyman rather than a mastercraftsman. The *1861*

AMD (p.167) listed him only as a piano dealer. After 1863, he was listed as working with "machines."

CAMMAYER/CAMMEYER, John C./Charles

1835-36	piano mkr	38 1/2 Division
1837	"	65 1/2 Bowery
1838	"	9 Elizabeth
1839	"	28 Catherine
1840-41	pianos	1 Duane
1842	piano mkr	"
1843-47	"	201 1/2 Division

Cammeyer or Cammayer, as it was occasionally spelled, was listed alternately as Charles and John C. throughout his career. **Spillane** (1890:162) wrote: "Carmeyer [*sic*] began on Walker Street in 1837 [and] was well known past 1850 as a maker of cheap instruments." Although not listed after 1847 in the *NYCD*, the 1854 *NYBD* did list him as a piano dealer at 335 Madison Avenue. After that date he was listed as a pianoforte maker at 6th n. North 5th in Brooklyn from 1857-58.

CANFIELD, Ardon V.

See *Cummings & Canfield*.

CANSCHAT/CANSCHET/CHANSCHET/
CONSHORT, Michael

1798	instr mkr	Second
1799-1801	pianoforte mkr	"

This maker changed the spelling of his name each year he was listed in the *NYCD*: 1798 Canschat; 1799 Conshort; 1800 Canschet; 1801 Chanschet. Perhaps unable to find another way to spell his name, he disappeared from the city records after 1801.

CARGILL

Several members of the Cargill family were involved in the importing and selling of musical instruments. Henry A. Cargill and Thomas S. Cargill were active as early as 1849, and they were later joined by Charles R. Cargill.

In 1850, with *Charles Bruno*, the Cargills established *Bruno & Cargill*. This partnership lasted until 1853, and the following year they formed *Cargill & Company*, which remained in business until 1858. In 1859, with importer *Hermann Sonntag*, they formed *Cargill & Sonntag*. Sonntag advertised in 1861 that he was "Formerly of Cargill & Sonntag" and since he was still located at their 11 Maiden Lane address, it is probable that he had taken over sole control of the firm. It is unlikely that any of the Cargills actually made instruments themselves, although their name was stencilled on instruments made by others. See *Bruno & Cargill*.

CARGILL & COMPANY

1854-56	importers/mus instrs	47 Maiden la.
1857-58	mus instrs	11 Maiden la.

See above *Cargill*.

CARGILL & SONNTAG

1859	mus instrs	11 Maiden la.

See above *Cargill*. *Hermann Sonntag* continued to work as an instrument importer and dealer past 1890.

CARHART, Jeremiah

1849	melodeons	77 E. 13th
1850	melodeon reeds	75 E. 13th
1851-54	melodeons	"
1855-66	"	97 E. 23rd
1867-68	organs & melodeons	143 E. 23rd

Carhart, an innovator in melodeon design, began his career in Buffalo c.1836. On December 28, 1846, he was granted an important patent (No. 4912) for the suction bellows used in many later melodeons. In 1849, Carhart and his partner *Elias Needham* established a factory in the city to manufacture reed organs and organ reeds. Their firm, *Carhart & Needham*, continued in operation until 1868, although its title was changed to *Carhart, Needham & Company* in 1855.

According to the *1855 New York Census*, *Carhart & Needham* owned $28,000 of real capital, $25,000 worth of tools, and had in stock 50,000 feet of rosewood, pine and black walnut worth $40,000. The firm employed 80 men at $50 per month and used steam-powered machines to produce 5,000 organ reeds and 1,500 melodeons that year, worth $190,000.

Carhart & Needham entered two "improved melodeons" in the 1853 New York Crystal Palace Exhibition. By 1866, the firm had produced 15,000 instruments, and was manufacturing new ones at a rate of 40 per week. Carhart died c.1869, and his widow was involved in patent fights for several years thereafter. For further information, see **Gellermann** (1976:9-10).

CARHART, NEEDHAM (& COMPANY)

1849	melodeons	77 E. 13th
1850-54	" / reeds	75 E. 13th
1855-66	melodeons	97 E. 23rd
1867-68	organs & melodeons	143 E. 23rd

In 1855, the name of this firm was changed from *Carhart & Needham* to *Carhart, Needham & Company*. See *Jeremiah Carhart*.

CARLES, Severin

1852	mus instr mkr	35 Murray
1853	not listed	
1854	mus instr mkr/ fancy articles	195 Fulton
1855	mus inst mkr/ fans	"
1856	accordeons	177 Williams
1857	mus intrs	"
1858	accordeons	"

Carles was also listed as a maker of musical instruments in the *NYBD*s of this period.

CAROLAN, Michael

"For many years there lived at No. 842 Greenwich Street, New York City, a good performer on the Union pipes [i.e. uilleann or Irish bagpipes], named Michael Carolan. A native of County Louth, he was born about 1810, and learned the art of pipe-making in his youth . . . Long past his eightieth milestone, he died in 1894, in comparative obscurity." (O'Neill 1973:160)

The only Michael Carolan listed in the *NYCD* during this period was a shoe and boot maker who worked for many years at 871 Broadway. It is not known whether this cobbler was the same person as the pipe maker, however, both crafts did require a knowledge of leather working.

CARTER, Alden J.

1830	mus instr mkr	10 Willet
1831-32	faucet-mkr	"

After a year as an instrument maker, Carter and his partner, William Robinson, Jr., redirected their firm, *Carter & Robinson*, to the manufacturing of "Block-tin Faucets." These men were in some way related to another instrument-making firm, *Jones & Gillespie*, and shared some of the same addresses. See *Jones & Gillespie*.

CARTER & ROBINSON

| 1830 | mus instr mkr | 10 Willet |
| 1831-32 | Block-tin Faucet Mkrs | " |

See above *Alden Carter*.

CARY, William

1817	pianoforte mkr	21 Division
1818-20	"	Essex c. Broome
1821	"	95 Mott
1822	carpenter	"
1824-26+	"	45 Elizabeth

After leaving the musical instrument trade, Cary continued to work in the city as a carpenter through the late 1820s.

CASING, John

| 1813 | pianoforte mkr | 279 Bowery |

Redway (1941:62) also listed Casing as a maker in 1812 and 1814, however, he was not listed in the *NYCD* during those years, and the source of her information has not been located.

CENTRAL PIANO-FORTE COMPANY

1867	pianos	87 E. 22nd
1868-70	"	51 Crosby
1871-72	not listed	
1873-74	pianos	152 Prince
1875	not listed	
1876-77	pianos	150 Prince

First listed in 1867 as "manufacturers of First Class Piano Fortes" (*CmRg* 1867:131), by 1869 Central had become the 25th largest piano-manufacturing firm in the nation, with gross annual sales of $44,000. (*New York Tribune*, March 15, 1869) **Pierce** (1965:49) claimed that the firm continued in operation until 1880, however, it was not listed past 1877 in the *NYCD*.

Given the size of this firm and the almost total lack of advertising and documentation available, it is probable that Central was primarily a "jobbing house" which provided unmarked pianos to be stenciled and sold by others as their own.

CERVENY/CZERWENY, Franz V./Francis

| 1850 | manuf of all kinds of Brass instrs, new inventions | 16 John |
| 1851 | mus instr mkr | " |

1852	mus instrs	r. 161 Bowery
1853-54	mus instructor/mus instrs	161 Chrystie
1855	mus instr mkr	"
1856-57	mus instrs	"

The Czerweny (Anglicized as Cerveny) brass instrument-manufacturing firm was founded at Hradec Králové, Bohemia by Václav Frantisck Cerveny in 1842. (For a biography of the founder see *New Grove* 1980:4:84.) Called by **Langwill** (1980:27) "the most important brass instrument factory in the second half of the 19th century," Cerveny sent a relative (probably his son) to New York to establish an American branch of the company.

Franz or Francis Cerveny was listed alone in 1850, but the firm was listed as *F.V. CERVENY BROTHERS* in 1851. The firm was probably more active as an importer of German instruments than as a manufacturer in New York.

CERVENY, F.V. BROTHERS

| 1851 | mus instrs mkr | 16 John |

See above *Franz Cerveny*.

CHAMBERS, Thomas H.

1835	piano mkr	31 Crosby
1836-37	music	167 Broadway
1838-41	"	285 Broadway
1842-56	pianos/music	385 Broadway
1857-63	pianos	8 Bible House
1864	"	10 Bible House
1865-67	"	8 & 10 Bible H. & 14 6th
1868-69	piano manuf	" & "
1870	pianos	99 Fourth & 219 Sixth
1871-73	"	101 Fourth & 221 Sixth
1874-78	"	306 Fourth
1879	------	h. 23 Gramarcy Park

Best remembered as a partner in *Dubois, Bacon & Chambers* (1836-40), Chambers was a practical piano maker who had begun as an apprentice c.1828. After leaving his first partnership, Chambers worked for *Dubois & Stodart* until 1863, when he joined *Emil Gabler* to establish the piano-manufacturing firm *Chambers & Gabler* which remained active until 1866. (In the 1865 *NYCD*, Chambers advertised himself as "Formerly practical partner of Dubois & Stodart and Dubois, Bacon & Chambers.")

During the late 1860s, Chambers headed his own firm. In 1870, he was joined by a son and their firm,

Chambers & Son, lasted until 1878. (The son was probably Maynard M. Chambers, but two other sons, Leonard M. and Samuel J., also worked in the trade.) See *Dubois, Bacon & Chambers*.

CHAMBERS & GABLER

1863-64	pianos	108 E. 25th
1865-66	"	14 Sixth

This firm consisted of *Thomas Chambers* and *Emil Gabler*. See above.

CHAMBERS & SON

1870	pianos	99 Fourth & 219 Sixth
1871-73	"	101 Fourth & 212 Sixth
1874-78	"	306 Fourth Ave.

Both father and son retired in 1879. See *Thomas Chambers*.

CHANSCHET, Michael

See *Michael Canschat*.

CHARTERS, George

1796-97	mus instr mkr	19 Barclay
1798-1804	see *Whaites & Charters*	
1805-13	not listed	
1814	------	30 Vesey
1815	pianoforte mkr	r. 40 Provost
1816	"	19 Barclay
1817	"	" & 138 Fulton
1818-19	"	33 Walker

According to **Spillane** (1890:106): "Among the piano-makers that came over from London about the beginning of the century were George Charters and Joseph Waites [*sic*]. They were in business in New York in 1804. In 1815—July 8—George Charters was granted the *first* patent issued to a New Yorker for a pianoforte improvement."

The partnership *Whaites & Charters* was active from 1796-1804, and after its dissolution, Charters apparently left the city for several years and was not listed again in the *NYCD* until 1814. He then spent five years in the city as a pianoforte maker before moving to Cincinnati, Ohio in 1819 where he operated a piano-making shop and circulating library on Fifth between Main & Sycamore until about 1825. He was "For many years the only piano-maker [Cincinnati] could boast." (**Greve** 1904:I:919)

Several examples of Charters' pianos are extant. A square piano with two pedals made in 1798 and labeled as Charters "from London" is in the Smithsonian Institution. (Cat. No. 31,569) See *Whaites & Charters*.

CHATAIN, Amand

See *Choplain & Chatain*.

CHESKY, Abraham

1844	accordeons	7 Division

Chesky probably moved out of the region after 1844 since there are no other listings of him in either New York or Brooklyn.

CHEVALIER/CHEVILIER, Louis Antoine

1817	------	31 Catherine
1818	------	14 Orange
1819	pianoforte mkr	"
1820-23	musician	101 Reede

Chevalier, whose name also appeared as A.L. Chevilier, was primarily a dancing master, music publisher and musician. (See **Wolfe** 1980:57.) His career as a piano maker was short-lived. A violinist of the same name played with the New York Philharmonic c.1842 (**Ritter** 1890:275), and there were also several piano dealers with the same surname active during the 1850s, however, their relation to this maker is not known.

CHILD(S), William

1798	grocer	219 William
1799-1800	not listed	
1801-03	mus instr mkr	"
1804-11	not listed	
1812-14	mus instr mkr	23 Chatham
1815-16	"	213 William
1817	"	30 Chapel

A relative of the violin maker *Richard Childs*, see below, with whom he shared the 23 Chatham Street address in 1812, Child added an "s" to his surname in 1812. He also shared the Chatham Street address with the well-known flute maker and publisher *Edward Riley*.

CHILDS, Richard

1811	violin mkr	17 Chatham
1812	"	23 Chatham

See above *William Child(s)*.

CHOPLAIN, Anthony

1854	pianos	r. 1 Marion & 63 Prince
1855-57	"	89 Mercer h. 63 Prince
1858-65	"	173 Prince
1866-68	organs	h. r. 117 Laurens
1869	piano mkr	"

Choplain was first listed in 1854 as a member of the piano dealership Dubreuil & Choplain. From 1856-58, Choplain joined Amand Chatain to establish *Choplain & Chatain*. In 1859, Choplain was listed alone, however, he shared his 173 Prince Street address with the piano maker *Jean Laukota*. Choplain was probably more active as a dealer than a manufacturer, although he did advertise himself as a maker in both the *1861 AMD* (p.170) and the 1865 *CmRg* (p.70).

CHOPLAIN & CHATAIN

1856-57	pianofortes	120 Amity place
1858	"	173 Prince

See above *Anthony Choplain*.

CHRISTIE, Jacob J.

1870	piano mkr	r. 85 Varick
1871	not listed	
1872	pianos	426 W. 19th
1873-75	"	78 Barrow
1876	"	1291 Broadway & 78 Barrow
1877	not listed	
1878-85	pianos	213-215 W. 36th
1886-87	"	520 W. 48th
1888	"	234 E. 44th & 158 E. 45th

Spillane (1890:252) wrote: "Mr Jacob Christy [*sic*], the originator of the business that up to a recent period bore his name, entered the trade over thirty years ago, and is in every sense a practical piano-maker. He built up a very large business meanwhile, and was well known up to a few years ago. Mr. Christy is at the present time connected with the Colby Piano Company at Erie, Pa."

During his New York career, Christie headed *Christie & Company* from 1878-81 and 1886-88. With his son John, he was a partner in *Christie & Son* from 1882-85. The *1885 AMD* (p.202) listed Christie as both a piano manufacturer and music dealer.

CHRISTIE & COMPANY

1878-81	pianos	213-215 W. 36th
1882-85	see below	
1886-87	pianos	520 W. 48th
1888	"	234 E. 44th & 158 E. 45th

See above *Jacob Christie*.

CHRISTIE & SON

1882-85	pianos	213 W. 36th

See above *Jacob Christie*.

CHRISTMAN, Charles G.1

1823	mus instr mkr	Bedford n. Burton
1824-25	"	64 & 80 Crosby
1826	"	Bedford n. Commerce
1827-28	"	79 Bedford
1829-36	"	398 Pearl
1837-42	"	404 Pearl
1843-51	importer/mus intrs	"
1852	mus instrs	605 Broadway & 404 Pearl
1853-54	"	404 Pearl
1855-56	"	391 Pearl
1857-58	music	"

Christman was a prominent maker who specialized in the manufacturing of wind instruments. Also involved in music publishing (**Dichter** 1977:180), Christman advertised in 1831 that he was a "Manufacturer of Accordeons, Harmonicas, and Musical Wind Instruments." (*American Advertising Directory* 1831:80)

Christman exhibited instruments at many of the American Institute Fairs: in 1835 he was awarded a silver medal for the best specimens of flutes, clarinets, trumpets and a post horn; in 1844 he received a silver medal for a double bass; in 1845 a silver medal was awarded for his flutes, clarinets and guitars; in 1846 a diploma was given to him for a 16 key-flute, a guitar and a keyed bugle; in 1851 he served as a judge; and in 1853 he won another silver medal for this clarinets, flutes, a cornet and a royal Kent bugle. (*American Institute Records*) The maker had entered instruments at the first Massachusetts Charitable Mechanics' Fair in 1837, and at the 1853 New York Crystal Place, Christman exhibited clarionets, flutes, trumpets, saxe-horns, bugles and a tuba. (*Official Catalogue* 1853:95)

According to the *1855 New York Census*, Christman owned $2,000 of real capital and $17,500 worth of tools. He had in stock $200 of brass, $200 of silver, $300 of wood and $500 of ivory. His shop employed 4 men, who were paid $40 a month and annually produced musical instrument worth $10,000. Little else is presently known about Christman, but many of his instruments survive. In 1844, Christman shared his 404 Pearl Street address with the instrument maker *James Clearman*, but the relationship of these artisans is not known.

CHRISTOPHER, William H.

1847-51	pianos	130 Ave. 3
1852	not listed	
1853-54	pianos	118 Ave. 3
1855-57	"	" & 109 E. 14th
1858	"	18 Ave. 4
1859	flowers	307 Broadway
1860	artificial flowers	153 E. 12th

Christopher and *Wales Grow* were partners from 1847-58 in the piano-manufacturing firm *Grow & Christopher*. **Spillane** (1890:189) wrote, "They made very good instruments and were known in the trade up to 1857, when they disappeared from notice." After Christopher left Grow, he became involved in the making of artificial flowers. See *Grow & Christopher*.

CLARK, John

1833-39	piano mkr	137 Broadway
1840-42	"	240 Broadway
1843-48	pianos	"
1849-53	"	257 Broadway
1854-58	"	785 Broadway

Clark immigrated from England c.1833 and joined the piano manufacturing firm of *Robert & William Nunns*. Soon, he was "taken into partnership, the firm becoming Nunns, Clark & Company." (**Spillane** 1890:152-53) Following the withdrawal of William Nunns in 1839, the firm became *Nunns & Clark*, and as such continued in operation until 1860. According to **Spillane**, "While much has been written about Nunns & Clark, they have never been identified with any reforms or innovations . . . They simply made average pianos after stereotypical principles . . . employed good men, and paid good prices." See *Nunns & Clark*; *Nunns, Clark & Company*.

CLARK, Joseph S.

1850	machinist	53 Mangin [*sic*]
1851	melodeons	293 Broadway
1852-54	mus instr mkr	264 Broadway

Despite his listings as an instrument maker, Clark probably was never a mastercraftsman. No further information is presently known about this artisan.

CLARKE, James A.

Clarke reportedly made banjos from 1855 until his death on February 20, 1880 (**Howard** 1959:46), however, the only person of this name listed in the *NYCD* during this period was an "agent" at 80 W. 26th Street. It is not known if the agent and the banjo maker were the same person.

Clarke made improvements to the first metal rim banjo, made by Wilson & Farnham of Troy, New York. (**Howard** 1957:11) It is recorded that the winner of a banjo contest held at the Chinese Assembly Rooms at 539 Broadway on October 19, 1857 was awarded a $100 banjo made by Clarke. (**Howard** 1959:35)

CLAUS(E), Christian

1789	mus instr mkr	Partition
1790	"	Dover
1791-93	"	9 Dover
1794-99	"	4 Dover

Clause was probably a native of Stuttgart, Germany. (See **Spillane** 1890:71.) Sometime before 1783, Clause moved to London where he worked for several years as a guitar maker. In 1783, he was awarded an important patent (G.B. No.1394), that was "the earliest evidence for a key-action for the English guitar mounted internally." (See *V. & A. Catalogue* 1968:II:51)

Clause—whose name occasionally was spelled without the final "e"—came to America c.1788. **Harding** (1933:71) claimed that the maker went first to Philadelphia, but his name does not appear in that city's directory during this period. In 1789, Clause was listed in New York, and from 1791-93 he was in partnership with *Thomas Dodds*. Their firm, *Dodds & Claus*, was located at 66 Queen Street.

It is probable that the partners split much of their work: Dodds building the keyboard instruments while Clause concentrated on the construction and repair of stringed instruments. The engraver Dr. Alexander Anderson noted in his diary that he was so pleased with a violin he had bought that he "put it in Mr. Claus's hands to repair and varnish." Anderson later recorded paying Clause $2.50 for this work. (**Anderson** March 24, June 8, 1795) In an advertisement from the same period, Clause informed "the ladies that he intends to manufacture piano-fortes and common guitars the same as he used to do in

London." (*The Diary: or, Loudon's Register* [N.Y.], June 10, 1793) See *Dodds & Clause.*

CLEARMAN, James

1838-41	mus instr mkr	19 James
1842-43	mus instrs	"
1844	"	404 Pearl

Clearman was a relative of *John Clearman*, see below, with whom he shared a home address at 44 Downing Street in 1844. The 1844 *NYBD* (p.184) listed Clearman as a maker of "flutes and clarionets." He was also associated with *Charles Christman*, an instrument maker who shared his business address at 404 Pearl in 1844.

CLEARMAN, John

1836-40	mus instr mkr	44 Downing
1841-42	"	23 Burton
1843-46	mus instrs	44 Downing
1847	not listed	
1848	mus instrs	108 Varick
1849-61	"	148 Elm
1862-63	smith	"
1864	mus instrs	"
1865-66	smith	"
1867	boxes	"
1868	mus instrs	"
1869	not listed	
1870-71	silver	432 Broome

A relative of *James Clearman*, see above, with whom he shared a home address at 44 Downing Street in 1844. From 1849-51, Clearman and his partner *David Bogert* headed the instrument-making firm *Clearman & Bogert*. In those years he was listed as a "smith," Clearman probably worked as a silversmith.

CLEARMAN & BOGERT

| 1849-51 | mus instrs | 148 Elm |

See above *John Clearman.*

COGER, Alexander

1818-19	stationer	20 Dey
1820	not listed	
1821	harmonic glass mkr	3 Spruce

The mysterious "harmonic glass" listing might indicate that Coger manufactured glass harmonicas.

COHEN, Jacob

1846	watchmaker	147 Spring
1847	not listed	
1848-49	watchmaker	102 Chatham
1850-52	mus instrs/mus instr mkr	26 W. Broadway
1853-54	" / "	80 Hudson
1855	" / "	" & 47 Downing
1856-58	" / "	166 Franklin

A small-time instrument maker, Cohen was awarded a diploma for the 2nd best banjo displayed at the 1852 American Institute Fair, and a silver medal "For the best Banjo and Drums" entered at the same organization's 1853 Fair. (*American Institute Records*) In 1853, with a partner named Pike, he founded the short-lived firm *Cohen & Pike* at 39 1/2 Canal Street.

COHEN & PIKE

| 1855 | mus instr mkrs | 39 1/2 Canal |

Nothing more is presently known about Pike, however, he might have been related to a family of the same name active in musical circles in Norwich and Duchess, New York. See *Jacob Cohen.*

COMB(E)S, Henry

1830	piano mkr	12 Rivington
1831	"	10 Rivington
1832-33	gratemaker	124 Norfolk
1834-35+	"	358 Pearl

Combes left the instrument trade in 1831 for gratemaking, a trade he followed into the 1840s.

COMPTON, William

1843	pianoforte mkr	292 Rivington
1844	"	386 Sixth
1845	"	385 Bowery
1846-48	pianos	"
1849-52	not listed	
1853	pianoforte mkr	E. 40th
1854	"	103 E. 40th
1855-64	pianos	101 & 103 E. 40th
1865	piano mkr	" & "
1866	------	" & "

Compton was a small-time piano manufacturer. (See *1861 AMD* p.170.) At the 1844 American Institute Fair, he was awarded a diploma "For a Cabinet Piano-Forte." (*American Institute Records*) Compton might have died c.1867, since an "Eliza, wid. of William" was listed at 321 W. 37th Street in the 1867 *NYCD*.

CONNOR, Francis

1871-73	tuner	574 Third Ave.
1874	pianos	"
1875	tuner	h. 155 E. 37th
1876-78	pianos	157 E. 37th
1879-90+	"	239 E. 41st

Connor was a practical piano maker who personally supervised his factory, and who was highly respected in the trade. His business was primarily wholesale. **Spillane** (1890:286-87) wrote: "Francis Connor, whose entry in the the sphere of the American piano trade dates back to 1871, had achieved an honorable reputation as early as 1878 as a manufacturer of excellent instruments sold at prices within the reach of the people." Connor's firm was listed as "& Company" only in 1874, and perhaps mistakenly, the *1885 AMD* (p.192) listed the maker's factory as being located at 247 E. 41st in Brooklyn.

CONNOR & COMPANY

1874	pianos	574 Third Ave.

See above *Francis Connor*.

CONOVER BROTHERS (James Frank, George H.)

1885-87	pianos	105 E. 14th
1888-90+	"	402 E. 14th & 37 Ninth

The Conovers were born at Mount Morris in Livingston County, New York, into a family "of Dutch extraction." James Frank was born on January 31, 1843, and his brother George H. on June 20, 1844. They began their careers in the trade as piano dealers in Kansas City, Missouri in 1870.

"Ten years later," wrote **Spillane** (1890:277-82), "they began the manufacture of pianos, the senior member [James] returning to New York for that purpose, while his brother conducted their Western business. They retailed nearly all of their own production until 1885, when they began to offer their pianos to the trade. Their business grew rapidly . . . so that to-day the Conover Brothers' pianos are recognized as a strong factor in the piano trade. In January, 1889, they sold their Western business, and G.H. Conover removed to New York to engage permanently with his brother in manufacturing."

CONSHORT, Michael

See *Michael Canschat*.

COOK, John J.

1856	piano mkr	h. 122 Lewis
1857	not traceable	
1858	mus instr mkr	37 Essex
1859-60	"	369 Grand
1861	mus intrs	"

In the *1861 AMD* (p.89), Cook was listed only as an instrument dealer. His relationship to the piano maker *Sebastian Cook*, see below, is not known.

COOK/KOOK, Sebastian

1841	pianos	11 Oliver
1842-43	"	28 Catherine
1844	not listed	
1845	pianos	142 Catham
1846-47	"	E. 21st. n. Broadway
1848	"	Ave. 6 c. W. 23rd
1849-50s	"	423 Ave. 6

Cook, a small-scale piano manufacturer, was awarded a diploma "for the second best piano in touch and tone," entered in the 1841 American Institute Fair. (*American Institute Records*)

For unknown reasons, Cook changed the spelling of his surname to Kook c.1845, and continued in the trade as a piano dealer into the 1850s. His relationship to the instrument maker *John J. Cook*, see above, is not known.

COQUILLAT, Emanuel

1828	pianoforte mkr	12 Lispenard
1829	"	87 Varick

No further information is presently known about this maker.

CORBETT, William

1832	piano mkr	525 Broome
1833-35	not listed	
1836	pianos	104 Laurens

Probably only a piano dealer, Corbett was a member of the partnership *Corbett & Briggs* in 1838. His partner in this venture was most likely *Gilbert V. Briggs*.

CORBETT & BRIGGS

1838	pianos	73 Centre n. Walker

Briggs was probably the same person as the piano maker *Gilbert Briggs*. William Corbett, see above, had been active as a piano dealer earlier in the decade.

COSTELLO, Patrick

1871	pianos	33 Greenwich
1872	"	92 Ave. 6 (*NYBD*)
1873-74	piano mkr	h. 30 W. Washington Pl.
1875	"	h. 559 W. 52nd
1876-80s	"	h. 569 W. 52nd

In the 1872 *CmRg* (p.120), Costello listed himself as a piano manufacturer as well as a dealer. After 1875, however, he apparently worked only as a journeyman.

COTTIER, Hugh

Cottier was a flute maker who began his career in New York c.1840. Although never listed in the *NYCD*, in 1841 and 1843, when he was awarded diplomas for the second best flutes exhibited at the American Institute Fairs, his address was given as 65 Mulberry Street. In 1845, when he entered another flute in the American Institute Fair, his address was listed as 209 Allen Street.

From 1849-53, Cottier owned a music and piano store at 162 Atlantic Avenue, Brooklyn. About 1854 Cottier moved to Buffalo where he was associated with James D. Sheppard. (PC:Eliason) The maker continued to enter instruments at exhibitions: in 1850 and 1851 his diatonic flutes won silver medals at American Institute Fairs; and at the 1855 Fair, the judges noted that a Cottier flute, entered by his New York agents *William Hall & Sons*, was "superior to any flutes we have ever examined," and awarded him a gold medal. (*American Institute Records*)

COUPA, John E./B.

1838-41	------	385 Broadway
1842-49	prof. guitar	"
1850	teacher	"

From 1840-41, the Spaniard Coupa, well-known in New York as a guitar teacher, entered into partnership with guitar maker *Christian F. Martin*. Coupa's studio probably served as a retail outlet for their *Martin & Coupa* guitars. There is no evidence that Coupa was personally involved in making instruments. See **Lawrence** (1988); **Longworth** (1975:2); *Martin & Coupa*.

CREGIER/CRIGIER, Michael V./N.

1826	pianoforte mkr	120 Canal
1827	"	117 Grand
1828-30	"	37 White
1831	"	414 Broadway
1832-37	"	395 Broadway

Cregier's name appeared as "Crigier" only in the 1826 *NYCD*. He also advertised in the *American Advertising Directory* (1831:81). On June 16, 1826, Cregier took on sixteen-year old *William Loomis* as an apprentice, but the apprenticeship was cancelled after a police examination on July 28, 1830. See *William Loomis*.

CROSS, John W.

| 1832 | piano mkr | Tenth n. Bowery |

No further information is presently known about this maker.

CRUSE, Francis

| 1833 | piano mkr | 122 Orange |

No further information is presently known about this maker.

CUFF, John

| 1831-33 | mus instr mkr | 474 Grand |
| 1834-36 | " | 166 Spring |

Nothing more is presently known about this maker.

CUMMINGS, Laurence P.

1853	pianos	103 E. 13th
1854	"	116 Ave. 3
1855-56	"	114 E. 14th & 116 Ave. 3
1857-64	see *Cummings & Canfield*	
1865	pianos	726 Broadway; 156 E. 21st
1866	"	156 E. 21st
1867-70	"	8 Union Pl. & 235 E. 21st

Cummings was probably more active as a piano dealer than as a maker. His first partnership was with the piano makers *Napoleon* and *William Haines*. Their firm, *Haines Brothers & Cummings*, was located at 116 Third Avenue from 1854-55. Cummings then joined *Ardon Canfield* from 1857-64 in the partnership *Cummings & Canfield*; and later, in 1865, with *John L.R. Jennys*, founded *Cummings & Jennys*. Cummings left the piano trade in 1870, and was later listed as the "Rev. Cummings." Also see *Haines Brothers & Cummings*.

CUMMINGS & CANFIELD

| 1858 | pianos | 158 E. 21st (*CmRg*) |

This partnership was listed only in the *CmRg* (1858:350). See above *Laurence Cummings*.

CUMMINGS & JENNYS

| 1865 | pianos | 726 Broadway & 156 E. 21st |

This firm also advertised that they were piano manufacturers in the *CmRg* (1865:113). See above, *Laurence Cummings*.

CURRIER, Nathaniel

See *Stodart & Currier*.

CZERWENY, Franz V.

See *Franz V. Cerveny*.

D

DALE, Benjamin B.

| 1885 | mus instr mkr | 29 Liberty (*AMD*) |
| 1886-90+ | " | 35 Liberty |

Dale was first listed in the *1885 AMD* (p.203). In 1886, his home address was listed as 335 South Fifth Street, Brooklyn, and during the 1890s, his residence was given as Cranford, New Jersey. Nothing more, however, is presently known about this maker.

DARLING, David

| 1823 | mus instr mkr | 196 Washington |

Nothing more is presently known about Darling's career in New York. In 1828, Darling was listed as a musical instrument maker in Providence, Rhode Island. (**Mangler** 1965:13) The well-known Providence-based brass instrument maker Thomas D. Paine married a woman name Ida Eleanor Darling, who might have been related to this artisan. (**Eliason** 1979:13)

DASH, John Balthus, Sr.

1765	see below	
1786	tin, copper & ironmongery store	67 Broadway
1787	"	68 & 26 Broadway
1788-90	hardware & ironmongery store	68 Broadway
1791-93	tinman	"
1794	tinsmith	138 Broadway
1795-1804	tin & copper-smith	"

Dash was in New York as early as March 1765, when he advertised: "John Balthus Dash Tinman from Germany, At his house near the Oswego Market, makes the best of French Horns...Philadelphia Buttons and Shoe Buckles, and will sell them very reasonably by wholesale or retail." (*New York Mercury*, March 18, 1765)

Later in his career, Dash operated a metal-working shop, but apparently continued to make instruments since a forester's horn, made by Dash and dated 1783, is extant in a Belgium collection. (**Langwill** 1980:36) In 1789, Dash was joined by his son, John Balthus Dash, Jr. (1754-1820). It is likely that only the elder Dash was involved in making instruments since the younger Dash was primarily concerned with the repairing of city fire fighting equipment.

The elder Dash died on September 25, 1804 at the age of 77, and his funeral cortege left from his house at 138 Broadway. (*Evening Post*, September 27, 1804)

DASH, John Balthus, Jr.

1789-90	hardware & iron mongery store	61 Broadway
1791	iron monger	"
1792-93	copper, tin-plate- worker & iron monger	"

1794	tin & coppersmith	147 Broadway
1795-1805	iron monger	"
1806-20	"	" & 72 Liberty

John Dash was the son of the instrument maker listed above. Whether or not the son was involved in the instrument-making trade is not known, and in fact, much of his career was spent repairing fire fighting equipment for the city. (**MCC**: 1917:passim) In 1815, Dash Jr. was joined by his own son, also named John B. Dash, and they established *Dash & Son*, which continued until the father's death on November 25, 1820 at the age of sixty-six. (*Evening Post*, November 25, 1820)

DAVIES, Edward J.

1835	piano mkr	142 Elm
1836-38	pianos	12th n. Ave. 6
1839-55	not listed	
1856	pianos	130 E. 28th

Davies was born in 1810 in England (**Kaufman** 1976:28), and was quite young when he began his own firm in New York in 1835. From 1836-38, he worked with his brother, *Julian Davies*, in the firm *Davies & Brother*.

Both brothers disappeared from city records in 1839; probably moving to New Jersey, where Edward was mentioned as a piano maker at Woodbridge, Middlesex County, in 1850. Although there is no record of Julian working in New Jersey, another relative, John E. Davies (b. England 1804), was active as a piano maker in Woodbridge (1850) and Rahway (1860). John E. is also known to have published a piece of music in New York c.1819. (**Wolfe** 1980:57)

Julian later returned to New York in 1854 to work as a piano dealer, and he was joined two years later by Edward who also returned to work as a dealer. Edward left the city after only a year, however, Julian continued to work in the trade until 1871. See **Kaufman** (1976:28).

DAVIES, Julian G.

1836-38	see *Davies & Brother*	
1839-53	not listed	
1854-59	pianos	773 Broadway
1860-61	"	6 Astor Pl.
1862-66	"	467 Broome & 49 Greene
1867-70	"	95 Prince
1871	piano agency office	109 Mercer h. N.J.

A member of the firm *Davies & Brother*, Julian G. was probably in New Jersey from 1839-53. (See *Edward Davies*.) Upon returning to the city in 1854, Julian apparently worked as a piano dealer (*1861 AMD* p.167), and from 1870-71, he headed his own firm, *Julian G. Davies & Company*.

DAVIES & BROTHER

| 1836-38 | pianos | 12th n. Ave. 6 |

This firm consisted of *Julian* and *Edward Davies*. See above.

DAVIES, JULIAN G. & COMPANY

| 1867 & 70 | pianos | 95 Prince |
| 1871 | piano agency office | 109 Mercer |

This firm was probably a dealership rather than a manufactory. See *Julian Davies*.

DAVIS, David

In the *1861 AMD* (p.158), Davis advertised as a manufacturer of hand organs at the New Bowery c. Oliver Street. His address was the same as that of another hand organ manufacturer, *Henry S. Taylor*, for whom Davis might have worked. A Davis family made hand organs in London during the first half of the nineteenth century (**Boston** 1967:53-54), however, their relationship to this craftsman has not been established.

DAVIS, Francis

1826	cabinetmaker	41 Forsyth
1827	mus instr mkr	242 Broome
1828	"	201 1/2 Division
1829	"	199 1/2 Division
1830-42	"	238 Bowery
1843-44	fancystore	"
1845-47	mus instr mkr	70 Clinton
1848	not listed	
1849	fancygoods	397 Grand, h. same

Nothing more is presently known about this maker or his relationship to others of the same surname. Fancygoods shops often stocked musical instruments, which might explain why Davis intermittently operated one.

DAVIS, Jesse J.

1844	piano mkr	25 Cornelia
1845	"	230 W. 17th
1846	"	24th n. Ave. 9

1847	piano mkr	175 Ave. 3
1848-49	"	212 12th
1850	"	331 5th
1851-54	piano action mkr	Fifth c. Lewis
1855	pianos	333 5th
1856	"	212 6th

Davis was one of "the many small makers" active during the 1840s. (**Spillane** 1890:197) After 1856, he continued in the trade as an action maker, and from 1856-59, he was a partner in the successful action-making firm *Rogers & Davis*. During the 1860s, Davis was listed as a journeyman piano maker and occasionally as a dealer. (*1861 AMD* p.167) See *Rogers & Davis*.

DAVIS, Morgan

1801-11	see *Gibson & Davis*	
1812-17	pianoforte mkr	63 Barclay
1818-20	"	61 Barclay
1821-33	"	63 Barclay
1834	"	201 Chambers
1835	"	64 Church
1836-38	pianos	"
1839	"	63 Northmoore
1840-41	"	30 Chapel

From c.1799-1822, Davis was a member of the well-known piano-manufacturing partnership *Gibson & Davis*. Although his partnership with *Thomas Gibson* officially ended in 1822, the two men probably remained on good terms since they continued to work at adjacent addresses until 1833. Thereafter, Davis moved to Chambers Street while Gibson remained at the 61 Barclay Street address until his retirement in 1843. Davis and Gibson were also neighbors at 30 and 32 Chapel Street during the 1840s.

Spillane (1890:102) wrote that both Gibson and Davis were "legitimate piano-forte makers" and assumed—possibly on the basis of his surname—that Davis was a Welshman. Both artisans immigrated from London c.1801, where they had worked together for at least two years previous to their arrival in America.

Davis' relationship to other instrument makers of the same surname is not known, however, he was certainly related to William H. Davis, a piano dealer and organ maker who took over the former's 63 Northmoore address in 1840. **Cameron** (1976:86) claimed they were father and son, however, this has not been proved. See *Gibson & Davis*.

DAVIS, W. J.

1839	music	367 Broadway
1840-42	not listed	
1843	flute player	24 White

Primarily a flutist, Davis was periodically involved with the making and selling of musical instruments. He was first listed in New York as a partner of the multi-talented singer, composer, conductor, music publisher and dealer *Charles Edward Horn*. Their firm, *Davis & Horn*, lasted only a year.

Although Davis was not listed in the *NYCD* from 1840-42, he did appear in several New York concerts during this period (see **Lawrence** 1988:136), and in 1841 he entered five flutes in the Third Massachusetts Charitable Mechanics' Association Exhibit, and was awarded a silver medal (*Catalogue* 1841). About this date, Davis became interested in the new Boehm-system gaining acceptance among European flutists. According to **Badger** (1853:iiiv-iv), the first Boehm-system flute was brought to this country "in the possession of a gentleman tourist [and] Mr. W.J. Davis, an eminent Flute professor of New York, examined the peculiarities of its construction, at once perceived its merits, and predicted that its ultimate destiny would be its general adoption. He immediately engaged in its manufacture, but the undertaking proved far from profitable. All proved too much . . . [Davis] has since relinquished both the profession and manufacture altogether."

It is probable that Davis moved to the South sometime after his appearance in an 1846 concert (**Lawrence** 1988:405). A music store owner and publisher of the same name was active in Richmond, Virginia, during the 1840s and 1850s. (**Stoutamire** 1972:138) This probability is strengthened because Horn, Davis' New York partner, had worked in Richmond before coming to the city.

DAVIS, William

1826-29	pianoforte mkr	r. 18 Thomas
1830-31	piano mkr	91 Chapel

Davis might have been the same person as the piano dealer and organ builder William H. Davis who **Cameron** (1976:86) claimed was the son of the piano maker *Morgan Davis*. That William Davis was active as an organ builder during the 1840s.

DAVIS & HORN

1839	music	367 Broadway

This firm consisted of the musicians *W.J. Davis* and *Charles Edward Horn*. Established primarily as a music publishing business at 411 Broadway, the partners also sold "piano-fortes, musical instruments, sheet music, fine prints, etc." (**Lawrence** 1988:56) See above *W.J. Davis*.

DAY, Charles M.

1816-24	cabinetmkr	various addresses
1825	"	Jones n. Herring
1826-27	not listed	
1828	piano forte mkr	65 Herring
1829	"	273 Bleecker
1830	piano mkr	"
1831	"	373 Bleecker
1832-33	"	117 Barrow
1834-37	not listed	
1838	organbuilder	r. 136 Mulberry
1839	Eliza wid. of Charles M.	74 Attorney

Day was a cabinetmaker who later became involved in musical-instrument making. He died on March 29, 1839, and his obituary listed his home address as 69 Anthony Street. (*Evening Post*, March 29, 1839) His relationship to *Jacob Day*, see below, is not known.

DAY, Jacob

1837-40	piano mkr	71 Hester
1841	not listed	
1842-43	piano mkr	104 Ave. 3

Several persons of this name, one of them a carpenter, were listed in the *NYCD* during the 1820s. Given the dates this maker was active, it is possible that he was a son of *Charles M. Day*, see above, but this has not been confirmed.

In 1842, Day was listed as a co-partner in the piano- manufacturing firm *Adam H. Gale & Company* at 104 Third Avenue. It is also probable that Day was a member of the *New York Pianoforte Manufacturing Company*, the cooperative that preceded *Gale & Company*. Day was not mentioned in city records after 1843; but the "Elizabeth, wid. Jacob, r.39 Watts [Street]" listed in the 1844 *NYCD* might have been his widow.

DE BAUN, Peter

1831	cabinet mkr	179 Bleecker
1832-34	piano mkr	"
1835-36	"	181 Bleecker

Redway (1941:64) mistakenly listed this maker as De Braun. After 1836, De Baun moved his shop from Manhattan to Flatlands, Long Island — now a part of Brooklyn. In 1838, he exhibited a piano "of excellent tone and handsome finish" (*Commercial Advertiser*, October 18, 1838), at the American Institute Fair and was awarded a gold medal. (*American Institute Records*)

DECKER BROTHERS (David and John Jacob)

1862-63	piano manuf	85 Varick
1864-68	"	91 Bleecker
1869-70	pianos	33 Union Pl. & 322 W. 35th
1871-90 +	piano manuf	" & 320-328 W. 35th

The Deckers were born in Germany and trained there as piano makers. They probably immigrated to America c.1850, since John Jacob Decker worked for *Raven & Bacon* and was "later admitted as a partner for eight years before joining his brother." (**Jones** 1971:47-48) *Decker Brothers* was founded c.1862 and, wrote **Spillane** (1890:249-50), "Having accumulated a small capital, and being attached to each other's interests . . . in addition to each being highly skilled craftsmen, it is no surprise to read the story of their subsequent success." David Decker probably did more of the firm's designing since he was the one granted a number of patents. When he retired during the 1880s, John Jacob took over as the firm's manager.

The Decker Brothers were not related to *Myron Decker*, a piano manufacturer whose firm, *Decker & Sons*, was also active in New York during the same period. In addition, neither of the above firms is known to have been associated with the piano dealers Decker & Brothers, who were in business on Bleecker Street from 1868-75.

In 1869, Decker Brothers was the fifteenth largest piano- manufacturing firm in the nation with annual sales of $118,000. (*New York Tribune*, March 15, 1869) A Decker Brothers piano fitted with a Janko keyboard and manufactured c.1890 is in the collection of the Smithsonian Institution. (*Smithsonian Institution Checklist*: Cat. No. 299,840)

DECKER, Myron A.

1863-65	pianos	87 E. 23rd
1866	"	419 Broome
1867	"	2 Union Pl.
1868	"	119 Ave. 3
1869-79	"	127 Ave. 3
1880-83	"	1550 Ave. 3
1884-89	"	" & 2374 Ave. 3
1890 +	"	" & 975 E. 135th

Decker was born in 1823 at Manchester, Ontario County, in the Catskill region of New York, and according to **Spillane** (1890:237), was "descended from good American stock of old standing." (This fact is significant since it rules out any relation to the German-born *Decker Brothers* listed above.) In 1844, Decker began a four-year apprenticeship at the New York piano-making shop owned by *Van Winkle* (probably *Abraham Van Winkle*), after which Decker moved to Albany where he found work with the piano makers *Boardman & Gray*. By 1856, he had established his own manufactory in Albany and was selling instruments throughout the region. The *1861 AMD* (p.169) gave the location of his shop as 45 Church Street, Albany.

Possibly discouraged by Albany's declining expansion, Decker returned to New York City c.1863, and by 1868 his firm was doing well enough for him to lease a large factory building at 119 Third Avenue which had previously housed the piano maker *John Osborne*. As his firm expanded, Decker moved to still larger quarters in 1880 and again in 1890.

From 1866-67, Decker headed *Decker & Company*, but, wrote **Jones** (1971:48), "The partnership did not last long . . . and in 1868 the business was closed up." Decker then worked alone for several years before joining with a Chickering & Company salesman named J.C. Barnes in 1871 to establish *Decker & Barnes*. "The partnership proved mutually agreeable," wrote **Jones** (1971:43), "and lasted until the winter of 1877 [1876?] when Mr. Barnes lost his wife, and his health being poor he withdrew." In 1882, Decker admitted his son, Frank C.—who had worked in his father's factory since 1873—to full partnership, and the title of the firm was changed to *Decker & Son*. The elder Decker died in 1901 and the firm was incorporated in 1909. For further information see **Dolge** (1911:317); **Spillane** (1890:237-42).

DECKER & BARNES

| 1871-76 | pianos | 127 Ave. 3 |

This firm consisted of *Myron A. Decker*, see above, and J.C. Barnes.

DECKER & COMPANY

| 1866 | pianos | 419 Broome |
| 1867 | " | 2 Union Pl. |

See above *Myron A. Decker.*

DECKER & SON

1882-83	manuf of Piano Fortes	1550 Ave. 3
1884-89	"	" & 2374 Ave. 3
1890+	"	" & 975 E. 135th

See above *Myron A. Decker.*

DEDERER, Levi

1835	pianoforte manuf; pianofortes tuned & repaired	67 Bayard
1836	jeweller	84 Bowery h. 67 Bayard
1837	not listed	
1838	piano mkr	198 Bowery

Dederer was working in the city, probably as an apprentice, as early as May 1829 when he is listed as resigning his position in a volunteer fire engine company. (MCC 1917:18:78) He was first listed as a master in 1835, and **Spillane** (1890:161-62) mentioned him among the makers "of lesser note."

DE HOOG, Peter

1845	piano manuf	242 1/2 Spring
1846	"	476 Hudson
1847-49	"	150 Barrow
1850	piano mkr	90 Thompson
1851-52	piano manuf & tuner of pianos with the aeolian	"
1853-55	piano manuf	"
1856-57	piano & mus instr mkr	693 Ave. 6
1858-62	"	697 1/4 Ave. 6
1863-64	"	486 Ave. 6
1865-66	pianos	Broadway n. W. 52nd
1867-72	"	h. Ave. 9 n. W. 61st
1873-75	piano mkr	h. Broadway n. W. 68th
1876	not listed	
1877-78	piano mkr	W. 68th c. 10th
1879-86	"	W. 67th n. 8th
1887-98	"	46 W. 67th

De Hoog began his career in partnership with *Richard Kernan*. Their piano-manufacturing firm, *De Hoog & Kernan*, lasted for only a year, after which De Hoog operated his own firm alone for many years. The *1855 New York Census* listed De Hoog's single-employee firm as having no real capital, $200 worth of tools, and $2,000 worth of lumber. The *1861 AMD* (p.170) listed this artisan as a manufacturer, but by the late 1860s he was apparently more active as a piano dealer (*NYCD*), and still later made his living as a journeyman.

DE HOOG & KERNAN

1845	piano manuf	242 1/2 Spring

This firm consisted of *Peter De Hoog*, see above, and *Richard Kernan*.

DE JANNON, Charles

1851-52	musician	385 Broadway
1853-55	not listed	
1856-57	guitarist	304 Broadway

De Jannon was listed as a musical instrument maker only in the 1857 *NYBD* (p.218), which gave his address as 385 Broadway. The rest of his listings indicate that De Jannon was primarily a musician, and it is possible that he merely sold stencilled instruments rather than manufacturing his own.

After leaving New York, De Jannon apparently moved to Brooklyn, where a Charles Dejanon [*sic*] "Piano Forte & Guitar Teacher," was listed at 15 Elm Place in the *1861 AMD* (p.108).

DELVEAU

See *John F. Browne*.

DENOBRIGA, Augustus

1878	piano mkr	Elton n. 159th
1879	not listed	
1880-81	piano mkr	h. Elton n. 159th
1882-90+	pianos	838 Elton Ave.

A small-time piano manufacturer (*1885 AMD* p.203), Denobriga was active as a maker and tuner into the 1890s. A relative of this maker, *Louis Denobriga*, was also active in the trade for several years (1876-78), and the two shared the same address in 1878.

DENOBRIGA, Louis

1876-77	piano mkr	h. 323 E. 21st
1878	"	Elton n. 159th

See above *Augustus Denobriga*.

DENT, James

1834-39	piano mkr	114 Orange
1840	"	118 Orange

Dent was related to the organ builder Robert Dent (active 1821-33), with whom he shared his Orange Street addresses, but nothing further is presently known about his work. See **Redway** (1941:64).

DIEHL, Justus

See *Behning & Diehl*.

DIERKES, Henry D.

See *Teufel & Dierkes*.

DIERTICHSEN, William

1866-67	pianos	33 W. 13th
1868	"	h. 273 W. 4th

In 1866, Diertichsen joined Herman Ludewig and Christopher Strothoff to form *Diertichsen, Ludewig & Strothoff*, manufacturers of "First Class Piano-Fortes." (*CmRg* 1867:133) The five year warranty offered by this firm was of little use since the partnership was disbanded the following year. All three partners vanished from city records after 1868.

DIERTICHSEN, LUDEWIG & STROTHOFF

1866-67	pianos	33 W. 13th

See above *William Diertichsen*.

DINGLE, John W.

1864	pianos	40 W. 18th
1865	piano mkr	h. 70 Eldridge
1866	pianos	73 Christopher
1867-68	"	Barrow n. Bleecker
1869	"	6 Marion
1870-71	"	183 Grand

Dingle was first listed as a partner of *James Steedman* in 1864. Their firm, *Dingle & Steedman*, lasted only a year, and although Steedman continued to be active as a piano manufacturer into the 1870s, it is likely that Dingle later worked as only a piano dealer rather than a maker. Dingle was specifically listed as a maker only in the 1867 *CmRg* (p.133).

DINGLE & STEEDMAN

1864	pianos	40 W. 18th

See above *John Dingle*.

DISBROW, William

1831	cabinetmkr	58 Mulberry
1833-40	"	118 Eldridge
1841-43	"	262 Houston
1844	"	126 Houston
1845-46	pianoforte	262 Houston
1847-51	"	334 Houston
1852-54	piano mkr	r. 387 Bowery

Nothing more is presently known about this maker.

DISTIN, Henry John

1878	mus instrs	255 & 386 Bowery
1879-80	"	115 E. 13th

Born July 22, 1819 in London, Distin was a member of a well-known family of musicians, musical instrument makers and dealers. With his father, John Distin (1793-1863), and brothers, Henry first toured the United States in 1849 as a member of the extremely successful Distin brass ensemble (see **Lawrence** 1988:593-95). In 1846, Distin began work as the English agent for the French instrument maker Adolphe Sax, and by 1851 he had his own factory at Great Newport where he manufactured brass instruments for Her Majesty's Army and Navy. During this period, Distin was awarded several British patents for improvements he designed for brass instruments and drums.

About 1877, Distin migrated to Philadelphia where he worked for instrument manufacturers W.J. Pepper and *Moses Slater*. Distin spent several years in New York as the superintendent of Slater's city-based brass instrument-making shop. An advertisement from the period mentions Slater's "steam factory in New York under the entire supervision of H. Distin" (**Krivin** 1961:243), and Distin's name appears on Slater's brass instruments. In 1882, Distin left New York for Cressona, Pennsylvania, and in 1887, he moved his operation again to Williamsport, Pennsylvania. Distin retired in 1890 and died on October 11, 1903. (PC:Eliason) Many instruments bearing Distin's label are extant.

DIXSON, Horatio

1845	piano forte mkr	291 Bleecker

In 1847, Dixson was listed as a machinist, and still later as a wheelwright in Brooklyn. His relationship to *John Dixson*, see below, is not known.

DIXSON, John

1828-29	pianoforte mkr	266 William
1830-39	"	40 Madison
1840-45	not listed/not traceable	
1846-47	piano mkr	49 E. 16th

Dixson later moved to Brooklyn where he was listed as a piano maker at 46 Carlton n. Park Avenue in 1849 and 1851-53. Dixson might have died c.1853 since in 1854 an "Ann, widow of John" was listed at 394 Hudson Street in the Brooklyn City Directory. His relationship to *Horatio Dixson*, see above, is not known.

DOANE, Richard

1869	pianos	427 Broome

Doane headed several firms during his career, see below. He was listed as a manufacturer only in the *1870 U.S. Federal Census,* and probably worked primarily as a piano dealer.

DOANE, CUSHING & SMITH

1870	pianos	423 Broome

See above *Richard Doane.*

DOANE, WING, CUSHING & SMITH

1871-72	pianos	423 Broome & 19 W. Houston

See above *Richard Doane.*

DOBSON, Charles Edgar

1861	banjo	561 Broadway
1863	"	h. 169 Wooster
1864	music	691 Broadway
1865	"	713 Broadway
1866	teacher	h. 156 W. 13th
1868	banjo	h. 681 Broadway
1873-74	eating house	141 Ave. 4
1877	banjo	260 Bowery
1879	liquor	50 W. 31st
1881-90+	musician	65 W. 33rd

One of the five Dobson brothers, Charles Edgar was primarily a musician and banjo dealer. In 1861, with his brother *Frank Dobson*, and again in 1865 with his brother *Henry Dobson*, Charles Edgar was a member of *Dobson & Brother*, music and banjo dealers. Their partnerships should not be confused with the 1863-66 partnership *Dobson Brothers*, which involved Charles Edgar and *George C.*, and actually manufactured instruments. In his later years, Charles Edgar worked as a music teacher and dealer and was joined in business by this son, Charles Edgar, Jr. **Howard** (1959:37) gives Charles Sr.'s dates as 1839-1910. See below *Henry C. Dobson*.

DOBSON, Edward Clarendon

1868	banjo	h. 681 Broadway
1870	music	h. 56 MacDougal
1871-72	teacher	h. 522 Broome
1873	musician	h. 213 Thompson
1874	banjoist	h. 48 Amity
1875	music	h. 48 W. 3rd
1876	banjo	400 W. 3rd
1878	music	r. 115 W. 15th
1879	teacher	h. 74 Bleecker
1880	musician	h. 396 Ave. 7
1881-85	banjo teacher	65 W. 33rd
1886-89	banjo	1399 Broadway
1890+	"	1428 Broadway

In the *1885 AMD* (p.203), Edward Dobson was listed as "Banjo College & Manufacturer" at 62 W. 33rd Street. See below *Henry C. Dobson*.

DOBSON, Franklin (Frank) Prescott

1861	banjo	561 Broadway
1863	police	h. 169 Wooster
1865	music	713 Broadway
1868	banjo	h. 681 Broadway
1870	"	h. 27 King

Apparently less successful in the banjo business than his brothers, Franklin joined his brother *Charles Edgar* in 1861 to form the short-lived firm *Dobson & Brother*. See below *Henry C. Dobson*.

DOBSON, George Clifton

1860	music	h. 190 Ludlow
1863	banjo	h. 169 Wooster
1864	musician	"
1866	banjo mkr	279 Bowery & 681 Broadway
1868	banjo	h. 681 Broadway

George C. Dobson was born in 1842 at Williamsburg, Brooklyn and died in 1890. (**Howard** 1959:37) In 1869, he left New York for Boston where, writes **Ayars** (1937:275), "Mr. Dobson was one of the most noted teachers of banjos not only in Boston but in the United States. He made banjos and guitars, mostly assembling them at his home." And, wrote

Jones (1971:49), "His numerous instrument books for the banjo are the best of their kind." He should not be confused with his nephew of the same name who later joined Henry C., see below, in the firm *Dobson & Son*.

DOBSON, Henry Clay

1860	music	h. 621 Fourth
1861	prof.	h. 317 Bleecker
1863	teacher	h. 649 Broadway
1864	"	h. 748 Broadway
1865-67	music	681 Broadway
1868	banjo	"
1869	"	260 Bowery
1870-72	mus instrs	"
1873	eating house	141 Ave. 4
1874-75	banjos	" & 340 Bowery
1876-78	"	466 Ave. 6
1879-81	banjos/music	1237 Broadway
1883-90+	banjos	1368 Broadway

Writing about the Ethiopian Opera House on the Bowery during the 1840s, **Harlow** in *Old Bowery Days* (1931:272) mentioned: "Among the constant gallery patrons were five boys named Dobson, who developed themselves into artists on the banjo. Henry invented a 7-sting banjo, and George could play a duet on two banjos at once, one with each hand. They became banjo teachers and later began to manufacture the instrument. In the seventies the 'studio' was at 260 Bowery."

Henry Clay Dobson, the most prominent of the Dobson brothers, was born in 1832 in New York. His parents were of old New England stock, but family tradition maintains that economic necessity forced young Henry to find work in the cloakroom of the Astor Hotel. Through his job, Dobson came into contact with Negro co-workers who taught him to play the banjo, and he, in turn, taught his brothers to play the instrument.

It is claimed that Henry Clay began to manufacture banjos as early as 1851 in what is now the Steinway section of Queens, New York. He designed a closed-back banjo and later, c.1870, is said to have been the first to manufacture banjos with raised frets. Some of Dobson's instruments were reportedly made by *John H. Buckbee*. (See **Howard** 1959:46)

Dobson was also active as a musician and teacher, and later in his career he estimated that he had taught 25,000 to 30,000 banjo students including such well-known and socially prominent New Yorkers as Lady Randolph Churchill, Lotta, and a large proportion of the Vanderbilt and Belmont families. After the turn of the century, however, Dobson was forced to file a petition of bankruptcy claiming the "the day of the banjo was over, the bicycle, golf and camera had proved too strong a combination for the banjo." (**Howard** 1957:10) Dobson died in New York on May 28, 1908 at the age of 77. [The author is indebted to Reeder Miller of Decatur, Georgia for supplying much of the above information about his grandfather Henry Clay Dobson.]

DOBSON & BROTHER

| 1861 | banjos | 561 Broadway |
| 1865 | music | 713 Broadway |

The firm was headed by *Charles E.* and *Franklin Dobson* in 1861, and Charles E. and *Henry C.* in 1865. See *Charles E Dobson*.

DOBSON BROTHERS

1863	banjos	160 Wooster
1864-65	not listed	
1866	banjo mkr	297 Bowery

This firm consisted of *Charles E.* and *George C. Dobson*. It should not be confused with *Dobson & Brother*, see above, which was headed by Charles E. and first *Franklin* and later *Henry C. Dobson*.

DOBSON & SON

| 1881-82 | banjo | 1237 Broadway |
| 1883-90+ | " | 1368 Broadway |

This firm was headed by *Henry C. Dobson* and his son George Clifton Dobson. (The latter should not be confused with his uncle of the same name who was then active in Boston.) The *1885 AMD* (p.203) listed Dobson & Son as musical instrument manufacturers at 1270 and 1368 Broadway. **Howard** (1959:46) claimed that at least some of Dobson's banjos were made for him by *John H. Buckbee*. See *Henry Clay Dobson*.

DODDS, Thomas

1785	see below	
1786	organ & mus instr mkr	76 Queen
1787	mus instr mkr	66 Queen
1789-93	" & mahogany merchant	"
1794-95	mus instr mkr	320 Queen
1796	not listed	
1797	mus instr mkr	287 Broadway
1798	not listed	
1799	mus instr mkr	221 Pearl

Dodds, whose name was occasionally misprinted as Dobbs, immigrated from London in the summer of 1785, and shortly thereafter advertised in the *Independent Journal* (August 13, 1785):

"Thomas Dodds, Arrived in the last Ship from London, Organ Builder, Harpsichord, and Piano Forte Maker begs leave to offer his best services to Ladies and Gentlemen who may have occasion for the above-mentioned Instruments specimens of his abilities in constructing which may be seen and tried at his House, No. 74, in Queen-Street.

"He humbly trusts from his regular education in these branches and having been employed upwards of twenty years in a very extensive line of business, he shall afford perfect satisfaction to all his employers.

"He repairs and tunes the above-mentioned, and every other kind of Musical Instruments, and has for sale, Organs, Harpsichords, Piano Fortes, Violincellos, Violins, German Flutes, Hautboys, Clarinets, Bassoons, French Horns, Fifes, and most kinds of Wires and Strings for Instruments, as Violin and Guitar Strings, Harpsichord and Piano Forte Wires, &c."

Little is known about Dodds' career in England. One source (**Boalch** 1974:35) claimed Dodds was active c.1756; and it is possible that he was related to, or was the same person as the musical instrument maker T. Dodd of 11 New Street, Covent Garden, London, who published some music in 1795. (**Humphries** 1970:134) If so, he was probably the younger brother of the bow maker John Dodd. (**Langwill** 1980:276) Dodds seems to have been quite successful in New York, and in 1788 he petitioned the New York House of Assembly "that the importation of Musical Instruments may be prohibited; and that he may be naturalized." (*Daily Advertiser* [N.Y.], January 25, 1788) This request, coming from a recent immigrant who apparently sold imported instruments in his own shop, was not granted, however, the Assembly did award him citizenship on March 1, 1788. (New York State *Journals* 1788:32, 102)

In 1789, Dodds sold a piano to New York's leading citizen, President George Washington, who bought it for his stepdaughter, Miss E. Custis. The piano cost 16 guineas, "4 Guineas being allowed for an old Spinnett" the President had brought with him from Virginia. When Washington left office, he took Dodds' piano back to Mt. Vernon. After his death, it became the property of G.W.P. Custis, who moved the instrument to his plantation at Arlington, Virginia. Custis, in turn, left the piano to his heir, Robert E. Lee. It was still at Arlington at the beginning of the Civil War when it was broken into pieces by souvenir hunters. (**Decatur** 1933:35)

From 1791-93, Dodds joined the German-born luthier *Christian Claus* in the partnership *Dodds & Claus*. (See below.) Claus, like Dodds, had previously worked in London, but unlike Dodds, who was a keyboard maker, Claus specialized in the making of stringed instruments. Several other New York piano makers like *Archibald Whaites* and *William Howe* were trained by Dodds.

Dodds disappeared from city records after 1799. The "widow of Thomas [Dodds]" listed in the 1800 *NYCD* was the wife of a shoemaker, not this craftsman. During the 1830s, a carpenter of the same name was again listed in the city directory, but his relation to the piano maker is not known.

DODDS & CLAUS(E)

1791-93   mus instr mkr   66 Queen

The partners, *Thomas Dodds* and *Christian Claus(e)*, advertised in *The Diary*, September 19, 1792: "Musical Instrument Manufactory. No. 66 Queen-Street, New York. Messrs. Dodds and Claus beg leave to inform the public, that they have lately imported, and have for sale, a complete assortment of well finished violins and flutes in all keys, voice flutes, concert flutes, clarinets, hautboys, bassoons, French- horns, trumpets, fifes proper to the field, stuado pastorellos, Eolian harps, books of instruments, and strings for every instrument, pitch-pipes, tuning forks and hammers, ruling pens, mutes in brass and ivory screws, bridges, music desks, &c. . . . At this manufactory every kind of musical instrument are finished according to the present taste, and with the latest improvements, as good and as cheap as in the city of London. Instruments sold on commission, taken on commission, taken in exchange, let out, repaired, and tuned, in the best manner . . . N.B. A good allowance is made to dealers in these articles."

An English guitar with a Dodds & Claus label is now in an Italian collection (**Gai** 1969:35, 147), and a piano built c.1791 by the firm is in the Metropolitan Museum of Art, New York. The latter instrument bears a signature which might be that of Dodds' apprentice *Archibald Whaites*.

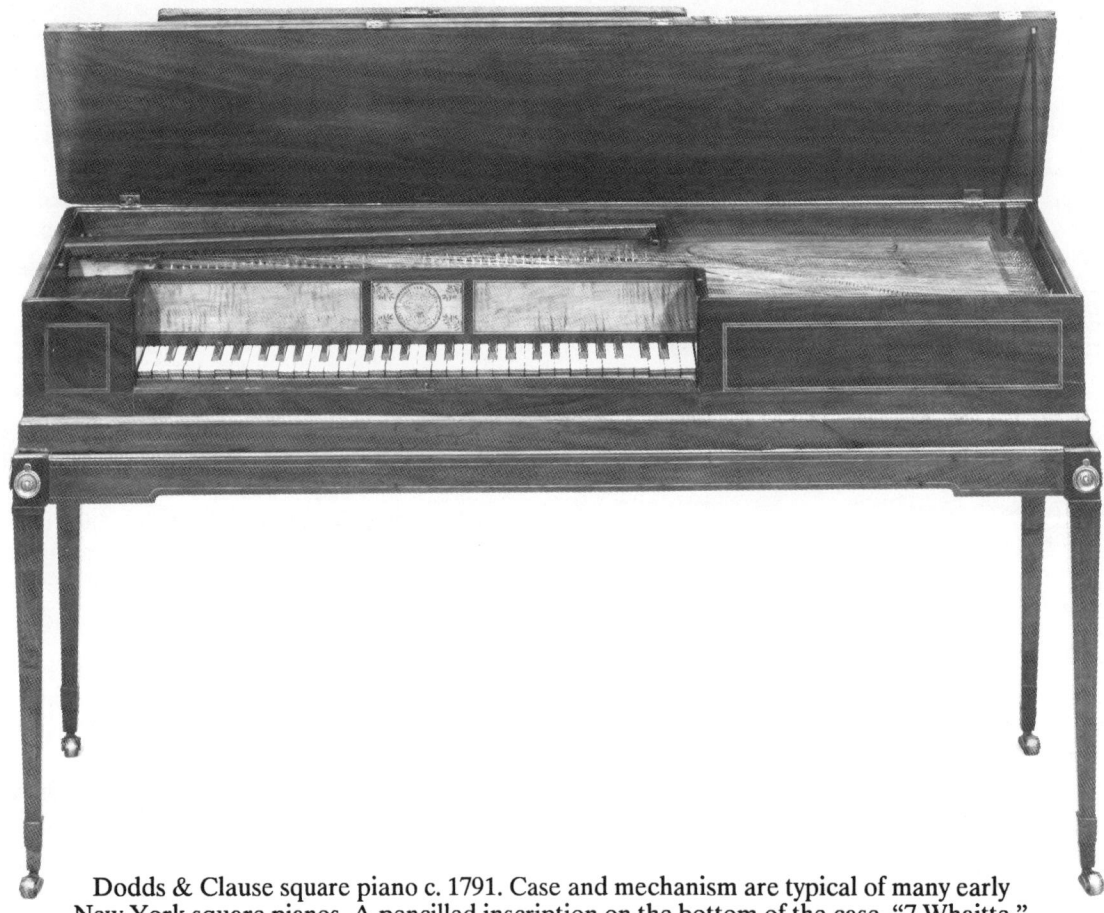

Dodds & Clause square piano c. 1791. Case and mechanism are typical of many early New York square pianos. A pencilled inscription on the bottom of the case, "7 Whaitte," apparently refers to Dodds' journeyman Archibald Whaites, who left the firm in 1792 to found his own shop.

DODGE, Samuel

1790	inspector	17 Franklin
1791	not listed	
1792	mus instr mkr	"

Several persons of this name were active in New York during the 1790s. He was probably the same Dodge who had witnessed the signing of instrument maker *Philip Pelton*'s will in 1765.

DODWORTH, Allen R.; Charles R.; Harvey B.; Olean H.; Thomas J.

Originally from England, this family of musicians, teachers, music publishers, and instrument dealers was active in the city for many years. Thomas J. Dodworth was listed as early as 1829; Allen (1817?-96), Charles and Harvey (1822-91), were listed during the 1840s, and Olean in 1866.

The brass instrument maker *Joseph L. Allen* used pump valves attributed to the Dodworths on his instruments, however, there is little evidence that the Dodworths were actually involved in manufacturing except for a listing of Allen R. and T. George [sic] as manufacturers at 47 Lafayette in the *1885 AMD* (p.203). Members of the family were active in the trade through 1890. See **Lawrence** (1988).

DOLL, Jacob

1884-85	piano strings	224 E. 22nd
1886-88	"	406 E. 30th
1889-90+	cases	"

Doll was born November 14, 1849 in Rohrbach, Baden, Germany, and immigrated to New York about the age of 14 where he found work as a carpenter and woodworker in the city's piano factories. In 1870, Doll established a piano dealership; in 1871 he began manufacturing piano cases; and by 1879, he was making pianos. (**NCAB** 16:438) None of Doll's activities were listed in the *NYCD* during the 1870s, and it is possible that his early successes were exaggerated in Doll's later years. After 1890, however, Doll became a prominent piano maker, and was joined by five of his sons in the firm Doll & Sons. The elder Doll died on November 13, 1911.

DOWLING

See *Hardman, Dowling & Peck.*

DOYLE, Thomas J.

| 1828 | pianoforte manuf | 534 Pearl |
| 1829-30 | not listed | |

1831	piano mkr	r. 534 Pearl
1832-34	not listed	
1835	piano mkr	277 Pearl
1836	"	69 Duane
1837-39	not listed	
1840	piano mkr	21 Canal
1841-42	"	23 Canal
1843	not listed	
1844	pianos	"
1845	not listed	
1846-51	pianos	"
1852-54	"	157 Centre
1855-57	"	Canal c. Centre
1858	piano mkr	h. 30 Goerck

A small-time piano maker mentioned by **Spillane** (1890:197), Doyle was awarded a diploma "For the 2nd best Piano Forte," at the 1844 American Institute Fair. (*American Institute Records*) From 1842-53, Doyle shared his 23 Canal Street address with the piano maker *Vivaldi Harrison*. A Doyle piano is reportedly owned by the Mission Inn, Riverside, California. (**Pierce** 1965:68)

DRIGGS, Spencer B.

1857	pianos	505 Broadway
1858-59	"	26 Wooster
1860	v. pres.	467 Broome & 26 Wooster
1861	not listed	
1862-63	pianos	538 Broadway h. N.J.
1864-65	"	3 Union Pl. & 252 Ave. 9

Born 1823 in Michigan (**Kaufman** 1976:28), Driggs experimented building pianos on the same principles as the violin in Detroit until 1855. Driggs moved to New York c.1856, and in 1859 he formed a short-lived partnership with the piano dealer Spencer Parmelee, *Driggs, Parmelee & Company.*

In 1860, Driggs served simultaneously as the head of his own firm, the *Driggs Piano Company*, and the vice president of the *William Wallace Piano* Company, both located at 467 Broome Street. There is also evidence that Driggs was actually manufacturing pianos in New Brunswick, New Jersey c.1860. (**Kaufman** 1976:23)

Driggs entered into another partnership in 1863 with Richard M. Tooker. Their firm, *Driggs & Tooker,* lasted only a year, and afterwards, wrote **Spillane** (1890:225- 26), "Mr. Driggs settled down to an acceptance of standard principles in piano construction . . . and became known as a small maker of some note." In 1865, Driggs formed the *Driggs Pianoforte Company*, which also lasted only for a year.

At some point, Driggs employed the well-known piano designer and mastercraftsman *Frederick Mathushek*, and in 1858, Driggs was awarded a British Patent for improvements he made to standard piano soundboards.

DRIGGS, PARMELEE & COMPANY

1859	pianos	26 Wooster

This firm was headed by Spencer Parmelee and *Spencer Driggs*. See above.

DRIGGS PIANO COMPANY

1860	pianos	467 Broome

Also listed as a piano-manufacturing firm in the *1861 AMD* (p.170). See above *Spencer Driggs*.

DRIGGS PIANOFORTE COMPANY

1865	pianos	252 Ave. 9

See above *Spencer Driggs*.

DRIGGS & TOOKER

1862-63	pianos	538 Broadway

Firm headed by Richard M. Tooker and *Spencer B. Driggs*.

DRUCKER, Sigmund

1860	jeweller	h. 293 Tenth
1864	importer	169 Broadway
1865-69	pianos	342 Ave. 2
1870	broker	25 Pine

Given his other professions, Drucker was probably a dealer rather than a practical maker of pianos. From 1865-68, however, *S. Drucker & Company* was listed as a piano-forte manufacturers at 340 & 342 Second Avenue. (*CmRg* 1867:133)

DRUCKER, S. & COMPANY

1865-68	pianos	342 Second Avenue

See above *Sigmund Drucker*.

DUBOIS, William

1813-14	------	33 White
1815-16	------	55 Hudson
1817	mus store	127 Broadway
1818-26	"	126 Broadway
1827	"	149 Broadway
1828-37	"	167 Broadway
1838-40	"	285 Broadway
1841-42	mus & pianos	"
1843	pianos	"
1844-50	"	315 Broadway
1851-53	"	300 Broadway
1854	late pianos	90 E. 26th

Primarily an instrument importer and dealer, Dubois took over the well-known New York music business originally founded by John Jacob Astor in 1789, and continued by John and Michael Paff from 1798-1817. According to **Spillane** (1890:107), Dubois "was born in the West Indies, but had handled pianos, as a ship merchant, between [New York] and London . . . he knew nothing practically about pianofortes and was not even a musician."

In 1822, Dubois joined the piano maker *Adam Stodart* as the financial backer of the partnership *Dubois & Stodart*. Dubois left Stodart in 1834 and joined *George Bacon*, another practical maker, to form *Dubois & Bacon*, which was in business from 1835-38. When *Thomas H. Chambers* was admitted in 1836, the firm's title was changed to *Dubois, Bacon & Chambers*.

Dubois, Bacon & Chambers was dissolved in 1840, and after working on his own for several years, Dubois joined *Charles S. Seabury* to form *Dubois & Seabury* from 1843-44. Later, Dubois joined *Daniel C. Warriner* from 1850-52 to establish *Dubois & Warriner*.

Throughout his career, Dubois remained primarily the financial backer of his many partnerships. "Dubois had little significance in connection with manufacturing after his separation from Bacon [1840] the latter retaining the bulk of the business and prestige." (**Spillane** 1890:150) Dubois did have a talent for choosing good craftsmen as partners, and because of this, his name is still remembered. Dubois was also active as a music publisher. (See **Wolfe** 1980:56.)

DUBOIS & BACON

1835-37	mus store	167 Broadway
1838	"	285 Broadway

See above *William Dubois*.

DUBOIS, BACON & CHAMBERS

1836	piano mkr	88 Centre
1837	piano warehouse	167 Broadway;factory 13 Crosby & 142 Elm
1838-40	pianos	285 Broadway

In 1836, *Thomas Chambers* was admitted to the firm *Dubois & Bacon*. Even so, Dubois & Bacon continued to be listed simultaneously with this firm for two more years. See above, *William Dubois*.

DUBOIS & SEABURY

1843	piano forte mkrs	r. 13 Crosby
1844	pianos	"

The partnership consisted of *William Dubois* and *Charles Seabury*. See above.

DUBOIS & STODART

1822-26	music store	126 Broadway
1827	"	149 Broadway & 39 Arcade
1828-34	"	167 Broadway

This firm was headed by *William H. Dubois,* see above, and *Adam Stodart*—not *Robert Stodart*, as **Spillane** (1890:107-08) mistakenly maintains. **Chickering** (1902:51) suggested that some of the pianos bearing this firm's label were actually made by the Nunns piano company on Long Island. This theory is confirmed by a square piano in the collection of the New York State Farm Museum, Cooperstown, New York, labeled as being made by *William & Robert Nunns* for *Dubois & Stodart*. Several other examples of the firm's pianos are in the collection of the Smithsonian Institution. (See *Smithsonian Institution Checklist* 1967; Catalog No. 315,697; 315,700)

DUBOIS & WARRINER

1850	pianos	315 Broadway
1851-52	"	300 Broadway

The firm consisted of *William Dubois*, see above, and *Daniel Warriner*. The latter was active in the city's instrument trade from 1846-63.

DUBREUIL

See *Anthony Choplain*.

DUCKER, Melchior

1858	grocer	596 Houston & 151 Mercer
1859	liquors	" & 194 Washington
1860-61	grocer & triolodeons	19 W. Houston & 618 B'way
1863	piano & triolodeon factory	19 W. Houston

1864-66	pianos	"
1867-68	------	"
1869-70	------	h. 144 W. 4th

Ducker had been listed in connection with taverns and grocery stores as early as the 1840s. About 1859, he entered into an instrument-making partnership with his neighbors at 21 West Houston Street, *Charles J.* and *Cornelius Van Oeckelen*, who were working on perfecting the triolodeon—apparently a type of harmonium. Their firm, *Van Oeckelen & Ducker*, lasted only two years, after which the Van Oeckelens withdrew and Ducker continued on his own. The *1861 AMD* (p.88) listed Ducker as a melodeon and triolodeon manufacturer at 618 Broadway. He probably retired from business c.1868. See *Van Oeckelen & Ducker*.

DUFFY, Peter

1883-87	pianos	423 Ave. 11

According to **Spillane** (1890:302), "Mr. Peter Duffy, a practical piano-maker of some originality and force of character, began business in 1880 in New York, and soon became known as a maker of good popular-priced pianos. Recently, however, he changed the title of his business to the firm name, the Schubert Piano Company, of which he is principle. The instruments bearing his name are meritorious for their price and character."

The *Schubert Piano Company*, see below, was first listed in 1886 at 423 Eleventh Avenue, and it continued in operation until the 1930s.

DUNHAM, John B.

1826	cabinet mkr	Jones n. Herring
1827	piano mkr	63 Herring
1828-34	not listed	
1835-37	piano mkr	Ave. 3 n. 26th
1838	"	375 Broadway
1839-47	"	361 Broadway
1848	"	343 Broadway
1849-53	"	79 E. 13th
1854	"	81 E. 13th
1855-58	"	79 E. 13th
1859-65	"	75-79 E. 13th
1866-67	pianos	111 E. 13th
1868-69	"	831 Broadway
1870-72	"	831 Broadway
1873+	see *Dunham & Sons*	

Born in 1799, Dunham was apprenticed as a cabinet maker in his youth, and "after travelling extensively in the South and working in Charlestown for some time, Dunham settled in New York in 1834, where he got employment in the factory of Nunns, Clark & Company as a case-maker." (**Spillane** 1890:180) His employment by Nunns, Clark & Company probably explains why he was not listed in the *NYCD* from 1828-34.

In 1836, Dunham entered into partnership with *Adam Stodart* and *Horatio Worcester* to form the piano-making firm *Stodart, Worcester & Dunham*. Their partnership lasted until 1844, when Worcester withdrew, and the company reorganized as *Stodart & Dunham*. They continued to manufacture pianos until 1849 when Stodart also withdrew, leaving Dunham to manufacture pianos under his own name for several years.

During this period, Dunham employed the noted piano designer *Frederick Mathushek*, who constructed one of the earliest over-strung square pianos for Dunham's company. (See **Dolge** 1911:322) His innovations did not go unnoticed by the press. In an February 19, 1852 article modestly entitled "New Era in Pianoforte Making," the *Evening Mirror* reported that "Mr. John B. Dunham . . . the well known pianoforte manufacturer, has patented and produced an improvement in Square Pianos, which will astonish and delight the musical world." The article goes on to describe an overstrung piano which "will make his name known from Maine to Georgia, not to mention California and other remote places." And it predicts, should Dunham's improvements be widely adopted, they "will be hailed with delight as the form and size of the Grand Piano are quite unpopular with the generality of purchasers."

Dunham & Company, as his firm was titled from 1854-58, "became very widely known in the course of time and . . . consequently assumed large proportions." (Spillane 1890:181) The *1855 New York Census* noted that Dunham & Company had $45,000 of real capital, $7,500 of tools and 300 meter feet of lumber worth $15,000. Dunham's steam powered factory employed 102 men and 11 boys at an average monthly wage of $44, and annually produced 600 pianos worth $145,000.

In 1867, the name of the firm was changed to *Dunham & Sons*, and after the founder's death on February 9, 1873, its title was changed twice more: to *Dunham Piano-Forte Manufacturing* in 1882; and then to the *Dunham Piano Company* in 1889. The firm continued in operation past 1890. See *Stodart, Worcester & Dunham*; *Stodart & Dunham*.

DUNHAM, J.B. & COMPANY

| 1854 | pianos | 81 E. 13th |
| 1855-58 | " | 79 E. 13th |

See above *John Dunham*.

DUNHAM PIANO COMPANY

| 1889-90+ | pianos | 412 E. 23rd |

See above *John Dunham*.

DUNHAM PIANO-FORTE MANU-FACTURING

| 1882 | pianos | Ave. 4 c. 155th |

See above *John Dunham*.

DUNHAM & SONS

1867	pianos	111 E. 13th
1868-69	"	831 Broadway
1870-72	"	17 Union Sq.
1873-77	"	18 E. 14 & 155 c. Morris.
1878-79	"	124 5th; manuf. Ave. 4 c.155
1880-81	"	155 c. RR Ave.

See above *John Dunham*.

DUPARGE, Luther

| 1796 | mus instr mkr | 159 William |

No further information is presently available, however, this maker might have been related to the Mirecourt violin maker Nicolas Remy Duparge, who was active from 1750-80. (See **Henley** 1960:2:85)

DUPUY, Guitan B.

1848-52	piano mkr	233 Fifth
1853-58	not listed	
1859-68	piano mkr	208 Sullivan
1869-71	pianos	" & 12 Carroll Pl.
1872-75	"	151 Bleecker
1876-80	"	101 Bleecker & 208 Sullivan
1881-83	"	42 Clinton Pl. & 178 Wooster
1884-86	"	36 Clinton Pl.
1887	not listed	
1888-89	pianos	16 E. 13th

From 1859-81, Dupuy and *Francis Taylor* headed the piano- manufacturing firm *Taylor & Dupuy*. In the *1885 AMD* (p.204), Dupuy was listed as heading his own firm at 42 Clinton Place, but soon thereafter he was joined by his son, John S. Dupuy, in the short-lived firm *Dupuy & Son* at 36 Clinton Place. See *Taylor & Dupuy*.

DUPUY & SON

1885-86	pianos	36 Clinton Place

See above *Guitan Dupuy*.

DUSINBERRE, Theodore

1884	piano mkr	h. 343 Willis Ave.
1885-90+	pianos	462 E. 136th

"Dusinberre & Company is a comparatively new concern," wrote **Spillane** (1890:302). "It came into existence in 1884, and is made up entirely of practical workmen of experience and skill. Mr. F.L. Dusinberre [*sic*], the head of the business, is a graduate of Haines Brothers' shop. He was born in Bradford, N.Y. in 1846, and entered the Haines brothers' employ in 1863. Since that time he has acquired a large and varied experience and is a thorough-going piano-maker . . . Mr. R.E. Small, Mr. Dusinberre's partner, is a New Yorker, and a practical man also. He attends to the business of superintending the factory and its necessities. Dusinberry & Company only manufacture uprights, and their instruments are, from a price standpoint, excellent and well made in every respect."

DUSINBERRE & COMPANY

1885-90+	pianos	462 E. 136th

See above *Theodore Dusinberre*.

DWYER, James

1829-32	cabinet mkr	341 Washington
1833	piano mkr	"
1834-36	"	13th n. Ave. 5

No further information is presently known about this maker.

E

EBNER, August (Augustus)

1855	mus instrs	h. 157 Stanton
1856-57	mus instr mkr	h. 27 Delancey
1858	violin mkr	"
1859	flutes	h. 38 Delancey
1860	mus instr mkr	"
1861	flutes	h. 111 Delancey
1862	flute mkr	r. "
1863	flutes	h. 38 Delancey
1864	instrs	"
1865-66	crockery	46 Delancey
1867	flutes	h. 88 Delancey
1868	flute mkr	"
1869-70	music	"
1871	flutes	"
1872-75	flute mkr	"
1876	"	h. 4 First
1877	flutes	h. 161 Christie
1878	instr mkr	"
1879	flute mkr	h. r. 13 Stanton
1880	mus instr mkr	"
1881	mus instrs	"
1882	musician	"
1882	mus instrs	"

Ebner was a small-time instrument maker and dealer. The *1861 AMD* (p.91) listed him as a flute manufacturer. He might have been related to Joseph Ebner (1791-1849), a flute maker active in Munich. (**Langwill** 1980:277)

EGAN, Michael

A maker of Irish [uilleann] bagpipes, Egan immigrated to New York from Liverpool, where he had been active as an instrument maker from c.1845-51. (**Langwill** 1980:45) He probably arrived in the city in the mid-1850s, and reportedly "kept a little shop on 42nd between 9th and 10th [Avenues] until his death in 1860 or 1861." (**O'Neill** 1973:159)

No instrument maker of this name is listed by the *NYCD*s of this period, however a "musician" of the same name was listed at Eleventh Avenue n. W. 47th Street in 1856.

EGGLESO, Arthur

| 1846-48 | pianoforte mkr | 81 Hammond |

Members of the Eggleso family had worked in the city as cabinet makers and upholsterers since the 1820s. Arthur Eggleso was first listed in the 1835 *NYCD* as an upholsterer, but in 1842 he turned to cabinet making. In 1846, he became a piano maker, but only a few years later he left the city, apparently to enlist in the military. On June 5, 1855, the *Evening Post* [N.Y.] reported the death of "Major Arthur Eggleso" at San Francisco, California in his 44th year.

EHRLICH, Edward

See *Altenburgh & Ehrlich*.

EISENBRAND, Henry

| 1815 | mus instr mkr | 15 Duane |

This maker is almost certainly the same person as the German-born wind-instrument maker Christian Heinrich Eisenbrandt (b.Göttingen, April 13, 1790;d.Baltimore March 9, 1860) who settled in Baltimore in 1822 and gained renown as a skilled instrument maker in the following decades. The son of a noted woodwind maker, Eisenbrandt escaped conscription in the Napoleonic Wars by emigrating to America and settling in New Castle, Delaware. He later taught flute students in Philadelphia and during the War of 1812 fought in the battle of North Point. Following the war, he moved to New York in 1815 for a short time, before deciding to return to Germany where he worked as a court musician before returning to America and settling in Baltimore in 1819. His career in New York was short-lived and he seems to have had little or no impact on the local instrument industry. For further information on his later career see:**Hart** (1974:76); **Langwill** (1980:46); **Libin** (1985:74-77).

EMPIRE CITY PIANO-FORTE COMPANY

| 1866-68 | manuf & wareroom | 178 Prince |

Listed primarily in the *NYBD*, this firm might have been a stencilled firm name, or might have produced instruments that were stencilled by others.

ERNST, Louis

See *Lighte & Ernst*.

ESTEY PIANO COMPANY

| 1888 | pianos | 403 E. 63rd & Southern Blvd. c. Lincoln Ave. |
| 1889-90+ | " | 5 E. 14th & 403 E. 62nd |

This firm was an outgrowth of the Estey Organ Company, which had been established by Jacob Estey in Brattleboro, Vermont in 1848. (**Dolge** 1911:363; **Jones** 1971:55) In December 1885, Estey took over the New York piano manufacturer *Simpson & Company*, and soon thereafter began to manufacture pianos on a large scale. Their New York factory was under the supervision of the respected mastercraftsman *Stephen Brambach*. (**Spillane** 1890:283-84) See *Simpson & Company*; *Stephen Brambach*.

EVANS, John

See *Newby & Evans*.

EXNER, Sebastian

1854	mus instr mkr	h. 169 Second
1855	mus instrs	"
1856	mus instr mkr	" (*NYBD*)

In 1856, Exner was listed only by the *NYBD*, and apparently left the city soon thereafter. In 1861, he was listed as a "musical instrument manufacturer" at 254 North 12th Street, St. Louis, Missouri. (*1861 AMD* p.69)

F

FAIRCHILD, Rufus

See *Zogbaum & Fairchild*.

FAKLER

See *Krall & Fakler*

FARRAND, Daniel M.

1833	piano mkr	41 Harrison
1834	"	6 Jay
1835-37	"	Ave. 3 c. 13th
1838	"	Ave. 3 n. 14th
1839	not listed	
1840	piano mkr	115 Ave. 3
1841-43	grocer	Broadway c. 19th
1844-45	hotel	Broadway c. 20th
1846	not listed	
1847	piano mkr	E. 24th n. Broadway
1848-49	not listed	
1850	piano forte mkr	247 Centre
1851-52	pianos	Ave. 3 n. 31st

Farrand was a small-time piano maker who might have been a member of the *New York Pianoforte Manufacturing Company*, the co-operative shop located near Third Avenue and 13th Street during the late 1830s. His relationship to the later Detroit organ builder William R. Ferrand is not known.

FERRIS, Benjamin

1818-19	silversmith	153 Duane
1820	"	Amos n. Hudson
1821	"	Dominick c. Varick
1822	"	Reed n. Chapel
1823	"	95 Crosby
1824	"	Crosby n. Spring
1825	not listed	
1826	mus instr shop	106 h. 67 Crosby
1827	"	Sixth n. MacDougal

Ferris had worked as a silversmith in Philadelphia (1802-11); Waterford, New York (1811); Wilmington, Delaware (1813); and Albany (1816), before coming to the city. (**Darling** 1964:74) In 1818, he shared his 153 Duane Street address with the instrument maker *Simon Giffin*, and in 1822 they

established the partnership *Ferris & Giffin*. A flute bearing their label is owned by Old Sturbridge Village. See **Langwill** (1980:51).

FERRIS & GIFFIN

| 1822 | mus instr mkr | 154 Fulton |

See above *Benjamin Ferris*.

FIRTH, John

1815-16	mus instr mkr	8 Warren
1817-19	"	9 Frankfort
1820	"	Hester n. Rynders
1821	"	362 Pearl
1822	"	Hester n. Rhynders
1823-24	"	215 Hester
1825-28	"	360 Pearl
1829-31	"	358 Pearl
1832	mus instrs	1 Franklin Sq.
1833-36	mus instr mkr	"
1837	"	41 Vanderwater
1838-42	"	1 Franklin Sq.
1843-45	music store	"
1846-56	music	"
1857-63	"	547 Broadway
1864	"	563 Broadway

Firth had a long and successful career as a musical instrument maker, dealer, importer and music publisher. His various activities and partnerships, which occasionally overlapped one another, make a history of his career confusing.

Firth was born in Yorkshire, England, on October 1, 1789, and immigrated to America in 1810. During the War of 1812 he served in the military with his future partner, *William Hall*. (PC:Eliason) After the war, both men found work in the New York shop of the flute maker and publisher *Edward Riley*, and both also married daughters of Riley — making them brothers-in-laws. In 1815, Firth left Riley and established his own shop at 8 Warren Street. Hall left Riley in 1820, and in 1821 their partnership, *Firth & Hall*, was established.

In 1833, Firth & Hall became *Firth, Hall & Pond* when *Sylvanus Pond* was admitted into partnership. Both Hall and Pond came from the Albany area, and it is possible that they knew each other before coming to New York. Although Firth, Hall & Pond was listed in the 1833 *NYCD*, it was not listed again until 1843. During the 1840s, the firm was immensely successful in music publishing, and the dealing and manufacturing of instruments.

Firth, Hall & Pond lasted until 1847 when William Hall withdrew and the firm was reorganized as *Firth, Pond & Company*. The "& Company" were *William A. Pond* and Thaddeus Firth, sons of the owners. The elder Pond was in charge of the piano department, and the firm's pianos were manufactured at their factory in Williamsburg, Long Island. (See **Jones** 1971:139.)

Firth, Pond & Company continued in business until 1863, when John and Thaddeus Firth withdrew to establish *Firth, Son & Company*. Their partnership lasted until John Firth's death on September 10, 1864 at the age of 75 in Newtown, Long Island. His son carried on alone for several years before selling the firm to Oliver Ditson Company of Boston on March 4, 1867.

Firth and his partners are probably best remembered as sheet music publishers, and especially as the principle publishers of Stephen Foster's works. Many extant instruments bear the stamp of Firth and his partners: some are stencilled instruments, others were actually manufactured by the firm. In 1834, for example, Firth & Hall bought into the woodwind-making firm headed by Asa Hopkins and Jabez Camp in Litchfield, Connecticut, and in 1845 they acquired the company outright. Woodwinds manufactured in the Connecticut shop were sold through Firth & Hall's New York store.

According to the *1855 New York Census*, Firth, Pond & Company's piano factory owned $2,000 worth of tools, and $10,000 worth of lumber. It employed 30 men and 2 boys at total wages of $1,200 and that year produced 450 pianos worth $20,000. A 7-octave semi-grand piano built in this shop was exhibited at the 1853 New York Crystal Palace (*Official Catalogue* 1853:95).

For additional information on Firth see **Spillane** (1890:154-56); **Langwill** (1980:51); **DMC**; **Jones** (1971:139); **Fisher** (1918).

FIRTH & HALL

1821-22	music store	362 Pearl
1823-26	"	358 Pearl
1827-28	"	358 & 360 Pearl
1829-31	"	359 Pearl
1832-46	"	1 Franklin Sq.

1847	manuf of piano-forte, with the new patent vibrating overbridge & importer of all kinds of mus instrs	" & 239 Broadway

The firm consisted of *John Firth*, see above, and *William Hall*. In 1833 and 1843-47 it was listed concurrently with *Firth, Hall & Pond*, even though the two firms shared the same address.

FIRTH, HALL & POND

1833	music store	1 Franklin Sq.
1843-44	mus warehouse	"
1845-47	"	239 Broadway

Sylvanus Pond joined partners *John Firth*, see above, and *William Hall* in 1833, but for some reason their firm, *Firth, Hall & Pond*, was not listed again in the *NYCD* until 1843.

FIRTH, POND & COMPANY

1848-50	manufs of pianofortes, flutes, guitars & c., also publishers and importers of all kinds of musical merchandise & special agents for Morrison's hygenia pills	1 Franklin Sq.
1851-53	music	"
1854	"	" & 407 Broadway
1855-56	"	1 Franklin Sq.
1857-58	music & instrs	547 Broadway
1859-60	music	"
1861-63	pianos	"

John Firth and *Sylvanus Pond* admitted their sons Thaddeus Firth and *William Pond* to partnership after the withdrawal of senior partner *William Hall* in 1847. See above *John Firth*.

FIRTH, SON & COMPANY

1864	music	563 Broadway
1865	publishers of music & importers of mus instrs	"

Headed by *John Firth*, see above, and his son Thaddeus. Another son, Edward J., was also involved in the concern. After the elder Firth's death in 1864, Thaddeus continued to run the business on his own for a short time before selling it to the Oliver Ditson Company of Boston. (See **Fisher** 1918)

FISCHER, Charles S.

1843	piano manuf	1 St. John's la.
1844-46	"	170 Greenwich
1847	pianos	"
1848-50	"	" & 95 Leonard
1851-53	"	176 Greenwich
1854-57	"	245 & 247 W. 28th
1858	"	325 Broadway & 245 W. 28th
1859-61	"	856 Broadway & "
1862-69	"	243 W. 28th
1870-80	"	425 W. 28th
1881-90+	"	417 & 427 W. 28th

From 1844 until 1873, Charles Fisher shared the above addresses with his brother, John U. Fischer. The Fischers' grandfather, Bernardo Fischer, a Viennese piano maker, had been appointed "Piano maker to King Ferdinand I of Naples" at the close of the eighteenth century. He trained his sons and grandsons in the craft, and about 1839 his young grandsons, *John*, aged 23, and *Charles*, 21, emigrated to New York. (Dolge 1911:289-90)

The brothers found work in the shop of *William Nunns*, and in 1843, they were admitted into partnership and the firm's name changed to *Nunns & Fischer*. After Nunns' retirement in 1848, the firm became *J. & C. Fischer*.

J. & C. Fischer was a large and successful concern. According to the *1855 New York Census*, the Fischers owned $17,000 of real capital; $5,000 of tools; and $20,000 worth of lumber. Their firm employed 40 men at wages of $45 per month, and that year produced $40,000 worth of pianos. By 1869, their firm was the 20th largest manufacturer of pianos in the country, with annual sales of $69,308. (*New York Tribune*, March 15, 1869)

John Fischer retired to his native Italy in 1873, and Charles admitted his four sons — Henry B., Bernardo F., Adolfo H., and Frederick G. — into partnership. The firm's title remained J. & C. Fischer and it continued operations into the 20th century. (**Spillane** 1890:199-200) See *Nunns & Fischer*.

FISCHER, John U.

See above *Charles Fischer*.

FISCHER, J. & C.

1849-50	pianos	170 Greenwich
1851-53	"	176 Greenwich
1854-55	"	245 & 247 W. 28th
1856	not listed	
1857-58	piano warerooms, manufactory	325 Broadway, 241-45 W. 28th
1859-61	pianos	856 Broadway & 243 W. 28th
1862-79	"	243-45 W. 28th
1880-90+	"	417-425 W. 28th

See above *Charles Fischer*.

FISK, Edward

1838	piano mkr	170 Mott
1839-40	"	21 Canal
1841	"	23 Canal
1842	not listed	
1843-44	piano mkr	49 Harrison
1845-46	"	113 Charlton
1847	not listed	
1848	pianos	"
1849	"	36 Charlton
1850	piano mkr	596 Washington

Fisk was a small-time maker who might have worked as a journeyman rather than a mastercraftsmen. **Pierce** (1965) did list the firm Fisk & Son as active c.1860, but no evidence of such a firm has been found in other sources. A journeyman piano maker, Williard A. Fisk, however, is also listed in *NYCD*s of this period. Edward's relationship to Williard Fisk or Samuel Fisk, who headed the *Union Piano-Forte Company* c.1866-75, is not known.

FLECHTER, Victor S.

1886	violins	23 Union Sq.
1887	mus instr	"
1888-90+	"	"

Flechter was a violin maker and dealer. Some bows bearing his label were actually made by the German craftsman Keil. (**Roda** 1959:160) The violin maker *Oswald Schilback* worked in Flechter's shop.

FLEMING, Joseph Adam

1785	harpsichords	27 Crown
1786-89	not listed	
1790	trunk mkr	18 Broad-street
1791-93	upholsterer, cabinet & trunk mkr	"

1794	"	43 Broad
1795	joiner & trunk mkr	64 Stone
1796-97	trunk mkr & upholsterer	116 Fly-market

In a 1785 flyer printed to advertise his work, the craftsman listed his many accomplishments:

"Joseph Adams Fleming who for many years carried on the HARPSICHORD making, CABINET UPHOLSTERY AND TRUNK WORK in Europe, begs leave to offer himself to the Gentry & Public in general, for their Patronage & Protection. He has taken the House No. 27 Crown Street, where he intends carrying on the above branches, vis.

"Harpsichords made, sold, bought, exchanged or lent at quarterly payments . . . desks, tallboys shaving tables, soffas, wardrobes, clock cases . . . state and canopy beds . . . parlour and fire screens, Venetian blinds, beds and window curtains, window cornishes in wood or paper mache, moulding gilt and plain, paper hung on shortest notice, feather beds, mattrasses with sacking bottoms, and umbrellas made and repaired: Trunk work in all its branches, vis. camp, couch, and portmanuta trunks . . . fiddle and guitar cases . . . canteens and valeeses, furr caps and band boxes . . . the best varnishes in oyl and spirits, gold lacker, fat oil . . . a few chests of toys . . . and a Bird Organ with twenty tunes on two barrels."

(This rare handbill from an 18th-century instrument maker was apparently extant at the New-York Historical Society as late as 1954 when a portion of it was quoted by **Gottesman** (1954:xi). The flyer was subsequently misplaced, but not before a member of the Society's staff made an incomplete typewritten copy of the document. This quote is a compilation of both extant copies, which overlap, but do not duplicate one another.)

Fleming's discission to specialize in trunk making after 1785 emphasizes the mercurial commitment to the musical trade practiced by many other "instrument makers."

FOOTE, John Howard

1855	salesman	31 Maiden la.
1856	clerk	"
1857-64	mus instr	"
1865-66	importer	" & 105 E. 22nd
1867	mus instrs	31 Maiden la.
1868-82	importer mus instrs	" & Chicago
1883-90+	"	31 & 33 Maiden la. & Chicago

Foote was born November 11, 1833 at Canton, Connecticut. As a boy, he was trained as a clock maker in one of the large clock factories of Bristol, Connecticut, and later worked as a journeyman in the machine works of Woodruff & Beach in Hartford. In January 1852, Foote left for New York City, where he found work as a clerk in a hardware store. In December 1853, he was hired by the musical instrument importers *Rohe & Leavitt*, and he continued to work for them until 1863 when the partners retired and Foote bought out their interests to become sole owner of the firm. Except for a short-lived partnership with *John F. Stratton* in 1865, Foote managed his large and successful importing business by himself until his death on May 17, 1896.

Foote is probably best remembered as the founding patron of the musical instrument collection of the Smithsonian Institution. In an 1882 letter to the Smithsonian, Foote wrote that "most of my goods, though not of my manufacture, are made to order by different makers from drawings, descriptions and in some cases models furnished by me." (PC:Eliason) In 1868, Foote established a branch store in Chicago. His firm served as the sole American agent for several French instrument manufacturers, including Antoine Courtois Mille. Many instruments bearing Foote's label are extant. For further information see: **NCAB** (IV:184); *Foote & Stratton*.

FOSTER, Caleb T.

1829	------	227 Sullivan
1830	------	225 Sullivan
1831	piano mkr	223 Sullivan
1832	"	29 Charlton
1833	plane mkr	"
1834	piano mkr	42 Amos
1835	"	Broadway h. 103 11th
1836	not listed	
1837	piano mkr	3 11th n. Ave. 5

Possibly a journeyman, his relationship to other instrument makers of this surname is not known, however, c.1837 he did live next door to *Edward Foster*.

FOSTER, David

| 1839 | piano mkr | 139 MacDougal |

Probably a journeyman piano maker, this Foster might very well have been related to the other Fosters who were active during the same period.

FOSTER, Edward

| 1838-39 | piano mkr | 5 Eleventh |

Probably a journeyman piano maker, this craftsman was almost certainly related to *Caleb Foster*, who was his neighbor on Eleventh Street c.1838.

FOX, John C.

| 1860-62 | pianos | 86 Walker |

Fox's firm, *John C. Fox & Company*, manufactured pianos on Walker Street between Broadway and Elm for several years. (*NYBD* 1861:46) His relationship to the piano maker *Joseph Fox*, see below, is not known.

FOX, JOHN C. & COMPANY

| 1860-62 | pianos | 86 Walker |

See above *John Fox*.

FOX, Joseph

1824-29	cabinet mkr	various addresses
1830	"	30 Burton
1831	piano mkr	102 E. Broadway
1832	"	307 Bowery
1833-34	cabinet mkr	105 Cannon

According to **Spillane** (1890:162), Fox was a partner of *Francis Gruss:*"Francis Gruss began as far back as 1833 at 13 Grand Street, in which year Joseph Fox had a repairing and small manufacturing place at 307 Broadway. They are known in an insignificant way up to 1845, and are remembered by old piano-makers as journeymen subsequently." Unfortunately, nothing has been found to confirm Spillane's date: there is no listing of the partnership, and neither man's name appeared in the *NYCD* after 1834. Fox's relationship to the other makers of the same surname had not been established.

FRIEDRICH, John

1884	mus instrs	80 Second
1885	violin mkr	"
1886	mus instrs	"
1887-88	violins	15 Cooper Union
1889	mus instrs	"
1890+	violins	16 Cooper Union

Born at Cassel, Germany in 1858, Friedrich learned violin making from Schonger in his hometown. He later worked for Möckel in Berlin, and Hammig in Leipzig, before immigrating to New York in 1883. In 1885, he formed a partnership with his brother *William*, see below, and their firm, *J. Friedrich & Brother*, soon rivalled *Gemunder* as the city's largest string instrument dealers.

Friedrich himself constructed about 300 chordophones before his death in 1943. He exhibited his work at the 1893 Chicago World's Fair, and the 1904 St. Louis World's Exhibition. Some bows bearing his label were manufactured abroad and stencilled. (**Henley** 1960:2:158)

FRIEDRICH, William

1885-86	mus instrs	80 Second
1887-88	violins	15 Cooper Union
1889	mus instrs	"
1890+	violins	16 Cooper Union

Brother of *John Friedrich*, see above, and partner in the firm *J. Friedrich & Brother*.

FRIEDRICH, J. & BROTHER

1885-86	mus instrs	80 Second
1887-88	violins	15 Cooper Union
1889	mus instrs	"
1890+	violins	16 Cooper Union

See above *John Friedrich*.

FRITZ, John

1835-37	cabinet mkr	80 Hester
1838-41	"	47 Allen
1842	pianos	105 Walker
1843-44	piano mkr	"
1845	"	---- Cedar
1846-47	"	105 Walker
1848-54	"	478 Broadway
1855-59	pianos	"
1860-63	"	h. 82 Eldridge
1864-71	------	"
1872	not listed	
1873	Ellen widow John	"

A German immigrant, Fritz worked for a while as a case maker in the shop of *Dubois, Bacon & Chambers*. (**Spillane** 1890:189) From 1842-59, Fritz and partner *William Linden* headed the firm *Linden & Fritz* (see below). Fritz probably retired c.1863 and died c.1872.

FROST, John

| 1816 | mus instr mkr | 7 Warren |

No further information is presently known about this maker, nor his relationship to the Boston music publisher John H.A. Frost, who was active during the 1790s. (**Wolfe** 1980:35)

FULLER, John I.

See *Grovesteen & Fuller.*

FURGUSON, Peter

1858	mus instr mkr	r. 276 Bowery
		(*CmRg*)

This maker was listed only in the 1858 *CmRg* (p.313), although the 1858 *NYCD* listed a butcher of the same name.

G

GABLER, Emil

1862	piano mkr	h 159 E. 21st
1863-64	pianos	108 . E. 25th
1865-66	"	14 Sixth
1867-69	manuf of up-right & square pianos	140 Centre
1870	not listed	
1871	pianos	h. 200 Third
1872	not listed	
1873	piano mkr	122 E. 22nd
1883-90+	see *Gabler & Brother*	

The less prominent of the Gabler brothers, Emil was a member of the piano-manufacturing firm *Chambers & Gabler* from 1863-66. He was not listed consistently after 1873, but in 1883 he joined his brother Ernest in the partnership *Gabler & Brother.* See below *Ernest Gabler; Chambers & Gabler.*

GABLER, Ernest

1856	pianos	165 Attorney
1857	piano manuf	127 Elm
1858	pianos	88 Walker
1859	"	311 Rivington
1860-63	"	129 E. 22nd
1864	"	" & 14 Amity
1865-76	manuf of pianos	122-126 E. 22nd
1877-82	pianos	220 E. 22nd
1883-90+	"	214-224 E. 22nd

Born in Glogau, Silesia, Gabler immigrated to New York in 1851, and began his own firm c.1854. (**Dolge** 1911:314) From 1858-59, he joined with *George Manner* to form the partnership *Manner & Gabler.* In 1883, after working alone for several years, he and his brother *Emile Gabler*, see above, established the piano-manufacturing firm *Gabler & Brother.*

Spillane (1890:236-37) wrote that Gabler & Brother were "makers of popular-priced instruments of good quality." Gabler was awarded several patents, and by 1869 his firm was the tenth largest piano manufacturer in the nation with annual sales of $149,484. (*New York Tribune*, March 15, 1869) After Ernest's death on February 27, 1883, Emil took control of the firm. (**Dolge** 1911:314) See *Manner & Gabler.*

GABLER & BROTHER

1883-90+	pianos	214-224 E. 22nd

See above *Ernest Gabler.*

GALE, Adam H.

1833	piano mkr	17 Mercer
1834-38	not listed	
1839-41	piano mkr	13th c. Ave. 3
1842-44	pianofortes	104 Ave. 3
1845	pianos	289 Broadway
1846	"	108 Ave. 3
1847-53	"	102-108 Ave. 3
1854-58	pianos & manuf	92 & 94 Ave. 3
1859-68	"	107 E. 12th
1869-71	"	207-215 E. 12th

From 1834-38, when Gale was not listed in the *NYCD*, he was apparently involved in the *New York Pianoforte Manufacturing Company*, a co-operative shop on Third Avenue near 13th Street. The co-operative ended in the 1840s when, wrote **Spillane** (1890:185-86), "like all such attempts of get a number of people with different qualities of education, taste, and character into the same harness, chaos came, and presently the firmest and most dominant mind came out uppermost and assumed management of the business under new basic conditions. This was A.H. Gale, a practical pianomaker and one of the workmen active in the concern. The name of New

York Pianoforte Manufacturing Company now changed to A.H. Gale & Company . . . [it] soon built up a large wholesale business. The Gale & Company piano was a familiar feature of the trade for upwards of thirty years, but like other concerns that practiced too conservative methods, A.H. Gale & Company disappeared from sight prior to 1870."

Gale & Company was listed in the *NYCD* only from 1842-44 and again from 1847-53, but it was probably in continuous operation during this period since it was mentioned in a number of other sources. The *1855 New York Census,* for example, listed Gale & Company as owning $35,000 of real capital, $7,000 worth of tools, and having in stock 250,000 [*sic*] feet of lumber worth $10,000. It employed 110 men and 7 boys at average monthly wages of $48, and that year produced 650 pianos worth $150,000.

In 1842, Gale's partners in Gale & Company were *Wales Grow, Edward Morgan,* Page T. Gale, and *Jacob Day.* (*NYCD Co-Partnership Directory* 1842:387) At the 1853 New York Crystal Palace, the firm exhibited a 7-octave piano in a serpentine case with carved plinth & Louis Quatorze legs, as well as a 7 1/4-octave upright piano. (*Official Catalogue* 1853:94)

GALE & COMPANY

1842-44	pianoforte	104 Ave. 3
1847-53	"	102-108 Ave. 3

See above *Adam H. Gale.*

GALLAN, Joel

1826	mus instr mkr	116 Franklin
1827	"	82 Elizabeth
1828	"	7 Anthony

No further information is presently available about this maker.

GALLY, Merritt

1876	printing presses	39 Park Row
1877-79	presses	"
1880-82	"	9 Spruce
1883	" & mus instrs	" & 25 E. 14th
1884-85	" & "	" & 76 Ave. 5
1886	presses, mus instrs & pianos	78 Ave. 5
1887-88	", ", ", & organs	95 Nassau
1889-90+	universal printing presses & automatic mus instrs	"

"Professor Merritt Gally . . . claimed to be the inventor of the organette and related instruments [although] no one person was responsible," writes **Bowers** (1972:739-40;757-61), who also contends that c.1880 Gally's organs were actually built by the Munroe Organ Reed Company of Worcester, Massachusetts and that Gally was better known as the inventor and manufacturer of the Universal printing press. Gally was listed as an instrument maker in the *1885 AMD* (p.204), and the same publication also listed a William A. Gally, instrument dealer, at 20 E. 14th Street.

GAMBLE, James E.

1851	accordeonist	375 Hudson
1852	"	h. 461 Hudson
1853	musician	151 Ave. 8
1855-56	music	304 Ave. 8
1857	"	h. 299 Ave. 8
1858	musician	295 Ave. 8
1860-61	music	"
1862-64	mus instrs	"
1865	Rosanna wid of James E. mus instrs	"

Primarily a musician and instrument dealer, Gamble was listed as an instrument maker only by the 1860 *NYBD* (p.320). Given his 1851 listing, it is possible that Gamble dealt in accordeons.

GARVIE, George D.

1883-84	mus instrs	12 Union Sq.
1885	clerk	h. 223 E. 124th
1886	machinist	"

Garvie's career as an instrument maker was short-lived, and he had probably already left the trade by 1885 when *Garvie & Wood,* "manufacturers of musical instruments" was listed in the *1885 AMD* (p.205). The 1885 *NYCD,* however, listed Garvie only as a clerk, and his partner, Wood, is not traceable. Both men might have worked as salesmen for a larger concern.

GARVIE & WOOD

1883-84	mus instrs	12 Union Sq.

See above *George D. Garvie.*

GASSIN, Andrew

1832	piano manuf	Crosby
1833-34	piano mkr	95 Crosby & 95 Wooster
1835-37	"	95 Wooster

1838	not listed	
1839-40	piano mkr	Ave. 3 n. 23rd
1841	not listed	
1842-43	------	Lexington c. 28th
1844	piano mkr	"
1845	"	26th n. Ave. 6
1846-68	"	103 Lexington Ave.
1869 +	"	Bleecker

Although Gassin began his career as a manufacturer, he seems to have later worked as a journeyman. His name continued to appear periodically during the early 1870s. He was related to *Joseph Gassin*, see below, with whom he shared several addresses.

GASSIN, Joseph

1833-34	piano mkr	95 Crosby
1835-36	"	94 Wooster
1837-43	not listed	
1844	piano mkr	Lexington c. 28th
1845	"	26th n. Ave. 6
1846-49	"	E. 27th n. Ave. 1
1850	"	172 E. 27th
1851-59	"	h. 172 E. 27th
1860	clerk	"
1862	piano mkr	"
1863	pianos	"
1864	u.s.n. [U.S. Navy?]	"
1865	piano mkr	"
1868-70s	pianos/piano mkr	h. 326 E. 27th

Gassin seems to have worked primarily as a journeyman. His name and the date August 20, 1853, are pencilled on the soundboard of a *Nunns & Clark* piano now in the collection of the MMA (Catalog No. 06.1312). He was apparently related to *Andrew Gassin*, see above, with whom he shared several addresses.

GEIB

The Geibs were prominent in the city's instrument industry for several generations. The most important members of the family were *John Geib, Sr.*, and his sons *John, Jr., Adam, George* and *William*. Their careers and partnerships, especially those with other family members often overlap and remain somewhat unclear.

JOHN (JOHANNES) GEIB, SR.

| 1798-99 | organbuilder | First |
| 1800-04 | " | Bowery c. North |

1805	"	Corres. Gard. Leonard
1806-09	"	Leonard
1810	"	95 Leonard
1811-12	"	" & 35 Sugar Loaf
1813-15	"	55 Sugar Loaf

Geib was born at Standerheim, Germany on February 27, 1744, and trained there as an organbuilder before emigrating to England c.1760. He was one of the "twelve apostles" who helped establish the craft of piano making in Britain, and he was apparently quite successful in London. He married an English woman on August 20, 1779, and lived in the Old Bailey, Tottengham Court, London for several years before moving to Southampton Road, London in 1792. On February 11, 1792, he was granted letters of denization.

While in London, Geib worked for such well-known piano firms as Schudi, Longman & Broderip, and was also in partnership with Lenkfeld. He was awarded several British patents, including an important one for the "grasshopper-action," and another for buff stops on square pianos.

Why Geib, and other successful European craftsmen decided to emigrate to the New World is not known, but on June 24, 1797, Geib and his family—including his 17 year-old twins sons *John, Jr.* and *Adam*; 15 year-old *George*; and 4 year-old *William*—sailed for New York on the ship Factor. He was first listed in the 1798 *NYCD*, and from 1800-1802 headed the organbuilding firm *Geib & Company*. Geib survived a bankruptcy in 1802, and also maintained a shop in Boston until 1804. (**Libin** 1985:173) From 1803-14, Geib and his son John, Jr. headed the firm *Geib & Son*.

The elder Geib died near Newark, New Jersey on October 30, 1819, at the age of 75, and was buried in St. Paul's churchyard at Broadway and Vesey Streets, New York. A portrait Geib is owned by the New-York Historical Society. For further information see **Spillane** (1890:104-05); **Boalch** (1974:49); and especially **Gildersleeves** (1945). See also *Geib & Company*; *Geib & Son*.

JOHN GEIB, JR.

The elder of *John Geib*'s twin sons, John Jr. was born in London on May 26, 1780. From 1803-14, he joined his father in the keyboard-making firm, *Geib & Son*, and c.1815, after his father's retirement, he was joined in the family business by his brothers *Adam* and *William*.

During the period John Jr. was in partnership with his father, he was also involved in a piano-manufacturing shop with his brother Adam. There was quite a lot of overlap among the various business ventures of the Geib family, and John Jr. was involved in *Geib & Son, J. & A. Geib, J. & A. Geib & Company*, and *J.A. & W. Geib*, see below. In 1816, a son, also named John Jr., was briefly involved in a partnership with his uncle, Adam. John Jr. died on September 10, 1821, at the age of 42, and like his father, was buried in St. Paul's churchyard. A portrait of John Jr. is owned by New-York Historical Society.

ADAM GEIB

The younger of *John Geib*'s twin sons, Adam (b. 1780) took over the family business after the deaths of his father and brother, with whom he had previously worked. About 1815, he became involved in publishing music, using printing plates he had acquired from John Appel. In 1816, Adam took his nephew, John Jr. into partnership, and in 1818, his brother *William* joined him in his publishing venture. (**Wolfe** 1980:55)

From 1822-27, Adam and William headed the piano and music store *A. & W. Geib* at 23 Maiden Lane. After William withdrew, Adam carried on by himself for a year before being joined by his son-in-law, *Daniel Walker*, a piano maker and one of the founders of the New York Philharmonic. Their partnership, *Geib & Walker*, lasted until 1843. On August 19, 1848, the *Mirror* noted that Geib had relocated and now was "smiling through the doors of Stodart and Dunham's old store" at 361 Broadway. (**Lawrence** 1988:559)

After Adam's death in 1849, the family business was continued by his son, *William Howe Geib*, who was primarily a dealer rather than a maker. See *John Geib, Sr.*; *J.& A. Geib*; *J.A. Geib & Company*; *J.A.& W. Geib*; *A.& W. Geib*; *Geib & Walker*.

GEORGE GEIB

The third son of *John Geib, Sr.*, see above, George was born March 31, 1782 in London. He travelled extensively and apparently had little connection with the family business. **Lawrence** (1988:660) believes he died c.1848.

WILLIAM GEIB

Born in London on March 5, 1793, William joined his elder brothers *John Jr.* and *Adam* in the family's music business in 1818. After withdrawing

from his partnership with Adam in 1827, William moved to Philadelphia to study medicine, and lived there until his death in 1860. See *J.A.& W. Geib*; *A.& W. Geib*.

WILLIAM HOWE GEIB

The son of *Adam Geib*, see above, William Howe was primarily a music store owner and instrument dealer. He took over the family's business after his father's retirement c.1845, and from 1849-58, with James Jackson Jr., was a partner in the firm *Geib & Jackson*. After Jackson withdrew, c.1858, Geib headed his own firm for several years before finally selling out to *Charles Betts* in the 1860s.

GEIB, A. & W.

1822-27	piano & music store	23 Maiden la.

Firm consisted of *Adam* and *William Geib*. See above.

GEIB J. & A.

1804	pianoforte mkrs	40 Barclay
1805	"	Mt. Vernon
1806-08	"	Leonard n. Broadway

Firm consisted of twin brothers *John Geib, Jr.* and *Adam Geib*. During this period, John, Jr. was probably primarily involved with his father's firm, *Geib & Son*. The brothers also worked together from 1816-17, see below.

GEIB, J. [&] A. & COMPANY

1816-17	music store	23 Maiden la.

Firm consisted of *John Geib, Jr.* and *Adam Geib*. The twin brothers also worked together from 1804-08, see above, but were probably occupied primarily with their father's firm, *Geib & Son*, during the earlier period.

GEIB, J., A. & W.

1818-21	music stores & pianos	23 Maiden la.

William Geib joined his brothers *John Jr.* and *Adam*. See above.

GEIB & COMPANY

1800-02	organbuilder	Bowery c. North

Members of this firm were *John Geib, Sr.* and one or more of his sons—probably *Adam* or *John, Jr.*

Although listed as organbuilders, the firm also advertised their ability to manufacture organized, grand and common pianos, and pedal harps. (See [N.Y.] *Spectator*, March 19, 1800.)

In 1802, a Commission of Bankruptcy was issued by the Judge of the District Court of the United States for the New-York District against John Geib "organbuilder and trader." (*American Citizen & General Advertiser* [N.Y.], October 2, 1802) Geib's business was reorganized the next year as *Geib & Son*, see below.

GEIB & JACKSON

1849-51	pianos	361 Broadway
1852-54	"	499 Broadway
1855-58	"	783 Broadway

This firm was headed by *Adam Geib*'s son *William Howe Geib*, see above, and James Jackson, Jr. It was primarily a dealership, and after its dissolution, Geib continued to sell pianos until 1872. Sometime during the 1860s, however, the bulk of the old Geib family's business was sold to *Charles Betts*.

GEIB & SON

1803	organbuilder	Bowery c. North
1804	"	Bowery
1805	"	Corres. Gard. Leonard
1806-09	"	Leonard
1810	"	95 Leonard
1811-12	"	" & 35 Sugar Loaf
1813-14	"	55 Sugar Loaf

This firm was headed by *John Geib, Sr.* and his son *John Jr.* It was probably a continuation of their earlier partnership, *Geib & Company*, which had been declared legally bankrupt in 1802. Although listed only as "organbuilders" in the *NYCD*s, Geib & Son also produced pianos. A square piano in the MMA's collection is a good example of their work (see **Libin** 1985:169). And a receipt for $270, dated September 19, 1812, records that the Geibs sold "an Elegant patent Piano- forte with drawers and two pedals" to a resident of Flatbush, Long Island. (**Vanderbilt** 1881:124)

GEIB & WALKER

1829-43	piano & music store	23 Maiden la.

This firm was headed by *Adam Geib*, see above, and his son-in-law *Daniel Walker*, a musician and one of the founders of the New York Philharmonic. **Spillane** (1890:160-61) wrote that the firm was "very well known past 1830 as piano manufacturers, and also as music publishers and importers." A piano of their manufacture was exhibited at the Mechanics' Institute in 1838.

GEMUNDER, August Martin

1865	piano mkr	705 Ave. 3
1866	violin mkr	h. 13 First
1867	mus instrs	h. 12 Stanton
1868	repairer & manuf of violincellos, bass,& etc.	158 E. Houston
1869	violins	"
1870	mus instrs	"
1871-73	"	261 Bowery
1874-86	"	393 Bowery
1887-90 +	violins	13 E. 16th

Gemunder was born at Ingelfingen, Würtemburg, on March 22, 1814, and was taught violin making by his father, Johann Georg Heinrich Gemunder. He emigrated to New England c.1846, and established a music shop in Springfield, Massachusetts. In late 1847, Gemunder and one of his brothers (Albert?) decided to form a touring musical group, and sent to Europe for their brother *George Gemunder*, see below, who was then working as a violin maker in Paris. The brothers and a fourth man formed a quartet, but it proved unprofitable and was soon disbanded. August, like his brother George, worked for a short while as an instrument maker in Boston before relocating to New York.

Both brothers became successful instrument makers in New York, although they apparently maintained separate workshops throughout their careers. In the *1885 AMD* (p.51), August advertised that "the celebrated AUGUST GEMUNDER violins are constructed strictly on the old Italian principals & are acknowledged to be the only instruments that are equal in quality of tone & superior in power to the famous Italians." Some of Gemunder's violins were quite good, and after his death on September 7, 1895, his three sons continued the operation of his shop. For further information see: **Baker** (1958); **Henley** (1960:2:198); **Ayars** (1937:198).

GEMUNDER, George

1853	violins	304 Broadway
1854	mus instr mkr	22 Howard
1855-57	violins	"
1858	not listed	
1859-64	violins	159 Ninth
1865-67	"	h. 174 Ninth

1868-69	"	205 Ninth
1870	violin mkr	"
1871	music	"
1872	not listed	
1873	violins	"

George Gemunder was born at Ingelfingen, Würtemburg on April 13, 1816, and like his brother *August Gemunder*, see above, he learned violin making from his father, the luthier Johann Georg Heinrich Gemunder. After working as a journeyman in several European nations, George found work in the Parisian shop of the noted luthier Vuillaume. All did not go smoothly there — for one thing, Gemunder was convinced that his fellow journeymen were jealous of his talents — and in 1847 he welcomed an invitation from his brothers in America to join them in a touring musical group.

Unfortunately, American audiences failed to fully appreciate the Gemunder brothers' musical talents, and "For George Gemunder, who had then very little knowledge of the English language . . . there remained no other choice but to settle as a violinmaker. He borrowed from a friend twenty-five dollars, and with this money he set out for Boston . . . [but] as his business in Boston did not prove sufficiently lucrative, Gemunder left the city after 18 months . . . and established business in New York" in 1851. (**Gemunder** 1881:11-12)

A skilled craftsman, if a difficult personality, George soon became an important part of the city's musical life. He apparently never worked with his brother August, who had also settled in the city. About 1873, he moved his shop to Astoria [now Queens], Long Island, and there continued to produce stringed instruments until his death on January 15, 1899. Never one to underestimate his own achievements, Gemunder wrote and privately printed a strange third-person account of his life. See **Gemunder** (1881); **Henley** (1960:2:198); **Ayars** (1937:198); **Mathews** (1970:347-48); **Jones** (1971:61-62).

GERBETH, August (Augustus) F.

| 1866-69 | mus instrs | 181 Chrystie |
| 1870-74 | " | 179 Chrystie |

Gerbeth was a small-time instrument maker. From 1868-72, he was in partnership with Ferdinand Seifert. Their firm, *Gerbeth & Seifert*, advertised as "manufacturers of Musical Instruments of All Kinds of German Silver, Brass, & c. 179 Chrystie Street, N.Y. Repairing done in a neat manner, & at the shortest notice." (*CmRg* 1870:111) Nothing more is presently known about Seifert, and Gerbeth con-

tinued on his own for several years after their partnership dissolved.

GERBETH & SEIFERT

| 1868-69 | mus instrs | 181 Chrystie |
| 1870-72 | " | 179 Chrystie |

See above *August Gerbeth*.

GERVAIS

See *Lacombe & Gervais*.

GEVER, Adam

Gever was listed as a "Manufacturer of Musical Instruments" at 150 E. 4th Street in the *1885 AMD* (p.205), however, no further information is presently known about this maker.

GIBSON, Thomas

1802-03	mus instr mkr	58 Warren
1804-06	"	63 Barclay
1807-13	pianoforte mkr	"
1814-24	"	61 Barclay
1825	"	196 Broadway
1826-28	"	61 Barclay
1829-32	"	" & 40 Robinson
1833-43	"	61 Barclay
1844-45	late piano mkr	h. 6 Union pl.

From 1802-22, Gibson and his partner *Morgan Davis* headed the prominent piano-manufacturing firm *Gibson & Davis*. The two men arrived from Britain, where they had apparently been partners as early as 1799, sometime before May 1801. On March 25, 1802, they advertised in the *Mercantile Advertiser* [N.Y.] that "Gibson & Davis, lately arrived in this country, after several years experience in the Piano Forte Business in the best manufactories in London, and having been established upwards of two years previous to coming here, have acquired such knowledge through adopted and steady perseverance in the upright and Horizontal Grand; and likewise, square Piano-Fortes; as they flatter themselves will do them credit."

Spillane (1890:102) wrote that Davis was probably a Welshman. Gibson was born in Scotland in 1763 (**Libin** 1985:169) and soon after arriving in New York, he joined the local St. Andrew's Society. (**MacBean**)

Many examples of *Gibson & Davis* pianos are extant. The case of a fine Gibson & Davis square piano in the MMA's collection is attributed to the workshop of the noted furniture designer Duncan Phyfe (**Libin** 1985:168-69). Another *Gibson & Davis*, owned by the Smithsonian Institution, had an unusual patented transposing keyboard. (Smithsonian Institution, Catalog No. 299,857)

Gibson's partnership with Davis ended in 1822, but the men apparently remained on good terms, and continued to live and work next door to each other for many years. Gibson retired c.1844 and later moved to upstate New York. He died in November 1858 at the age of 95 in Southeast Putnam, New York. (*N.Y. Spectator*, November 22, 1858)

GIBSON & DAVIS

1802-03	mus instr mkrs	58 Warren
1804-06	"	63 Barclay
1807-13	pianoforte mkrs	61 Barclay
1814-16	not listed	
1817-22	pianofortes	"

The firm was headed by partners *Thomas Gibson* and *Morgan Davis*. See above.

GIFFIN, Simon M.

1818	mus instr mkr	153 Duane
1819	"	Varick n. Broome
1820	"	Jones n. Herring
1821	"	Arden n. Herring
1822	"	165 Duane
1823-24	not listed	
1825	mus instr mkr	Delancey n. Forsyth
1826-27	"	52 Rivington

Giffin, whose name was occasionally misspelled as *Griffin*, was probably a wind-instrument maker. In 1818, he shared his 153 Duane Street shop with the silversmith *Benjamin Ferris*, and in 1822 they were listed as partners in the firm *Ferris & Giffin*. A flute made by this firm is in the collection of Old Sturbridge Village. (**Langwill** 1980:51) See *Benjamin Ferris*; *Ferris & Giffin*.

GILLESPIE

See *Jones & Gillespie*.

GINOCCHIO, Antonio (Anthony)

1855	mus instrs	19 Baxter
1856	mus instr mkr	h. r. 41 Hester
1857-58	mus instrs	"
1859-61	instrs	"
1862	organ mkr	"
1863-66	mus instrs	r. 41 Hester

1867	organs	"
1868-72	mus instrs	"
1873-78	organs/organ mkr	"
1879-85	organs	r. 112 MacDougal
1886-90 +	mus instrs	"

A manufacturer of hand organs and cylinder melodeons, in 1861 Ginocchio headed the firm *Ginocchio & Brother* with his brother John. (*1861 AMD* p.157) Antonio continued to work in the instrument trade, however, John was later listed as a "stencil maker." (*NYCD* 1863)

GINOCCHIO, John

1863	organ mkr	41 Hester

See above *Antonio Ginocchio*.

GINOCCHIO & BROTHER

1861	[hand] organs	r. 41 Hester

See above *Antonio Ginocchio*.

GIRKIN, William

See *Pethick & Gerkin*.

GLASEL/GLAESEL, August

1870	see *Busch & Glaesel*	
1871-76	not listed	
1877	mus instrs	175 Bowery
1878	violin mkr	h. "
1879	violins	"
1880-87	mus instrs	363 Bowery
1888-90 +	violins	"

Glasel might have been a member of the guitar and violin-making Glaesel family of Markneukirchen, Germany, who were also active during the second half of the nineteenth century. In 1870, the New York instrument maker and dealer *Frederick Busch* had a partner named August Glaesel, and despite the difference in spelling, this maker was probably the same person.

Assuming Glasel to have been a member of *Busch & Glaesel*, it appears that after the dissolution of the partnership, the maker left the city for several years. In 1884, he advertised himself as a manufacturer and repairer of violins, cellos, double basses and guitars. (*CmRg* 1884:54) See *Busch & Glaesel*.

GLENN, Robert

1839-41	piano mkr	168 Fulton
1842-43	pianos	"
1844-45	"	152 Fulton
1846-52	"	194 Fulton
1853-55	"	83 Spring
1856	Hester A. widow of Robert	h. 107 Allen

In 1839, Glenn and his partner, *John Wake*, headed the piano-manufacturing firm *Wake & Glenn*. The two men continued to work at the same address until 1844, although their partnership was not listed after 1842.

In 1844, Glenn joined *Abel Rogers* in the piano-making firm *Glenn, Rogers & Company*. This concern lasted until 1846, when Glenn withdrew to establish his own firm, *Robert Glenn & Company*. In 1847, a "Mahogany Music Stand" made by Glenn's firm was awarded a diploma at that year's American Institute Fair. (*American Institute Records*) Glenn died c.1855. See *Wake & Glenn*; *John Wake*.

GLENN, ROBERT & COMPANY

1846-50	pianos	194 Fulton

See above *Robert Glenn*.

GLENN, ROGERS & COMPANY

1844-46	pianos	152 Fulton

See above *Robert Glenn*.

GLEITZ, August

1861-63	mus instrs	r. 173 Suffolk
1864	pianos, citherns guitars & strings	107 Fifth

During his years in New York, Gleitz was apparently more active as an instrument dealer than builder. According to **Pierce** (1965:91), Gleitz immigrated from Germany in 1857, and with his son Richard (b.1861), and another son (b. Bloomfield, New Jersey), began to manufacture pianos in Bloomfield in the late 19th century.

GLOR, Peter (Pierre) P.

1855	------	132 Leonard
1856	not listed	
1857	joiner	h. 53 1/2 Greene
1858	not listed	
1860	fancygoods	29 Greene
1861	accordeons	"
1862	fancygoods	"
1863	manuf	h. 31 Greene
1864	fancygoods	30 W. 4th
1865	repairer	"
1866	fancygoods	"
1867-70	pearl	"
1871	repairer of artists' articles	"
1872	fancygoods	"
1873	artist	"
1874	fans	"

In the 1857 and 1860 *NYBD*s, Glor was listed as a "musical instrument maker"; and the *1861 AMD* (p.91) listed him a "guitar manufacturer." His other *NYCD* listings seem to indicate that instrument making and repairing were only two of several varied occupations.

GODFREY, Cornelius

1834	piano mkr	r. 29 Thompson
1835-36	"	53 King
1837	"	Carmine n. Varick

Probably a journeyman, Godfrey might have been related to the organ, harpsichord, and barrel organ maker George Godfrey, who had been active in London earlier in the century. (See *V.& A. Catalogue* 1968:209)

GODONE, Gasper (Jasper)

1830-31	piano mkr	63 1/2 Canal
1832-34	"	412 Broadway
1835	"	412 1/2 Broadway
1836-37	mus instrs	"
1838	"	403 Broadway
1839-49	"	403 1/2 Broadway
1850	music store	"
1851-52	mus instrs	"
1853-55	"	773 Broadway
1856	music	"
1857	not listed	
1858	music	599 Broadway
1859-61	mus instrs	"
1862	not listed	
1863-66	music	278 W. 24th
1867	------	h. 60 W. 28th
1868	music	"
1869	"	h. 112 W. 28th

Godone apparently began as a piano maker and later became an instrument dealer specializing in violins, cellos, and music stands. He was in business as early 1827, since on May 27th of that year the 18-year-old Antonio Torione was legally apprenticed to "Gasparo Godone, musical instrument maker." (**NYGBR** 115:1:11) The *NYBD* listed Godone as an instrument maker well into the 1850s.

GOETTING, A.H.

Goetting was listed as a "Manufacturer of Musical Goods" at 122 and 124 Duane Street only in the *1885 AMD* (p.205).

GOETZE, Frederick

1860-64	music	h. 203 Bowery
1865	not listed	
1866	mus instrs	177 Bowery
1867	accordeons	"
1868	not listed	
1869	mus instrs	h. 98 Bowery
1870	accordeons	202 Chatham
1871-74	not listed	
1875	mus instrs	h. E. 76th n. E.R.
1876-77	not listed	
1878-80	------	h. 447 E. 76th
1881	accordeons	r. 453 E. 76th
1882	music	1483 Ave.3, h. 553 E. 76th
1883-85	accordeons	453 E. 76th
1886-87	mus instrs	"
1888-90 +	"	511 E. 76th

Goetze was primarily a "Manufacturer of Accordeons" (*NYBD* 1867:111). According to the *1855 New York Census*, he owned $500 of real capital, and $3,000 of raw materials [wood and leather]. He worked alone, and paid himself $400 in annual wages. In 1855, his shop produced $3,000 worth of accordeons.

A Brooklyn-based piano-making firm, Goetz & Company, was active during the 1860s—but no connection between this maker and the piano firm has been established.

GOODMAN & BALDWIN

1854	mus instr mkrs	333 Broadway (*NYBD*)

This firm was listed only in the 1854 *NYBD* (p.129), and nothing further is known about either partner. Their 333 Broadway address, however, was also the address of the well- known music dealer Horace Waters, and the latter might have employed the partners or acted as their retail outlet.

GORDON, James

1865-66	musician	h. 34 Sixth
1867-68	"	h. 22 Sixth
1869-70	music	"
1871-72	pianos	196 Bleecker
1873	"	157 Bleecker
1874	not listed	
1875-78	pianos	"
1879-80	"	111 Clinton pl.

In the 1873 *NYBD*, Gordon advertised as a "Manufacturer of the 7 1/2 Octave Piano Fortes, having Agraffe & Silver Trebles." He had probably left the trade before 1885 when his name appeared as a piano manufacturer at 111 Clinton Place in the belatedly printed *1885 AMD* (p.205).

GORDON, Stephen T.

Gordon was a well-known and successful music dealer who came to New York from Hartford, Connecticut, where he had worked from 1846-53. (**Ditcher** 1977:196) In 1854, with Thomas S. Berry, he established the New York dealership Berry & Gordon.

From 1867-68, Gordon and *Moses Slater* headed the instrument-making firm *Gordon & Slater* (**Redway** 1941:39-40). Following the dissolution of this company, Gordon headed his own firm until 1874, when he was joined by his son, Stephen F., and established the dealership S.T. Gordon & Son. Their partnership lasted past 1890. Throughout his career, Gordon worked as a dealer; only during his short-lived partnership with Moses Slater was his name associated with instrument manufacturing. See *Moses Slater*.

GORTON, Cephas

1830	cabinet mkr	39 Wooster
1831	carpenter	83 Chapel
1832	"	66 Bayard
1833	"	93 Grand
1834	piano mkr	114 Spring
1835	"	172 Spring
1836-37	pianos	55 Greene
1838	"	112 Laurens
1839	not listed	
1840	pianos	99 Norfolk
1841	not listed	
1842	piano mkr	54 Clinton
1843	not listed	
1844	pianoforte mkr	62 Broome
1845	"	93 Lewis

1846	"	97 Lewis
1847-50	"	92 Houston
1851	"	107 Houston

Gorton, whose name was occasionally given as *Gordon*, might have been a journeyman rather than a mastercraftsman. Nothing further is presently known about his career.

GOULD, Napoleon W.

Gould, instrument inventor and manufacturer at 100 Grand Street, entered an improved transposing guitar, and an improved banjo in the 1853 New York Crystal Palace Exhibition. (*Official Catalogue* 1853:95) Nothing further is presently known about his career, and his relation to the music publisher John E. Gould of the well-known firm Gould & Berry, has not been established.

GRIFFIN/GRIFFEN, Charles

1835	piano mkr	27 Second
1836-38	"	20 Sixth
1839	"	436 Bowery
1840	"	98 Ave. 3
1841-43	"	13th n. Ave. 3
1844	"	12 Stuyvesant pl.
1845-49	"	96 Ave. 3
1850	pianofortes	
1851	not listed	
1852-53	piano mkr	11 Tenth
1854	"	260 & 262 W. 32nd
1855	pianos	262 W. 32nd; h. 11 Tenth
1856	"	" & 815 Broadway
1857	"	260 W. 32nd
1858	"	160 W. 29th

From 1854-57, Griffin and Egbert Scudder headed the piano-manufacturing firm *Griffin & Scudder*. Griffin seems to have been the practical partner. According to the *1855 New York Census*, the firm owned $1,000 worth of tools, and had $10,000 worth of stock—including 50,000 feet of lumber. Their steam-powered plant employed 35 men, at total monthly wages of $840; and that year they produced 200 pianos worth $9,000.

A small square piano, manufactured by Griffin & Scudder and numbered 2131, was reported by **Pierce** (1965:95). After 1848, Griffin's name occasionally appeared as *Griffen*; however, nothing more is presently known about this maker or his partner Scudder.

GRIFFIN & SCUDDER

1854-56	mus instr mkrs	260 & 262 W. 32nd
1857	"	" & 815 Broadway

The firm headed by Egbert Scudder and *Charles Griffin*. See above.

GRIM, David

1821	carpenter	543 Pearl
1822	"	Delancey n. Forsyth
1823	cabinet mkr	Chapel c. Murray
1824	"	39 Robinson
1825	"	27 Chapel
1826	"	120 Chapel
1827-30	pianoforte mkr	117 Grand
1831	"	103 Allen
1832	"	Reade c. Greenwich

Probably a journeyman rather than a mastercraftsman, nothing more is presently known about Grim.

GROVESTEEN, James H.

1846	pianos	120 Grand
1847	"	" & 44 W. 14th
1848	"	117 Grand & 38 W. 14th
1849-51	"	122 Grand & 44 W. 14th
1852	"	481 Broadway
1853	"	" & 48 Mercer
1854-57	"	505 Broadway
1858	"	26 Wooster
1859	"	h. 211 W. 35th
1860	"	h. 333 W. 35th
1861	"	211 Hudson
1862-63	"	478 Broadway
1864-68	"	499 Broadway
1869	"	55 Mercer
1870-71	"	354 W. 27th
1872	president & pianos	194 Broadway & 55 Mercer
1873-74	pianos	55 Mercer
1875-85	"	71 Mercer
1886	------	r. 430 W. 23rd
1887-89	------	604 W. 22nd
1890 +	------	h. 430 W. 23rd

Grovesteen was trained as a piano maker in New York, and c.1838 he moved to Albany to establish his own shop. In 1846, he returned to the city and entered into partnership with the piano maker *William Senior*. Their firm began as *Grovesteen &*

Senior, but in 1847, its title was changed to *Senior & Grovesteen*.

After ending his partnership with Senior in 1848, Grovesteen headed his own firm, *Grovesteen & Company*, from 1852-53. In 1854, he joined piano dealer William Truslow in the partnership *Grovesteen & Truslow*. According to the *1855 New York Census*, the firm owned $20,000 of real capital; $6,000 worth of tools; and had $40,000 worth of veneers in stock. Their steam-powered factory employed 50 men and 4 boys at total monthly wages of $2,500 who that year produced $100,000 worth of pianos.

After the dissolution of Grovesteen & Truslow in 1857, Grovesteen spent several years without a partner before joining with *Joseph Hale* from 1861-63 to form *Grovesteen & Hale*.

Grovesteen again worked alone for several years, but in 1869, with instrument dealer John I. Fuller, he founded the piano-making firm *Grovesteen, Fuller & Company*. After only a few months of operation, it was cited as the 17th largest piano-manufacturing firm in the nation, with gross annual sales of $96,825. (*New York Tribune*, March 15, 1869) Grovesteen seems to have been the president of this partnership, as well as the person in charge of daily operations, since Fuller's home address was listed by the *NYCD* as Schenectady, New York. In 1873, the "& Company" was dropped from the firm's title, and it became *Grovesteen & Fuller*.

Instruments made by Grovesteen firms were awarded medals at American Institute Fairs in 1848, 1850 and 1851 (*American Institute Records*); and a Grovesteen & Company piano was exhibited at the 1853 New York Crystal Palace (*Official Catalogue* 1853:94). For further information see **Spillane** (1890:139-40); **Dolge** (1911:286); *William Senior*; *Senior & Grovesteen*; *Joseph Hale*.

GROVESTEEN & COMPANY

1852-53	pianos	481 Broadway
1865-68	"	499 Broadway

Grovesteen used the title "& Company" from 1852-53, and then again from 1864-68. During both periods, he headed his own firm. See above *James Grovesteen*.

GROVESTEEN & FULLER

1873-74	pianos	55 Mercer
1875-86	"	71 Mercer

See above *James Grovesteen*.

GROVESTEEN, FULLER & COMPANY

1869-72	pianos	55 Mercer

See above *James Grovesteen*.

GROVESTEEN & HALE

1861	pianos	211 Hudson
1862-63	"	478 Broadway

See *James Grovesteen*; *Joseph Hale*.

GROVESTEEN & SENIOR

1846	pianos	120 Grand
1847-48	see *Senior & Grovesteen*	

Firm consisted of *James Grovesteen*, see above, and *William Senior*. After their first year, for unknown reasons, the names of the partners were reversed, and the firm was thereafter known as *Senior & Grovesteen*.

GROVESTEEN & TRUSLOW

1854-57	pianos	505 Broadway; factory 24 & 26 Wooster

The partners in this firm were *James Grovesteen*, see above, and William Truslow.

GROW, Wales F.

1842-43	piano mkr	104 Ave. 3
1844	not listed	
1845	pianofortes	"
1846-47	"	4 E. 21st & 130 Ave. 3
1848	"	130 Ave. 3
1849-50	piano manuf	111 E. 14th
1851	"	14th c. Ave. 3
1852	"	130 Ave. 3
1853	pianos	"
1854-56	piano manuf	118 Ave. 3 & 109 E. 14th
1857-58	"	18 Fourth
1859	pianos	h. 67 E. 23rd
1860	------	"
1861	not listed	
1862-63	------	h. 76 E. 26th
1864	------	h. 17 W. 26th
1865	boardinghouse	17 W. 26th
1866	------	"

Grow was a practical piano maker, and since he was a partner of *Adam H. Gale & Company* in 1842, it is also likely that he had previously been involved with the co-operative *New York Pianoforte Manufacturing Company* at Third Avenue and 13th Street.

In 1847, Grow joined another practical maker, *William Christopher*, to establish the firm *Grow & Christopher*, which continued in operation until 1858. According to the *1855 New York Census*, Grow & Christopher owned $2,037 worth of real capital; $2,719 of tools; and had in stock $6,000 of lumber, $2,407 of hardware, $550 of woolen cloth, and $700 of ivory. The firm employed 30 men and 4 boys and monthly wages of $40 each, and that year, their steam-powered factory constructed 164 pianos worth $75,000 [?].

After the dissolution of Grow & Christopher, the maker seems to have gradually drifted out of the trade. The partners' pianos were exhibited at various fairs and exhibitions. (See **Spillane** 1890:189)

GROW & CHRISTOPHER

1847-48	piano manufs	130 Ave. 3
1849-50	pianos & piano manuf	11 E. 14th
1851	"	14th c. Ave. 3
1852-53	"	130 Ave. 3
1854-56	"	118 Ave. 3
1857-58	"	18 Fourth

The firm was headed by *Wales Grow*, see above, and *William Christopher*.

GRUSS, Francis

1831-32	pianoforte mkr	13 Grand
1833	piano mkr	436 Washington
1834	"	52 Howard

Little else is presently known about this maker, however, **Spillane** (1890:162), suggests he might have established a partnership with *Joseph Fox*: "Francis Gruss began as far back as 1833 at 13 Grand Street, in which year Joseph Fox had a repairing and small manufacturing place at 307 Broadway. They are known in an insignificant way up to 1845, and are remembered by old piano-makers as journeymen subsequently." No other information has been found about this partnership.

GUCK, Paulus

1844	piano manuf	76 Pitt

No further information is presently known about this maker.

GUETTER, Moritz

1881	instr mkr	h. 205 Forsyth
1882-84	violin mkr	"
1885	------	"

A member of the violin-making family of Markneukirchen, Guetter was born in Germany in 1857, and worked in Warsaw and London before his death c.1883. (**Henley** 1960:3:10) Although the date of his death is variously reported, Guetter apparently worked in New York for a very short time, and had probably died long before his name appeared as a "Musical Instrument Manufacturer" in the *1885 AMD* (p.205).

GUTTWALDH/GUTWALDT, Joseph A.

1819-20	pianoforte mkr	50 Courtlandt

Spillane (1890:106-07) provides the only information presently available about this maker: "A clever German named James Alois Gutwaldt [*sic*] came to this country in 1811 and began making musical instruments in Brooklyn, some of which were sold by the Paffs [New York music dealers] on Broadway. A good many music teachers and musicians in New York at this time were Germans, and they came to Gutwaldt's aid. He sprang into rapid esteem and his pianos created quite a furor. His grands were frequently mentioned with great commendation by the press in connection with concerts from time to time past 1813. Through some unknown cause his popularity died out finally, and we hear little about him after 1830. It is asserted, however, that he was employed past this period in Firth & Hall's piano shop as their foreman for several years, but this I find is erroneous. Gutwaldt took out a patent on August 27th, 1818, for 'an improvement in the framework of a grand'."

GUTWENNYER, Peter

1835	mus instr mkr	129 Grand

No further information is presently known about this maker.

H

HAFELY(E), Frederick

1853	instrs	214 Walker
1854-55	mus instrs	"
1856	brass instrs	h. 179 Mott
1857	not listed	
1858	mus instr mkr	145 Elm
1859-63	mus instrs/manuf	r. 151 Eldridge
1864	mus instrs	58 Greene
1865	brass	38 Lispenard
1866	finisher	h. 20 Dowing

Hafely, whose name occasionally appeared as *Hafelye*, was listed as a "Brass Instrument Manufacturer" in the *1861 AMD* (p.90). Nothing more is presently known about his career.

HAINES, Francis W.

See below *Napoleon Haines*.

HAINES, Napoleon J.

1852	pianos	128 E. 14th
1853-56	"	116 Ave. 3
1857-65	"	334 Ave. 2
1866-86	"	360 Ave. 2
1887-88	"	362 Ave. 2 & 25 E. 17th
1889-90 +	"	S. Blvd. n. Alexander

Throughout his career, Haines worked with his brother, Francis W. Haines (b.1822). Napoleon Haines was born in London in 1824, and at the age of eight, c.1834, his family emigrated to America. In 1839, both brothers went to work in the co-operative shop of the *New York Pianoforte Manufacturing Company*. (This firm claimed its pianos were built only by mastercraftsmen, but the young Haines brothers must have been employed as apprentices.) They continued to work for this concern even after it was taken over by *Adam Gale*. In 1852, the Haines joined piano maker *William Miller* to establish the firm *Haines & Miller*; and later, from 1854-55, with *Laurence Cummings*, they headed the partnership *Haines Brothers & Cummings*.

In 1855, the Haines established their own firm, *Haines Brothers*, which was to be an important factor in the city's instrument trade. According the *1855 New York Census*, Haines Brothers began as a sub-stantial concern, owning $10,000 of real capital, $2,000 of tools, and $3,000 of lumber. The brothers employed 50 men and 4 boys, at an average monthly wage of $44; and that year they produced 250 pianos worth $60,000. By 1869, Haines Brothers was the fourth largest piano manufacturer in the nation with gross annual sales of $287,051. (*New York Tribune*, March 15, 1869)

Among their other innovations, Haines Brothers was credited with being the first American manufacturer to cease building square pianos. (See **Spillane** 1890:204-10) Napoleon Haines became a prominent citizen, and even served for a while as the president of the Union Dime Saving Bank, an institution he had helped found. Francis Haines died on September 18, 1887 at the age of 65. Napoleon, with the assistance of his sons, continued to head the firm until his own death on April 19, 1900. (**Dolge** 1911:295)

HAINES BROTHERS

1856	pianos	116 Ave. 3 & 340 Ave. 2
1857-58	"	334 Ave. 2
1859-60	"	" & 626 Broadway
1861-63	"	334 Ave. 2
1864-65	"	" & 758 Broadway
1866-76	"	360 Ave. 2
1877-78	"	" & 145 Fifth
1879-81	"	" & 124 Fifth
1882-84	"	" & 95 Fifth
1885-86	"	" & 41 Union Sq.
1887-88	"	362 Ave. 2 & 25 E. 17th
1889-90 +	"	S. Blvd. n. Alexander

See above *Napoleon Haines*.

HAINES BROTHERS & CUMMINGS

| 1854-55 | pianofortes | 116 Ave. 3 & 112 E. 14th |

See above *Napoleon Haines*.

HAINES & MILLER

| 1852 | pianos | 128 E. 14th |

See above *Napoleon Haines*.

HALE, Joseph P.

1861	pianos	211 Hudson
1862-65	"	478 Broadway
1866	"	Ave. 10 c. W. 36th
1867	"	453 W. 36th
1868	agent Great Union Piano Forte Co.	"
1869	"	479 Ave. 10
1870-73	pianos/broker	" & 30 Broadway
1874-77	pianos	523 W. 35th
1878-80	"	549 W. 35th
1881-83	president/pianos	519 W. 35th & 31 Pine
1883	Lucy A. wid of Jos. P.	h. 112 W. 34th

The "father of the commercial piano," Hale began his career selling crockery in Worcester, Massachusetts. Accumulating a small fortune of $35,000, Hale came to New York in 1861 and became the financial backer of the respected mastercraftsman *James Grovesteen* in the piano- manufacturing firm *Grovesteen & Hale*. After his partnership with Grovesteen ended in 1863, Hale continued on his own for several years before founding *Joseph P. Hale & Company* in 1877.

Hale's major innovation was to buy all parts of his pianos ready-made from subcontractors and merely assemble them in his factory. His success was phenomenal, but he elicited vitriolic outrage from other piano makers, who claimed that "unhampered by tradition or prejudice of any kind . . . [Hale] manufactured pianos as he would have manufactured bedsteads." (**Dolge** 1911:179-80) Although Hale's practices might have shocked the trade, his low-priced pianos delighted the public, who bought Hale's pianos in vast quantities. By 1869, Hale's firm was the seventh largest in the nation with gross annual sales of $207,355. (*New York Tribune*, March 15, 1869)

Hale's connection with the (Great) *Union Piano-Forte Company* in 1868 is unclear; it might have been one of the dozens of stencilled firm names Hale used to market his instruments. Hale's piano empire apparently collapsed after his death in 1882, but resentment of his methods and success ran so high in the New York piano trade that his name rarely appeared in print even following his death. For further information see **Dolge** (1911:179-80); **Groce** (1982:73-80); **Loesser** (1954:526-32); **Ehrlich** (1976:137); *Grovesteen & Hale*.

Advertising lithograph of the Haines Brothers factory at 2nd Avenue & 21st Street c. 1860. Vignettes of the firm's showrooms at 626 Broadway are included below.

HALE, JOSEPH P. & COMPANY

1877	pianos	523 W. 35th

See above *Joseph Hale*.

HALL, William

1820	mus instr mkr	Wooster n. Prince
1821-22	"	362 Pearl
1823-24	"	358 Pearl
1825	"	39 Roosevelt
1826	"	494 Pearl
1827-31	"	358 Pearl
1832-42	"	1 Franklin Sq.
1843-47	music	"
1848-49	music warehouse	239 Broadway
1850	piano mkr	237 Broadway & 16 White
1851-53	music warehouse	239 Broadway /1 Oak pl.
1854-57	music/pianos	" / 16 White
1858	mus instrs	" & "
1859-64	pianos/music	543 Broadway
1865	Agents for Driggs patent pianofortes, publishers of sheet music & agents for Prince Co.'s melodeons & school organs	"
1866-70	music	"
1871-74	"	751 Broadway

Hall was born in Tarrytown [then Sparta], New York on May 13, 1796, and apprenticed to an Albany musical instrument maker; possibly to John Meacham. He worked in Albany until the War of 1812 when he left to join the militia. Hall might have met *John Firth* in the service, and after the war, both men went to work for the New York flute maker *Edward Riley*. In addition to working together in the shop, both Firth and Hall married daughters of Riley, making them brothers-in-laws.

In 1820, Hall followed Firth's lead and left Riley to establish a shop of his own. The next year, 1821, the friends joined to form the extremely successful partnership *Firth & Hall*. In 1833, they admitted *Sylvanus Pond*, a music dealer from Albany, who might have known Hall during his apprenticeship in that city. Their newly formed firm, *Firth, Pond & Hall*, lasted until 1847 and played an important role in the city's musical trade.

In 1847, Hall withdrew and his ex-partners reorganized as *Firth, Pond & Company*. Hall entered into partnership with his son, James F. Hall, to establish *Hall & Son*, a success venture which lasted until 1874. *Hall & Son* entered flutes in the American Institute Fairs of 1849, 1850, 1859 and 1869. (*American Institute Records*) At the 1853 Crystal Palace Exhibit, the firm displayed a "French grand action pianoforte, of 7 1/4 octaves in a double serpentine case of crotch and mottled oak, with carved plinths." (*Official Catalogue* 1853:94) According to the *1855 New York Census*, Hall & Son owned $700 worth of tools, and had in stock $2,000 worth of wood and iron. The factory employed 25 men and 5 boys at average monthly wages of $28 — a much lower wage than the average $40 paid to workers at the piano-making shops of the day — and that year produced $20,000 worth of pianos.

James Hall withdrew from his father's firm in 1870 to join the army, and William continued to head the business on his own until his death in New York on May 3, 1874. Hall, who was often respectfully referred to as "General Hall," was a prominent citizen and an active member of New York musical life, even serving for a while as the president of the prestigious Sacred Music Society. (**Jones** 1971:71) For further information see **Spillane** (1890:155-56); *Firth & Hall*; *Firth, Hall & Pond*.

HALL & SON

1848-49	music warehouse	239 Broadway
1850	piano mkr	237 Broadway & 16 Oak
1851-53	music warehouse	239 Broadway & 1 Oak pl.
1854-58	music/pianos	239 Broadway & 16 Oak
1859-70	music/pianos	543 Broadway
1871-74	music store	751 Broadway

See above *William Hall*.

HALLES, William

Although never listed by the *NYCD*, the *1870 United States Census* reported Halles as a banjo and tambourine manufacturer. His shop employed 3 men at annual wages of $2,000; and he had in stock 2,000 feet of lumber worth $600; 1,000 pounds of brass worth $375; and $100 worth of other materials. Halles' total [real?] capital came to $5,000. In 1870, his shop produced 1,000 banjos worth $3,000, and 1,500 tambourines worth $2,500. It is possible that his instruments were stenciled and sold by others.

HALLIDAY, Thomas

"Thomas Halliday, Musical Instrument Maker, 205 Church Street" was probably an apprentice when he joined Volunteer Fire Company No. 16 on December 14, 1829. (*MCC*:18:395) Halliday resigned his membership in the Engine Company on April 18, 1831 (*MCC*:19:650), but was never listed in the *NYCD* – unless the carver listed in 1833 at 479 Broome Street was the same person as the instrument maker. Halliday's relationship to Joseph Halliday, a Boston bugle designer and musician (**Ayars** 1937:222) has not been established.

HAMM, John

1834	mus instr mkr	r. 78 Grand
1835	"	36 Thompson
1836-38	"	56 Thompson

Nothing more is presently known about this maker or his relationship to *Tobias Hamm*.

HAMM, Tobias

1854	piano mkr	264 W. 37th
1856	not listed	
1857-60	cabinet mkr	h. r. 66 Wooster
1861-64	not listed	
1865-69	pianos	19 W. Houston h. 95 same
1870	"	h. 95 Houston
1871	piano mkr	"
1872	cabinet mkr	h. 112 Houston

Hamm spent his career wavering between cabinet making and piano building. In 1866, he was listed as a partner of *Kraushaar & Company*. His relationship to *John Hamm*, see above, is not known.

HAMMING, E.

| 1885 | mus instr manuf | 215 Forsyth |

Listed only in the *1885 AMD* (p.206), Hamming was in business as early as 1870 when the United States Census reported "H.H. Hamming, banjo jobbing and repairing". Working alone with hand tools and a stock of lumber and silver worth $200, Hamming earned $1,500 that year by producing $3,500 worth of musical instruments. (*1870 U.S. Manuf. Census*, ms.) A fretless banjo with 30 brackets and friction pegs by this maker is now in the Smithsonian Institution's collection. (*Smithsonian Institution Banjo Checklist*)

HAMMOND, Achiloe

| 1835 | piano mkr | 172 Spring |

Nothing further is presently known about this maker.

HANLEY, James

1841	harp mkr	22nd n. Ave. 3
1842-43		premium patent double
	action harps	"
1844-45	"	85 Anthony
1846	"	413 Broadway
1847-48	harp	196 Fulton
1849	"	233 Broadway
1850	harp manuf	8 N. William & 549 B'way
1851-52	harps	10 N. William
1853	not listed	
1854-55	harp mkr	13 Ave. 3
1856	harps	293 Bowery

Hanley claimed to be a pupil of the famous harp maker Sebastien Erard of London, and advertised as the "maker of the patent double action harp." (*NYBD* 1846:170) In 1841, he was awarded a silver medal for a harp he exhibited at the Third Massachusetts Charitable Mechanics' Association Exhibition; the judges noting that "This instrument was made by an English artist, who has recently established a manufactory of harps in the city of New York." (*MCMA*:83) Also in 1841, Hanley received a silver medal for a "superior harp" exhibited at the American Institute Fair; and in 1850, at the same fair, Hanley was awarded a diploma for a "Double Harp of Elegant Workmanship." (*American Institute Records*)

At the 1853 New York Crystal Palace, Hanley, whose named appeared in the catalog as *Hawley*, entered a "Grand gothic double action harp of 6 1/2 octaves." (*Official Catalogue* 1853:95)

HANSEN/HANSON, Henry P.M.

1853-54	coal	238 Mulberry
1855-56	not listed	
1857	pianos & coal	100 Centre & 572 Washington
1858-61	pianos	100 Centre

Perhaps the only person in the New York instrument trade to combine coal dealing with piano making, Hansen was listed in the *1861 AMD* (p.170) as a "piano manufacturer." At the 1856 American Institute Fair, Hansen received a diploma "For the third best square Piano Forte." (*American Institute Records*) The maker's surname frequently appeared as "Hanson".

HARISON, Frederick V.

See *Frederick Harrison*.

HARDMAN, Hugh

1849	piano mkr	Washington n N. Moore
1850	"	255 Washington
1851	pianos	103 W. Broadway
1852	"	62 White
1853-56	not listed	
1857	piano mkr	h. W. 52nd n. Ave. 9
1858	"	233 W. 26th
1859-60	pianos	120 Amity
1861	"	118 Amity
1862-65	"	120 Amity
1866-68	agent, pianos	" & 19 Broadway
1869-70	piano mkr	118 Amity
1871-72	pianos	120 Amity & 126 Mac-Dougal
1873	piano manuf	248 Ave. 6
1874-75	"	524 W. 55th
1876	not listed	
1877	pianos	W. 57th n. Ave. 10
1878-79	"	494 W. 57th h. England
1880 +	see *Hardman, Dowling & Peck*	

Born in 1815 at Liverpool, England, Hardman began work in the New York piano trade in the early 1840s. In 1877, after heading his own firm for many year, he admitted his son John into partnership to form *Hardman & Company*. **Dolge** (1911:290) wrote "The firm was among the first to manufacture good commercial upright pianos, and met with distinctive success." Hardman retired c.1879, and might have returned to his native England. Under his son's guidance, the firm met with continued success. See *Hardman, Dowling & Peck*.

HARDMAN & COMPANY

1877	pianos	W. 57th c. Ave. 10
1878-79	"	494 W. 57th

See above *Hugh Hardman*.

HARDMAN, DOWLING & PECK

1880-82	pianos	492 W. 57th
1883-84	"	618 W. 49th

John Hardman, who took over *Hardman & Company* following his father, *Hugh*'s retirement c.1879, took in partners *Leopold Peck* and a man named Dowling (a dealer?) to establish *Hardman, Dowling & Peck* in 1880. Hardman, said to be "an excellent tuner and a practical piano- maker . . . as well as an inventor," was granted several patents. With his partners, he upgraded the Hardman piano to "a new artistic character and standing." (**Spillane** 1890:301-02) In 1884, Dowling withdrew, and the firm was reorganized as *Hardman, Peck & Company*, see below.

HARDMAN, PECK & COMPANY

1885-86	pianos	146 Fifth & 618 W. 49th
1887-90 +	"	138 Fifth & 618 W. 49th

A continuation of the earlier firm, *Hardman, Dowling & Peck*. After Hardman's death on November 10, 1889 at the age of 46, the firm continued in operation without a change of title. (**Spillane** 1890:302)

HARLASS, Frederick W.

1864	drums	h. 73 Division
1865	not listed	
1866	banjos	20 Wooster
1867	mus instrs	"
1868	banjos & mus instrs	102 Grand
1869	banjos	h. 512 Broome
1870-72	mus instrs	"

Harlass advertised as the "Inventor and Manufacturer of PATENT AMERICAN LADIES' & PARLOR BANJOS . . . Also, Manufacturer of all kinds of the Common Banjos, and other Musical Instruments." (*CmRg* 1871:125)

HARPER, John

1846	pianoforte mkr	265 Ave. 6
1847	not listed	
1848	pianoforte mkr	"
1849	"	277 Ave. 6
1850	"	344 Greenwich
1851-52	"	401 Ave. 1

A relative of *Robert Harper*, see below, John Harper headed the piano-manufacturing firm *John Harper & Company* from 1849-50. **Spillane** (1890:197) mentioned Harper among the small makers active during the 1840s. His relationship to the Philadelphia maker piano of the same name, active c.1802, is not known. (**Mann** 1977:107) His name disappeared from the *NYCD* after 1852, and he might have followed Robert Harper to Fordham, New York.

HARPER, Robert

1849-50	piano tuner	277 Ave. 6

Robert Harper, a relative of *John Harper*, see above, had probably already moved out of the city before the following notice appeared in the *1861 AMD* (p.262): "Robert Harper, Pianoforte Maker. For the past 20 years in the employ of the first establishments in the city, in the Manufacture, and also Tuning... Orders left at 927 Broadway, 174 Wooster Street, or by mail to Fordham, Westchester County, N.Y. will be attended to with care and dispatch."

HARPER, JOHN & COMPANY

1849-50	pianos	334 Greenwich

See above *John Harper*.

HARRINGTON, Elbridge G.

1875-77	broker/agent	115 Broadway
1878	agent	145 Broadway
1879-82	pianos	701 First Ave.
1883-86	"	453 W. 41st
1887	"	449 W. 41st
1888	"	828 Ave. 7
1889-90 +	"	830 Ave. 7

Harrington apparently began as a piano dealer, and c.1879 became a manufacturer. (*1885 AMD* p.206) His firm *Harrington & Company*, founded in 1881, continued in operation part 1890. In 1899, Harrington was listed as a member of the National Piano Manufacturing Association.

HARRINGTON & COMPANY

1881-82	pianos	702 First Ave.
1883-86	"	453 W. 41st
1887	"	449 W. 41st
1888	"	828 Ave. 7
1889-90 +	"	830 Ave. 7

See above *Elbridge Harrington*.

HARRISON, Frederick Vivaldi/Vivaldi Frederick

1829	cabinet mkr	45 Robinson
1830-33	piano mkr	"
1834-38	not listed	
1839	------	Ave. 3 c. 28th
1840-41	not listed	
1842-53	piano mkr	23 Canal
1854	"	h. 106 Varick
1855	"	37 Mercer
1856-57	pianos	"
1858-61	"	357 Canal

1862-65	"	539 Broome
1866	"	261 W. 24th

Harrison, whose name occasionally appeared as Harison, was a small-time piano maker, whose instruments were awarded diplomas at the 1843 and 1847 American Institute Fairs. (*American Institute Records*) From 1842-52, he shared his 23 Canal Street shop with piano maker *Thomas Doyle*, however, the two men were never formally listed as partners. According to the *1855 New York* Census, Harrison owned $12,000 of real capital, and $500 worth of tools. He had in stock 12,000 feet of lumber worth $300; 50 sets of actions worth $400; 50 sets of pearl and ivory worth $400; and 24 gallons of varnish worth $60. He employed 8 men at total monthly wages of $384, and that year produced 50 pianos worth $15,000.

HARTMANN, Alfred & Rudolph

1881-85	mus instrs	Foot E. 26th
1886-87	"	255 Bowery & 446 E. 26th
1888-90 +	"	255 Bowery

According to their *1893 Catalogue*, the partnership between Frederick Reinhard and the Hartmanns, *Hartmann Brothers & Reinhard*, was founded in 1880. By 1893, the firm had a factory at 106-112 Cambridge Avenue, Jersey City, New Jersey. Although listed as "Musical Instrument Manufacturers" in the *1885 AMD* (p.206), it is probable that most of their goods were imported. It is also likely that all three of the partners were from Germany.

HARTMANN BROTHERS & REINHARD

1881-85	mus instrs	Foot of 26th
1886-87	"	225 Bowery & 446 E. 26th
1888-90 +	"	225 Bowery & 312 E. 75th

See above *Alfred & Rudolph Hartmann*.

HASTINGS, A.H.

Hastings was a respected mastercraftsman in the New York piano trade, who was listed as an independent manufacturer only in the 1873 *CmRg* (p.105), when his shop's address was given as 426 West 19th Street with warerooms at 47 & 49 University Place.

Later, Hastings served as the superintendent of the *Braumueler Piano Company*. **Spillane** (1890:303-04) wrote: "In connection with [Braumueler Piano Company] A.H. Hastings, superintendent, a very clever piano-maker and inventor, may be spoken of. The latter learned the business in Albany many years ago, and subsequently became a tuner, in which capacity and as a dealer he travelled all over South and North America and Cuba. He later came to New York and spent several years in Raven & Bacon's [shop], and another period in Chickering & Sons' New York house as a tuner and tone regulator. Mr. Hastings is a prolific inventor . . . At present [1890] he is in charge of the Braumueler factory. For many years past he has been known extensively as a scale draughtsman and pattern-maker to the trade. Mr. Hastings was born in Malone, N.Y. in 1834, and comes of New England parentage." See *Braumueler*.

HATTON, Paul

1820	mus instr mkr	18 Vandewater
1821	"	451 Broadway
1822-23	"	45 Warren
1824-25	"	452 Broadway
1826	"	12 Fifth n. Bowery
1827-28	"	Roosevelt c. Oak
1829	"	69 Catherine
1830	"	198 Grand
1831	Charlotte widow of Paul	118 Centre

Hatton was apparently a woodwind maker; several extant oboes bear his label. (See **Langwill** 1980:74) His relationship to *William Hatton*, see below, is not known. The maker died sometime in 1830.

HATTON, William

1793	mus instr mkr	3 Peck-slip
1794	"	358 Broadway
1795	"	360 Broadway

Hatton was almost certainly the same person was the actor of the same name who appeared at London's Haymarket Theatre in 1789. He migrated to America with his wife, Ann Julia, an actress and the author of the libretto for *Tammany*, the earliest recorded Indian play. (**Mates** 1962:153-55, 190)

Hatton was first listed as an instrument maker in 1793, but he was apparently not a successful businessman, and in 1795 the New York auctioneer Gerard Steddiford offered for sale, "the lease of that extensive building called Hatton's Musical Instrument Manufactory, pleasantly situated at the upper end of Broad Way, near the White Conduit House.

This place has a large improveable garden, and would answer for a tavern or tea garden, or any business that requires room . . . The above premises contain three lots of ground, each 25 feet front to rear, and in depth 100 feet, subject to a ground rent of 4£-10s—per annum for each lot. Thirteen years of the lease unexpired from the first of May last." (*The Argus* [N.Y.], July 14, 1795) His relation to the instrument maker *Paul Hatton*, see above, is not known.

HAUGAARD

See *Narvesen, Bergman & Haugaard*.

HAUGH, Casper

| 1826 | pianoforte mkr | Renwich n. Spring |

In 1825, Haugh had worked as an instrument maker on North Fifth Street, Reading, Pennsylvania. (PC:Historical Society of Berks County) In 1830 and again 1833, Haugh was listed as a piano maker in Philadelphia (**Catalano** 1979:109), but nothing more is presently known about his career.

HAUSMANN, Christian

1866-67	pianos	1 Broome
1868	"	240 W. 27th
1869-73	"	244 W. 27th
1874	"	r. 225 W. 28th

From 1867-73, Hausmann and his partners *Adam Schmitt* and *John Miller* headed the piano-manufacturing firm *Hausmann & Company*. He also worked with the piano maker *Bernard Kroeger*, from 1867-69, in the firm *Kroeger & Hausmann*.

HAUSMANN & COMPANY

| 1867 | pianos | 1 Broome (*CmRg*) |
| 1872-73 | " | 244 & 246 W. 27th (*CmRg*) |

Never listed in the *NYCD*, this firm consisted of *John Miller, Adam Schmitt*, and *Christian Hausmann*. See above.

HAWES, George

1834	turner	Ave. 5 n. 12th
1835	mus instr mkr	12th n. Broadway
1836	"	383 Broome

Hawes might have been the same person as the music engraver of that name who was active in Boston c.1823-26. (**Wolfe** 1980:63) Hawes worked in New York for only a few years before moving to 15 Court Street, Newark, New Jersey, where he first worked as a flute maker from 1843-48, and later found employment as a wood and ivory turner from 1848-60. (**Kaufman** 1976:29)

Langwill (1980:75) lists a flute maker of the same who was active in London from 1834-37, but his relationship to this maker has not been established.

HAWKEY, Henry

1842	cabinet mkr	18 Hamersley
1843	not listed	
1844-48	pianoforte mkr	r. 126 Amity
1849-55	"	118 Amity
1856-62	pianos	31 King
1863-64	not listed	
1865-66	piano mkr	"

A small-time piano manufacturer, Hawkey also advertised in the *NYBD* and *CmRg* from 1846-60. The *1861 AMD* (p.170), listed Hawkey as a "Pianoforte Manufacturer" at 31 King Street. A grand square piano with mother-of-pearl keys and inlay made c.1840 by this maker was exhibited at the Chickering Exhibition of 1902. (*Chickering Catalog* 1902:56)

HAWLEY, James

Misprint of the name of harpmaker *James Hanley*, see above.

HAZELTON, James & Frederick

1849	piano mkr	20 Vandam
1850	"	h. 9 Carlton
1851-53	pianos	219 Centre & 9 Carlton
1854-58	"	209 Centre
1859	not listed	
1860-63	pianos	" & 114 Eliz., 99 Prince
1864	"	" & 119 Mercer, "
1865-68	"	140 Greene, 119 Mercer
1869-90 +	"	34 University pl.

Henry Hazelton was born in 1816 in New York and apprenticed in 1831 "in an old legal manner" to *Dubois & Stodart*. In 1838, he moved to Albany where he first worked for William Boardman and later took

on partners to form his own firm, Hazelton, Lyon & Talbot. **Spillane** (1890:201) claimed Hazelton returned to New York in 1841, but if so, he was not listed in the *NYCD* before 1849.

In 1851, he joined his brother *Frederick Hazelton*, also a trained piano maker, to establish *H. & F. Hazelton*. The firm's title was changed to *Hazelton Brothers* in 1852 when a third brother, John E. Hazelton, was admitted into partnership.

According to the *1855 New York Census*, Hazelton Brothers owned no real capital, but did have $1,000 worth of tools; and a stock of 3,000 feet of hard wood and leather worth $6,000. The firm employed 25 men at total monthly wages of $1,000, who that year produced 2,000 pianos worth $35,000. By 1869, Hazelton Brothers was the sixteenth largest producer of pianos in the nation, with gross annual sales of $104,661. (*New York Tribune*, March 15, 1869)

Henry Hazelton was a respected member of the trade and the community. Among his other activities, he served on the jury that convicted the New York politician "Boss" Tweed. (**Hershkowitz** 1977:235) After Frederick retired in the 1880s, Henry and John continued to run the firm with the help of other family members. See **Spillane** (1890:201-04).

HAZELTON, H. & F.

1851	pianos	219 Centre & 9 Carlton

See above *Henry & Frederick Hazelton*.

HAZELTON BROTHERS

1852-53	pianos	219 Centre
1854-58	"	209 Centre
1859	not listed	
1860-63	pianos	", 114 Eliz., 99 Prince
1864	"	", 119 Mercer, "
1865-68	"	140 Greene, 119 & 99 Mercer
1869-90 +	"	34 University pl.

See above *Henry & Frederick Hazelton*.

HEARNE, Edward

1834-36	piano mkr	13th n. Ave. 5

No further information about this maker is presently known.

HEERS & PIRSSON

This firm is mentioned only by **Spillane** (1890:195-96), who wrote that they exhibited a double-grand piano at the London Crystal Palace Exhibition of 1851 and that their instrument "won much notice, owing to its features of originality." Heers' name does not appear in the Exhibition's *Official Catalogue* (1851), however, he might have worked on the Pirsson piano exhibited.

HEGARTY, Michael

Hegarty was listed as a "Musical Instrument Manufacturer" at 461 W. 27th Street only in the *1885 AMD* (p.206). The 1883 *NYCD* listed the profession of a person of that name and address as "clothing," and after 1884, listed an Ellen Hegarty "clothing and garments" at 461 W. 27th Street.

HENDERSON, John (Y.)

1835	piano mkr	145 Grand
1836	"	143 Grand
1837	"	57 Crosby
1838-39	not listed	
1840-42	music	549 Broadway
1843-44	piano mkr	"
1845	music	r. 59 Marion
1846-53	"	549 Broadway & 59 Marion
1854-55	pianos	" & "
1856-58	"	547 Broadway

Before 1838, Henderson was listed as John, and after 1840 as John Y. He also advertised as a piano maker in the 1850 *CmRg* (p.226).

HERRICK, Hiram

1846	pianofortes	297 Broadway
1847	pianos	W. 27th n. Ave. 9

From 1846-47, Herrick and partners *John Wake* and *John Myer* headed the piano-manufacturing firm *Wake, Myer & Herrick*. **Spillane** (1890:180) wrote: "This Herrick, I find, was in business in 1838 on Canal Street. In 1839 he was granted patent No. 1379 for a 'square' action. He afterwards was superintendent of several prominent factories, but he died recently [1890] in Brooklyn." (Despite Spillane's claim, no record of Herrick's Canal Street shop has been found.) The maker was granted another patent in 1868, at which time his home address was given as Boston. (**Spillane** 1890:366) See *Wake, Myer & Herrick*.

HESS, Daniel

1864-65	Importer of Mus Instrs & Strings, Manuf of accordeons, concertinas & mouth harmoniums. Depot	19 Maiden la.
1866-69	mus instrs	49 Maiden la.
1870-75	"	33 Maiden la.
1876	importer	"
1877-81	mus instrs	"
1882-84	"	41 Maiden la.
1885-86	"	22 Maiden la.

Hess was both an importer "especially of Accordeons, Concertinas, & bandonions," (*CmRg* 1867:111), and a manufacturer (*1885 AMD* p.206). A rotary-valve Bb cornet with a string action made by Hess is in the collection of the Shrine to Music, Vermillion, South Dakota.

HEYER, Frederick

Heyer was primarily an organbuilder. In 1773, he advertised that: "FREDERICK HEYER, Organ Builder, in the Broad- Way, in the same House where Mr. George Cook, Saddler lives, near St. Paul's Church, Makes and repairs Harpsichords and Spinets in the neatest Manner, and with Dispatch. Has some new and very neat Harpsichords for Sale. Also a Chamber Organ, which may, in a short Time, be compleatly finished, and enlarged (if tho't necessary) so as to suit a Place of public Worship." (*Rivington's New-York Gazetteer*, November 11, 1773)

HICKS, George

1849-54	cylinder piano mkr & organ builder	Brooklyn
1856	organ builder	Chatham Sq. c. E. Broadway 4 1/2 E. Broadway
1857	piano mkr/organs	4 1/2 E. Broadway
1858	hand organ mkr/organs	"
1859-62	organbuilder	101 Jay St., Brooklyn
1863	Harriet widow	"

Hicks (b.England 1818) was a hand-organ and cylinder-piano maker, who might have been related to the hand-organ making family of the same name then active in Bristol, England. It is possible that his New York addresses were merely retail outlets for goods produced in a Brooklyn factory. Instruments made by Hicks are in the collections of the MMA, SI and HFM. See **Libin** (1985:190).

HILL, Warren

1835	mus instr mkr	185 Chapel
1836	"	159 Forsyth
1837-38	"	28 Renwich
1839-40	"	24 Sullivan
1841	"	246 Spring
1842	"	36 Watts
1843	mus instrs	"
1844-45	"	370 Hudson
1846-47	"	68 1/2 Greene
1848	music	h. 92 Vandam
1849	"	h. 168 Spring
1850-52	not listed	
1853	clerk	239 Broadway
1854-56	publisher	"
1857-58	music	241 Broadway

After 1847, Hill apparently left the instrument-making trade to work in music publishing. Several men of this surname were active as instrument dealers during the 1850s, but their relationship to this maker is not known.

HINGSTON, John

See *Pethick & Hingston*.

HINTZ, Adolph(us)

1859-63	pianos	709 Fourth
1864-69	"	393 E. 4th
1870-71	"	173 Lewis
1872	"	10 Ave. 2

From 1859-62, Hintz and his partner *Charles Sieh* headed the piano-making firm *Sieh & Hintz*. In 1862, *A. Hintz & Company* was also listed; and in 1867, Hintz joined a new partner, *Louis Schraidt*, to establish *Hintz & Schraidt*.

In 1868, Hintz founded his own firm. According to the *1870 U.S. Census*, he owned $10,000 of real capital, and $3,000 of raw materials. His shop employed 8 men at total annual wages of $6,000, and that year produced $9,800 worth of pianos. Hintz was not listed in the *NYCD* after 1872, however, he might have been a member of *Schnabel, Hintz & Lambert* from 1875-76. See *Sieh & Hintz*; *Schnabel, Hintz & Lambert*.

HINTZ, A. & COMPANY

Listed only in the 1862 *CmRg* (p.36), this piano-manufacturing firm had warerooms at 86 Walker Street and a factory at 709 Fourth Street. The "& Company" might have been *Charles Sieh*. See above *Adolphus Hintz*.

HINTZ & SCHRAIDT

This firm, headed by *Adolphus Hintz* and *Louis Schraidt*, was listed only in the 1867 *CmRg* (p.134). See above *Adolphus Hintz*.

HOEY, James (W.)

1837-39	mus instrs	215 Orange
1840	"	29 Marion
1841-54	not listed	
1855	organbuilder	49 Grand
1856	mus instr mkr	241 E. 18th

In 1838, Hoey was in partnership with an instrument maker named *Toomey*; their shop was located on Spring Street. At the 1838 American Institute Fair, they were awarded a diploma for "the second best specimen of flutes." (*American Institute Records*). The James W. Hoey who reappeared in the 1855 *NYCD* was quite probably the same person. See **Langwill** (1980:81); *Toomey & Hoey*.

HOFFMAN(N), Charles E.F./Frederick

1843-46	piano mkr	355 1/2 Canal
1847	not listed	
1848	piano mkr	360 Grand h. 355 1/2 Canal
1849-50	"	381 Grand
1851-54	"	r. 368 Grand
1855-56	not listed	
1857-58	pianos	169 Prince
1859	not listed	
1860-62	pianos	h. 512 Fourth

Hoffman's surname was occasionally spelled with a double "n," and after 1843, he was consistently listed as "Charles E.F." His relationship to *Theodore Hoffman*, see below, is not known.

HOFFMAN, Theodore

1854	piano mkr	32 Second
1855-56	not listed	
1857-58	pianos	h. 32 Second
1859-63	"	161 Mercer
1864-71	"	78 Barrow

In 1858, Hoffman and a maker named Eckert—probably *Charles Eckert* who later manufactured piano keys—established the partnership *Hoffman & Eckert*. Hoffman headed his own firm from 1859-62 and again from 1869-71; but c.1861-68 he joined with Joseph Stuehler in the firm *Hoffman & Stuehler*. The *1861 AMD* (p.170) listed their factory as located in Brooklyn.

Hoffman advertised that he was a "Manufacturer of Piano-Fortes, 78 Barrow Street near Hudson. The newest improvements of the Overstrung Metal Frames, & c. warranted of the best workmanship. Eighth Avenue Cars pass right by door." (*CmRg* 1866:114)

HOFFMAN, T. & COMPANY

1859-62	pianos	161 Mercer
1869-71	"	78 Barrow

See above *Theodore Hoffman*.

HOFFMAN & ECKERT

1858	pianos	159 Mercer

See above *Theodore Hoffman*.

HOFFMAN & STUEHLER

1861-63	piano manuf	161 Mercer (*AMD*)
1864-68	"	78 Barrow

This firm was headed by Joseph Stuehler and *Theodore Hoffman*, see above.

HOGER/HOJER, George W.

Hoger or Hojer was probably an apprentice piano maker when he was appointed to Engine Company No. 46 as a volunteer fireman on August 24, 1829. His address was given as 26th Street near Third Avenue (*MCC*:18:231), however, his name never appeared in the *NYCD*.

HOLDER, Charles J.

1831	cabinet mkr	49 Orchard
1832-33	"	5 Orchard
1834	"	372 Broome
1835	piano mkr	193 Mott
1836	"	62 Spring
1837	not listed	
1838	piano mkr	123 Sullivan
1839-40	"	30 Lispenard
1841-42	"	r. 137 Spring
1843-46	pianos	"

1847-50	not listed	
1851-56	pianos	188 Spring
1857	collector & pianos	Front c. Coenties slip
1858	pianos/liquors	188 Spring/80 Pine
1859-60	not listed	
1861	------	188 Spring
1862-63	pianos	"
1864	"	100 & 188 Spring
1865-68	"	100 Spring
1869-70	"	h. 13 Varick

Pianos made by Holder were awarded silver medals at American Institute Fairs in 1841, 1844 and 1852. In 1842, Holder received only a diploma, the "silver medal having been before awarded"; and in 1852, for a "Superior Piano Forte Case," the Institute presented Holder with a copy of Webster's Dictionary. (*American Institute Records*) The maker also exhibited a piano at the 1853 New York Crystal Palace. (**Rimbault** 1860:402) Holder taught the trade to *Albert Weber* (**Dolge** 1911:296), and as late as 1870, his advertisements still proudly mentioned the awards given to him a generation earlier by the American Institute.

HOLLYER, Alexander

See *Steedman & Hollyer*.

HOLMES, George F.

1832	cabinet mkr	568 1/2 Pearl
1833	not listed	
1834	piano mkr	125 Sullivan
1835-36	"	22nd n. Ave. 3
1837-39	"	Ave. 3 n. 14th
1840	"	96 Ave. 3
1841-42	"	14 Ave. 3
1843	not listed	
1844-46	piano mkr	"
1847-52	pianos	"
1853	"	385 Bowery & 20 Sixth
1854-58	"	20 Sixth
1859	pianos & action mkr	"
1860-63	pianos	"
1864-65	"	385 Bowery
1866	piano mkr	"
1867-68	pianos	"
1869	"	75 University pl.

Holmes was awarded a diploma for the third best piano exhibited at the 1855 American Institute Fair: the judges noting his was a "fine instrument only inferior to the two previously named" [i.e. a *Steinway & Sons* and *Schuetze & Luedolff*]. (*American Institute Records*)

According to the *1855 New York Census*, Holmes owned $12,000 of real capital and $2,000 worth of tools. He had in stock $10,000 of wood and iron; 2,080 actions worth $20,000; 48 1/2 tons of coal worth $315 to run his steam-powered shop; and $11,000 worth of other materials. Holmes employed 20 men at total monthly wages of $600, and that year his shop produced 75 pianos worth $20,000. (*U.S. Manufacturing Census*, ms.) In addition to making pianos, Holmes also manufactured piano actions — probably selling them to other New York shops. (*NYBD* 1861:47)

HOLSTROM, Andres

See *James & Holstrom*.

HOOPER & BALL

1826-27   mus instr mkr   557 Broadway

Several Hoopers, all of them carpenters, were listed in the 1826 and 1827 *NYCDs*, but which one was a partner in this instrument-making firm is not clear. The other partner was probably *William Ball*, an instrument maker active through 1832.

HORN, Charles Edward

Born in London on June 21, 1786, Horn was an actor, singer composer, teacher and music publisher who toured widely in England, Ireland and North America. He first came to New York on tour in 1827, and lived in the city for short periods of time during the ensuing years. He was active as a music publisher, (**Dichter** 1977:207), and apparently worked in Richmond, Virginia c.1838 (**Stoutamire** 1972:155), before returning to New York in 1839, where he joined the instrument-making firm *Davis & Horn*. After its first year of operation, Davis withdrew from the concern, but Horn's Music Store at 411 Broadway continued in business for a few years before Horn return to London. Horn later moved to Boston where he became the conductor of the Boston Handel and Haydn Society before his death on October 21, 1849. See **Lawrence** (1988:220); *New Grove* (1980:8:712-13); *Davis & Horn*.

HORNE, Robert

Horne first advertised his abilities in the *New-York Mercury* on September 14, 1767: "Robert Horne, Musical Instrument-Maker, from London, at Mr. Francis Cooley's on Golden- Hill; Makes and repairs violins, bass viols, tenor viols, AEolius harps, gauiters, German flutes, Kitts, violin bows, &c. in the neatest and compleatest manner. All orders punctually obey'd, with the quickest dispatch: The favor of Gentlemen and Ladies shall be duly honour'd with any of the above. N.B. Merchants may be supplied with any of the above, cheaper than in London on proper notice given."

Later, in an 1772 notice which appeared through 1773, Horne advertised: "Robert Horne, Musical Instrument-Maker, from London, on Golden-Hill, near Burling's Slip, Makes and repairs musical instruments, vis. Violins, tennors, violoncellos, guittars, kitts, aeolus harps, spinnets, and spinnet jacks, violin bows, tail-pieces, pins, bridges, bows hair'd, and the best Roman Strings, & c. N.B. Country stores supply'd on the shortest notice." (*New-York Gazette and the Weekly Mercury*, January 6, 1772)

Horne was probably the same man who worked as "Drum maker to his Majesty's Office of Ordinance" at 20 Barbican Street, London in the mid-eighteenth century. (See *V.& A. Catalogue* 1973: 210.)

HOUSEMAN/HOUSMAN, Abraham

1825	carpenter	Laurens n. Canal
1826	"	King n. MacDougal
1828	not listed	
1829	carpenter	192 Varick
1831-32	"	9 Burton
1833-36	piano mkr	"
1837-40	not listed	
1841-50s	carpenter	97 Bedford

Houseman continued to work as a carpenter through 1853. His relationship to the later piano maker *Christopher Hausman*, see above, is not known.

HOWE, William

1796	organbuilder & mus instr store	326 Pearl
1797-98	" & "	320 Pearl
1799	widow of William, music store	"

An instrument maker, music store owner, and music publisher who apprenticed in the shop of *Thomas Dodds*, Howe advertised in the *Daily Advertiser* [N.Y.] on July 5, 1797: "New Music and Piano Fortes of superior quality, just arrived by the Brig Mary, from London, William Howe, No. 320 Pearl street, late Mr. Dodd's, respectfully informs the ladies and gentlemen of New-York, that he is publishing all Songs, Duets, & c. in the Comic opera of the Shipwreck performed with universal applause at the Theatre Royal, Drury Lane. W.H. has for sale, every article in the musical line, wholesale, retail, and for exportation. Also a general assortment of umbrellas. N.B. . . .Old instruments taken in exchange or repaired."

Howe died in November 1798, probably still a young man, leaving "To my wife Sarah, all the profits arising from my shop of musical instruments & all the rest of my income real and personal estate for the maintenance of my children till the youngest arrives at the age of twenty-one years." (**NYHS** "Abstract of Wills" 1902:15:109-10) Sarah Howe [later Terrett] was apparently successful at running the store, and continued in business until 1805. Her shop was one of the first to advertise the sale of musical-instrument-making tools: "Mrs. Howe . . . still carries on the business at No. 320 Pearl-Street, and has for sale, Barrel organs, Piano Fortes, fine Tone Pedal Harp, Trumpets, Flutes, Clarinets, French Horns, Bugle Horns, Hautboys, Bassons [*sic*], Concert Trumpets, & c. with a general assortment of all kinds of Musical Instruments . . . Likewise, different kinds of working Tools, Turning Takle [*sic*], Ivory, Ebony, Working benches, & c." (*New-York Gazette and General Advertiser*, December 28, 1799) For further information on Sarah Howe's activities as a music publisher see **Wolfe** (1980:144-45).

HUMEL

See *Adam Kern*.

HUNER, John F.

1883-84	pianos	r. 515 W. 42nd
1885	"	449 W. 38th
1886-90 +	"	507 W. 36th

Although Huner listed himself as a piano manufacturer in the 1883 *CmRg* (p.61), he was probably more active as an instrument dealer in the early 1880s. By the 1890s, however, he had established the *Huner Piano Company* at 71 University Place.

HUZZA, George

Huzza, a drum manufacturer, was not, strictly speaking, a city maker since his shop was located at Fordham, Westchester County [now part of the Bronx], according to the *1861 AMD* (p.90).

HYDE

See *Warner & Hyde*.

HYSLOP, Samuel C.

1815	pianoforte mkr	218 Church
1816-18	not listed	
1819-21 +	cabinet mkr	12 Beaver

Hyslop continued to work in the city as a cabinet maker and later as a merchant at various addresses until his death, c.1834.

I

IHLSENG, Lars G.

1857	piano mkr	h. r. 149 E. 25th
1858-60	not listed	
1861	pianos	Fulton, Brooklyn
1862-63	pianos	156 E. 21st
1864	piano mkr	" & 103 E. 33rd
1865-66	piano manuf & warehouse	156 E. 21st
1867-69	pianos	h. 151 E. 33rd
1870	not listed	
1871	pianos	"
1875	"	233 E. 23rd
1878	"	151 E. 33rd
1883 +	"	142 E. 86th

From 1860-62, Ihlseng and partners *Conrad Narvesen* and *J.E.L. Linsted* headed the piano-manufacturing firm *Ihlseng, Narvesen & Linsted* at 16 Fulton Street, Brooklyn. (*1861 AMD* p.169) Linsted left the firm in 1863, and it was reorganized as *Ihlseng & Narvesen*. In 1865, Ihlseng was again listed alone (*CmRg* 1865:71). During the late 1860s, the maker seems to have retained a shop at 16 Fulton Street, Brooklyn, in addition to his retail store in the city. During the 1870s and 1880s, Ihlseng apparently continued his involvement in the trade solely as an instrument dealer.

IHLSENG & NARVESEN

1862	pianos	156 E. 21st
1863-64	Piano Forte Makers	156-58 E. 21st

See above *Lars Ihlseng.*

IHLSENG, NARVESEN & LINSTED

From 1860-62, this firm was located at 16 Fulton Street, Brooklyn. (*1861 AMD* p.169) The firm was reorganized as *Ihlseng & Narvesen* after Linsted withdrew in 1863, even though the latter continued to be listed at the new firm's address until 1867. See above *Lars Ihleseng.*

IHNE, John

1857	piano mkr	h. 11 Crosby
1858	grocer	198 Chrystie
1859-61	pianos	57 Crosby
1862	piano mkr	h. 163 Mott
1863	pianos	h. 52 Crosby
1864	"	79 Ave. 3
1865	"	111 E. 14th & 79 Ave. 3
1866	"	82 E. 14th
1867-73	"	112 E. 14th
1874-75	------	h. 201 E. 13th

In 1864, Ihne admitted his son, the piano tuner John Ihne, Jr., into partnership, establishing the firm *Ihne & Son*. **Spillane** (1890:252) mentioned Ihne & Son as "among the other piano-making firms that had attained some note towards 1870 as makers of instruments for the masses." In 1865, they were listed in the *CmRg* (1865:71) as "Manufacturers of Square Overstrung Piano Fortes".

IHNE & SON

1864	pianos	79 Ave. 3
1865	piano manuf	" & 111 E. 14th
1866	piano fortes	82 E. 14th
1867-73	pianos	112 E. 14th

See above *John Ihne.*

ILSLEY, FERDINAND I. & COMPANY

1861	pianos	286 Bowery h. Newark
1862-65	"	430 Broome

The "& Company" was probably Ilsley's relative, George F. Ilsley, who was listed as a piano dealer at the same address. Both men might have been related to the music dealer E.C. Ilsley, who had a shop on Broadway in 1856. Although the *NYBD* listed *Ilsley & Company* as piano makers, the *1861 AMD* (p.168) listed them only as piano dealers.

IVES, Seth

1827	fife-maker	55 Bedford
1828	"	71 MacDougal
1829	porter house	148 Christopher
1830	cabinet mkr	63 Carmine
1831-33	"	66 Carmine
1834	"	44 Downing
1835	Eliza widow of Seth	27 Charlton

No further information is presently known about this maker.

J

JACKSON, James Jr.

See *Geib & Jackson*.

JACOB BROTHERS(John F.; Charles;

C. Albert)

1881	pianos	r. 515 W. 42nd
1882-85	"	1329 Broadway
1886	"	"& 817 Broadway
1887	"	819 Broadway
1888	"	453 W. 36th
1889-90+	"	542 W. 40th

"Among the firms that succeeded in producing high- grade pianos and scoring at the same time a remarkable financial success," wrote **Dolge** (1911:321), "Jacob Brothers stand preeminent. Charles Jacob studied piano making with Calenberg & Vaupel . . . while his brother, John F. Jacob, worked for years with Hardman, Peck & Company, and Billings & Wheelock. They started their business in 1878. After the death of John F. in 1885, the youngest brother, C. Albert, was admitted to the firm, and in 1902 the business was incorporated. Besides their own extensive factory, this corporation owns the Wellington Piano Case Company, the Abbott Piano Action Co., and the old established business of James & Holstrom." In addition to their shop in mid-town Manhattan, in 1885 Jacob Brothers also maintained a shop at 51 & 53 Bushwick Avenue, Brooklyn. (*1885 AMD* p.206)

JACOBS, Christian J.

1837-39	piano mkr	125 Mulberry
1840	"	57 Elizabeth
1841-43	"	123 Mulberry

Apparently not a relative of the Jacobs family who were involved in the sale of musical instruments, see below, this craftsman was later listed as a cabinet maker.

JACOBS

A large family involved in selling jewelry, watches, and fancy goods, as well as musical instruments during the 1840s and 1850s, the Jacobs included:

Angel Jacobs

Angel Jacobs, probably the patriarch of the Jacobs family, was first listed in 1820 as a watchmaker. Not listed for many years, his name reappeared as a jeweler during the 1840s. From 1850-52, he advertised accordeons among the goods he sold in his shop at 98 1/2 Chatham Street. He was listed as a "Musical Instrument Dealer" at 100 Chatham in the *1861 AMD* (p.89), although it is likely that Angel's widow, Rachael, was actually running the shop by that date. (See *NYBD*.) In 1856, the musical instrument-making firm *Angel Jacobs' Sons* was listed at 100 Chatham in the *NYCD*.

David L. Jacobs

1851	banjos	149 Hester
1852	mus instrs	145 Hester
1853-55	"/ banjos	149 Hester
1856-60	"/ banjos	90 Chatham

Mentioned as a banjo maker by **Howard** (1959:46), David Jacobs was also listed in the *1861 AMD* (p.90) as a maker of "Banjos & Tambourines."

Henry P. Jacobs

Primarily listed as a "teacher" and a "clerk," Henry P. Jacobs was only mentioned as an instrument maker in the 1856 *NYBD* (p.286), which gave his address as 92 1/2 Chatham Street.

John Jacobs

1846-47	fancygoods	55 & 78 1/2 Chatham
1848	"	102 Chatham
1849-51	not listed	
1852	music	h. 461 Pearl
1853-54	jeweler	102 Chatham
1855	accordeons	407 Broadway
1856+	jeweler	"

More active as an instrument maker than the other members of the Jacobs family, John was awarded a diploma "For the Best Banjo" at the 1850 American Institute Fair. At the 1852 Fair he was awarded another diploma "for the best Tambourine & Banjo," and at the 1855 Fair he entered a banjo, bass drum, and accordeon reeds. (*American Institute Records*) At the 1853 New York Crystal Palace,

Jacobs exhibited: "Accordeons with improved reeds; banjo with new arrangements for tuning; tambourine with flush screws." (*Official Catalogue* 1853:95) From 1846-57, with Lionel Jacobs, John headed the instrument dealership *J. & L. Jacobs*.

Lionel Jacobs

1846-49	fancygoods	55 & 78 1/2 Chatham
1850-51	"	102 Chatham
1852	accordeon depot	"& 264 Canal
1853-54	jeweler	102, 190 & 92 Chatham
1855	accordeons	92, 102, 407 Broadway
1856-59	jeweler	407 Broadway
1860	mus instrs	" & 67 William

From 1846-57, Lionel and John Jacobs headed the instrument dealership *J. & L. Jacobs*. Lionel was also listed as a dealer in the *1861 AMD* (p.89).

JACOBS, J. & L.

See above *Lionel Jacobs* and *John Jacobs*.

JACOBUS & WHITING

| 1822 | pianoforte mkrs | 39 Chapel |

Whiting was probably *Luther Whiting*, a piano maker active from 1823-47. Jacobus might have been one of the two carpenters of that name listed in the 1822 *NYCD*, but this has not been confirmed.

JAMES, Amos C.

1870	merchant	77 Franklin
1871	"	54 Lispenard
1872-75	not listed	
1876	pianos	195 Seventh
1877-90+	"	233 E. 21st

James was apprenticed in *James Grovesteen*'s Albany shop. He later worked for the Albany piano makers Boardman & Gray, and was a partner in the Albany firm Marshall, James & Traver. About 1870, James arrived in New York, "under contract with Mr. F.G. Smith, to superintend the manufacture of his instruments." (**Spillane** 1890:140,144,275) In 1876, James joined partner *Andres Holstrom* to form the piano-manufacturing firm *James & Holstrom*.

JAMES & HOLSTROM

| 1876 | pianos | 195 Seventh |
| 1877-90+ | " | 233 E. 21st |

This partnership was headed by *Amos James*, see above, and *Andres Holstrom*.

JARDINE, John

1833	piano mkr	451 Broadway
1834	"	449 Broadway
1835	"	465 Broadway
1836-39	"	459 Broadway

Jardine was born in 1804, probably in Dartford, England, and was the brother of the well-known New York organbuilder George Jardine. (See *New Grove* 1984:2:323; **Oches** 1975:161; **Jones** 1971:80.) In 1833, John Jardine joined *James Bridgeland* in the piano-manufacturing firm *Bridgeland & Jardine*. Jardine was apparently the practical member of this partnership (**Spillane** 1890:158), and after it was dissolved in 1837, his name disappeared from city records, except for an 1844 *NYBD* (p.184) listing which gives his address as 103 Spring Street.

During the 1840s, Jardine was primarily based in New Jersey, where he was listed as a pianoforte maker at 145 Mercer Street, Jersey City in the *1861 AMD* (p.85). (In August 1848, however, he advertised in the *Herald* that he would tune pianos for fifty cents and gave his address as 457 Hudson Street. See **Lawrence** 1988:559.) According to **Kaufman** (1976:21-22,29), Jardine was listed as "insane" in the *1850 Federal Census*, and died c.1860. **Spillane** (1890:158-59) credits Jardine with exhibiting an overstrung square piano in 1833 "that antedates European overstringing by two years." See *Bridgeland & Jardine*.

JENNYS, John L.R.

| 1869-72 | pianos | 233 E. 21st |

Jennys had been active in the city's musical trade as early as 1865 when, with partner *Laurence Cummings*, he headed the piano-manufacturing firm *Cummings & Jennys*. In 1869, he and his son, John Jr., established *Jennys & Son*, which advertised as "manufacturers of Grand, Square, and Upright Piano-Fortes. Ranks first in this city. The Patent Agraffe Treble is introduced in every instrument without extra charge." (*CmRg* 1869:113) See *Cummings & Jennys*.

JENNYS & SON

| 1869-72 | pianos | 233 E. 21st |

See above *John L.R. Jennys*.

JOERDONS, John F.M.

1858	broker	49 Nassau
1859-60	importer/com. mer.	
1861-62	not listed	
1863	merchant	51 Maiden la.
1864-65	importer	131 Williams
1866	fancygoods	60 Maiden la. & 21 Liberty
1867-68	"	63 Liberty
1869	mus instrs	"
1870	merchant	97 Reade
1871	mus instrs	83 Chambers & 65 Reade
1872	"	25 Murray
1873-74	"	4 Courtlandt

It is probable that Joerdons was only an importer and dealer, however, **Krivin** (1961:246) quotes an 1868 advertisement which claimed Joerdons also made "guitars, banjos, tambourines, military drums, flutes of all kinds, etc." The *1861 AMD* (p.90) lists Joerdon only as an importer.

JOHNSON, William

1833	piano mkr	342 Washington
1834	not listed	
1835	piano mkr	15 Thomas

Nothing further is presently known about this maker.

JOHNSTON, Robert

1848	mus instr mkr	279 Ave. 3

No further information is presently known about this maker.

JOLLIE, Allen R.

1829	mus instr mkr	104 Bedford
1830-31	"	221 Bleecker
1832-33	"	402 Broadway
1834-35	"	105 Elm h. 403 Broadway
1836-40	music	385 Broadway
1841-42	mus instrs	401 Broadway
1843-46	"	66 Walker
1847	"	169 Fulton
1848-49	"	122 Fulton
1850-54	"	300 Broadway
1855	"	519 Broadway
1856	mus/mus instr mkr	" & 157 Elm
1857	mus instrs	157 Elm
1858	"	h. 101 Charlton
1859-61	"	h. 55 Vandam
1862-66	"	h. 10 King
1867-68	not listed	
1869	ivory	143 Grand
1870	tuner	"
1871-77	ivory/turner	"
1878	Jeannette, widow Allen R.	h. 7 Leroy

Allen Jollie and his relative, *Edward Jollie*, see below, made woodwind instruments, and although they were never officially listed as partners, they and a third relative, Samuel C. Jollie, shared many of the same shop addresses. Allen was in the city as early as April 10, 1826, when the "musical instrument maker" of 81 Gold Street was appointed as a volunteer fire fighter to Engine Company No. 12. (*MCC* 15:339) He resigned his commission on September 8, 1828. (*MCC* 17:368)

Either Allen or Edward Jollie might have been connected with the instrument dealer William E. Millet in the partnership *Jollie & Millet*; however, it is more probable that Samuel C. was the Jollie involved with this venture since in 1836 the firm became *Jollie & Company* under the direction of the latter.

Allen Jollie was awarded a diploma for the best flute exhibited at the 1843 American Institute Fair (*American Institute Records*), and examples of his instruments can be found at various museums. See **Langwill** 1980:87

JOLLIE, Edward (Jr.)

1823	mus instr mkr	Christopher n. Greenwich
1824-25	"	Amos c. Washington
1826	instrs	"
1827-30	not listed	
1831	mus instr mkr	27 Morton
1832-35	not listed	
1836	mus instrs	40 Oliver
1837	"	118 Bowery
1838	"	347 Bleecker
1839	"	274 Spring
1840	"	r. 11 Clarke
1841-42	"	401 Broadway
1843-46	turner	66 Walker
1847	instrs	169 Fulton
1848-49	"	122 Fulton
1850-53	"	300 Broadway
1854	music	"
1855	express	519 Broadway
1856	mus instrs	157 Elm

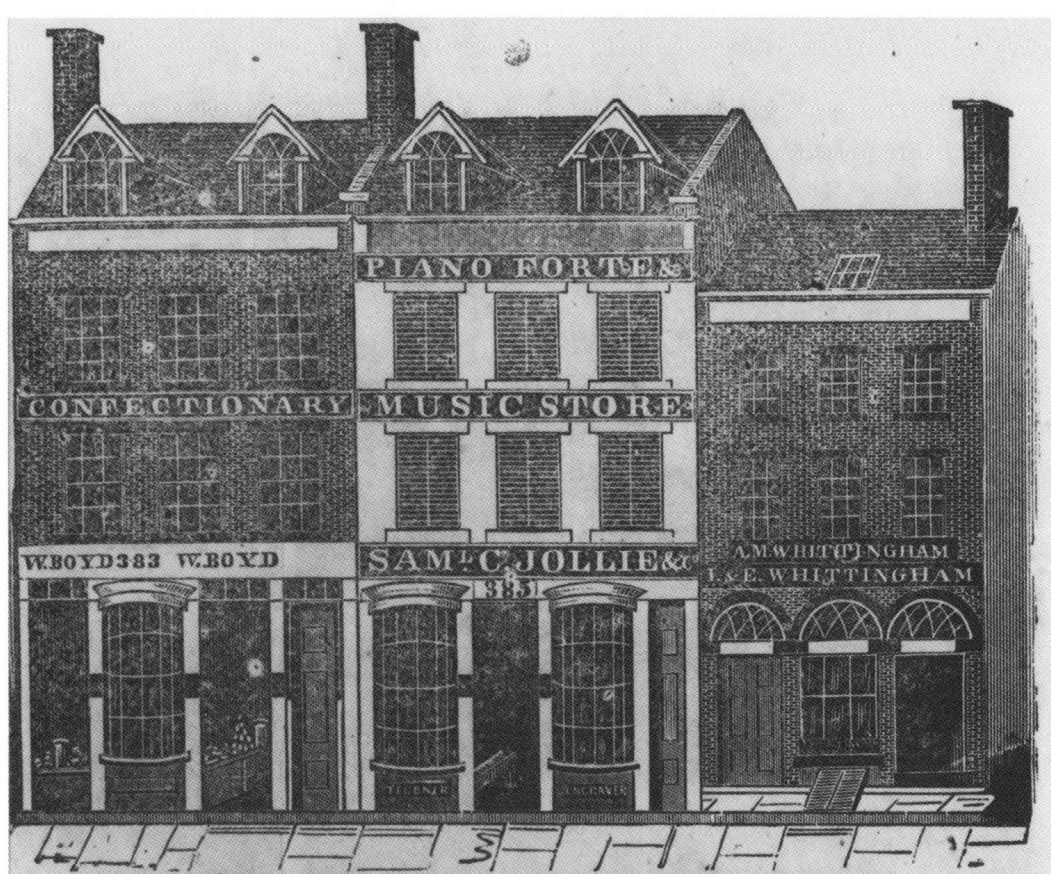

Advertising broadside showing Samuel Jollie & Company's shop at 385 Broadway c. 1836-40. The firm's activities and wares are detailed in the fine print.

| 1857-58 | music | 140 Varick |
| 1859-63 | express | 2 Harrison |

A relative of *Allen Jollie*, see above, it is likely that this woodwind maker, or a third relative, Samuel C. Jollie, was the partner of *Joseph Secor* in the 1829 firm *Jollie & Secor*.

JOLLIE & COMPANY

| 1836-40 | music store | 385 Broadway |

See above *Allen Jollie*.

JOLLIE & MILLET

| 1835 | music store | 385 Broadway |

This partnership was headed by one of the Jollies and William E. Millet. See above *Allen Jollie*.

JOLLIE & SECOR

| 1829 | mus instr mkr | 17 Stanton |

It is unclear which of the Jollies was involved in this firm, but *Joseph Secor* was an instrument maker active in the city from c.1826-31. See above *Edward Jollie*.

JONES, Daniel L.

1835-38	spirit gas	18 Monroe
1839-43	"	499 Pearl
1844-50	"& lamps	30 City Hall pl.

In 1842, Jones was awarded a silver medal for an "improvement in the Cambrian Harp" exhibited at the American Institute Fair. (*American Institute Records*) The only other indication that Jones was interested in music was his listing under "harps" in the 1844 *NYBD* (p.184) Given his name and interest in harps, it is possible that Jones was of Welsh background.

JONES, Luther

1821-22	grocer	Broome c. Arundel
1823	"	137 Allen
1824-25	drum mkr	"
1826	mus instr mkr	"
1827	"	104 Allen
1828-31	"	6 Willet
1832	faucetmaker	"
1833	------	"
1834	------	76 Bowery

From 1826-29, Jones was a member of the instrument-making firm *Jones & Gillespie*. Both partners had some connection with the instrument-making firm *Carter & Robinson*, of 10 Willet Street, whose members also turned to faucetmaking.

JONES & GILLESPIE

1826	mus instr mkr	137 Allen
1827-28	not listed	
1829	------	6 Willet

See above *Luther Jones*.

K

KAEMPF, Reinhardt A.

| 1881-84 | mus instrs | 180 Chrystie |
| 1885-90+ | " | 297 Bowery |

Kaempf was listed as a "Musical Instrument Manufacturer, 180 Chrystie Street" in the *1885 AMD* (p.207). Trombones made by Kaempf are now in several collections. See **Langwill** (1980:88).

KALLENBERG, Henry

1869	music	1 Jackson
1870	not listed	
1871	mus instrs	"
1872-90+	"	518 Grand

Kallenberg's firm advertised as "Importers and Manufacturers of all Kinds of German & French Accordeons, Bandonions, Concertinos, Violins, Fine Italian Strings, & c., at Wholesale & Retail. Buyers will find our assortment in German Accordeons of great variety, as well as one of the largest in the city." (*CmRg* 1870:112) In 1871, Kallenberg added guitars, banjos, hand organs and trumpets to this list. (*CmRg* 1871:125) The *1885 AMD* (p.207) listed Kallenberg as a "Manufacturer of Accordeons & music publisher." He was apparently not related to the piano maker *Henry Calenberg*.

KARR, William H.

See *Francis Bacon*.

KEARSING, George W.

1838	piano mkr	13 Second
1839	"	r. 24 Jones
1841	"	13 Second
1842	"	133 Amity
1844	"	74 Charles
1847	pianos	88 Walker
1854-58	"	71 Ave. 1

This maker probably worked for his father *John Kearsing*, see below, before 1838. **Spillane** (1890:106) wrote "In recent years the name of George Kearsing . . . appeared. This old maker was in business in 1868 and upward, but got crowded out by more modern methods and larger facilities." Given the above *NYCD* listings, Spillane's dates are probably incorrect.

According to the *1855 New York Census*, Kearsing owned $8,000 of real capital, and $1,500 worth of tools. He had $2,000 worth of woods, iron, steel, etc. in stock; and his firm employed 3 men at total monthly wages of $120 who that year produced 24 pianos worth $4,500. See below *John Kearsing*.

KEARSING, John

1804	pianoforte manuf	Bowery
1805-06	"	Bowery c. North
1807-16	"	279 Bowery
1818	pianos	177 Broome
1819	"	279 Bowery
1820	pianoforte mkr	"
1821-23	"	96 Chatham
1824	"	Third Ave.
1825	"	50 Courtlandt
1826-28	"	Herring c. Burton
1829	"	293 Bowery
1830-31	"	456 Broadway
1832	not listed	
1833	piano mkr	2 Greene
1834	"	13 Mulberry
1835	"	107 Attorney
1836	"	3 Second

John Kearsing and his sons *Thomas*, *William*, *George*, and John Jr., arrived in New York, possibly from London c.1804. (**Pierce** 1865:200) They established a successful piano-manufacturing shop, which was reportedly the largest in the city before 1830. (**Spillane** 1890:106) The family business began as *J. Kearsing & Sons* from 1804-09; and then, from 1810-16, the firm became *J. Kearsing & Son*. Thereafter, the senior Kearsing apparently worked alone until 1836. On June 13, 1831, H.O., G.F., and W.F. Kears-

ing were granted a patent for improved piano actions. (**Spillane** 1890:106) A square piano made by Kearsing & Sons is now in the collection of the Smithsonian Institution. (*Smithsonian Institution Catalogue* No. 315,693)

KEARSING, Thomas

1809	------	Nicholas William
1811-13	------	Bowery n. 2 mile stone
1814-16	not listed	
1817	pianoforte manuf	Ave. 3 n. Nicholas
1818	not listed	
1819-21	pianoforte mkr	Ave. 3
1822-23	not listed	
1824	pianoforte mkr	"
1825-28	not listed	
1829-31	pianoforte mkr	Sixth n. Ave. 3
1832	piano mkr	175 Broadway
1833-35	"	259 Broadway
1836	pianos	"
1837-39	"	Sixth n. Ave. 3
1840-42	"	12 Sixth
1843	piano mkr	"
1850	late pianos	"
1854	"	8 Sixth

After leaving his father's firm, *J. Kearsing & Sons*, c.1816, Thomas went into business for himself. From 1832-42, with his own sons, he established the piano-making firm *T. Kearsing & Sons*. The firm was awarded a diploma for the "third best specimen of horizontal pianofortes" at the 1836 American Institute Fair. (*American Institute Records*)

KEARSING, William (F.)

1817	pianoforte manuf	270 Bowery
1818-19	"	279 Bowery
1820-35	not listed	
1836-37	pianos	561 Houston

Kearsing was probably the same person as the piano maker, tuner, and instrument repairman of the same name who was active in Richmond, Virginia c.1838-44. (**Stoutamire** 1972:139) See above *John Kearsing*.

KEARSING, J. & SON

1810-16	pianoforte manuf	279 Bowery

See above *John Kearsing*.

KEARSING, J. & SONS

1804	piano manuf	Bowery
1805-06	"	Bowery c. North
1807-09	"	279 Bowery

See above *John Kearsing.*

KEARSING, T. & SONS

1832	piano mkr	175 Broadway
1833-35	"	259 Broadway
1836	pianos	"
1837-39	"	6th n. Ave. 3
1840-42	"	12 Sixth

See above *Thomas Kearsing.*

KELL, Charles

1856	drum mkr	h. 200 Seventh
1857	mus instrs	343 Ninth
1858	"	h. 200 Seventh

In addition to drums, Kell also made banjos, and he was awarded a diploma for the second best banjo exhibited at the 1856 American Institute Fair. (*American Institute Records*) In 1859, Kell was listed as a drum maker at Ainslie n. Union Avenue, Brooklyn; and still later was listed as a cabinet maker.

KELLY, Joseph E.

1852	mus instr mkr	90 Fulton (*NYBD*)

Kelly was listed only in the 1852 *NYBD* (p.223), and no further information about him is presently known.

KENARD, Isaac

Kenard was probably still an apprentice when he joined Fire Engine No. 46 as a volunteer fire fighter on October 8, 1827; the *MCC* (16:543) listed his occupation as "pianoforte maker," and his address as 26th Street. Two other piano makers, *Jacob Smith* and *Isaac Van Horne*, were members of the same Fire Engine Company. Kenard was never listed in the *NYCD*.

KERN & HUMEL

Adam Kern was listed as a piano maker at 213 W. 40th Street in 1869. According to the *1870 U.S. Census*, his firm, *Kern & Humel*, owned $8,000 of real capital. It had in stock 17,000 feet of wood worth $1,900; and 200 tons of brass and ivory worth $2,000. The shop also contained 6 molding machines, 2 planing machines, and a 50-horse-power steam engine; it employed 9 men at annual wages of $2,800 who that year produced $10,000 worth of pianos.

KERNAN, Richard

1844	cabinet mkr	274 Greenwich
1845	pianoforte manuf	242 1/2 Spring
1846	piano manuf	25th n. Ave. 2
1847	"	266 Ave. 3

Kernan is best remembered for his 1845 partnership with *Peter De Hoog.* See *De Hoog & Kernan.*

KERRISON, Robert

1835-36	stables	21 Dey
1837	"	" & 36 Oak
1838-39	"	21 Dey

Kerrison is credited with the invention of the "ascending" or "cut-off" valve on brass instruments (**Dodworth** 1853:23), and was also awarded several patents for improvements in piano actions. (PC:Eliason) In 1841, Kerrison moved to Philadelphia where he worked as a watchmaker for many years.

KINDT, Louis

1863	pianos	79 Third
1864-65	"	20 Sixth
1866	"	865 Broadway
1867-68	"	" & 22 E. 18th
1869-71	"	413 W. 42nd
1872	piano manuf	"
1873	pianos	"

From 1863-65, Kindt and William Grupe, a grocer, headed the piano dealership Grupe & Kindt. Kindt then joined George M. Manz in the partnership *Kindt & Manz*, which continued in operation until 1870; after which, he spent several years on his own before establishing *Kindt & Company*, see below. It is possible that throughout his career Kindt was a dealer rather than a manufacturer.

KINDT & COMPANY

1873	pianos	413 W. 42nd

See above *Louis Kindt.*

KINDT & MANZ

1866	pianos	865 Broadway
1867-68	"	" & 22 E. 18th
1869-70	"	413 W. 42nd

The firm was headed by *Louis Kindt*, see above and George Manz.

KINDSTROM, Gustave W.

See *Pease & Kindstrom*.

KING, Matthew (Matthias)

1801	musician	Cross
1802-06	"	333 Broadway
1807	not listed	
1808	mus instr mkr	34 Essex
1809-10	not listed	
1811-16	mus instr mkr	"
1817-21	"	36 Essex
1822	widow of Matthew	"

Possibly the same person or the son of the British composer Matthew P. King (1733-1823), whose son Charles M. was active in New York during the 1840s. (See **Lawrence** 1988:228)   A carpenter of the same name is sometimes confused with this maker. His relationship to *Peter King*, see below, is not known.

KING, Peter

1824	mus instr mkr	Bedford n. Arden
1825	"	King n. MacDougal
1826	"	Bedford n. Burton

Redway (1941:70) lists a cabinet maker of the same name who was active from 1828-30, but no proof has been found to establish they were the same person. This maker's relation to *Matthew King*, see above, is not known.

KINKELDEY, Carl

See *Mathushek & Kinkeldey*.

KLIX, Albrecht

See *Behning & Klix*.

KNAPP, John H.

See *Ward & Knapp*.

KNAUF(F), Frederick

1864-70	pianos	228 Ave. 3
1871-73	piano mkr	h. 240 E. 25th

Before 1863, Knauf was listed as a piano tuner, and in 1865 he was briefly involved in the partnership *Knauf & Schmidt* — possibly with the piano maker *Adam Schmidt*.

KNAUF & SCHMIDT

Listed as a manufacturer of pianofortes at 228 Third Avenue only in the 1865 *CmRg* (p.72) See above *Frederick Knauf*.

KNOPF, Henry Richard

1881	violins	116 E. 4th
1882	mus instr mkr	"
1883	violins	"
1884	violin mkr	h. 349 E. 12th
1885	violins	"
1886-90+	"	92 Third

Born in 1860 at Markneukirchen, Germany, son of the violin maker Heinrich Knopf, this maker worked for Bausch at Dresden and Christian Adam in Berlin, before immigrating to Philadelphia in 1879 where he found work with the luthier John Albert. In 1880, Knopf moved to New York where he remained until his death in 1939. Knopf is credited with personally making 450 violins, 50 violas, 50 cellos, and 1,000 bows in the course of his long career. See **Henley** (1960:3:150); **Roda** (1959:189-92).

KOBER, George

See *Stark & Kober*.

KOCH, John J.

Koch was listed as a manufacturer of musical instruments at 174 First Avenue only in the *1885 AMD* (p.207).

KOENIG, Herman

See below *Herman Konig*.

KOHNLE, Joseph

1856	pianist	h. 196 W. 37th
1857	piano mkr	"
1858-59	not listed	
1860-62	pianos	173 Prince
1863-64	pianos/piano mkr	"
1865-67	pianos	"
1868	"	MacDougal n. 4th
1869-71	not listed	
1872-73	piano mkr	h. 441 W. 37th

In 1860, Kohnle and the piano dealer Francis Riedel headed the firm *Kohnle & Riedel*; and in the *1861 AMD* (p.170), Kohnle was listed as a piano manufacturer. A piano made by Kohnle is in the collection of the Smithsonian Institution (*Catalogue* No. 315,701).

KOHNLE & RIEDEL

1860	pianos	173 Prince

See above *Joseph Kohnle*.

KOMPFF, Philip H.

1859-60	pianos	h. 203 Ave. 3
1861-63	not listed	
1864	piano mkr	h. 133 E. 20th
1865	new & second hand pianos	162 Ave. 3
1866-68	pianos	"
1869	"	125 Ave. 3
1870-72	"	174 Ave. 3
1873-74	drums	116 Elizabeth
1875	drums & banjos	"
1876	drums	129 Ave. 4
1877-83	pianos	"
1884-85	music	"
1886-87	pianos	"
1888	piano mkr	h. 340 E. 15th
1889-90+	pianos	50 Ave. 3

Kompff was a piano dealer (*1861 AMD* p.168) and manufacturer (*NYBD* 1870:131) who also made "all kinds of Drums, Banjos, Tambourines, & c." (*NYBD* 1873:87) On his business cards, c.1876, Kompff also advertised he was a manufacturer of "Military Brass and Bass Drums." (New-York Historical Society, Landauer Collection 16:C) With his son William, Kompff headed the firm *Kompff & Son* from 1876-77.

KOMPFF & SON

1876	drums	129 Ave. 4
1877	pianos	"

See above *Philip Kompff*.

KONIG/KOENIG, Herman

1863	mus instr mkr	h. 147 Sixth
1864	mus instrs	"
1865	not listed	
1866-67	instr mkr	254 E. Houston
1868	mus instrs	h. 249 Stanton
1869	"	h. 230 E. 4th
1870	violins	h. 12 Stanton
1871-72	"	h. 17 Stanton
1873	music	391 Bowery
1874	mus instrs	"
1875	violins	387 Bowery
1876-77	violin mkr	"
1878-85	mus instrs	"
1886-90+	violins	"

The *1885 AMD* (p.207) listed Konig as a "String Instrument Importer," and he seems to have worked primarily as a dealer. His son, *Herman Jr.*, see below, was also in the business.

KONIG, Herman, Jr.

Listed only as a string dealer in the *NYCD*s of the 1880s, the *1885 AMD* (p.207) gave his profession as "Violin Manufacturer & repairer" at 884 Bowery. Konig was probably trained by his father, *Herman Konig*, see above.

KOOK, Sebastian

See *Sebastian Cook*.

KRAKAUER, Simon

1855	------	163 Stanton
1856	music	h. 163 Stanton
1858	musician	h. 47 Clinton
1859-60	"	h. 578 Fourth
1861	"	h. 106 Sixth
1862-63	segars	h. 6 Clinton
1864	musician	"
1865	teacher	h. 409 Fifth
1866-73	musician	218 Broome
1874-90+	"	40 Union Sq.

Simon Krakauer was a piano manufacturer and the father of *David*, *Daniel*, and *Julius*, who later headed the firm *Krakauer Brothers*, see below. According to **Dolge** (1911:326-27): "Educated as a musician, becoming a violinist and orchestra conductor of note, Simon Krakauer was born at Kissingen, Germany, in 1816, came to America in 1854 and started manufacturing pianos in 1869, with his son David, who had learned in A.H. Gale's shop." When his other sons joined them, c.1884, the title of the firm was changed to *Krakauer Brothers*. The elder Krakauer died in 1905.

KRAKAUER BROTHERS (David, Daniel, and Julius)

1884	pianos	40 Union Square East
1885-88	"	", 412 E. 23, 729 Ave. 1
1889	"	", 703-09 Ave. 1
1890+	"	", 159 E. 126th

David Krakauer, who had been trained as a piano maker in the shop of *A.H. Gale* and possibly *Kindt & Grube*, joined his father, *Simon Krakauer* in a piano-manufacturing venture c.1869. Their business was not listed until 1884, when they were joined by two other Krakauer brothers, Daniel and Julius, and the firm *Krakauer Brothers* established. **Spillane** (1890:284-85) wrote that the Krakauers were "manufacturers of popular-priced instruments of very excellent character ... Mr. David Krakauer, the practical member of the firm, learned piano making in this city at Kind & Grube's [Kindt & Grube], and subsequently worked in many of the leading shops. At twenty-one he began business in a modest manner as a small maker, and meanwhile opened a musical instrument store at the upper end of the Bowery. He was joined in partnership by his brothers ... they leased a small factory and opened a retail warerooms on Union Square." David Krakauer died in 1900 (**Dolge** 1911:326-27), but the firm continued in operation until the 1960s. See above *Simon Krakauer.*

KRALL, Charles

1854	piano mkr	r. 85 Varick
1855-57	not listed	
1858	pianos	h. 139 Laurens
1859-61	not listed	
1862-63	piano mkr	h. 171 Wooster
1864	not listed	
1865	piano mkr	h. r. 144 Sullivan
1866-67	pianos	r. 291 W. 24th
1868	piano mkr	r. 431 W. 24th
1869	pianos	"
1870-71	piano mkr	305 Seventh

Krall and his partner [Otto?] *Schuetze* established the piano-manufacturing firm *Schuetze & Krall* in 1854. Their partnership lasted only a year, after which Krall worked alone until 1867 when he joined a man named Fakler in the partnership *Krall & Fakler.* Krall probably died c.1871 when a widow named Emily Krall was listed in the 1871 *NYCD* as doing "sewing" at 174 Division Street. See *Schuetze & Krall.*

KRALL & FAKLER

This firm consisted of *Charles Krall,* see above, and Fakler, who was probably a dealer. The partners, "Manufacturers of Piano-Fortes. Factory & Warerooms No. 291 W. 24th Street, Between 9th & 10th Avenues," were listed only in the 1867 *CmRg* (p.135).

KRANICH, Hellmuth

1865-66	pianos	394 Hudson
1867-68	"	106 Bleecker & 57 Downing
1869-73	"	241 E. 23rd
1874-79	"	241 & 243 E. 23rd, 218 E. 26th
1880-90+	"	235 E. 23rd

Kranich was named as a trustee of the *New York Piano Forte Company* in 1864, and was first listed in the 1865 *NYCD.* Kranich is probably best remembered as the partner of piano maker *Jaques Bach,* with whom he established the piano-manufacturing firm *Kranich, Bach & Company* in 1867. In 1872, the title of the firm was changed to *Kranich & Bach.* By 1869, they were the 26th largest piano-manufacturing concern in the nation with gross annual sales of $42,622. (*New York Tribune,* March 15, 1869) According to the *1885 AMD* (p.192), the firm's factory was located at 593 Fulton Street, Brooklyn.

Spillane (1890:250-51) wrote: "Mr. H. Kranich and J. Bach ... were both born in Germany [Bach was actually from Alsace], and were practical piano-makers, each skilled in a special department. Their first start in business was unpretentious, but towards 1875 they had become steadily established as manufacturers of reputable instruments. Since that period their business has progressed very uniformly. They have bought out many detailed improvements, and their pianos appeal to a large constituency of intelligent patrons, while in some sections of the country they enjoy great popularity among the masses."

KRANICH & BACH

1873	pianos	241 E. 23rd
1874-79	"	"& 218 E. 26th
1880-90+	"	235 E. 23rd

The successor to *Kranich, Bach & Company,* see below.

KRANICH, BACH & COMPANY

1867-68	pianos	106 Bleecker & 57 Downing
1869-72	"	241 E. 23rd

Partners *Hellmuth Kranich*, see above, and *Jaques Bach* headed this firm which was reorganized in 1872 as *Kranich & Bach*.

KRAUSHAAR, Anthony (Anton)

1864	piano mkr	86 Walker
1865-70	"	19 W. Houston

From 1865-68, with Charles J. Schonemann, Albert Schneider, and *Tobias Hamm*, Kraushaar headed *Kraushaar & Company*. (*CmRg* 1866:144)

KRAUSHAAR & COMPANY

1865-68	pianos	19 W. Houston

See above *Anthony Kraushaar*.

KREUTZER, Carl

1879	railings	344 W. 39th
1880-83	violins	321 W. 42nd
1884	mus instrs	"
1885-87	"	344 W. 42nd
1888	violins	"
1889-90+	violin mkr	926 Ninth

Kreutzer, a violin manufacturer (*1885 AMD* p.207), joined his son William in 1883 to establish *Kreutzer & Son*. In 1885, another son joined the firm, and its title was changed to *Kreutzer & Sons*.

KREUTZER & SON(S)

1883	violins	321 W. 42nd
1884	mus instrs	"
1885-90+	"	344 W. 42nd

The firm consisted of *Carl Kreutzer* and his son William. In 1885, it briefly became *Kreutzer & Sons* when a second son, Frank, joined the firm. See above.

KRINER, Alois L. [Lorenz?]

1879	mus instrs	h. 310 Sixth
1880-81	not listed	
1882-87	mus instrs	84 Second
1888	violins	"
1889	"	89 Second
1890+	violin mkr	h. 87 Second

Kriner was almost certainly the same person as Lorenz Kriner, a member of a Mittenwald violin-making family who was born in 1838, worked at Stut-tgart in 1863 and settled in New York, where he was active as a maker from 1873-1906. See **Henley**(1960:3:164).

KROEGER, Bernard

1856	pianos	h. 198 W. 27th
1865	"	161 Ave. 5 & 156 W. 27th
1866	"	156 W. 27th
1867-69	"	240 W. 27th
1874-78	"	260 E. 46th
1879	piano mkr	"

Kroeger was apparently a piano dealer who was involved in several partnerships. In 1865, Kroeger and Theodore Schmidt were partners in the firm *Kroeger & Schmidt*. In 1876, with a new partner, he headed *Kroeger & Sivert*, and at the same time was involved with *Christian Hausmann* in the firm *Kroeger & Hausmann*. He was not listed consistently in the *NYCD*, and his relationship to the piano manufacturer *Henry Kroeger*, see below, is not known.

KROEGER, Henry C.

1861	pianos	h. 768 Ave. 3
1862-65	not listed	
1866	pianos	E. 52nd c. Fourth
1867-69	"	214 E. 52nd
1870-79	"	h. 411 E. 58th
1880-83	"	24 Union Sq.
1884	"	" & 435 Ave. 7
1885-86	"	" & 234 E. 44th
1887-88	"	" & 360 Ave. 2
1889-90+	"	360 Ave. 2

Henry Kroeger was born in 1827 in Germany, and at the age of fifteen was apprenticed to a piano maker in Hamburg. He worked as a journeyman in "many of the leading factories of Hamburg" before coming to New York in 1855 where he worked for *Steinway & Sons* in an "important position" before joining with his son, Henry Jr., to establish *Kroeger & Son* in 1880. (**Spillane** 1890:290-91) According to Henry Z. Steinway, Kroeger was first employed by Steinway & Sons in 1855. In 1860, he became a foreman tone regulator, and by 1864 was promoted to be a superintendent, probably following the death of Theodore Vogel, the husband of Wilhelmina Steinway (1833-1875). Kroeger left the firm in 1879, probably due to difficulties with Charles son's Henry. (PC: Henry Z. Steinway) In 1885, the firm became *Kroeger & Sons* when another son, Otto, was admitted to partnership. The relation of this family to *Bernard Kroeger*, see above, is not known.

KROEGER, B. & HAUSMANN

1867-69	pianos	240 W. 27th

This firm consisted of *Bernard Kroeger*, see above, and *Christian Hausmann*. The latter was a piano maker active from 1866-73, but it is likely the Kroeger was only a piano dealer. In 1867, Kroeger also headed the dealership *Kroeger & Sivert*.

KROEGER, B. & SCHMIDT

This partnership was listed only in the 1865 *CmRg* (p.72) as "Manufacturers of Grand Square & Upright Piano Fortes, Warerooms 22nd Street c. Fifth Ave. Manufactory 156 W. 27th. B. Kroeger ... Theodore Schmidt." See above *Bernard Kroeger*.

KROEGER, B. & SIVERT

Listed only in the 1867 *CmRg* at 156 W. 27th Street, this firm was probably a piano dealership. See above *Bernard Kroeger*.

KROEGER & SON

1880-83	pianos	24 Union Square
1884	"	" & 435 Seventh

This firm consisted of *Henry Kroeger*, see above, and his son, Henry Jr. It later became *Kroeger & Sons*, see below.

KROEGER & SONS

1885-86	pianos	24 Union Sq. & 234 E. 44th
1887-88	"	" & 360 Ave. 2
1889-90+	"	360 Ave. 2

A continuation of the earlier *Kroeger & Son*. See above and *Henry Kroeger*.

KUBIN, Joseph

1882	jeweler	837 Courtlandt
1883	mus instrs	625 N. Third
1884	"& marble	"
1885	music	244 N. Third
1886+	jeweler & marble	"

Kubin and his son, Joseph Jr., were listed as "Manufacturers of Musical Instruments" in the *1885 AMD* (p.207), however, it is likely that both were dealers rather than craftsmen.

KUBIN & SON

1883-84	mus instrs	625 N. 3rd
1885	music	224 N. 3rd

See above *Joseph Kubin*.

KUDER, Joseph

See *Hugo Sohmer & Company*.

KUHNER, Leopold

See *Mathushek & Kuhner*.

KUYPERS, Henry

1812-13	mus instr mkr	55 Nassau
1814	"	99 Beekman

Nothing further is presently known about this maker.

KYES, Charles H.

1848-50	cabinet mkr	35 Hammersley
1851	"	r. 2 W. 31st
1852-53	refrigerators	r. 107 W. 31st
1854-58	not listed	
1859+	refrigerators	30 Clark

Instrument making might have been only a part-time pursuit for Kyes; however, he was awarded a diploma for the best banjo exhibited at the 1848 American Institute Fair. The judges listed his address as 35 Hammersley. (*American Institute Records*)

L

LACOMBE, Hypolite

1856	mus instrs	76 Leonard
1857	manuf	h. 39 Wooster
1858	mus instr mkr	32 Wooster
1860-62	mus instrs	h. 39 Wooster
1863	"	h. 35 Wooster
1864	"	31 Marion
1865	not listed	
1866	mus instrs	h. 114 St. Mark's pl.
1867	brass	"
1868	not listed	
1869	mus instrs	"

From 1857-60, Lacombe was also listed as an instrument maker in the *NYBD*. In 1861, the maker was a member of the brass-instrument-manufacturing firm *Lacombe & Gervais*; and in 1862, he headed *H. Lacombe & Company*.

LACOMBE & COMPANY

| 1862 | mus instrs | 39 Wooster |

Possibly a continuation of the earlier firm *Lacombe & Gervais*, see below, which previously occupied the same Wooster Street address. See above *Hypolite Lacombe*.

LACOMBE & GERVAIS

Listed as "Brass Instrument Manufacturers" at 39 Wooster Street in the *1861 AMD* (p.90). Nothing further is presently known about Gervais. See above *Hypolite Lacombe*.

LAMBERT, Henry

See *Schnabel, Hintz & Lambert*.

LAMSON, Paul

1816-18	mus instr mkr	208 Broadway
1819	not listed	
1820-21	mus instr mkr	5 Frankfort
1822	"	76 Gold
1823	"	17 Dutch
1824	"	10 Bancker
1825	not listed	
1826-27	mus instr mkr	15 Leonard
1828	"	North c. Clinton

Lamson was listed in the Boston City Directory as an umbrella maker in 1810; and as a woodwind and violin maker at 23 Court Street in 1813. (**Johnson** 1943:282) First listed in the 1816 *NYCD*, Lamson probably made woodwinds and strings in New York as he had in Boston. He was possibly the same Paul Lamson who served as the city's "Register of Dogs" c.1826. (*MCC* 15:635)

LANDRES, Michael W.

1868-70	mus instrs	206 Spring
1871-79	"	208 Spring
1880-88	"	244 Spring
1889-90+	"	432 Hudson

Landres was probably an instrument dealer, although the *1885 AMD* (p.208) did list him as a "Musical Instrument Manufacturer" at 244 Spring Street.

LANZER, Charles

| 1881-83 | violins | 48 E. 4th |
| 1884 | Elizabeth widow Christian | h. 862 Ave. 6 |

From 1881-83, Lanzer joined his son, Charles Jr., in the partnership *Lanzer & Son*. In the *1885 AMD* (p.208) their firm was mistakenly and belatedly listed as "Lanzer & Sun."

LANZER & SON

| 1881-83 | violins | 48 E. 4th |

See above *Charles Lanzer*.

LARRABEE, James D.

1844-45	flute mkr	110 Fulton
1846	gold pencil mkr	bds. 85 Mercer
1847	Helen wid. of James D.	85 Mercer

Badger, in his *Illustrated History of the Flute* (1853:30), credited Larrabee with being the maker of one of the earliest Boehm-system flutes built in America.

In 1844, Larrabee was awarded a silver medal "For the best Boehm system flute" exhibited at the American Institute Fair; and in 1846, the same organization awarded him another silver medal "for an

Ivory Octave Flute." (*American Institute Records*) In 1846, the *NYCD* listed the maker's home address as Newark, New Jersey, but in 1847, his widow was again living in New York City. Larrabee apparently died in 1846, and on May 7th of that year, the *Tribune* noted that Larrabee's business had been bought out by flutemaker *Alfred G. Badger* (**Lawrence** 1988:405).

LAUKOTA, Jean

1851	piano manuf	18 Harrison
1852	not listed	
1853	pianos	"
1854-55	piano manuf	"
1856-58	pianos	5 Mercer
1859	"	173 Prince

Laukota exhibited a seven-octave rosewood-square piano at the 1853 New York Crystal Palace (*Official Catalogue* 1853:402). In 1855, with a partner named Marschall—who was probably the piano maker *Theodore Marschall*—he headed the partnership *Laukota & Marschall*. There is reason to think their firm was the successor to *John Bornhoeft* c.1855. According to the *1855 New York Census*, their firm owned $200 worth of tools; and had in stock 11,000 feet of lumber worth $400, 60 sets of hardware worth $600, and 60 sets of ivory worth $360. The firm employed 11 men at total monthly wages of $440, and that year produced 60 pianos worth $24,000. **Spillane** (1890:251) mistakenly referred to this maker as "Locotte."

LAUKOTA & MARSCHALL

1855-56	pianos	5 Mercer

See above *Jean Laukota.*

LAUTER, Edward A.

1861	mus instrs	193 Grand
1862-66	"	431 Broome
1867	not listed	
1868	music	h. 255 Bowery

Listed as a "violin & guitar manufacturer" in the *1861 AMD* (p.91), Lauter seems to have been less prominent than his relative *Franz Lauter*, see below, however, the two shared several addresses during the 1860s. Edward might have been the "& Co." in the 1866 firm *Lauter & Company*.

LAUTER, Franz/Francis E.

1851	machinist	30 Chrystie
1852-57	mus instrs	21 Chrystie
1858	manuf & mus instr importer	"
1859-60	mus instrs	53 Maiden la.
1861	"	21 Chrystie
1862-65	not listed	
1866	mus instrs	431 Broome
1867	"	62 Bleecker
1868	not listed	
1869-85	mus instrs	225 Bleecker

In the *1861 AMD* (p.41), Lauter advertised as an "Importer and Manufacturer of Musical Instruments, vis: Violins, Guitars, Flutes, Accordeons, Flutinas, Concertinas, Drums, Banjos, Tambourines, Brass Instruments, Clarionets, &.... All Brass and Silver Instruments are made under my own supervision, and I have the best workmen employed."

Lauter claimed to have won prize medals at the 1853 New York Crystal Palace Exhibition, and the 1844 Berlin World's Fair (*CmRg* 1870:112). He also entered wind instruments in the American Institute Fairs of 1851, 1855, 1856 and 1857. (*American Institute Records*)

In 1859, Lauter was in partnership with William A. Wermerskirch. Their firm, *Lauter & Wermerskirch*, lasted only a year, after which Wermerskirch was listed as a clerk. In 1866, Lauter headed *Lauter & Company*, a firm which also included *Edward Lauter*, see above, and possibly Bernard Lauter, an instrument dealer whose address was given as 27 E. Houston.

LAUTER & COMPANY

1866	mus instrs	431 Broome

See above *Franz Lauter.*

LAUTER & WERMERSKIRCH

1859	mus instr mkrs & importers	53 Maiden la.

See above *Franz Lauter.*

LEAVITTE

See *Rohe & Leavitte.*

LECOCQ, Jules/Julius

1845	brass instr mkr	92 Leonard
1846-54	instr mkr	132 Leonard
1855-56	music	"
1857-63	mus instrs	"
1864-65	not listed	
1866-72	mus instrs	"
1877-79	------	"

According to the *1861 AMD* (p.90), Lecocq was a "Manufacturer of Metal Musical Instruments with Piston, Pump, and Rotary Valves." This maker was probably the same person as the saxhorn maker J. Lecocq who worked in Paris, (see **Langwill** 1980: 103). In 1845, Lecocq shared his 92 Mercer Street address with the violin maker *Charles Mercier*. The two men were never listed as partners, however, both were probably French immigrants.

LENDEN, William

1824	pianoforte mkr	401 Broadway

Nothing further is presently known about Lenden. It is possible that he might have been the same person as, or a relative of the piano maker *William Linden*, who was active in the city from 1837-61.

LESIEUR, John D.

1834	piano mkr	Ave. 3 n. 22nd

Nothing further is presently known about this maker.

LETT/LETE

See *Vallate & Lett*.

LEUCHTE, Ferdinand C.

See *Ferdinand C. Lighte*.

LEWIS, Henry

1835	piano mkr	73 Hammersley

Nothing further is presently known about this maker.

LEWIS, Laban

1848	harp mkr	15 Rose
1849	"	97 Mott
1850-51	"	r. 141 Chrystie
1852	harps	47 Eldridge
1853	"	293 Bowery
1854-56	harps & daguerreotypes	"
1857-58	harps	"
1859-60	"	554 Broadway
1861-63	"	626 Broadway
1864	"	2 Leroy pl.
1865	"	9 Leroy pl.
1866-68	"	99 Bleecker

Laban Lewis and his relative, *Reese Lewis*, see below, were harp manufacturers. Although they claimed to have been established in New York as early as 1846, there is no record of their firm, *R.& L. Lewis*, before 1853. Early in their careers, both men worked in other crafts, e.g. watchmaking and daguerreotypes.

In 1853, R. & L. Lewis exhibited a "Grand double action harp" at the New York Crystal Palace. (*Official Catalogue* 1853:94) The same source listed music dealer A.J. Kendall of 62 White Street as the Lewises' sales agent.

LEWIS, Reese

1842-45	watch mkr	5-7 Doyers
1846-47	not listed	
1848	harp mkr	15 Rose
1849	watch mkr	295 Broadway
1850-51	"	r. 325 Broome
1852	fish reels	47 Eldridge
1853	"	293 Bowery
1854-56	"& harps	293 & 297 Bowery
1857-58	harps	293 Bowery
1859-60	"	554 Broadway
1861-63	"	626 Broadway
1864	"	2 Leroy pl.
1865	"	9 Leroy pl.
1866-68	"	99 Bleecker

Possibly the only person ever to have made both harps and fishing reels, Reese worked with his relative *Laban Lewis*. See above.

LEWIS, R. & L. (& COMPANY)

1853	harp manuf	293 Bowery
1854-56	harps & daguerreotypes	293 & 297 Bowery
1857-58	harps	293 Bowery
1859-60	"	554 Broadway
1861-63	"	626 Broadway
1864	"	2 Leroy pl.
1865	"	9 Leroy pl.
1866-68	"	99 Bleecker

From 1857-58, and again in 1864, "& Company" was added to this firm's title. See above *Laban Lewis*.

LICK, James

1821	pianoforte mkr	198 Broadway

It is claimed that Lick was apprenticed to piano maker Joseph Hisky in Baltimore, and that he later worked as a journeyman in New York and Philadelphia before making a fortune on South American railroads and moving to San Francisco where he became a philanthropist, and among other things, founded the famous Lick Observatory. See **Spillane** (1890:127); **Stieff** (1946:26); **Pierce** (1965:146).

LIGHTE, Ferdinand C.

1847	pianofortes	43 Greene
1848	not listed	
1849	pianofortes	111 Elm
1850-51	"	20 & 22 Canal
1852-53	"	22 Canal & 123 Elm
1854-63	pianos	421 Broome & 124 Wooster
1864	"	421 Broome
1865	"	421 Broome & r. 13 Crosby
1866-69	"	421 Broome
1870-72	"	"& manuf 524 W. 43rd
1873-78	"	12 E. 14th & 524 W. 43rd
1879-83	"	10 Union Sq. & 524 W. 43rd
1884	"	E. 17th & 524 W. 43rd

Lighte was a respected and innovative mastercraftsman who was a member of a number of successful partnerships during his career. He was probably of German background, and before 1851 his surname appeared as "Leuchte."

In 1850, Lighte entered into his first partnership with *Henry Newton*. The title of their firm, *Leuchte & Newton*, was changed to *Lighte & Newton* c.1851, when the maker's surname was Anglicized. The partners exhibited a 7 1/4- octave piano at the 1853 New York Crystal Palace Exhibition (*Official Catalogue* 1853:94), and also won a gold medal that same year for a piano exhibited at the American Institute Fair. (*American Institute Records*)

William Bradbury was admitted into partnership in 1854, and the firm's title changed to *Lighte, Newton & Bradbury*. According to the *1855 New York Census*, the firm owned no real capital, but did have $16,000 worth of tools. It employed 164 men and 1 boy at average monthly wages of $50 each.

In 1858, Newton withdrew, and the firm was reorganized as *Lighte & Bradbury*. It continued in operation until 1863, after which Lighte established his own firm, *F.C. Lighte & Company*. The *1870 United States Census* recorded Lighte & Company as owning $150,000 of real capital and $60,000 of raw materials. It employed 100 men and 1 boy at annual total wages of $75,000, and that year it produced 500 pianos worth $150,000. In 1869, Lighte & Company was the ninth largest piano manufacturer in the na-

tion with gross annual sales of $155,000. (*New York Tribune*, March 15, 1869)

The "& Company" of Lighte & Company might have been the piano maker *Louis Ernst* (see *CmRg* 1864:48), who joined Lighte in the overlapping partnership *Lighte & Ernst*. Although Lighte & Ernst continued in operation until 1884, it is likely that Lighte died c.1879. For further information on Lighte's contributions to piano design, see **Spillane** (1890:198).

LIGHTE & BRADBURY

1859-63	pianos	421 Broome & 124 Wooster

See above *Ferdinand Lighte*.

LIGHTE, F.C. & COMPANY

1864-72	pianos	421 Broome
1873-78	"	12 E. 14th & 524 W. 43rd
1879	"	10 Union Sq. & 524 W. 43rd

See above *Ferdinand Lighte*.

LIGHTE & ERNST

1874-78	pianos	12 E. 14th & 524 W. 43rd
1879-83	"	10 Union Sq. & 524 W. 43rd
1884	"	E. 17th & 524 W. 43rd

See above *Ferdinand Lighte*.

LIGHTE & NEWTON

1850-51	pianos	20 & 22 Canal
1852-53	"	22 Canal & 123 Elm

See above *Ferdinand Lighte*.

LIGHTE, NEWTON & BRADBURY

1854-58	pianos	421 Broome & 122 Wooster

See above *Ferdinand Lighte*.

LINDELL, Eric J.

1837-41	piano mkr	1 St. John's la.
1842	"	343 Broadway
1843-44	pianos	115 Franklin
1845-46	"	1 St. John's la.
1847-51	"	36 White
1852	piano tuner	75 W. 11th

1853-54	pianos	"
1855-58	music	"
1859-63	pianos	44 W. 15th

From 1837-45, Lindell and his partner, *Peter Andrew Wennerstrom*, headed the firm *Lindell, Wennerstrom & Company*. It is likely that Lindell later worked primarily as a piano dealer.

LINDELL, WENNERSTROM & COMPANY

1837-41	piano mkrs	1 St. John's la.
1842	"	343 Broadway
1843-44	"	115 Franklin
1845	"	1 St. John's la.

See above *Eric Lindell*.

LINDEMAN, William

1835	piano mkr	48 William
1836-42	not listed	
1843	pianos	19 James
1844-50	"	139 Centre
1851-58	"	56 Franklin
1859-60	"	636 Broadway
1861-64	"	173 Mercer
1865-70	"	2 Leroy & 112 Wooster
1871	not listed	
1872	------	92 Bleecker

William Lindeman was born at Dresden in 1795 and trained as a piano maker in Germany before he immigrated to New York c.1834. (**Dolge** 1911:279-80) He established a successful piano manufactory in New York, and was credited by **Spillane** (1890:186-87) with being one of the first immigrant German craftsmen to overcome the local Anglo-American prejudice in the instrument trade. In 1847, a Lindeman piano was awarded a diploma at the American Institute Fair. (*American Institute Records*)

In 1850, and then again from 1857-58, Lindeman and his son Henry, headed the firm *Lindeman & Son*. Henry (b. New York, August 3, 1838) was the inventor of the firm's liver-shaped "Cycloid" piano (U.S. Patent No. 29,502). According to the *1855 New York Census*, William Lindeman's firm owned $10,000 of real capital; $800 worth of tools; and had 2,000 feet of lumber in stock. It employed 15 men at average monthly wages of $40, and that year produced $18,000 worth of pianos.

Lindeman pianos won awards at American Institute Fairs in 1855 and 1857. (*American Institute Records*) In 1859, the firm became *Lindeman & Sons*

when sons Harmon and Ferdinand were admitted to partnership. By 1869, Lindeman's firm had become the 21st largest manufacturer of pianos in the nation with gross annual sales of $62,980. (*New York Tribune*, March 15, 1869) After the elder Lindeman's death on December 24, 1875, his sons William, Harmon, and Ferdinand continued in the trade. See below *Lindeman & Sons*.

LINDEMAN & SON

1850	pianos	56 Franklin
1851-56	not listed	
1857-58	pianos	"

See above *William Lindeman*.

LINDEMAN & SONS

1859-60	pianos	636 Broadway & 171 Mercer
1861-64	"	173 Mercer
1865-70	Patent Cycloid & Square Pianos	" & 2 Leroy pl. & 112 Wooster
1871-72	pianos	92 Bleecker
1873-75	"	", 173 Mercer, 14 E. 14th
1876-80	"	"
1881-86	"	", factory 201 Mercer
1887-90+	"	146 Fifth & 409 Eighth

See above *William Lindeman*.

LINDEN, William

1837	piano mkr	399 Broome
1838	"	91 Mott
1839	"	154 Walker
1840	not listed	
1841	pianos	138 Walker
1842	piano manuf	105 Walker h. 138 Walker
1843-46	pianos	"
1847	not listed	
1848-52	piano mkr	478 Broadway
1853-59	pianos	"
1860-62	"	192 Prince
1863-64	not listed	
1865	Mary widow William	h. 192 Prince

From 1842-59, Linden, with his partner *John Fritz*, headed the piano-manufacturing firm *Linden & Fritz*. Both men were trained piano makers and German immigrants, and wrote **Spillane** (1890:189),

"They made very good instruments in their time . . . Linden was formerly [i.e. before 1842] employed in the shop of Dubois, Bacon & Chambers as a key-maker, while Fritz was employed in the same place as a case-maker." Linden's relationship to the piano maker *William Lenden*, who was active as a piano maker in 1824, is not known, although they might have been the same person.

LINDEN & FRITZ

1842-46	piano mkrs	105 Walker
1847	not listed	
1848-59	pianofortes	478 Broadway

See above *William Linden*.

LINSTED(T), J.E.L.

See *Ihlseng, Narvesen & Linsted*.

LOHR, Frederick

1855	cabinet mkr	h. 26 Ave. B
1856	"	h. 84 Ave. A
1858	banjos	5 1/2 Bayard
1859-62	mus instrs	h. 38 Division
1863	music	"
1864	instrs	"
1865	organs	"
1866-71	music/mus instrs	"
1872-73	not listed	
1874-76	mus instrs	92 Chambers
1877	clerk	h. College Ave. n. 145th
1878	musician	"
1879	mus instrs	"
1880	Christiana wid. Frederick	"

In 1858, with partner *George Unruh*, Lohr established the short-lived banjo-manufacturing firm, *F. Lohr & G. Unruh*. Lohr was probably related to the banjo maker *Theodore Lohr*, see below, although the two were never listed at the same address.

According to the *1870 United States Census*, Lohr owned $1,000 of real capital; and had in stock 1,000 feet of rosewood worth $300, as well as $50 worth of 10-inch sheep-skins. His shop employed 2 men at annual wages of $1,200 who that year produced 200 banjos worth $1,800.

LOHR, Theodore

1868	mus instrs	19 Sixth Ave.
1869	instr mkr	94 Forsyth
1870	manuf of banjos	"
1871	music	"
1872-73	mus instrs	"
1874-76	"	294 1/2 Grand
1877-90+	"	294 Grand

According to the *1870 United States Census*, Lohr was a banjo manufacturer who owned $1,800 of real capital; and had in stock 1,500 feet of walnut worth $150, and $200 worth of silver. He employed one workman (probably himself), and 2 boys at annual wages of $1,456. That year, his shop produced 150 dozen banjos worth $3,200, and 50 dozen tambourines worth $300.

The *1885 AMD* (p.208) listed Lohr as a "Musical Instrument Importer," at 298 Grand Street, and **Henley** (1960:3:210) wrote that Lohr also made violins, guitars and harmonicas. He was probably related to banjo-maker *Frederick Lohr*, see above, however, the two never shared an address.

LOHR, F. & G. UNRUH

1858	banjos	5 1/2 Bayard

See above *Frederick Lohr*.

LONGHURST, Thomas

1833-35	mus instr mkr	471 Pearl
1836	"	469 Pearl
1837	not listed	
1838	flute mkr	"
1839	"	469 Pearl & 169 Broadway
1840	"	164 Broadway
1841	not listed	
1842-46	flute mkr	"

In 1847, Longhurst was listed, with no given occupation, at 53 Front Street, Brooklyn. From 1851 onwards, he was listed as an ivory turner at 101 Fulton Street, Brooklyn. Longhurst probably died sometime before 1856, when his wife, Elizabeth, who had previously been listed as a "lacedresser" in the 1842 *NYCD*, was listed alone as an "upholstress" at 67 Prospect, Brooklyn.

There are Longhurst flutes in several instrument collections, including a 9-keyed rosewood C-flute with silver fittings in the *DMC* (*Catalog*, No. 877).

LOOMIS, William J.

1831	piano mkr	387 Third Ave.
1832	"	22 Clarke

All that is presently known about Loomis is that on June 16, 1826, at the age of 16 years, 5 months, and 21 days, Loomis was apprenticed to the piano manufacturer *Michael N. Cregier*. On July 28, 1830, however, the apprenticeship was cancelled "on examination by the police" and the boy was discharged. (*New York Genealogical & Biographical Record*, 115:1:8, January 1984) The reason behind the cancellation of the apprenticeship is not known, although it is possible that the boy was being mistreated.

LOUD, Thomas Sr.

1826-27	pianoforte mkr	102 Canal
1828	"	280 Broadway
1829-31	"	453 Broadway
1832	------	61 Vandam
1833	Harriet widow of Thomas	228 Varick

Loud's fame rests on an important patent for overstringing pianos which he received in 1802 while he was still working in England. Loud is often confused with members of the piano-making Everdon family of Philadelphia, who, for unknown reason, used the surname Loud after they immigrated to the United States. **Libin** (1985:177) suggests that Thomas Loud Everdon of Philadelphia was the son of the New York maker and adopted his wife's or mother's surname to differentiate himself from his father. This remains conjectural, however, in 1817 the Philadelphians dropped the use of the Everdon name and returned to Loud. (See **Mann** 1977:183)

Spillane (1890:178), in addition to a great deal of misinformation about Loud, wrote: "Mr. Henry Hazelton remembers Loud's place on Broadway perfectly well. In order to emphasize his national origin as a piano-maker, the latter had over his store the sign, 'Thomas Loud, pianoforte-maker from London.' Other old piano-makers of New York remember Loud distinctly on this account, but he was never known as a maker of significance." Loud died at the age of 71 at 61 Vandam Street on January 2, 1833. (*Evening Post* [N.Y.], January 3, 1833)

LOVE, James H.

1842-43	tuner	259 Williams

Although only listed in the 1842-43 *NYCD*s, Love was active for many years in the piano trade. He first appeared in city records as an apprentice when he joined and later resigned from a volunteer fire engine company in 1827. (**MCC** 16:425,543) At that time, his occupation was listed as "pinnaforte maker" [*sic*], and his address was given as 184 Canal Street. From 1835-38, with *Otto Torp*, he headed the piano-manufacturing firm *Torp & Love*.

LOWENDALL/LOWENTHAL, Lewis

Lowendall was born in 1836, the son of a draper in a small North Prussian town. He studied music as a child, and string instrument making with Bansch at Leipzig and Heinrich Knopf at Berlin. In 1855, he opened a successful retail music shop in Berlin, and in 1867, he opened a shop in the United States. "He soon became aware that his German-spelled name was pronounced by his new American friends differently from the original and accustomed sound, so he changed it to the English version, Lowendall." (**Henley** 1960:3:216-17)

After six years of working as an importer and violin dealer in America, Lowendall returned to Europe and thereafter divided his time between England and the United States. Although Lowendall was a friend of *George Gemunder* and apparently worked in New York City, his name never appeared in the *NYCD*.

LUCAS, John

1833-34	turner	134 Spring
1835-41	mus instr mkr	"
1842	"	57 Second

This man might have been the same John Lucas as the flute maker who had been active in London c.1795. (See *V. & A. Catalogue* 1968:205) A 1-keyed flute by the London maker is in the Yale Collection (Catalog No. 324). The New Yorker's listing as a turner suggests he was also involved in woodwind making since the two professions required similar wood-working skills.

LUDEWIG, Herman

See *Dietrichsen, Ludewig & Strothoff*.

LUDKE, Ferdinand

pre-1865	teacher	287 1/2 Bowery
1866	pianos	3 Rivington
1867-68	"	h. 27 Rivington
1869-70	"	367 Broome
1871-72	not listed/ (*CmRg*)	45 Second Ave.
1873-74	pianos & melodeons	"
1875-77	pianos	60 E. 40th

From 1869-70, Ludke and his partner *Charles Schuler*, headed the piano-manufacturing firm *Ludke & Schuler*. In 1871, Ludke was listed as the head of his own shop at 45 Second Avenue. (*CmRg* 1871:151)

LUDKE & SCHULER

1869-70	pianos	367 Broome

See above *Ferdinand Ludke*.

LUDOLFF, August

See below *August Luedolff*.

LUEDOLFF, August(us)

1854	piano keys	206 W. 37th
1855	pianos	85 Varick
1856-63	"	452 Broome
1864-65	frames	"
1866-78	pianos	"
1879	"	64 Mercer
1880	"	452 Broome
1881	not listed	
1882	------	h. 128 Forsyth

In addition to "piano keys," the 1854 *NYCD* also listed Luedolff as a partner of *Ernst Aleithe* in the instrument-making firm *Aleithe & Luedolff* at 206 W. 37th Street. In 1855, he joined *Otto Schuetze* in the piano- manufacturing firm *Schuetze & Luedolff*. Their partnership lasted until 1876 when it was ended, probably by Schuetze's death. Among other innovations, this firm should be remembered for Luedolff's 1866 patent (No. 52,725) of the Civil War-inspired "Monitor Plate" piano. See *Aleithe & Luedolff*; *Schuetze & Luedolff*.

LUDWIG/LUDWIK, Francis

1857	accordeons	h. 192 Eldridge
1858	not listed	
1859	accordeons	430 Houston
1860-63	"	131 E. Houston
1864-66	mus instrs	r. 311 1/2 Bowery
1867-68	"	h. 120 E. Houston
1869	accordeons	h. 122 E. Houston
1870	accordeon mkr	h. 120 E. Houston
1871	accordeons	210 Forsyth
1872	music	h. 144 Chrystie

In 1866, Ludwig—whose name occasionally appeared as Ludwik—advertised as a "Repairer of all kinds of Musical Instruments. Accordeons always on hand." (*CmRg* 1866:94) In the 1871 *CmRg* (p.128) he was listed as a "Manufacturer and Repairer of Accordeons."

LUTHER, John Frederick

1842	piano mkr/tuner	116 Rivington
1843	piano mkr	"
1844-48	"	104 Ludlow
1849-53	"	116 Rivington
1854-59	"	349 Broome
1860-83	pianos	"
1884	"	h. 330 E. 58th
1885	------	"

Luther appears to have been more active as a piano dealer and tuner, however, the *1861 AMD* (p.171) listed him as a manufacturer, and **Pierce** (1965) does give plate numbers for Luther pianos. The *1885 AMD* (p.208) lists Luther only as a piano dealer, however, he had apparently retired by that date.

LYNCH, Patrick

1853	pianos	559 Broadway
1854-57	"	" & 833 Broadway
1858-73	"	921, 927, 932 Broadway
1874-76	"	1291 Broadway
1877	"	1164 Broadway
1878-80s	"	1329 Broadway

Lynch's *NYCD* listings suggest that he was only a dealer, however, the *1861 AMD* (p.171) did list him as a manufacturer. He apparently tried to attract the Catholic piano trade by offering references from "numerous Seminaries, Convents, & c., who have long had his Pianos in use." (*NYBD* 1861:47)

In 1866, Lynch and a dealer named Gomien, founded the piano dealership *Lynch & Gomien*, which continued in business into the 1880s. Several journeymen named Lynch were active in the city's instrument trade during the 1870s and 1880s.

LYNCH & GOMIEN

1866-73	pianos	921, 923, 927 & 932 Broadway
1874-76	"	1291 Broadway
1877	"	1164 Broadway
1878-80s	"	1329 Broadway

See above *Patrick Lynch*.

M

McDONALD, James and John

1847	piano mkrs	r. 119 Walker
1848	pianos	177 Prince
1849-55	piano manuf	293 Bowery
1856-57	pianos	132 Twelfth
1858-59	"	1161 Broadway
1860	not listed	
1861-67	pianos	358 Bowery & 108 E. 25th
1868	not listed	
1869-70	pianos	26 Fourth

James and John McDonald were involved in a number of small piano-manufacturing firms: from 1849-54 as *McDonald & Brother*; 1855-56 as *McDonald Brothers*; and 1861-70 as *McDonald & Company*.

McDonald & Brother exhibited a piano with a patent "Euterpean" attachment at the 1853 New York Crystal Palace Exhibition. (*Official Catalogue* 1853:94) According to the *1855 New York Census*, the McDonalds owned no real capital, and had only $200 worth of tools. They had in stock $5,400 worth of lumber, hardware, ivory and leather; and employed 8 men at total monthly wages of $364, who that year produced 72 pianos worth $18,000.

In the 1863 *CmRg* (p.43), the McDonalds advertised that their firm was initially established in 1845 — two years before they were first listed in the *NYCD*. Also active during this period, was a piano stool maker, P.M. McDonald, and a piano dealer, Thomas McDonald, however, their relation to the McDonald brothers is not known.

McDONALD BROTHERS

| 1855 | pianos | 293 Bowery |
| 1856 | " | 132 Twelfth |

See above *James and John McDonald*.

McDONALD & BROTHER

| 1849-54 | piano manufs | 293 Bowery |

See above *James and John McDonald*.

McDONALD & COMPANY

1861-67	pianos	358 Bowery & 108 E. 25th
1868	not listed	
1869-70	pianos	26 Fourth

See above *James and John McDonald*.

MAHON, John

1872	piano manuf	314 E. 39th
1873	pianos	"
1874-76	"	701 Ave. 1
1877	"	224 E. 39th & 1st c. 40th
1878-79	"	701 Ave. 1

Mahon did advertise as a "Piano-Forte manufacturer" in the 1874 *NYBD* (p.104), however, he was probably more active as a piano dealer.

MALLET/MALLAT, Francis D.

1819	musician	22 Reed
1820-28	not listed	
1829	dancing master	49 Lispenard
1830-31	"	85 Varick
1832-33	not listed (see below)	

Mallet had been active in Boston from 1798-1811, and again in 1824 as a musician, music teacher, music publisher and music shop owner. (See: **Johnson** 1943:268,284,292; **Ayars** 1937:9,107,147; **Wolfe** 1980:59-60.) Even though several sources, e.g. **Ayars**, give the date of Mallet's death as 1832, he is included in this study because of his probable relationship to *Francis Malley*, the instrument maker listed immediately below.

MALLEY, Francis D.

1834	mus instr mkr	21 Leroy
1835-37	"	32 Tenth
1838	"	260 Hudson

See above *Francis Mallet*. No further information about this maker is presently known.

MALTHANER, John C.

1834	piano mkr	r. 6 Willct

Nothing further about this maker is presently known.

MANHATTAN PIANOFORTE COMPANY

1866-67	pianos	129 E. 22nd
1868-78	"	229 E. 29th

The 1867 *CmRg* (p.135) listed this firm as the *Manhattan Piano-Forte Manufacturing Company*, but little else about its operations is presently known. It is quite possible that the name was a "stencil" used on instruments produced by smaller firms and marketed by this concern.

MANNELLO, Angelo

A mandolin maker, Mannello was born at Morcone, Italy on December 11, 1858. The son of a carpenter, Mannello was apprenticed to a woodworker in Naples, and in 1885 immigrated to New York where he opened a luthier shop which quickly prospered. Although not listed before 1890, prior to 1900 his shop is known to have occupied sites on Elizabeth Street between Grand and Broome, at 18 Spring Street, and at 355 1/2 and 360 Bowery. Several of Mannello's magnificently decorated mandolins are now in the collection of the Metropolitan Museum of Art. He died in the city on July 4, 1922. See **Libin** (1985:119-125).

MANNER, George Charles

1854	pianos	361 Broadway, 311 Rivington
1855	"	311 Rivington
1856-57	"	78 Third Ave.
1858-61	"	311 Rivington
1863	"	481 Broadway
1864-65	"	" & 48 Mercer
1866-69	"	187 Bowery
1870-72	"	" & 554 Broadway
1873	supt. (for Arion)	5 E. 14th
1874	piano mkr	h. St. Anne's n. 147th
1877-78	pianos	143 n. Third

From 1858-59, Manner and piano maker *Ernest Gabler* headed the piano-manufacturing firm *Manner & Gabler*. In 1866, Manner established his own firm, *Manner & Company*, and began to produce "arion piano fortes." The term "arion" apparently referred to an innovation patented by Manner, and it proved so successful that in 1870 the firm's title was changed to the *Arion Piano-Forte Company*. Soon thereafter, c.1870, the firm was apparently sold to Covell & Company, entrepreneurs who had previously dealt in fancy goods, gas fixtures, china, cut glass and bronzes. Although C.H. Covell was listed as Arion's president in 1870, Manner worked as the firm's superintendent until at least 1873.

In 1874, Manner was listed only as a journeyman, and it is possible that he lost his position with Arion when the firm was bought by *J. Simpson & Company*. In 1876, he joined his sons, Charles G. and George C. Jr., in the short-lived firm *Manner & Sons*. See *Arion Piano-Forte Company*.

MANNER & COMPANY

1866-68	pianos	187 Bowery
1869	arion piano fortes, patented, grand & square 7 1/4 octave, rosewood, plain & richly moulded cases, carved & gothic legs, overstrung bass & c.	187 & 189 Bowery

See *George Manner*; *Arion Piano-Forte Company*.

MANNER & GABLER

1858-59	pianos	311 Rivington

See above *George Manner*.

MANNER & SONS

1876-78	pianos	143 n. Third

See above *George Manner*.

MANZ, George M.

See *Kindt & Manz*.

MARCHAL, James C.

1877-78	pianos	47 University Pl.
1879-82	"	8 W. 11th
1883-85	"	453 W. 36th
1886-90+	"	235 E. 21st

Throughout his career, Marchal was the partner of a man named Smith. Their firm had a number of different titles: 1877- 79, *Marchal & Smith*; 1880-82, *Marchal & Smith Piano Company*; 1883-90 +, *Marchal & Smith Piano & Organ Company*. In the 1884

NYCD, the partners claimed their firm had been established in 1859, but no evidence of its existence has been documented before 1877. The *1885 AMD* (p.208) listed the partners as manufacturers, and **Pierce** (1965) mentions them as makers of the "University Piano" — presumably named after their location on University Place. Nothing further is presently known about Smith.

MARCHAL & SMITH

| 1877-78 | pianos | 47 University Pl. |
| 1879 | " | 8 W. 11th |

See above *James Marchal*.

MARCHAL & SMITH PIANO COMPANY

| 1880-82 | pianos | 8 W. 11th |

See above *James Marchal*.

MARCHAL & SMITH PIANO & ORGAN COMPANY

| 1883-85 | pianos | 453 W. 36th |
| 1886-90+ | " | 235 E. 21st |

See above *James Marchal*.

MARSCHALL, Theodore

1856	see *Laukota & Marschall*	
1865-66	pianos	88 Walker
1867-69	"	125 E. 14th
1870-71	"	149 E. 14th

Marschall arrived in New York from his native Bavaria in 1851, and in 1856 he joined the piano maker *Jean Laukota* in *Laukota & Marschall* — a firm which apparently succeeded *John Bornhoeft's* shop c.1855.

After the dissolution of their partnership, Marschall served as the superintendent of *Lighte & Bradbury* until 1866, when he joined *George Mittauer* in the firm *Marschall & Mittauer*. Both partners were "practical" craftsmen, and "within a short period became noted as makers of excellent instruments." (**Spillane** 1890: 251) In 1869, Marschall & Mittauer was the 19th largest piano manufacturer in the nation with gross annual sales of $80,172. (*New York Tribune*, March 15, 1869) Their success was relatively short-lived, since in 1872 *Sohmer & Company* advertised in the *NYCD* as "Successors to Marschall & Mittauer." Marschall was awarded several patents during his career. See **Spillane** (1890:365); *Laukota & Marschall*.

MARSCHALL & MITTAUER

1866	pianos	88 Walker
1867-69	"	125 E. 14th
1870-71	"	149 E. 14th

See above *Theodore Marschall*.

MARTIN, Christian Frederick

1834-35	violin & guitar mkr	196 Hudson
1836	mus instrs	"
1837	"	" & 212 Fulton
1838	"	212 Fulton
1839	"	320 Broadway & 212 Fulton
1840-41	"	385 Broadway
1842+	guitar manuf	"

Martin, son of the guitar maker Georg Martin, was born in Markneukirchen, Saxony, on January 11, 1796. He worked in the shop of Johann Stauffer in Vienna, and eventually rose to become foreman of the latter's atelier. Restrictive German guild regulations led Martin to emigrate, and on September 9, 1833, he left for New York, where he established a music store and continued his trade as a musical instrument maker. On May 29, 1839, Martin sold his stock to music dealers Ludecus & Wolter, 320 Broadway, and moved to Nazareth, Pennsylvania to join other members of the Moravian community.

Martin's fame and contributions to American guitar making are too great to be adequately dealt with by this study, (see **Longworth** 1975), however, it should be mentioned that though Martin left the city in 1839, he continued to print "New York" on his labels until 1898 — possibly because most of his instruments were sold through New York distributors. Instruments made by Martin during his residence in the city tend to have paper labels.

Martin was involved in several partnerships during his stay in the city. The first of these was with *Henry Schatz*, a violin maker Martin had known in Saxony. Their firm, *Martin & Schatz*, made violins at 196 Hudson Street in 1835. From 1845-51, Schatz worked as an instrument maker in Boston, (see **Ayars** 1937:277, 230), before settling in Nazareth and going to work for Martin's Pennsylvania factory.

From 1838-39, Martin and a partner named Bruno — almost certainly the instrument dealer *Charles Bruno* who had arrived from Germany in 1834 — headed the firm *Martin & Bruno*. And later, from 1840-41, Martin established *Martin & Coupa*, in partnership with *John Coupa*, a well-known guitar teacher with studios at 385 Broadway. It is unlikely that Coupa was actually involved with the construction of instruments; it is more probable that Coupa's studios served primarily as a retail outlet for Martin's guitars, since the maker had already left the city by 1840. Years later, the instrument dealers *Zoebisch & Sons* — a firm whose members apparently came from and belonged to the Nazareth Moravian community — served as Martin's distributors in New York. The maker's Pennsylvania shop is still in operation.

MARTIN, Gotfried Robert

1852	instr mkr	1 Franklin Sq.
1853	not listed	
1854	instr mkr	"
1855-56	instrs	r. 34 Forsyth
1857	not listed	
1858	brass	r. 59 Forsyth
1859-63	instrs	"
1864-66	mus instrs	43 Greene
1867-68	"	41 Greene
1869-70	"	221 Greene, h. Germany
1871	importer	"
1872	not listed	
1873-76	mus instrs	31 Courtlandt
1877-78	not listed	
1879-84	mus instrs	"
1885	------	h. 177 E. 111th

Martin was a "Brass [instrument] Manufacturer." (*1861 AMD* p.90) In 1866, he advertised as a "Manufacturer of Brass & German Silver Piston & Rotary Valve Musical Instruments. Also, Cavalry & Infantry Trumpets or Bugles." (*CmRg* 1866:94) In 1868, Martin joined the instrument dealer and importer *Moses Slater* in the firm *Martin & Slater*. The following year, the firm's title was changed to *Slater & Martin*, and as such, it continued in operation until 1871. From 1873-78, with the dealer *August Pollman*, Martin headed the firm *Martin, Pollman & Company*.

Martin, who occasionally used the shortened name Robert Martin, was probably a German immigrant, and from 1869-70, his home address was given as Germany. Also active during this period was a woodwind-making and importing firm, Martin & Martin, which had branches in London, New York and Philadelphia. (See **Langwill** 1980:115.) Their relationship to this maker is not known. Several

instruments bearing G.R. Martin's labels are now in museum collections. See *Slater & Martin*.

MARTIN & BRUNO

1838-39	mus instrs	212 Fulton

See *Christian Frederick Martin*.

MARTIN & COUPA

1840-41	mus instrs	385 Broadway

See *Christian Frederick Martin*.

MARTIN & SCHATZ

1835	violin mkrs	196 Hudson

See *Christian Frederick Martin*.

MARTIN & SLATER

1868	mus instrs	41 Greene

In 1868, the title of this firm was changed to *Slater & Martin*. See *Gotfried Martin*.

MARTIN, POLLMAN & COMPANY

1873-78	mus instrs	31 Courtlandt

See *Gotfried Martin*.

MARTINS, Martin

1846	pianos	r. 90 Leonard
1847-48	"	334 Greenwich
1849-51	"	83 Leonard
1852-53	see *Martins & Ouvrier*	
1854-59	pianos	539 Houston
1860	see *Martins & Ouvrier*	
1861-72	pianos	34 E. Houston
1873-90+	"	17 E. 16th

From 1846-67, Martins and his partner, the mastercraftsman *Peter Ouvrier*, headed the piano-manufacturing firm *Martins & Ouvrier*. After the firm's dissolution, Martins admitted his son, Eugene, into partnership, and their company, *Martins & Son*, continued in operation past 1890.

Martins was a "practical" maker, and was awarded a patent for an improved piano frame. (See **Pierce** 1965:158.) Throughout the 1860s, Martins & Ouvrier listed themselves as makers of upright and square pianos, but their firm was not mentioned by either the Census reports or the *1861 AMD*.

MARTINS & OUVRIER

1846	pianos	r. 90 Leonard
1847-48	"	334 Greenwich
1849-52	"	83 Leonard
1853-59	"	539 Houston
1860-67	"	34 E. Houston

See above *Martin Martins*.

MARTINS & SON

1868-72	pianos	34 E. Houston
1873-90+	"	17 E. Houston

See above *Martin Martins*.

MATHUSHEK, Frederick M.

1855	piano mkr	E. 34th c. Ave. 3
1856-57	pianos	188 Mercer & 72 Prince
1858	saloon	252 Fourth
1859-60	pianos	"
1861	not listed	
1862-65	pianos	34 Second Ave.
1866-74	not listed	
1875	piano mkr	h. 159 n. Courtlandt
1876	not listed	
1877	piano mkr	"
1878	not listed	
1879-87	*Mathushek Piano Manuf Co.*	23 E. 14th; factory New Haven, Conn.
1888-90+	"	80 Fifth Ave.
1882-85	*Mathushek & Kinkeldey*	210 E. 129th; 216 E. 128th
1886	*Mathushek & Son*	
		" & "
1887	"	242 E. 122nd
1888-90+	"	216 E. 128th & 313 W. 125th

Mathushek, a talented piano designer and inventor, was born on June 9, 1814 in Mannheim, and learned the piano trade at Worms. After his apprenticeship, Mathushek traveled through Germany and Austria, and then spent some time working in Henri Pape's Paris shop. Returning to Worms, he built several experimental pianos similar to those constructed by Pape, including an octagonal "table piano." Mathushek immigrated to New York in 1849, and was hired to draw scales and perfect other innovations for the shop of *John Dunham*. One of his innovations from this period was a hammered-covering device which was later widely used in the trade. (See **Dolge** 1911:321-25.)

Mathushek apparently tried working as a saloon keeper in 1858—several other Mathushek were active in that trade during the 1850s and 1860s—but soon returned to instrument making. In 1863, he entered into partnership with Leopold Kuhner; their firm, *Mathushek & Kuhner*, was in operation through 1865. During the late 1850s, Mathushek also worked for the noted piano designer *Spencer Driggs*.

In 1866, a group of German businessmen in New Haven, Connecticut, headed by instrument dealer Morris Steinhart, decided to establish a piano factory. They raised sufficient capital and invited Mathushek to head the concern, which they titled the *Mathushek Piano-forte Company*. However, the firm quickly ran into trouble and, wrote **Steinhart** (1900:171-72), "certain difficulties regarding our Superintendent, and the fear of my German partners lest they lose their money, made 'The Mathushek Piano-forte Company,' as created by us, short-lived; and as we were all weary of the venture, we virtually presented our successor with the stock, providing that he would assume our responsibilities." Under new owners, the firm continued in operation past 1890 as the *Mathushek Piano Manufacturing Company*. Although the firm's factory remained in New Haven, the concern did maintain New York showrooms. It is unclear how long Mathushek continued to be associated with the firm that bore his name, but it likely that he had severed his association with it c.1875 when he returned to New York.

From 1882-85, with the piano dealer Carl Kinkeldey, he headed the New York firm *Mathushek & Kinkeldey*. Then in 1886, with Victor H. Mathushek, he established *Mathushek & Son*. (Despite its title, Dolge claimed Victor was actually the maker's grandson.) On November 9, 1891, "like his master Pape, Mathushek died a poor man." (**Dolge** 1911:325) Following his death, his firm was incorporated, and still later, consolidated with *Jacob Brothers*. A book of clippings compiled by Mathushek is in the collection of the Museum of the City of New York. For further information, see **Spillane** (1890:226-27); **Steinhart** (1900:169-72).

MATHUSHEK & KINKELDEY

1882-85	pianos	210 E. 129; 216 E. 128th

See above *Frederick Mathushek*.

MATHUSHEK & KUHNER

1863-65	pianos	34 Second Ave.

See above *Frederick Mathushek*.

MATHUSHEK & SON

1886	pianos	210 E. 129th; 216 E. 128th
1887	"	242 E. 122nd
1888-90+	"	216 E. 128th; 313 W. 125th

See above *Frederick Mathushek.*

MATHUSHEK PIANO MANUFACTURING COMPANY

| 1879-87 | pianos | 23 E. 14th |
| 1888-90+ | " | 80 Fifth Ave. |

Originally established in 1866 as the Mathushek Piano-forte Company in New Haven, Connecticut, only its warerooms were located in the city. See above *Frederick Mathushek.*

MAUL, George

1850	guitars	388 Broadway
1851	segars	"
1852-57	guitars	"
1858-59	"	382 Broadway
1860-66	guitars/guitar mkr	h. 12 White

From 1839-58, Maul and partner *Louis Schmidt* headed the guitar and violin-making firm *Schmidt & Maul.* After leaving Schmidt, Maul opened a small instrument- manufacturing firm of his own. According to the *1855 New York Census*, the maker owned $10,000 of real estate, and $500 worth of tools. He employed 8 men at monthly wages of $36, and that year, reportedly produced $5,000 worth of "brass." (This appears to be a mistake on the part of the census taker, since no evidence exists that Maul made any instruments other than guitars and violins.) Two organ builders, Henry and Ludwig Maul, were active in Newark, New Jersey during the late 1850s (**Kaufman** 1976:30), but their relationship to this maker is not known. See *Schmidt & Maul.*

MAXWELL, Charles M.

1879	marble	176 Broadway
1880-84	pianos	83 E. 13th
1885+	storage	74 University & 33 E. 13th

Although listed as a piano manufacture in the *1885 AMD* (p.209), given Maxwell's other professions it is likely that he was involved in the instrument trade only as a dealer.

MAXWELL, Samuel

1849	cabinet mkr	66 University
1850	pianos	r. 259 Bowery (*NYBD*)
1851	piano mkr	2 W. 12th
1852	"	272 West
1853	"	42 W. 14th
1854	"	84 Ave. 9
1855-56	"	h. 282 W. 18th

Maxwell might have been a piano dealer or a journeyman throughout his career. Nothing further is presently known about his career.

MEDCALF/METCALF, Charles E.

1826	cabinet mkr	Bowery-hill
1827	piano mkr	215 Mulberry
1828	"	189 Mulberry
1829	"	Sixth n. Ave. 3
1830	not listed	
1831-33	piano mkr	142 Elm
1834-38	"	77 Delancey

After 1831, Medcalf's name usually appeared as Metcalf. No further information is presently known about this maker.

MEEKS, Henry S.

1824	cabinet mkr	Arden n. Bedford
1825	mus instr mkr	King n. MacDougal
1826	"	Bedford n. Commerce
1827	"	390 Bowery
1828	"	36 Amity
1829	not listed	
1830-32	piano mkr	Bowery n. Art
1833	"	767 Bowery
1834	"	396 Bowery
1835	weigher	318 Bowery c. Bleecker
1836	pianos	Tenth n. Bowery
1837	"	Bowery
1838	"	Anthony
1839	"	464 Bowery
1840	"	432 Bowery

Meeks might have been related to the well-known New York cabinet maker Joseph Meeks (**Heatherington** 1973:7), or the piano maker William E. Meeks, who was listed as a journeyman in 1842, however, no further information about this maker is presently known.

MEHLIN, Paul G.

1889	pianos	461 W. 40th
1890 +	"	467 W. 40th

Mehlin was born on February 28, 1837, in Stuttgart. He was trained there as a piano maker and worked in the shop of Frederick Doerner, before immigrating to New York where he worked for *Raven & Bacon* and *Lighte & Bradbury*. After serving in the Union Army during the Civil War, he went to work for *Chambers & Gabler*. In 1889, with his sons Henry Paul and Charles H., he established *Mehlin & Sons*, which, according to **Pierce** (1965), continued in operation through the 1960s. For further information see **Spillane** (1890:292-96).

MEHLIN & SONS

1889	pianos	461 W. 40th
1890 +	"	467 W. 40th

See above *Paul G. Mehlin*.

MEIN, Robert

1830-31	piano mkr	109 1/2 Canal
1832-33	not listed	
1834-35	piano mkr	96 Varick
1836	"	81 Sullivan
1837-39	"	391 Grand
1840	Margaret wid of Robert	"

Mein died sometime in 1839, but nothing else is presently known about his career.

MEINELL, William R.

1876-82	flutes	64 Nassau
1883-90 +	mus instrs	"

The *1885 AMD* (p.209), listed Meinell as a "Manufacturer of Boehm flutes." From undated notes in the *DMC,* it is known that Meinell spent seven years working with Krupse in Germany, and that his son, W.F. Meinell, succeeded him as head of the firm c.1903. (See **Krivin** 1961:248.)

MEINS, Richard

Strictly speaking, Meins was not a "city" instrument maker since his drum manufactory was located in Flushing, Queens (*1861 AMD* p.90), however, his drums might have been labeled "New York."

MEISENHARTER/MISENHARTER/ MISSENHARTER, Charles

This brass-instrument manufacturer was in business as early as 1877, when a euphonium he made was presented to a George Wiegands by Crooks Amateur Cornet Band of New York on December 28th. On the instrument, Meisenharter claimed to have been awarded "Medallions 1st Class" at Philadelphia, London, and Paris [exhibitions]. (PC:Eliason) Meisenharter was listed as a "Musical Instrument Manufacturer" at 204-208 E. 23rd Street in the *1885 AMD* (p.209).

MEISTER, DELIUS & COMPANY

1886	pianos	218 W. 37th
1887	"	453 W. 36th

The 1887 *CmRg* (p.58) listed D. Meister & Company as manufacturers of "Grand, Upright & Square Pianos." Nothing else is presently known about the firm.

MERCIER, Charles

1842-43	guitars	156 Fulton
1844	"	92 Duane
1845	violins	92 Leonard
1846-49	"	44 Canal
1850	violin mkr	"
1851-53	violins	422 1/2 Broadway
1854-55	instrs	"
1856	violin mkr	"
1857-63	violins	"
1864-65	mus instrs	"
1866	mus instr mkr	"
1867-68	mus instrs	409 Broome

Mercier claimed to have established his New York shop in 1840, and in addition to guitars and violins, he advertised his importation of "Turkish Cymbals from Constantinople." (*1861 AMD* p.91) In 1845, he shared his 92 Leonard Street shop with the brass maker *Jules Lecocq*. Although there is no record that the two men were ever partners, it is probable that both were French immigrants. Mercier might have been related to A. Mercier, a violin maker who was active at Mirecourt, France from 1860-62. (See **Henley** 1960:3:21.)

MERRILL, James F.

1820	------	80 Nassau
1821	------	73 Henry
1822	cabinet mkr	"
1823-24	"	Arden n. Bedford

1825	mus instr mkr	King n. MacDougal
1826	"	Burrows n. Sixth
1827-28	cabinet mkr	123 Nassau
1829-32	"	40 N. Moore
1833	------	31 Renwick
1834	Martha wid James, boar- dingh.	197 Franklin

Only one person of this name was listed in the *NYCD*s of this period, so the widow listed in 1834 was almost certainly his. In 1824-25, his addresses were the same as those of the piano maker *Henry Meeks*, however, no further information is presently known about Merrill.

METCALF, Charles E.

See *Charles Medcalf*.

MILLER, William

1853	pianos	128 E. 14th
1854-56	"	156 E. 21st
1857-58	"	E. 28th n. Ave. 3
1859-61	"	h. 137 E. 21st
1862-64	"	h. 160 E. 21st
1865	piano mkr	"

In 1852, Miller was probably the craftsman who joined the piano maker *Napoleon Haines* in the firm *Haines & Miller*. Miller was listed as the head of his own firm in 1853, and in 1856, he was awarded a diploma for the 3rd best piano shown at that year's American Institute Fair. (*American Institute Records*)

According to the *1855 New York Census*, Miller had several shops in New York, which primarily produced piano cases and stools. At one of his shops, Miller owned $8,000 of real capital; $500 worth of tools; and $7,500 of lumber and veneers. He employed 10 men and 1 boy at average monthly wages of $45, and that year produced 312 pianos worth $15,600. In another shop, Miller had $3,000 worth of lumber and hardware, and he employed 40 men and 8 boys at total (monthly?) wages of $1,440, who that year produced 100 pianos and 10,000 piano stools worth $50,000.

In 1858, a maker named John Miller advertised himself as the "Manufacturer of the William Miller Pianoforte." (*NYBD* 1858:350) Although no documentation has been found, it is reasonable to assume that John was a son or close relative of William Miller. See *Haines & Miller*.

MILLET, William E.

See *Jollie & Millet*.

MILLS, James B.

1830	piano mkr	23 Downing
1831	"	55 Bedford
1832-42	"	27 Morton
1843	not listed	
1844	Caroline wid of James B.	"

No further information is presently known about this maker.

MIREMONT, (Claude) Augustin

1853	see below	44 Forsyth
1854-57	violins	544 Broadway
1858-60	"	h. 542 Broadway
1861	violin manuf	"

Miremont was born in Mirecourt, France in 1827, and learned violin making from his father Sebastian Miremont. After working for several violin-making shops in Paris, the maker emigrated to New York in 1852. At the 1853 New York Crystal Palace Exhibition, he entered violins, altos, a bass and counter-bass "in imitation of the violins of the 15th century." (*Official Catalogue* 1853:94) After 1861, Miremont returned to Paris where he worked as a violin maker at 20 rue Faubourg, Poissonnière until his death at Pontorson in 1887. See **Roda** (1959:218); **Henley** (1960:3:35-36).

MITCHELL, William

1836-40	see below	
1841-42	mus instrs	66 Charlton
1843	instr mkr	6 Vandam
1844-50	"	26 Vandam

Mitchell was still an apprentice at 72 Eldridge in 1836 when he entered an octave flute in the American Institute Fair and was awarded a diploma. At the 1839 American Institute Fair, he won a silver medal for the second best specimens of keyed flutes; his address was then given as 26 Vandam Street. At the 1842 Fair, Mitchell entered five flutes and was awarded a diploma, again for exhibiting the second best specimens. (*American Institute Records*) A wind-instrument maker of the same name was active in Glasgow, Scotland about this time (see **Langwill** 1980:121), but their relationship, if any, has not been established.

MITTAUER, George

See above *Marschall & Mittauer*.

MIXSELL, Aaron

1843	------	27th n. Ave. 3
1844-45	pianos	"
1846-50	"	91 Lexington Ave.
1851-52	"	186 Ave. 3
1853	"	112 Ave. 3
1854-59	"	79 E. 13th
1860	"	252 Fourth
1861-64	"	95 E. 13th
1865-66	piano mkr	"

Mixsell was related to *Peter Mixsell*, see below, with whom he headed in the piano-manufacturing partnership *A. & P. Mixsell* in 1860. In 1861, Mixsell was listed as heading his own firm at 305 Fourth c. Greene. (*1861 AMD* p.171)

MIXSELL, Peter

1860	pianos	252 Fourth
1861	"	117 E. 19th
1862-63	formerly *Mixsell & Company*	"
1864	pianos	" & 12 W. 4th
1865-66	"	12 W. 4th & 92 E. 13th
1867-70	"	209 E. 19th
1871-72	"	h. 411 W. 42nd

Peter Mixsell was a brother-in-law of the piano maker *Alfred Newby*, and a relative of *Aaron Mixsell*, see above. He had worked as an instrument maker in Albany before moving to New York. (**Spillane** 1890:291) In 1860, Peter and Aaron Mixsell established the piano-manufacturing firm *A. & P. Mixsell*, and shortly thereafter Peter left to head *Mixsell & Company*.

In 1861, Mixsell and an instrument dealer named Flood founded the short-lived partnership *Mixsell & Flood*. Then, from 1864-71, Mixsell headed *P. Mixsell & Company*, manufacturers of "Carpenter's Patent Harmonium Grand Pianos." (*CmRg* 1867:136) Peter left the trade in 1872, selling out his interests to *J. F. Stone*. During this period, there were several other Mixsells active in the piano trade: Philip Mixsell, a piano maker listed from 1859-60; Isaac Mixsell, a piano dealer listed in 1856; and Aaron J. Mixsell, a piano agent listed in 1860.

MIXSELL, A. & P.

1860	pianos	252 Fourth & 247 Thompson

The Mixsells advertised themselves as manufacturers of "New Style Parlor Grand Piano-Fortes," and mentioned that they had received a patent on October 2, 1860 for an improvement to the piano (*CmRg* 1861:47). See above *Aaron Mixsell*; *Peter Mixsell*.

MIXSELL, P. & COMPANY

1864	pianos	117 E. 19th
1865-66	"	12 W. 4; 92 E. 13; 117 E. 19th
1867-70	"	209 E. 19th
1871	piano manufactory	411 & 413 W. 42nd

There might have also been an earlier firm of this title since in 1863 *Peter Mixsell*, see above, advertised that he was "formerly of Mixsell & Company." (*NYCD* 1863)

MIXSELL & FLOOD

1861	pianos	252 Fourth & 247 Thompson

See above *Peter Mixsell*.

MOENNIG, Henry W.

1857-61	mus instr mkr	141 Forsyth (*NYBD*)
1862-63	instrs	r. 99 Forsyth
1864-66	music	97 Forsyth
1867-70	mus instrs	99 Forsyth
1871-72	"	97 Forsyth
1873-74	"	309 Bowery
1875-79	"	198 & 309 Bowery
1880-83	"	294 Bowery h. 23 Ave. 2
1884	Mary wid of Henry W.	h. 23 Ave. 2

Moennig was listed as a "brass manufacturer" in the *1861 AMD* (p.90), and belatedly listed as a "Band Instrument Manufacturer" after his death by the *1885 AMD* (p.209). **Langwill** (1980:121,123) suggests this maker was related to the Monnig family of brass-instrument makers in Leipzig. Robert Eliason (PC:Eliason) reports finding a listing for the firm Moennig & Company from 1872-73. The piano maker Robert Moennig, and musical instrument dealer William Moennig listed in the 1871 *NYCD*, might have been members of this firm.

MONGANI, Theobald F.

See *Theobald Monzani*.

MONNIOT, PELOUBET & COMPANY

What little information is known about this firm comes from an advertisement which appeared in the *Morning Chronicle* [N.Y.] on November 6, 1803: "Monniot, Peloubet & Co. Lately from France, have the honor to inform the public, that they make and repair all sorts of Musical Instruments, viz. Violins, Piano Fortes, Harpsichords, Organs, Clarinets, Flutes, Octaves, Flageolets, & c. They likewise alter and put such new tunes on Hand Organs as may be wished for. As they intend to settle in this City, they wish for a fair opportunity to make their talents known, and the public may rely on their best endeavours to give satisfaction. For further particulars apply at no. 253 Broadway, opposite the new City Hall." Monniot's name thereafter disappears from New York records, but *Louis Peloubet* remained active in the city until at least 1812.

MONROE, Peter

1832-33	piano mkr	r. 135 Amity

No further information about this maker is presently known.

MONTGOMERY, John C.

1800	mus instr mkr	355 Pearl
1801	"	55 Cherry
1802-04	"	64 Nassau
1805	"	255 Broadway
1806	" & tuner	Elm
1807	widow of John C.	3 Ann

Spillane (1890:104) claimed that Montgomery was a maker of harpsichords and pianos who originally came from Dublin, but if so, his name was not included by **Teahan** (1963). An advertisement placed by the maker in *The New-York Gazette and General Advertiser* on January 1, 1800, suggests that he had worked in Charleston, South Carolina before coming to the city: "John Montgomery, Musical Instrument Maker and Tuner, Takes this method to inform the public, that he has lately arrived in [from?] Charleston, and has commenced business at No. 23 Rose- Street, where he makes and repairs all kinds of Wind and String Instruments, in the neatest manner. He hopes from his experience in the above business he shall merit the favour of the public in general." His widow was listed in 1807, but no obituary has yet been located for the maker.

MONZANI/MONGANI, Theobald P.

1835	flute manuf	73 Leonard
1836-43	flute mkr	113 Elm
1844	mus instr mkr	32 E. 13th
1845-47	"	284 W. 17th
1848	"	r. 217 1/2 Varick

Monzani was probably a son of the well-known London flute maker Tebaldo Monzani, who was active from 1790-1839. The younger Monzani's activities in the city are somewhat unclear: he was first listed as the head of *Monzani & Company* in 1835, but thereafter, he apparently worked alone.

A flute in the Yale University Collection of Musical Instruments (*Catalog* 1968:162) bears the label Monzani & Reed. Actually, Reed was the publisher and music dealer George P. Reed who acted as Monzani's retail distributor in Boston c.1839. (See **Ayars** 1937:15,17.) There is no record that the two men ever worked together in New York. The **DMC** reportedly contains a flute labeled Badger & Monzani which was made in New York c.1858-59. No record of such a firm has been found, however, it is possible that Monzani continued to work as a journeyman or subcontractor for *Alfred Badger* after the former's name disappeared from the *NYCD* in 1848. See *Alfred Badger*.

MONZANI & COMPANY

1835	flute manuf	73 Leonard

See above *Theobald Monzani*.

MORAN, Edward G.

1842-43	piano mkr	104 Ave. 3

According to the 1842 *Co-Partnership Director*, Moran was a partner of *Adam H. Gale & Company*. Given his partnership with Gale, it is also likely that he had earlier been a member of the *New York Piano Forte Manufacturing Company*, the co-operative shop located on Third Avenue that had been active in the late 1830s. *Gale & Company* continued in operation through 1844, however, Moran's name does not appear in the *NYCD* after 1843.

MORGENROTH, Christopher

1849	piano mkr	21 W. Broadway

Possibly the same person as *Gustavus Morgenroth*, see below, nothing further is presently known about this maker's career.

MORGENROTH, Gustavus A.

1850-53	pianos	112 W. Broadway
1854	"	195 E. 20th
1855-56	"	212 Ave. 3

Possibly the same person as the piano maker *Christopher Morgenroth*, see above. In 1854, this maker and a partner named Soebbeler established the piano firm *Morgenroth & Soebbeler*. The latter might have been either the piano dealer *Nicholas Soebbeler*, or the piano maker *William Soebbeler*.

MORGENROTH & SOEBBELER

1854	pianos	228 Ave. 3 (*NYBD*)

See above *Gustavus Morgenroth*.

MORRELL, Charles Sr.

1855	bookbinder	132 Amos
1856	book marbling	94 Fulton

Morrell was born in Augusta, Maine in 1826. He operated a bookbinding shop in New York, but also made and played the banjo. His shop served as a headquarters for the city's banjo players, and he specialized in building "prize banjos" and fitting new vellum heads on instruments. In 1858, Morrell moved to San Francisco, where he remained until his death on April 26, 1890. (**Howard** 1959:24)

MORRIS, Charles A.

See *Stodart & Morris*.

MORRIS, Richard M.

See *Bruno & Morris*.

MORRISON, James

According to **Howard** (1959:48), Morrison was active as a banjo maker in New York from 1883-1910. His banjos "were constructed with a steel hoop 5/16" in thickness, resting on steel pins inserted in the rim." This maker can not be traced in the *NYCD*, however, there were several woodworkers of the same name active in the city during this period.

MORSE, E. L.

See *Bristow, Morse & Company*.

MOSER, Daniel

1859	mus instrs	34 Bayard
1860	"	14 Division
1861	banjos	h. 117 St. Mark's Pl.
1862	turner	"
1863	cabinet mkr	"
1864	mus instrs	"
1865	Margaret wid. Daniel	"

From 1859-60, Moser and the instrument maker *George Unruh* headed the partnership *Moser & Unruh*. Unruh had previously worked with the banjo maker *Frederick Lohr*, and it is likely that *Moser & Unruh* were also involved in manufacturing banjos. Nothing further is presently known about Moser's activities; he apparently died sometime in 1864.

MOSER & UNRUH

1859	mus instrs	34 Bayard
1860	"	14 Division

See above *Daniel Moser*.

MUNDY, Edward N.

1820	cabinet mkr	17 Dominick
1821	"	Arden n. Herring
1822-23	piano mkr	74 Reed
1824	"	92 Reed
1825-27	"	154 Fulton
1828-31	"	641 Greenwich
1832-35	"	234 Bleecker
1836	"	559 Houston
1837	"	204 Bleecker
1838-39	pianos	"

From 1822-28, Mundy and *Alickam Robb* headed the piano-making firm and music dealership *Robb & Mundy*. After the dissolution of their partnership, Mundy worked alone for several years before joining *John Pethick* in the firm *Mundy & Pethick* from 1832-39. See *Robb & Mundy*.

MUNDY & PETHICK

1832-35	piano mkrs	234 Bleecker
1836	"	559 Houston
1837-39	pianos	204 Bleecker c. Hancock

See above *Edward Mundy*.

MUNROE, Thaddeus

1821	cabinet mkr	8 Thomas
1822-23	"	40 Thomas
1824-26	"	Herring n. Raisin
1827	not listed	
1828	pianoforte manuf	Art c. Bowery
1829-30	"	Bowery n. Art
1831	not listed	
1832-33	piano mkr	"
1834	"	438 Bowery n. Art

Nothing further is presently known about this maker, however, the piano maker *Thomas Richardson* was also listed at what appears to be the same address, Herring n. Raisin, in 1826.

MYER, John

1827	piano mkr	39 Jones
1828	"	60 Forsyth

Myer might have been a member of the later firm, *Wake, Myer & Herrick* from 1846-47, but this awaits documentation. Nothing further is presently known about Myer.

N

NARVESEN, Conrad

1863	pianos	156 E. 21st
1864-66	"	71 E. 22nd
1868-71	"	121 E. 22nd
1872-76	"	233 E. 21st
1877-79	"	157 E. 44th
1880	"	232 E. 36th
1881	piano mkr	"
1882-83	pianos	"
1884-85	supt.	23 W. 13th
1885-88	see *Narvesen Piano Co.*	University c. 12th
1889-90+	pianos	56 W. 13th

Narvesen was born in Norway and emigrated to America as a youngster. **Spillane** (1890:251) claimed that he began working in the piano trade in 1845, but he was not listed in the *NYCD* before 1861 when he became a partner in the Brooklyn-based piano-manufacturing firm *Ihlseng, Narvesen & Linstedt*. (*1861 AMD* p.169) In 1863, Linstedt withdrew, and the firm, reorganized as *Ihlseng & Narvesen*, continued in operation through 1864 at 156-158 E. 21st Street, Manhattan.

After the dissolution of Ihlseng & Narvesen, Narvesen worked alone for several years before joining with his son Nicholas to establish *Narvesen & Son* from 1869-77. In 1880, with two other Scandinavian piano makers, *John Bergman* and *August Haugaard*, he formed *Narvesen, Bergman & Haugaard*. Sometime later, probably c.1885, *Richard Walters* purchased Narvesen's business interests and continued to produce instruments labeled the *Narvesen Piano Company* past 1890. It is likely that all of this maker's

many partners were Scandinavian immigrants. See *Ihlseng, Narvesen & Linstedt*; *Ihlseng & Narvesen*.

NARVESEN, BERGMAN & HAUGAARD

1880	pianos	232 E. 36th

See above *Conrad Narvesen*.

NARVESEN PIANO COMPANY

1885-88	pianos	University Pl. c. 12th
1889-90+	"	56 W. 13th

A continuation of the Conrad Narvesen piano firm under the ownership of *Richard Walters*. See above *Conrad Narvesen*.

NARVESEN & SON

1869-71	pianos	121 E. 22nd
1872-76	"	233 E. 21st
1877	"	157 E. 44th

See above *Conrad Narvesen*.

NASH, Isaac

1826	cabinet mkr	Cornelia n. Herring
1827	not listed	
1828	pianoforte mkr	Ave. 3 c. 11th
1829	not listed	
1830	carpenter	647 Greenwich
1831	"	66 Grove
1832	"	Tenth

Nothing further is presently known about this maker, however, he was probably related to the piano maker *Thomas Nash*, see below, with whom he apparently shared an address in 1832.

NASH, Thomas

| 1832 | pianoforte mkr | Bowery & Tenth |

Nothing further is presently known about this maker, however, he was probably related to *Isaac Nash*, see above.

NEEDHAM, Elias Parkman

1849	melodeons	77 E. 13th
1850	melodeons reeds	75 E. 13th
1851-54	melodeons	"
1855-66	"	99 E. 23rd
1867-83	organs	143 E. 23rd
1884	supplies	"
1885-86	photo materials	"
1887	------	"

A member of the well-known melodeon-making firm *Carhart & Needham* from 1849-54, and *Carhart, Needham & Company* from 1855-68. After the death of *Jeremiah Carhart* in 1869, Needham entered into partnership with his son to establish *Needham & Son*, which had apparently dissolved before it was belatedly listed in the *1885 AMD* (p.210). During the 1890s, a Needham Piano Company was active in Washington, New Jersey, but its relation to this maker is not known. See *Carhart & Needham*; *Carhart, Needham & Company*.

NEEDHAM, E.P. & SON

| 1869-83 | organs | 143 E. 23rd |
| 1884 | supplies | " |

See above *Elias Parkman Needham*.

NEILSON, James

| 1838 | piano mkr | 508 Greenwich |
| 1839 | " | 86 Vandam |

Possible a relative of the instrument maker *Samuel Neilson* listed below, nothing else is presently known about this maker.

NEILSON, Jason

1829	pianoforte mkr	112 Amos
1830	"	52 Courtlandt
1831	not listed	
1832-33	piano mkr	453 Broadway
1834	"	127 Troy
1835	"	289 Washington
1836	not listed	
1837	piano mkr	1 Vesey

A relative of the piano maker *Samuel Neilson*, see below, whom he succeeded at the latter's 453 Broadway address in 1832.

NEILSON, John

| 1828 | pianoforte mkr | 111 Fulton |

Possible related to *Samuel Neilson*, see below, however, nothing further is presently known about this maker.

NEILSON, Samuel

1805	mus instr mkr	21 Barclay
1806	"	71 Chambers
1807-15	"	19 Barclay
1816	"	r. 15 Barclay
1817-18	"	96 Chambers
1819	" & pianoforte mkr	"
1820-25	pianoforte mkr	"
1826-27	"	140 Chambers
1828-33	"	154 Chambers
1834-35	piano mkr	453 Broadway
1836	"	1 Vesey h. 110 Spring
1837	"	110 Spring
1838	not listed	
1839	piano mkr	203 Varick

Neilson probably learned the piano-making trade from *Archibald Whaites*. The two men might have been related, but they were certainly friends as early as 1796 when Whaites named his infant son Samuel Neilson Whaites. (**Kelby**) In 1807, both men shared the 19 Barclay Street address; however, there is no record that they ever were formally listed as partners. After Whaites' death in 1815, William Neilson—who was almost certainly a relative of Samuel— was appointed by the court to be "guardian of the infant children of Archibald Whaites." (*MCC* 1917)

Little else is known about Samuel Neilson's life, except that he joined a volunteer fire department on June 2, 1828, and resigned on October 19, 1829. (*MCC* 17:255;18:297) A square, one-pedal piano stencilled "Saml Neilson, 19 Barclay, Patent," is in the collection of the Smithsonian Institution. (*Catalog* No.315,694) The James, Jason, and John Neilsons listed above were apparently related to this maker, and given their dates, it is possible that they were Samuel's sons. In fact, since the years of their listings do not overlap, they might possibly have been a single person. (The *NYCD* was not always meticulously accurate about the listing of first names.) See *Archibald Whaites*.

NEUHARDT, Julius

1866-67	piano mkr	h. 161 Eldridge
1868	"	h. 171 Forsyth
1869-70	"	h. 187 Bowery
1871	"	h. 171 Forsyth
1872	tuner	h. 135 Essex
1873-74	piano mkr/pianos	"
1875	tuner	h. 363 Bowery
1876	piano mkr	365 Bowery
1877	tuner	"
1878-80	pianos	"
1881-82	tuner	h. 331 Fifth
1883-90+	pianos	363 Bowery

Neuhardt was listed as a piano tuner in the *1861 AMD* (p.173) and in the years that followed, he worked primarily was a journeyman piano maker and a dealer. From 1883-84, with his brother Robert C. Neuhardt, he headed the piano firm *Neuhardt & Brother*. Although it is likely that this concern was only a dealership, the *1885 AMD* (p.210) did list the Neuhardts as piano manufacturers.

NEUHARDT & BROTHER

1883-84	pianos	363 Bowery

See above *Julius Neuhardt*.

NEW YORK PIANO-FORTE COMPANY

1866	pianos	394 Hudson
1867-68	"	88 Walker
1869	"	340 & 342 Ave. 2

This firm should not be confused with the earlier *New York Pianoforte Manufacturing Company*, see below. Like the earlier concern, the *New York Piano-Forte Company* was also a co-operative, but it seems not to have been a continuation of the former, since not only had several decades elapsed, but a letter of incorporation for the firm was registered at the Office of the County Clerk of New York on March 24, 1864. The letter named William Tabel, William Haubner and *Justus Diehl* as trustees, and bore the signatures of the seventeen other artisans who each contributed $1,000 of capital stock to become members of the corporation.

An 1866 advertisement explained that: "The principal reason why the Pianos of the Company are Superior to Others, is that the firm is composed of the most expert artisans from the largest establishments in the city, who invent all their own improvements and under whose personal supervision every part of the Instrument is made." (*NYBD* 1866:115) It is not known if pianos produced by this company bore the firm's title or the names of the individual artisans involved.

NEW YORK PIANOFORTE MANUFAC-TURING COMPANY

1840	[pianos]	c. 3rd Ave. & 13th (*NYBD*)

Although never listed in the *NYCD*, this co-operative was apparently in business as early as 1837. It continued in operation until it was taken over by *Adam Gale* in 1842. The firm consisted of twenty mastercraftsmen, and although its advertisements assured the public that no apprentices were used in the construction of its pianos, a number of prominent New York craftsmen claimed to have received their training at the shop, including piano manufacturer *Francis Haines*. Other craftsmen involved with the organization were *Jacob Day*, *Wales Grow*, and *Edward Morgan*.

During the 1830s, co-operative shops were a popular solution to increasing labor unrest in many industries. The piano maker's co-operative was organized about 1837, possibly in response to the continuing employer-employee tensions that had resulted in the publication of the 1835 *New York Book of Prices for the Manufacture of Piano-Fortes*, which sought to establish fair and agreed upon wages for workers in piano shops. The general economic panic of 1837 might have also stimulated the formation of the cooperative. See **Groce** (1982:101-09).

Much of what is known about the co-operative comes from **Spillane** (1890:184-85), who wrote: "This was the first attempt at establishing a piano manufacturing business upon co-operative lines ever attempted in the United States . . . the New York Pianoforte Company had been started by some twenty of the best workmen of Nunns & Clark . . . These 'twenty workmen' undoubtedly made very excellent pianos in their time, as I find mention of their instruments in the exhibitions of 1839 and 1840 [i.e. American Institute Fairs] . . . Immediately after that date [October 1840] they went out of existence nominally. Like all such attempts to get a number of people with different qualities of education, taste and character into the same harness, chaos came and presently the foremost and most dominant mind came out uppermost [i.e. Gale] and assumed management of the business under new basic conditions."

Additional information about the firm is found in the advertisements of George Endicott, a music dealer, who had been appointed 'sole agent' for the enterprise. In the *Commercial Advertiser* [N.Y.] of

August 30, 1838, for example, he wrote that the members of the cooperative, "In coming before the public, in competition with manufacturers of established fame . . . are resolved to build their reputation of the excellence of their Piano Fortes and the fairness of their prices and terms. . . It may not be amiss to inform purchasers and all concerned that this is a chartered company and the stockholders consist principally of regularly bred Piano Forte makers, many of whom have been for years engaged in the first situations of the best manufacturers in the country, that all alike are interested in the success and reputation of the company and that no boys or apprentices are employed in any part of their work."

NEWBY, Alfred J.

1885	pianos	472 W. 43rd
1886-87	"	528 W. 43rd
1888	not listed	
1889-90+	pianos	E. 136th n. Southern Blvd.

In 1885, Newby entered into partnership with *John Evans* to form the piano-manufacturing firm *Newby & Evans*. Spillane (1890:291-92) wrote: "Mr. Newby is a well-known piano-maker. He served his time to Mr. Peter Mixsell, his brother-in-law, an old time Albany and later New York maker. He too, is a native of Albany . . . Mr. John Evans, the intellectual and business partner, to whose ability so much of their success is due, is a native of Wales, where he was born in 1846 . . . He first entered the banking business, and for five years held a position in the National Provincial Bank of England . . . He arrived in New York in 1868, and with his scholastic acquirements and cultivated tastes turned towards journalism . . . he was successful, both as a writer and as a publisher . . . He became connected with Mr. Newby in 1884 . . . Their quick rise into eminence as makers of reputable instruments sold at popular prices may be judged from the fact that, in 1888, they erected a factory with a capacity of forty instruments per week [on 136th Street] . . . and are not yet satisfied with building space."

NEWBY & EVANS

1885	pianos	472 W. 43rd
1886-87	"	528 W. 43rd
1888-90+	"	E. 136th n. Southern Blvd

See above *Alfred Newby*.

NEWMAN, Edward G.

1867	pianos	113 Fourth Ave.
1868	not listed	
1869	piano mkr	h. 39 St. Mark's Pl.
1870	pianos	486 Ave. 2
1871-74	"	87 Ave. 3
1875-76	piano manuf	154 Ave. 4 c. E. 14th
1877-90+	pianos	54 E. 13th

Newman advertised in the 1873 *CmRg* (p.106) that he had "for several years been with the celebrated Steinway & Sons, employed on the most important branches of the business, and is therefore competent to make a first class instrument." He was also listed as a piano manufacturer in the *1885 AMD* (p.210).

NEWTON, Henry J.

1850-52	pianofortes	20 & 22 Canal
1853	"	22 Canal & 59 Spring
1854	"	421 Broome
1855	piano mkr	"
1856-60	pianos	" & 120 Wooster
1861	"	" & 40 Ave. 4
1862-72	"	" & 120 Wooster
1873-74	"	12 E. 14th
1875-79	------	h. 128 W. 43rd
1880+	pres. (dry plating)	

Newton was born on February 23, 1823, at Hartleton, Pennsylvania, and was apprenticed at the age of 17 to learn the piano-making trade at the Wittlesey Brothers' shop in Salem, Connecticut. In 1850, Newton came to New York, and with *Ferdinand Lighte*, founded the successful piano-manufacturing firm *Lighte & Newton*.

In 1854, *William Bradbury* was admitted to the firm, and its title changed to *Lighte, Newton & Bradbury*. The partnership lasted until 1858, when Newton withdrew to head his own company, which he continued to manage until his retirement from the trade c.1875. Newton later developed an improved printing process which earned him a reputation as the "Father of the Dry Plate Process in America." An eminent citizen, Newton was nominated to run for mayor by the Greenback Labor Party in 1878, and also headed several photographic and reform societies. He died on December 23, 1895, after being run down by a cable car on Broadway. (**NCAB** 7:23-24) See *Lighte & Newton*; *Lighte, Newton & Bradbury*.

NITSCHKE, Frederick W.

1856	pianos	r. 165 W. 29th
1857	piano mkr	150 Fourth
1858	see *John & William Nitschke*	
1859-70	pianos/piano mkr	h. 139 E. 28th
1871-75	piano mkr	h. 237 E. 28th
1876	Elizabeth wid Frederick W.	"

Nitschke was listed as a piano manufacturer in the *1861 AMD* (p.171). He was not listed in 1858, but he was probably the same person as the piano maker *William Nitschke*, see below, who was listed that year. In 1856, he was a member of *Nitschke & Son*, although it is not known whether he was the father or the son.

NITSCHKE, JOHN & WILLIAM

| 1858 | pianos | h. 139 E. 28th |

See above *Frederick Nitschke*.

NITSCHKE & SON

| 1856 | pianos | 150 Fourth Ave. |

See above *Frederick Nitschke*.

NUGENT, James B.

1869	piano mkr	524 Third Ave.
1870	pianos	h. 475 Tenth Ave.
1871	piano mkr	h. 465 1/2 Tenth Ave.
1872	cabinet mkr	"
1873	not listed	
1874-75	pianos/piano mkr	h. 519 W. 35th
1876	not listed	
1877	pianos	r. 225 E. 36th
1878-79	"	145 E. 42nd
1880-81	"	142 E. 36th
1882	"	232 E. 40th
1883	agent	h. 154 E. 41st
1884-85	not listed	
1886	collector	"

According to the *NYCD*, Nugent was apparently a piano dealer, however, the *1885 AMD* (p.210) listed him as a piano manufacturer. His firm, *James B. Nugent & Company*, was listed in 1880, 1882, and 1885. **Pierce** (1965) claimed that the firm continued in operation until 1913, but the above listings suggest that Nugent left the trade before 1885.

NUGENT, JAMES B. & COMPANY

| 1880 | pianos | 142 E. 36th |
| 1882 | " | 232 E. 40th |

This firm was also belatedly listed at 232 E. 40th Street in the *1885 AMD* (p.210). See above *James Nugent*.

NUNNS, Francis/John F.

| 1831-32 | piano mkr | 57 Orchard |

See below *Robert Nunns*.

NUNNS, Robert

1823-24	piano mkrs	172 Chambers
1825-28	"	3rd Ave.
1829	"	3rd Ave. c. 26th
1830-39	"	137 Broadway
1840-41	"	240 Broadway
1842-47	pianos	"
1848-53	"	257 Broadway
1854-55	"	785 Broadway
1856-60	"	" & 98 E. 26th
1861-63	"	97 E. 26th
1864	"	h. 97 E. 26th
1865	late Nunns & Clark pianos	581 Broadway
1966-68	pianos	h. 97 E. 26th

Robert Nunns and his brother, *William Nunns*, see below, emigrated from London c.1821. William is known to have arrived on November 21, 1821, on board the Cincinnatus. (**Lancour** 1963) Both brothers found work in the shop of *Kearsing & Sons* on Broome Street, before establishing their own firm, *Robert & William Nunns*, in 1823. Their firm was a success, and, wrote **Spillane** (1890:151), "they initiated a radical departure immediately after starting into the trade by introducing the present French action." Besides producing pianos for themselves, the Nunns manufactured pianos for *Dubois & Stodart*. (A piano bearing the label "Made for Dubois & Stodart by R. & W. Nunns," is in the collection of The Farmers Museum, Cooperstown, New York.) During this period, the Nunns operated a piano factory in Setauket, Long Island. (**Chickering** 1902:51)

In 1833, the piano maker *John Clark*, also from England, was admitted into partnership, and the title of the firm changed to *Nunns, Clark & Company*. Their partnership lasted until 1839, when William Nunns withdrew, and the concern was reorganized as *Nunns & Clark*.

Nunns & Clark was an extremely successful firm. They exhibited a piano at the 1853 New York Crystal Palace. (*Official Catalogue* 1853:94) According to the *1855 New York Census*, the partners owned $150,000 of real capital; $15,000 of tools; and had in stock 40,000 feet of pine and mahogany worth $20,000. The firm employed 80 men and 3 boys, who each earned $40 a month, and who that year produced 300 pianos worth $150,000. **Spillane** (1890:152-53) wrote that "while very much is written and spoken about Nunns & Clark, they have never been identified with any reforms and innovations in piano structure or acoustics after 1840 . . . They simply made average pianos after stereotyped principles first produced by other makers, employed good men, [and] paid good wages."

Nunns & Clark continued in business until 1860, although Clark was not listed after 1858. In the *1861 AMD* (p.171), Nunns was listed alone, and described as a piano manufacturer with a factory at Setauket, Long Island. Other members of the Nunns family, William, Jr., Robert, Jr., and John Francis, worked in the trade as journeymen and piano dealers through the 1860s. See below, *William Nunns*.

NUNNS, William

1823-32	see *Robert Nunns*	same addresses
1833-35	piano mkr	137 Broadway
1836	"	83 Anthony
1837-41	not listed	
1842	piano mkr	109 King
1843	"	1 St. John's Pl.
1844-47	"	170 Greenwich
1848	"	" & 95 Leonard
1849	"	300 Broadway
1850	"	88 Walker
1851	pianos	"
1852-53	piano mkr	379 Broadway & 88 Walker
1854	pianos	97 E. 26th

William's career was more uneven than that of his brother Robert. After heading *R. & W. Nunns* from 1823-32, and *Nunns, Clark & Company* from 1833-38, William and the piano tuner *Augustus Brumley* formed the firm *Nunns & Brumley* in 1836. In 1839, Nunns withdrew entirely from *Nunns, Clark & Company*, and apparently left the city for several years.

In 1843, Nunns joined the firm *John & Charles Fischer*, which was then reorganized as *Nunns & Fischer*. Their partnership lasted until 1848, when Nunns withdrew to head his own firm, *William Nunns*

& Company, which remained in business until 1853. William Steinway wrote that as a young apprentice, "he had lost all his savings of $300 by the bankruptcy of his employer, William Nunns, in 1853." (**Steinway** 1895:513) The following year, Nunns retired from the trade, possibly moving to Setauket, Long Island, where he and his brother had established their factory many years before. Many examples of pianos built by Nunns are now extant. See above, *Robert Nunns*.

NUNNS, R. & W.

1823-24	pianoforte mkrs	172 Chambers
1825-28	"	3rd Ave.
1829	"	3rd Ave. c. 26th
1830-31	"	137 Broadway
1832	piano mkrs	"

See above *Robert Nunns*.

NUNNS, W. & A. BRUMLEY

1836	piano mkrs	83 Anthony

See above *William Nunns*.

NUNNS & CLARK

1840-42	piano mkr	240 Broadway
1843-47	pianos	"
1848-53	"	257 Broadway
1854	"	785 Broadway
1855-60	"	" & 98 E. 26th

See above *Robert Nunns*.

NUNNS, CLARK & COMPANY

1833-39	piano mkrs	137 Broadway

See above *Robert Nunns*.

NUNNS, WILLIAM & COMPANY

1849	pianos	300 Broadway
1850-51	"	88 Walker
1852-53	"	379 Broadway & 88 Walker

See above *William Nunns*.

NUNNS & FISCHER

1843	piano manuf	1 St. John's La.
1844-47	"	170 Greenwich
1848	"	" & 95 Leonard

See above *William Nunns*.

O

O'BRIEN, John

1831	piano mkr	393 Pearl
1832	"	445 Pearl
1833	"	393 Pearl

No further information is presently known about this maker, however, a cabinet maker of the same name was listed at 9 Spring Street in 1828.

OCHSNER/OEKSNER, Sebastian

1854	mus instr mkr	r. 167 Second
1855-58	"	r. 169 Second

Although also listed as a musical instrument maker in the 1858 *NYBD* (p.611), Ochsner might have worked only as a journeyman.

OEHRLEIN, Gustave

1881-83	mus instrs	322 E. 9th

The son of *John Oehrlein*, see below, nothing further is presently known about this maker.

OEHRLEIN, John

1872	piano mkr	313 Sixth
1873-75	beer	"
1876-77	mus instrs	"
1878	"	19 Third
1879	"	320 E. 9th
1880	violins	"
1881-85	mus instrs	"
1886-87	"	87 E. 4th

Oehrlein was listed during the 1860s and 1870s as a beer seller and saloon owner at 416 Sixth. From 1881-83, he joined his son *Gustave Oehrlein*, see above, in the firm *John Oehrlein & Son*. Although their firm was probably a dealership, they were belatedly listed as "Musical Instrument Manufacturers" at 320 E. 9th Street in the *1885 AMD* (p.210).

OEHRLEIN, JOHN & SON

1881-83	mus instrs	322 E. 9th

See above *John Oehrlein*.

OEKSNER, Sebastian

See *Sebastian Ochsner*.

OGDEN, Cornelius G.

See *Brainard & Ogden*.

OLDENDORF, Henry

1876-84	drums	219 Centre
1885-86	"	220 Centre

Oldendorf was listed as a "Drum & Musical Instrument Manufacturer" at 219 Centre Street in the *1885 AMD* (p.210).

OLIER, T.

1859	mus instr mkr	16 Stanton

No further information is presently known about Olier.

O'NEILL, Patrick C.

1852-53	harpist	180 Hester

At the 1853 New York Crystal Palace, this musician exhibited an "American portable harp, capable of transposition into various keys, and of being played without tuning." His name was mistakenly listed in the exhibition's catalog as P.C.O. Neill, "manu. & prop." (*Official Catalogue* 1853:94)

OSBORNE, John

1830	piano mkr	406 Broome
1831	not listed	
1832-34	piano mkr	184 Chambers c. Greenwich
1835	"	201 Broadway

Osborne was an important and innovative piano maker who spent most of his career working outside the city. Born c.1792 in New England, he was apprenticed in Benjamin Crehore's Boston instrument-making shop, and from 1815-26, headed his own shop in that city. During this period, Osborne trained such noted American piano makers as Chickering, John Dwight, and the Gilberts. After leaving Boston, Osborne moved to Albany, and then, in 1830, to New York. In 1831, Osborne returned briefly to Albany to head the short-lived piano firm Meacham & Osborne. (AAD 1831:4)

In 1832 Osborne returned to New York. **Spillane** (1890:156) claimed that the maker, who "was a man of superior intellect and belligerent to a high degree," was awarded gold medals for his pianos at Mechanic Institute (American Institute?) fairs in 1833 and 1834—however, no supporting documentation has been found. Spillane also quotes an 1833 business announcement in which Osborne charged that the foreign-born makers then in New York and Boston had "pilfered American methods in piano-building, and acoustic development, without any justice or gratitude, but sneers at native Americans and their abstract intelligence [which] has been in the past effective enough to create a nation, and fearless enough to fight for its honor."

Osborne's New York firm was successful, and in 1834 he built a large factory on Broadway. On May 27, 1835, however, Osborne died in a fall from his factory, and it was rumored in the trade that he had committed suicide. Probably because of his questionable death and his difficult personality, Osborne's contributions have been undervalued. His factory building was later used by *Stodart, Worcester & Dunham*. For further information on the maker and his activities in Boston, see: **Ayars** (1937:106-09,285,290); **Johnson** (1943:282).

OTIS, Dwight P.

1868	pianos	678 Broadway & 29 King
1869-70	"	199 Wooster
1871-75	"	209 E. 19th
1876	piano manuf	"
1877-78	Successor & manuf of the Celebrated Bloomfield & Otis Pianos	"
1879	pianos	"
1880	not listed	
1881	pianos	27 Union Sq.

From 1868-77, Otis and *Edward Bloomfield* headed the piano- manufacturing firm *Bloomfield & Otis*. About 1877, Bloomfield apparently moved to the Midwest, leaving Otis to advertise himself as the "Successor and Manufacturer of the Bloomfield & Otis Piano-Forte." (***CmRg*** 1877:52) In the same advertisement, Otis also noted his pianos had been awarded a first premium (medal) at the 1850 American Institute Fair, and were exhibited at the 1869 Ohio State Fair, and the 1870 Georgia State Fair. In 1879, Otis' firm was listed as *D. Otis & Company*. See *Bloomfield & Otis*.

OTIS, D. & COMPANY

1879	pianos	209 E. 19th

See above *Dwight Otis*.

OTTES, Joseph

1863	musician	h. 141 Elizabeth
1864	drums	211 Grand
1865-66	"	209 Grand
1867	"	211 Grand
1868	drummer	h. 141 Elizabeth
1869	music	"
1870	not listed	
1871	music	h. 117 E. 4th
1873+	musician	"

Ottes continued to be listed as a musician through the 1870s. From 1864-68, Ottes and *William Sempf* led the drum-manufacturing firm *Sempf & Ottes*. See *Sempf & Ottes*.

OUVRIER, Peter

1846	pianos	r. 90 Leonard
1847-48	"	334 Greenwich
1849-51	"	83 Leonard
1852-53	not listed	
1854-59	pianos	539 Houston
1860-67	"	34 Houston
1868-74	"	33 W. 13th
1875-76	"	27 W. 13th
1877-78	"	6 E. 14th
1879-80	"	44 W. 14th

From 1846-67, Ouvrier and *Martin Martins* were the owners of the successful piano-manufacturing firm *Martins & Ouvrier*. After the end of their partnership, Ouvrier joined his sons Julius J., Louis, and Charles A., in the firm *Ouvrier & Sons*. Ouvrier left the trade in 1880, and his firm was reorganized by Louis and Charles A. as *Ouvrier Brothers* in 1882. See *Martins & Ouvrier*.

OUVRIER BROTHERS

1882-83	pianos	1 Union Sq.
1884-86	"	3 Union Sq.
1887-90+	"	21 E. 14th

See above *Peter Ouvrier*.

OUVRIER & SONS

1868-74	[pianos]	33 W. 13th
1875-76	"	27 W. 13th
1877-78	"	6 E. 14th
1879-81	"	44 W. 14th

See above *Peter Ouvrier*.

OVERIN, John

1829	mus instr mkr	Art n. Ave. 3

Overin was listed separately only in 1829. His name reappeared in 1831 as the partner of *William Ball* in the instrument-making firm *Ball & Overin*, located at 96 Walker Street. See *Ball & Overin*.

P

PAGE, John H.

1851	mus instr mkr	181 Broadway
		(*NYBD*)
1854	------	h. 114 Sixth Ave.

Page's 1851 address—which was listed only in the *NYBD* (p.218)—was the same as that of the flute maker *Alfred Badger*, for whom Page might have worked as a journeyman. During the early 1850s, a musician of this name was listed at 249 Fifth Avenue, but their relationship is not known.

PAILLARD, M.J. & COMPANY

M.J. Paillard & Company manufactured music boxes and mechanical instruments. The firm was established at Ste. Croix, Switzerland in 1814, and a New York branch was opened at 80 Nassau Street in 1850. See **Jones** (1971:126).

PALMER, H. & COMPANY

This piano-manufacturing firm was listed only in the *1885 AMD* (p.210). It was located at 368 Bleecker Street, but that address might have served only as their retail outlet for instruments manufactured outside the city.

PAPPENBERGER, Andrew

1876	pianos	r. 515 W. 42nd
1877	piano mkr	h. 532 W. 35th
1878	not listed	
1879	piano mkr	h. 514 W. 46th

From 1876-77, Pappenberger and the piano dealer Edward Taubald headed the piano-making firm *Pappenberger & Taubald*. Anton Pappenberger, a piano maker active from 1913-49 in Korneburg, Austria, might have been a relative. (**Pierce** 1965:184)

PAPPENBERGER & TAUBALD

1876-77	pianos	r. 515 W. 42nd

In 1877, this firm advertised that they manufactured "Upright & Grand 11 3/4 Octave Patent Pianos." (*CmRg* 1877:52) See above *Andrew Pappenberger.*

PARMELEE, Spencer

See *Driggs, Parmelee & Company*.

PATENT VIOLIN COMPANY

This violin-manufacturing firm, located at 15 Beaver Street, was listed only in the *1885 AMD* (p.210). The company was granted a patent on August 19, 1879 (No. 218,761), however, no further information about the firm is presently available.

PAULUS, William

See *Baack & Paulus*.

PEASE, Chauncey D.

1871-72	piano mkr	h. 550 W. 36th
1873-74	pianos	244 W. 27th
1875-76	"	265 W. 17th
1877-88	"	320 W. 43rd

Pease might have been the same person as the one working in the area of Cooperstown, New York c.1844, but this has not been confirmed. (See **Pierce** 1965). In 1873, Pease and Gustavus W. Kindstrom established the short-lived partnership *Pease & Kindstrom*; and in 1874, he founded *Pease & Company*, "Practical Piano Forte Manufacturers." (*CmRg* 1875:91) Pease retired c.1888, and his firm continued in operation for a short while under the direction of Harry D. and Samuel C. Pease—who were probably his sons. The elder Pease died sometime before 1892 when "Mary, widow of Chauncey D. Pease" was listed in the *NYCD*. **Spillane** (1890:252,368) mentioned Pease "among the other piano-making firms that had attained some note towards 1870 as makers of instruments for the masses." The maker was awarded Patent No. 344,677 on June 29, 1886 for an improved piano action-rail.

PEASE & COMPANY

1874	pianos	244 W. 27th
1875	"	" (*CmRg*)
1876	pianos	265 W. 17th
1877-88	"	320 W. 43rd

See above *Chauncey Pease.*

PEASE & KINDSTROM

1873	piano manuf	224 W. 27th

See above *Chauncey Pease*.

PECK, Leopold

See *Berh & Peck*; *Hardman, Peck & Company*.

PEEK, David C.

1820-21	cabinet mkr	36 Rhynders n. Broome
1822	see *Peek & Burns*	98 Leonard
1823	cabinet mkr	30 Rhynders
1824	"	Vandam n. Varick
1825	"	11 Leonard
1826	"	30 Rhynders
1827	"	60 Rhynders
1828	piano tuner	6 Willet c. Grand
1829	"	41 Delancey
1830-35	"	55 Delancey
1836	"	385 Broadway
1838	"	2 Barclay
1840-41	"	136 Amity
1842	"	307 Bowery
1843-45	piano warehouse	"
1846	piano tuner	"
1847	"	125 Amity
1848	piano mkr	142 Ave. 6
1849	piano tuner	106 Ave. 6
1853	"	15 W. 27th
1856	"	119 Greenwich

In 1822, this maker was a partner in the organ-building firm *Peek & Burns*. He then worked for many years as a cabinet maker and piano tuner before joining *William Brennison* in the piano-manufacturing concern *Peek & Brennison* in 1842. That same year, the partners were awarded a citation for their piano cases and a diploma for the second best piano exhibited at the American Institute Fair. (*American Institute Records*) Peek was probably the father of the piano maker *David T. Peek* listed below.

PEEK, David T.

1859-63	pianos	106 W. 29th
1868	"	152 W. 29th
1872	"	146 Bleecker
1876	"	23 Clinton Pl.
1880	"	213 W. 36th
1884	"	124 W. 35th
1888	"	216 W. 47th

Peek was probably the son of the organ and piano builder *David C. Peek* listed above. From 1859-68, Peek headed the piano-manufacturing firm *Peek & Company*; and in 1872 he joined his son in the firm *Peek & Son*. **Spillane** (1890:285) wrote that Peek & Son were "makers of the 'opera' piano [which] loomed up as a good popular-priced instrument, with a large circulation." Peek himself was a practical maker who had begun "in an unpretentious manner," and by 1890 held a "very respectable place" in the trade.

PEEK & BRENNISON

1842	pianos	197 Mercer

See above *David C. Peek*.

PEEK & BURNS

1822	organbuilders	98 Leonard

See above *David C. Peek*.

PEEK, DAVID T. & COMPANY

1859-63	pianos	106 W. 29th
1868	"	152 W. 29th

See above *David T. Peek*.

PEEK & SON

1872	pianos	146 Bleecker
1876	"	23 Clinton
1880	"	213 W. 36th
1884	"	124 W. 35th
1888	"	216 W. 47th

See above *David T. Peek*.

PELOUBET, Louis Alexander (Joseph Alexander)

1803	mus instr mkr & repairs	253 Broadway
1805	mus instr mkr	190 William
1812	"	222 Greenwich

Peloubet was born in France on March 10, 1764. He fought with the King's army during the French Revolution, and was later tried and sentenced to death by a revolutionary tribunal. With the help of friends, he escaped to Germany where he learned to make wind instruments, and in October 1803, he immigrated to New York. In the city, he joined a man named *Monniot*, who was very likely another French refugee, to form the partnership *Monniot & Peloubet*, instrument makers at 253 Broadway.

In 1805, as Joseph Peloubet, he was again listed in the *NYCD*. He was married in the city in 1805, but his son, *Louis Michel Francois (Chabrier) Peloubet,* see below, was born the following February in Philadelphia. Peloubet worked as an instrument maker for the rest of his career, moving often. He is known to have worked in Athens, Albany, and Hudson, New York before returning to the city in 1812. His activities after 1812 await documentation, but he apparently died c.1833, perhaps at Bloomfield, New Jersey. (See **Kaufman** 1979:15-16) See *Monniot & Peloubet*.

PELOUBET, Louis Michel Francois (Chabrier)

| 1829-31 | mus instr mkr | 150 Walker |
| 1832-36 | " | 204 Hester |

The son of *Louis Alexander Peloubet,* see above, from whom he probably learned the craft of instrument making, Louis Michel Francois, or Chabrier Peloubet, as he was better known, was born on February 22, 1806 in Philadelphia. He specialized in the making of flutes, and his instruments were exhibited at the New York Mechanics' Fairs of 1844, 1847, and 1850. In 1847, his entry was awarded a silver medal. (PC:Eliason)

In 1836, Peloubet moved his workshop to Bloomfield, New Jersey, where, in the late 1840s, he began to manufacture medoleons and parlor organs. During the 1850s, he was associated with Jeremiah M. Pelton, a city-based instrument dealer whose shop at 841 Broadway served as a retail outlet for Peloubet's instruments. Peloubet died at Bloomfield on October 30, 1885. See **Kaufman** (1979:15-16); *New Grove* (1984:3:31).

PELTON, Daniel and Philip

On October 5, 1775, drum makers Daniel and Philip Pelton ran the following advertisement in the *New-York Journal: or General Advertiser:* "Drums Made and sold by Phillip [sic] Pelton, upper end of Queen-street, and by Daniel Pelton, in Chappel street, now called Beekman Street, equal to any that have been imported for sound or beauty. As said Persons have great variety on hand any gentleman may be served at the shortest notice, and on the most reasonable terms. The purchaser may depend upon having their Drums tun'd to sound well."

It is not known how the Peltons were related; they were probably brothers or father and son. Philip's name appeared on several legal documents.

On October 28, 1765, he witnessed the signing of John Walcott's will. Walcott was a mariner on the British sloop Gaspee, and interestingly, the instrument maker *Samuel Dodge* was another witness to the signing. (**NYHS** *Abstracts of Unrecorded Wills* 1902:11:188) On December 5, 1774, the intestate will of Thomas Montanye from the West Indies was granted to Philip Pelton. (**NYHS** *Abstracts of Wills* 1899:8:373) Daniel Pelton's name appeared on the muster role of the New York City Militia on April 25, 1775. (**NYHS** *Revolutionary Muster Rolls* 1915: 2:502)

PEMBERTON, Jacob

1835	piano mkr	142 Elm
1836	"	16 Munroe
1837	"	61 Oliver
1838	not listed	
1839	pianoforte mkr	28 Cherry
1840-41	not listed	
1842	Ann widow of Jacob	66 Roosevelt

A piano maker of the same name was active at 38 Fleet Street, Dublin from 1793-97, and the same man was probably also a member of the piano-making firm Pemberton & McDonnell at 26 Fleet Street, Dublin from 1789-92. (**Teahan** 1963:31) Nothing more is presently known about the New York maker, and his relationship to the Dublin Pemberton has not been established.

PENZEL, Gustav L.

1882-84	mus instrs	216 Sixth
1885-86	"	354 Bowery
1887-90+	"	368 Bowery

More prominent after 1890, Penzel and his brother, Louis G., were importers and later manufacturers of woodwind instruments. Their firm, *G.L. Penzel & Brother,* was listed as flute dealers in the *1885 AMD* (p.211). **Langwill** (1980:134) claims the firm was founded in 1880 and lists oboes and clarinets made by the brothers.

PENZEL, G.L. & BROTHER

1883-84	mus instrs	216 Sixth
1885-86	"	354 Bowery
1887-90+	"	368 Bowery

See above *Gustav L. Penzel.*

PERRIN, David

1834-35	piano mkr	44 Norfolk

Although listed for only two years in the *NYCD*, Perrin apparently continued to work for many years thereafter in the piano trade. The lowest key of a *Nunns & Clark* piano, built in 1853 and now in the collection of the Metropolitan Museum of Art (*Catalog* No. 06.1312), bears the signature D. Perrin.

PERRY, Richard

1809	piano mkr	42 Barclay
1810-11	"	50 Harman

A Perry square piano "profusely inlaid with maple lines" and made by a "New Patent" method is now in the collection of the Smithsonian Institution (*Catalog* No. 303,521). Perry might have been related to several piano makers of the same surname who worked in Dublin and Belfast during this period (**Teahan** 1963:31), but nothing else is presently known about his activities.

PETERSON, Garret

1795	blacksmith	124 Chatham
1796-97	"	Bowery-lane
1800-06	smith	126 Chatham
1807-26	not listed	
1827	cabinet mkr	155 h. 203 Bowery
1828	"	44 Catherine
1829	piano mkr	Sixth n. Ave. 3
1830	not listed	
1831	piano mkr	299 Mulberry
1832	Amelia widow of Garret	240 Elizabeth

There were two Garret Petersons: a Jr. and a Sr., both of whom worked as blacksmiths during the early 1800s. It was probably the younger man who became a cabinet and later a piano maker. His wife, Amelia, was first listed as a widow in 1832.

PETHICK, John

1832-35	piano mkr	234 Bleecker
1836	"	559 Houston
1837-41	"	204 Bleecker
1842	"	146 Waverley
1843-45	piano manuf	4 Cottage Pl.
1846	not listed	
1847	pianos	204 Bleecker
1848	not listed	
1849-51	pianos	Cottage Pl. c. Bleecker h.17 Cottage Pl.
1852	Julia widow of John	

From 1832-39, Pethick and *Edward Mundy* headed the piano-manufacturing firm *Mundy & Pethick*. In 1840, Pethick joined John Hingston in *Pethick & Hingston*, and after its dissolution in 1841, Pethick worked alone until his death c.1851. On February 12, 1836, he was granted a patent for "improvements in the grand action invented by Pape, of Paris." (**Spillane** 1890:189) Pethick was probably related to *William Pethick*, see below, but their relationship awaits documentation.

PETHICK, William

1843-44	piano mkr	181 Houston
1845-47	"	h. 179 Stanton

Pethick was probably related to the piano maker *John Pethick*, see above, and certainly related to the piano dealer Thomas Pethick, who was active from 1842-57, and from 1852-57 headed the dealership Pethick & Girkin. Nothing further is presently known about William Pethick.

PETHICK & HINGSTON

1840-41	pianos	204 Bleecker c. Hancock

See above *John Pethick*.

PFAFF BROTHERS , Christian C. & Frederick (Christian F.)

1858-59	mus instr mkrs	44 Stanton	
1860-65	mus instrs	"	
1866-90+	"	"	
	Christian C.	148 E. Houston	
	Frederick	135 Third	

The Pfaffs were makers of brass instruments (*1861 AMD* p.90), and were probably related to the Bavarian wind-instrument-making family of the same name. After 1866, the brothers were listed at separate addresses. Their relation to the flute maker John Pfaff, who worked in Philadelphia during the same period, is not known. See **Langwill** (1980:136).

PHYFE, Isaac M.

1822	pianoforte mkr	100 Chapel
1823-28	not listed	
1829	piano mkr	215 Mulberry
1830-31	paper hanger	Tryon-row c. Chatham

Phyfe was either the brother or the nephew of the famous furniture maker Duncan Phyfe. He was involved in the piano trade for only a short while, and later worked as an upholsterer until the 1870s. Phyfe died on October 22, 1881 in Brooklyn at the age of 86. (**MacBean**:ms)

PIKE

See *Cohen & Pike*.

PIRSSON, Alexander T.

1822	pianoforte mkr	26 Church
1823-24	not listed	
1825	teacher [of] piano	"
1826	"	5th n. Ave. 6
1827-28	"	585 Broome
1829	music teacher	193 Hudson
1830-31	"	329 Hudson
1832	not listed	
1833-35	organist	146 Wooster
1836-43	not listed	
1844	prof of music	14 Bedford

Pirsson was the brother of the piano maker *James Pirsson*, see below, and might have been related to the music engraver William Pirsson, who had been active in the city from 1799-1812. (See **Wolfe** 1980:57.) Alexander Pirsson was more active as a musician than as an instrument maker, although from 1836-43, he unsuccessfully tried to establish a piano-manufacturing firm at 204 Broad Street, Newark, New Jersey. (**Kaufman** 1976:15) There is a possibility that this maker and *Talbot Pirsson*, see below, were the same person, given Alexander's middle initial was "T" and their listings do not overlap.

PIRSSON, James

1829	pianoforte mkr	193 1/2 Hudson
1830	"	Hudson n. Leroy
1831	"	214 Broadway
1832-33	not listed	
1834	piano tuner	116 MacDougal
1835	"	132 Perry
1836	"	124 Perry
1837	"	167 Broadway
1838-39	"	192 Amos
1840	piano manuf	Hammond
1841-42	"	85 Hammond
1843-44	piano mkr	104 Elm
1845-47	"	88 Walker
1848-53	"	87 Leonard
1854	pianos	480 Broadway
1855-56	"	748 Broadway

James Pirsson was a successful and innovative piano maker. In 1831, he headed *James Pirsson & Company*, but otherwise appears to have worked alone. **Spillane** (1890:195) wrote of a piano shown at the 1851 London Crystal Palace Exhibition by the firm Heers & Pirsson, but no record of this partnership has been found. Pirsson did receive gold medals for pianos he exhibited at the American Institute Fairs in 1839 and 1847. (*American Institute Records*) The maker was awarded several patents (**Spillane** 1890:198-99), and was also active as a double-bassist. (See *Bio-Bibliographical Index* 1956:297). An early member of the first New York Philharmonic, Pirsson's house at 80 Leonard Street was known as a Mecca for chamber music ensembles during the late 1840s. (See **Lawrence** 1988:608-09.)

One of Pirsson's innovations was the "American Double Grand Piano Forte" which was introduced on May 22, 1850, at the Apollo Rooms. The instrument, which could accommodate seven pianists, was described in *The Albion* as "not so large as two grands . . . its appearance is by no mean cumbersome or unwieldy . . . [and it] would provide a magnificent ornament in the drawing rooms of any of the large mansions of the upper ten." (**Minor** 1947:25) Pirsson was the brother of *Alexander Pirsson*, see above, and although last listed in the 1856 *NYCD*, a musician and instrument dealer of the same name, who was possible the same man, was reported in Wilmington, North Carolina in 1861. (*1861 AMD* p.177)

PIRSSON, Talbot

1845	lawyer	89 Elm
1848	pianos	87 Leonard
1852-54	"	490 Hudson
1856	"	480 Broadway
1857+	lawyer/merchant	"

Possibly the same person as *Alexander T. Pirsson*, see above, Talbot was apparently more active as a dealer than as a maker. He is best remembered for his partnership with the piano maker *Peter Provost*; their firm, *Provost & Pirsson* was active from 1852-54. Another member of the family, Joseph P. Pirsson, was a lawyer, which might explain Talbot's somewhat unusual combination of trades in 1857. See *Provost & Pirsson*.

PIRSSON, JAMES & COMPANY

1831	piano mkrs	214 Broadway

See above *James Pirsson*.

PITT, John B.

1843-49	harp mkr	75 Sands, Brooklyn
1850	harps	295 Broadway, h. 75 Sands

No further information is presently known about this maker, however, in 1848, he was probably associated with the harp-making firm *Lewis Pitt & Company*, see below.

PITT, LEWIS & COMPANY

| 1848 | harps | 15 Rose |

Listed as "Manufacturers of double action harps, repairing, strings, &c." in the 1848 *NYBD* (p.176). The "& Company" might have been the harp maker *John B. Pitt*, listed above.

PLESLIN, William

1827	cabinet mkr	92 Mott
1828	"	90 Reed
1829	"	375 Greenwich
1830-33	"	57 Bedford
1834-37	piano mkr	"
1838	not listed	
1839	piano mkr	"
1840-42	"	144 Barrow
1843-51	pianos	"
1852-53	piano mkr	"
1854-55	pianos	"
1856-58	"	r. 72 Barrow
1859	"	56 Troy
1860	"	72 Barrow
1861	"	296 W. 12th
1863-64	"	71 Barrow
1865	Eliza widow William	h. 296 W. 12th

Pleshin was listed as a piano manufacturer in the *1861 AMD* (p.171) at 56 Troy Street. His was apparently a small operation, and he worked without partners until his death, c.1864.

PLOWMAN, John

| 1834-35 | piano mkr | Third n. Ave. 2 |

In 1840, Plowman was active as a piano maker in Philadelphia (**Catalano** 1979:124), but nothing further is presently known about his activities in New York.

POLLMANN, Henry August

1872-78	mus instrs	31 Courtlandt
1879-84	"	58 Maiden La.
1885	merchant	"
1886-89	mus instrs	"
1890+	importer	70 Franklin

Pollman(n) was an importer and dealer of wind instruments. From 1873-78, with partner *Gotfried Robert Martin*, he headed the importing firm *Martin, Pollmann & Company*. After leaving Martin, he worked alone through 1905, advertising at one point this his firm was the sole U.S. representative of Rudall, Carte & Company of London. (See **Krivin** 1961:250.) Many instruments bearing his stencil are extant. See *Martin, Pollmann & Company*.

POND, Sylvanus Billings

1833	------	121 Hester c. Forsyth
1834-35	mus instr mkr	102 Henry
1836	"	36 Vandwater
1837-41	"	1 Franklin Sq.
1842-46	music	"
1847-49	"	" & 238 Broadway

Pond was born at Milford, Worcester County, Massachusetts on April 5, 1792. He moved to Albany, New York in 1819, and opened a music and military goods store there in 1825. From 1828-32, Pond was a member of the Albany instrument firm Meachan & Pond. During this period, Pond also headed the Albany Sacred Music Society, and in 1829, he unsuccessfully ran for sheriff of Albany County on the Anti-Masonic ticket. (PC:Eliason)

In 1832, Pond was invited to take charge of the piano department of *Firth & Hall* (**Jones** 1971:139), and in 1833 the new partnership *Firth, Hall & Pond* was listed. This association was a long and extremely successful one. When *William Hall* withdrew in 1847, the two remaining partners and their sons, *Thaddeus Firth* and *William Pond*, reorganized as *Firth, Pond & Company*. This firm continued in operation until 1863, although the elder Pond apparently retired c.1850. After the dissolution of Firth, Pond & Company in 1863, William Pond and his brother-in-law, John Mayell, established a music publishing house, Pond & Company, which remained in business into the present century.

Sylvanus Pond was also active as a musician, conductor and the arranger-composer of Sunday School hymns. He served as the director of the New York Academy of Music and the New York Sacred Music Society. There is no evidence that he was ever a practical musical instrument maker. Pond died on March 12, 1871 at his home in Brooklyn. For further information, see **Baker** (1958); **Jones** (1971:138-39). See *Firth, Hall & Pond*; *Firth, Pond & Company*.

POND, William A.

The son of *Sylvanus B. Pond*, see above, William Pond joined the firm *Firth, Pond & Company* in 1848 and remained with that firm until 1863 when it was disbanded. In 1864, he established his own firm, Pond & Company, which specialized in music publishing and instrument dealing, and remained in business at 547 Broadway and 39 Union Square until the early 20th century. William Pond died in December 1885 at New York. See *Firth, Pond & Company*.

POYNER, Joseph

1828-29	carpenter	16 Doyer
1830-33	not listed	
1834	piano mkr	Ave. 3 n. 24th

No further information is presently known about this maker.

PRIEST, John C.F.

Priest was listed as a "musical instrument manufacturer" at 96 Fulton Street only in the *1885 AMD* (p.211). A musician of the same name was listed at 292 Elizabeth Street in the *NYCD*, but their relationship is not known.

PRODDOW, Robert

See *Simpson & Proddow*.

PROVOST/PROVOOST, Peter

1833	piano mkr	7 York
1834	"	15 Commerce
1835	"	9 Commerce
1836-37	"	Vestry h. 9 Commerce
1838	"	32 Vestry
1839-42	"	15 Desbrosses
1843-45	"	51 Morton
1846-51	"	490 Hudson
1852-57	pianos	"

Provost, who used both spellings of his surname, was said to have "carried on a modest business for a number of years, when he drifted into being a journeyman." (**Spillane** 1890:162) Despite Spillane's contention, the *NYCD* listings indicate that Provost remained active as a master. In 1837, he was awarded a silver medal for the second best square pianoforte exhibited at that year's American Institute Fair. (*American Institute Records*) In 1846, he advertised as the "inventor & maker of the improved iron frame [piano] attachment." (*NYBD* 1846:170)

From 1852-54, with partner *Talbot Pirsson*, Provost headed the piano-manufacturing firm *Provost & Pirsson*. According to the *1855 New York Census*, their firm owned $6,000 of real capital; $500 worth of tools; and $2,000 worth of lumber. They employed 15 workmen at average monthly wages of $40, and that year produced $8,000 worth of pianos.

Provost seems to have been associated with the piano maker *John Randell*, who took over the former's shop at 15 Commerce Street in 1835. Randell's relative, Culver Randle, was married to a Sophia Provost, who was probably the link between the two men.

PROVOST & PIRSSON

1852-54	pianos	490 Hudson

See above *Peter Provost*.

PUGH, Thomas

Possibly the only bell founder to work in New York during the colonial period, Pugh was born in 1731 at Birmingham, England. On May 2, 1768, Pugh ran the following advertisement in *The New-York Gazette, or Weekly Post-Boy*: "Thomas Pugh, Brass and Bell-Founder, from Birmingham, at his Shop in Maiden-lane, N.Y. Makes & casts all sorts of Work in the Brass founding Way; also makes & sells all Sorts of soft and hard white Metal; likewise Pinchbeck, and Bath Metal, in all its kinds; He will make House Bells, Clock Bells, or Chiming Bells, for any that shall please to employ him, at the most reasonable Rates."

Pugh manufactured approximately 598 bells, many stamped with the inscription "Struggle for Freedom & Happiness." His shop was located "in a very small room" on Maiden Lane and most of casting work was done in his yard. He used an alloy that was 22% tin and 78% copper. In an undated notice, Pugh promised his customers that: "1. Each bell, whether sold singly or part of a set, is subject to trial before acceptance. This trial can either be at our foundry, before it is released for use or not. 2. Each bell is guaranteed against fracture or failure of tone for a period of fifteen years. 3. All mechanical parts are guaranteed as to satisfactory operation and against defects in workmanship or materials for a period of one year. 4. Inscriptions in tablet form are placed on bells without extra charge." (**Zankovich** 1956:295-97)

In addition to founding bells, Pugh also worked as an engraver and silversmith. He closed his New York shop in 1792, and in 1794, Pugh returned to England where he remained until his death in 1805. For further information, see **Zankovich** (1956).

PULLIS, Conrad

1858	mus instr mkr	129 Ave. 3 (*NYBD*)

No further information about Pullis is presently known.

R

RANDEL, Culver

    See *Culver Randle*.

RANDELL, John

1835	piano mkr	15 Commerce
1836-37	"	143 Delancey
1838	"	5 Roosevelt
1839	"	52 Harrison
1840-41	not listed	
1842-43	piano mkr	7 Barclay
1844	"	15 Commerce
1845-46	"	166 Madison
1847	"	72 Monroe

Probably the half-brother of *Culver Randle*, see below, John was born in Florida, New York in 1813 and lived until 1892. He might have been the "Randal" mentioned by **Spillane** (1890:161-62) as a partner of *John Tallman* on White Street in 1838, however, confirmation of this partnership is yet to be found. Randell was also associated with the piano maker *Peter Provost*, whose shop preceded Randell's at 15 Commerce Street in 1834. Recent correspondence with the maker's descendant Gary Randall indicates that John's relative, Culver, was married to a Sophia Provost, who was almost certainly related to the piano maker Provost. (PC:Gary Randall)

RANDLE/RANDEL, Adonijah

1832-33	piano mkr	21 Cornelia
1834-35	"	120 Barrow & 10 Grove
1836	"	Burton
1837-41	not listed	
1842	piano mkr	9 Morton
1843	not listed	
1844	matches	161 Bleecker
1845	"	48 Gold
1846	not listed	
1847	piano mkr	267 E. 25th

A brother of *Culver Randle* and cousin of *Jesse Randle*, see below, Adonijah was born in 1808 at Florida, New York. After working in the city, he returned to Florida and later moved to Troy, New York, where he died in 1862. (PC:Gary Randall)

RANDLE/RANDEL, Culver

1828-32	piano mkr	112 Amos
1833	"	82 Grove
1834	"	342 Bleecker
1835	"	111 Amos
1836	"	103 Amos
1837	"	71 Amos
1838	"	129 Amos

Randle was born in 1806 at Florida, New York, (now part of the town of Warwick), and was apprenticed to a New York piano maker. After heading his own piano-making shop in the city for several years, Randle returned to his hometown when the newly constructed Erie Rail Road made transportation of products from the Goshen area easier. About 1841, at Randelville—near Florida—he established a saw mill and instrument shop to produce pianos, piano cases, and music boxes. When Culver died on September 1, 1888 at the age of 82, his piano-making tools and half his estate were willed to his son, piano maker Jesse Randel.

Despite a variation of spellings, Randle was related to the other piano makers of that name who were active in New York. *Adonijah* was Culver's brother, and son of the piano maker *Jesse Randle*, who is probably the one listed below. *John Randell* was apparently Culver's half-brother. In addition, Culver married Sophia Provost, who was almost certainly a sister of the piano maker *Peter Provost*, and members of the Randle family had business dealing with Provost; John apparently taking over Peter's lease on 15 Commerce Street in 1834. [The author is indebted to Gary Randall of Goshen, New York for providing information about his ancestors.]

RANDLE/RANDEL, Jesse

1828-29	piano mkr	112 h. 86 Amos

Probably the father of *Adonijah*, *Culver*, and possibly the *John Randle* listed above. There is some chance that Jesse was the son of another piano maker named Jesse Randle, and thus a brother and/or half-brother to the other Randles. See *Culver Randle*.

RASENBERGER, Carl/Charles

1860	music	h. 312 E. 13th
1861	accordeons	319 E. 12th
1863	musician	h. 224 E. 11th
1864	accordeons	h. 165 Ave. A
1865-68	instrs	"
1869	mus instrs	"
1870	harmonicas	h. 183 Ave. A
1871	mus instrs	"
1872	accordeons	"
1873-83	mus instrs	19 Ave. A
1884-85	"	3 Ave. A
1886-87	"	108 Chambers
1888-89	importer	"

Rasenberger, or as it occasionally appeared Rosenberger, was a "teacher of accordeons," (*1861 AMD* p.116), who became involved with importing, selling and manufacturing the instrument. In 1876, Rasenberger and his son, Henry, founded *Rasenberger & Son*: "Manufacturers & Importers of Accordeons, and teachers in the Art of Playing on Accordeons and Guitars." (*CmRg* 1876:73) After Rasenberger's retirement, c.1889, the firm was continued by his son.

RASENBERGER & SON

1876-83	mus instrs	19 Ave. A
1884-85	"	3 Ave. A
1886-87	"	108 Chambers & 3 Ave. A
1888-90+	importers	"

See above *Carl Rasenberger*.

RATZ, Godthold/Gotthold

1842	piano tuner	542 Pearl
1843-45	instr mkr	564 Pearl
1846-47	piano tuner	37 Howard
1848	"	88 Grand
1849-53	"	86 Grand
1854	piano mkr	"
1855-56	manuf	"
1857	tool mkr	"

Primarily a piano tuner and repairer, in 1857 Ratz advertised that he "Tunes, lets, and sells pianos & melodeons at Philadelphia Hall, 147 Bowery." (*CmRg* 1857:311)

RAVEN, Richard M.

1832	piano mkr	189 Mulberry
1833-37	"	68 Sullivan
1838-39	"	240 Elizabeth
1840	"	---- Centre
1841-42	"	164 Centre
1843-47	pianos	"
1848-49	"	162 Centre
1850-56	"	160 Centre
1857	"	135 Grand
1858-59	"	" & 149 Baxter
1860-66	"	135 Grand
1867-70	"	644 Broadway
1871-72	"	149 Baxter
1873	Mary widow of Richard	46 W. 28th

Raven, for many years a respected member of the New York trade, began his career as an apprentice with *William Geib & Company*. In 1841, he joined piano maker *George Bacon* in the successful firm *Bacon & Raven*. After Bacon's death in 1855, *Francis Bacon*, the founder's son, was admitted into partnership, and in 1856, the firm's title was changed to *Raven, Bacon & Company* — probably to reflect Raven's role as the senior partner. The concern's title was changed again in 1862, and as *Raven & Bacon* it continued in operation through 1872.

According to the *1855 New York Census*, Raven & Bacon owned $50,000 of real capital; and it had $17,500 worth of raw materials in stock. The firm employed 350 (?) workmen at annual wages of $28,000, who that year manufactured $15,000 worth of pianos.

Raven died c.1872, and the firm was taken over by Thomas Raven, who had previously shared several work addresses with Richard Raven, and who might have been the "& Company" in the earlier concern. Under Thomas' leadership, from 1873-79, the title of the firm became *Raven & Company*; and when he left in 1878, the name of firm was changed again, this time to *Raven Piano Works*. See *Bacon & Raven*.

RAVEN & BACON

1862-66	pianos	135 & 149 Baxter
1867-69	"	646 Broadway & 149 Baxter
1870-72	"	149 & 151 Baxter

See above *Richard Raven*.

RAVEN, BACON & COMPANY

1856	pianos	160-64 Centre
1857-61	"	"
	manufactory	149 Baxter

See above *Richard Raven*.

RAVEN & COMPANY

1873	pianos	118 W. 14th
1874-75	"	" & 145 Baxter
1876-77	"	145 Mulberry & 13 E. 16th

See above *Richard Raven*.

RAVEN PIANO WORKS

1878-84	late *Raven & Bacon*	13 E. 16th
1885-86	"	20 E. 23rd

See above *Richard Raven*.

RAY, J.S.

Ray, of 100 Second Avenue, was awarded a diploma "for the 2nd best banjo" exhibited at the 1848 American Institute Fair. (*American Institute Records*) His name never appeared in the *NYCD*s of this period.

REICHARD, Henry

1838	piano tuner	422 Broadway
1839	"	106 Wooster
1840	"	40 1/2 Chatham
1841	"	165 Reade
1842	pianoforte mkr	100 h. 251 Broadway
1843	"	251 Broadway
1844-45	"	251 E. Broadway
1846	pianos	"
1847	piano mkr	r. E. 25th bet. Ave. 1 & 2

The German-born Reichard was a small-scale piano manufacturer. An innovative piano of his construction, which consisted of a two-octave pedal keyboard, similar to that of an organ, appended to a regular piano, was played by pianists Timm and Alpers on an April 20, 1843 concert reviewed by Henry C. Watson. (See **Lawrence** 1988:183.) In 1843, he joined piano maker *John Ruck* in the firm *Reichard & Ruck*. In 1844, again on his own, he was awarded a silver medal "for a beautifully finished Piano Forte" exhibited at the American Institute Fair. (*American Institute Records*)

REICHARD & RUCK

1843	pianofortes	251 E. Broadway

See above *Henry Reichard*.

REID, William T.

1844	piano mkr	40 W. 14th
1845	not listed	
1846-49	piano mkr	"
1850-51	pianos	44 W. 14th
1852-53	"	" & 548 Broadway
1854	"	385 Bowery
1855-58	"	155 & 157 Centre

Possibly the same person as the music dealer William Reid who was listed at 515 Pearl Street in 1840. **Spillane** (1890:197) mistakenly referred to this maker as "W. T. Reed."

REINHARD, Frederick

See *Hartmann Brothers & Reinhard*.

REMY, John

1841	instrs	42 Dey
1842-43	mus instrs	45 Dey
1844-45	"	165 William
1846	violin mkr	" (*NYBD*)

In 1844, Remy advertised as a maker of guitars and violins at 183 William Street. (*NYBD* 1844:184-85) He might have been a member of the Remy family of violin makers, who were active in London and Paris during the late-eighteenth and early-nineteenth centuries. (See **Henley** 1960:3:197-98.)

REWALD, Justus H.

1872	music	h. r. 36 First
1873	mus instr mkr	"
1874-79	mus instrs	133 Bowery h. 96 Allen
1880-81	mus instr mkr	h. 88 Chrystie
1882	not listed	
1883-86	mus instrs	88 Chrystie
1887-90+	"	83 Chrystie

In 1876, Rewald advertised as a "Manufacturer & Repairer of Musical Instruments, Musical Boxes & Accordeons a Specialty." (*CmRg* 1876:73) In the *1885 AMD* (p.212), Rewald was also listed as a "Musical Instrument Manufacturer." In 1874, a "H'y Rewald," musical instrument dealer, was listed as sharing Justus' shop at 133 Bowery. (*NYCD*)

RICHARDSON, Thomas

1826	pianoforte	Reason n. Herring

In 1826, the future piano maker *Thaddeus Munroe* was listed at the same address, but the connection between these two as well as further information about Richardson awaits documentation.

RICHMOND

See *Billings & Richmond*.

RICHTER, Adam

1860-62	banjos	h. 196 Forsyth
1863	"	h. 24 Clinton
1864	musician	h. r. 48 Clinton
1865	banjo mkr	"
1866	cabinet mkr	"
1867	"	25 Clinton
1868	"	h. 543 Fifth Ave.
1869	laborer	"
1870-71	toys	143 E. 14th

Described as a "Manufacturer of Banjos & Tambourines" at 194 Forsyth Street in the *1861 AMD* (p.90), Richter was probably the same person as the "A. Richter" of New York who was awarded patent No.408,852 on August 13, 1889, for an improved piano action. (**Spillane** 1890:369)

RIEDEL, Francis

See *Kohnle & Riedel*.

RILEY, Edward, Sr.

1806	music teacher	13 Broad
1807	"	3 Courtlandt
1808	"	28 Dey
1809-10	"	31 Dey
1811	music publ & engraver	17 Chatham
1812	music store	23 Chatham
1813-18	music engraver & publ	"
1819	" & "	29 Chatham
1820-31	music publ/mus instr mkr	"
1831	Elizabeth wid of Edward, mus store	"

Riley was born in England in 1769 and began his career as a music publisher and engraver in London c.1795. He immigrated to New York c.1805 where he continued publishing music, taught music lessons, performed as a flutist and singer, and sold musical instruments. By 1820, he had become one of the city's foremost music publishers. (See **Wolfe** 1980:55.)

From 1812-20, Riley and the copper-plate printer Thomas Adams headed the publishing firm *Riley & Adams*. It is unlikely that Riley actually made instruments himself, but many wind instruments bear his stamp. Riley's contributions to the trade include his three sons, *Edward C.*, *Frederick*, and *Henry*, who were active as music dealers and instrument makers; and his son-in-laws *John Firth* and *William Hall*. After Riley's death in 1829, his widow and sons continued to operate the family business.

RILEY, Edward C.

From 1823-71, Edward C. was listed as a professor of music at various addresses. The son of *Edward Riley, Sr.*, see above, he was involved in music publishing, and from 1836-42, he headed the publishing concern Edward C. Riley & Company at 29 Chatham Street. There is no evidence that Edward C. actually made instruments, but he apparently patented improved flute and clarinet keys. (See *Franklin Institute Journal*, June 1835, p.406.)

RILEY, Frederick

1843	music	29 Chatham
1844-50	"	297 1/2 Broadway
1851	instrs	52 Ann

The son of *Edward Riley, Sr.*, see above, Frederick was probably involved in instrument making from 1845-47, when he headed *Frederick Riley & Company*. In the 1845 **NYCD**, his firm advertised as "Manufacturers of Musical Instruments ... Military Bands supplied with setts [sic] of Instruments at reasonable prices. Brass & Side Drums of extra size made to order. N.B. Riley & Co. are not merely vendors of Instruments and Music, but are practical manufacturers."

RILEY, Henry

1826	mus instr mkr	Renwick n. Canal
1827-28	"	217 Broome
1829	"	3 Allen
1830	"	66 Norfolk
1831	"	64 Eldridge
1832-34	"	29 Chatham & 117 Wooster
1835	not listed	
1836	mus instrs	94 Laurens
1837	not listed	
1838	mus instrs	12 Bedford
1839	"	10 Clarkson
1840-42	"	29 Chatham

The son of *Edward Riley, Sr.*, see above, Henry was probably more active than his brothers in the making of instruments. He was not listed in New York after 1842, however, **Langwill** (1980:147) lists the firm "Henry Riley & Sons" as active in Birmingham, England from 1851-90. It is not confirmed that the English firm was headed by the New Yorker, but it is conceivable that Henry might have returned to his family's homeland.

RILEY & ADAMS

1812	music store	23 Chatham
1813-14	coppersplate printers	"
1815	not listed	
1816-20	copperplate printer & engravers	"

See above *Edward Riley, Sr.*

RILEY, FREDERICK & COMPANY

1845-47	music publ & mus instr manuf	297 Broadway
1848-50	music & store	"

See above *Frederick Riley.*

ROBB, Alickam T./Elickim T.

1822	------	Chapel
1825	------	154 Fulton
1828	------	h. 641 Greenwich
1829	piano mkr	235 Henry
1830	"	643 Greenwich
1831-36	mahogany-yard	22 Canal

From 1822-28, Robb and *Edward Mundy* headed the piano-manufacturing firm *Robb & Mundy*. A one-pedal piano made by this firm is now in the collection of the Smithsonian Institution (*Catalog* No. 315,695). After the firm was dissolved in 1828, the partners remained next-door neighbors for several years. Robb might have been the same person as the piano dealer, instrument maker and tuner E.T. Robb who had worked in Richmond, Virginia c.1820. (**Stoutamire** 1972:98)

ROBB & MUNDY

1822-24	music store	154 Fulton
1825-27	piano manuf	"
1828	pianoforte mkrs	641 Greenwich

See above *Alickam Robb.*

ROBERTSON, John C.

1831-35	piano pin maker	10 Rivington
1836-38	piano mkr	"

From 1831-32, Robertson was also a member of the iron-railing-manufacturing firm Robertson & Combes at 10 Rivington Street. His activities past 1838 are not traceable.

ROBERTSON, William

1853	see below	181 Broadway
1854	piano mkr	h. 334 Bleecker
1855	"	h. 40 Eighth Ave.
1856	"	h. 108 Perry
1857-58	"	383 Eighth
1860	not listed	
1861	pianos	h. 815 Greenwich
1862-70s	pianos/key mkr	h. 60 Hammond

At the 1853 New York Crystal Palace, Robertson displayed a "keyed stop violin, a new invention, greatly facilitating the process of playing." The *Official Catalogue* (1853:94) listed the maker's address as 181 Broadway, which was also the workshop of the noted flute maker *Alfred Badger*, and it is possible that the piano maker worked in the latter's shop. He continued to work as a journeyman into the 1870s.

ROBINSON, William, Jr.

See *Carter & Robinson.*

ROGERS, Able

1840	piano mkr	16 Mercer
1841	"	402 Broome
1842-43	"	1 Marion
1844-48	"	152 Fulton
1849-52	"	148 Fulton
1853	"	" & 9 Mercer
1854-56	"	9 Mercer
1857-58	"	"
1859	see *Rogers, Davis & Co.*	94 E. 31st
1860	pianos	334 Fourth

In 1841, *A. Rogers & Company* was awarded a diploma for the third best piano exhibited at that year's American Institute Fair. (*American Institute Records*) From 1844-46, Rogers joined *Robert Glenn* in the piano-manufacturing firm *Glenn, Rogers & Company*; and then, from 1846-48, with partner *William Bennett*, he headed the firm *Bennett, Rogers & Company.*

After leaving Bennett, Rogers and the wood-worker and billiard-table maker Daniel D. Winant founded the firm *Rogers & Winant*. According to the *1855 New York Census*, their company owned $1,000 worth of tools, and had in stock 800 feet of lumber worth $300, 52 sets of piano hardware worth $520, and 12 gallons of varnish worth $36. The firm employed 6 men, who earned total monthly wages of $216, and that year it produced 50 pianos worth $11,250.

Rogers & Winant continued in operation through 1857; in 1859, Rogers entered into the partnership *Rogers, Davis & Company* which specialized in the manufacturing of piano cases. See *Glenn, Rogers & Company*; *Bennett, Rogers & Company*.

ROGERS, Charles H.

1856	action mkr	212 Sixth
1857-60	"	Foot E. 24th
1861	case manuf	"
1864	pianos	"
1865	piano mkr	h. 129 E. 28th
1866	not listed	
1867	piano mkr	h. 228 E. 35th
1868-71	not listed/not traceable	
1872-73	pianos	"
1874-78	piano manuf	"

Rogers began to make piano actions with *Jesse Davis* c.1856. Their partnership, *Rogers & Davis*, continued in operation until 1859; and in 1858, they shared their address on 24th Street with the small-time piano manufacturer *James Brainard*. Rogers was listed as the head of a piano-case factory in the *1861 AMD* (p.165); and in 1874, with partner *Charles Borst*, Rogers returned to making pianos as the head of *Rogers & Company*. Rogers' relationship with the other makers of this surname is not known, although he was probably related to *Able Rogers*, see above, since they worked about the same time and both had partners named Davis.

ROGERS, George

| 1835 | piano mkr | 287 Fourth |
| 1836 | " | 254 Wooster |

Nothing further is presently known about this maker.

ROGERS, A. & COMPANY

| 1841 | pianos | 402 Broome |

See above *Able Rogers*.

ROGERS, C. & COMPANY

| 1874-78 | piano manuf | 226 E. 42nd |

See above *Charles Rogers*.

ROGERS & DAVIS

| 1856 | action mkrs | 212 Sixth |
| 1857-c.60 | " | Foot E. 24th |

See above *Charles Rogers*.

ROGERS, DAVIS & COMPANY

| 1859 | piano cases | 94 E. 31st |

It is not known if the Davis active in this firm was *Jesse Davis*, who had previously been *Charles Rogers'* partner in the action-manufacturing firm *Rogers & Davis*, see above. See also *Able Rogers*.

ROGERS & WINANT

| 1849-53 | pianos | 148 Fulton |
| 1854-57 | " | 9 Mercer |

See above *Able Rogers*.

ROHÉ, Joseph Anton

1840-41	music	44 Maiden La.
1842	"	46 Maiden La.
1842-47	importer mus instrs	44 Maiden La.
1848-51	mus instrs	"
1852-63	"	31 Maiden La.

From 1838-39, Rohé operated a music-importing business in Philadelphia. In 1840, he moved to New York where he advertised in 1846 that, in addition to importing instruments, he also manufactured "cornets, trombones, hibocornos, clavicor, neocor, bombardon, valve trumpets, & etc; also guitars and all kinds of woodwind instruments." (*NYBD* 1846:135)

In 1851, Rohé and a partner named Leavitte — a member of a family of importers then active in the city — established the firm *Rohé & Leavitte*. They advertised as "Manufacturers of Superior Quality saxhorns and other brass instruments." (*NYCD* 1854) Their firm remained in business until 1863, when it is probable that they were bought out by *Stratton & Foote*. Rohé might have been the same person as "J.A. Rohe" who was active in Paris during this period. (See **Langwill** 1980:149.) Rohé died in New York in 1869; instruments bearing his stamp are found in several collections.

ROHÉ & LEAVITTE

1851	mus instrs	44 Maiden La.
1852-63	"	31 Maiden La.

See above *Joseph Anton Rohé*.

RÖNNBERG, William

1834-38	mus instr mkr	13 Thompson
1839	"	13 Sullivan
1840-44	mus instrs	92 Fulton
1845	"	187 Broadway
1846-48	"	16 John
1849	"	150 Broadway
1850-54	not listed	
1855-58	mus instr mkr	298 Broadway
1859	instrs	"
1860-65	mus instrs	r. 298 Broadway
1866-68	"	52 John
1869	not listed	
1870	Boehm flute mkr	"
1871-72	flutes	"
1873	flute mkr	"
1874-78	flutes	"
1879-89	flutes/mus instrs	"

Rönnberg, a prominent New York wind-instrument maker, was born in Germany in 1803. **Kaufman** (1976:32) writes that he was listed at 12 Dodd Street, Bloomfield, New Jersey c.1815 (although this seems too early), and again c.1835 and 1850. He was first listed working in New York in 1834, and except for the years he apparently worked in New Jersey, he headed his own shop in the city. From 1844-89, he lived in Brooklyn. (**Libin** 1985:72)

In 1857, Rönnberg was awarded a diploma "For a Boehm Flute" exhibited at that year's American Institute Fair. (*American Institute Records*) He was listed as a "Flute & Clarionet Manufacturer" in the *1861 AMD* (p.91). An inscription on a flute now in the (*DMC Catalog* No. 491) suggests Rönnberg had a partner named Schroeder c.1857. Schroeder might have been an instrument dealer outside of the city who stamped a Rönnberg flute sold in his shop, or perhaps the mark of instrument-maker *Luke Schroeder* who had been active in the city and might have worked as a journeyman in later years. In either case, no other trace of this partnership has been found. Rönnberg made high quality flutes, many of which are extant.

ROSEBECK/ROSENBERG, John C.

1838	instr mkr	81 Division
1839	"	1 Orchard

In 1836, "John Rosenbeck of Utica" won an award for a trombone he had made "for Cioffi" and exhibited at that year's American Institute Fair. In 1838, after he had moved to New York, he was awarded a silver medal at the American Institute Fair for "an elegant silver slide trumpet," and in 1839, he won a diploma from the same organization "for a silver cornopian." (*American Institute Records*) It is not known if he returned to upstate New York after leaving the city in 1839.

ROSS, John J./John G.

1833	piano mkr	153 Duane
1834	"	r. 51 Norfolk
1835	"	94 Clinton
1836-41	not listed	
1842-46	organbuilder	r. 94 Clinton
1847-48	not listed	
1849-50	organbuilder	r. 114 Clinton
1851-54	not listed	
1855	organbuilder	h. r. 114 Clinton
1856	manuf of patent wheels, worked by ebb & flow of tide, and patent handpropellers for boats, used in fishing, sporting, &c.	"
1857	wheels	"
1858-60	machinist	"

Apparently the same person as the inventor of the "Ross" water motor for organs. **Ayars** (1937:257) wrote that Ross, of Albany, designed a water motor which was "used considerable by Boston organ builders." Perhaps this maker spent time in Albany and Boston during those years he was not listed in the *NYCD*.

ROSS, William H.

In 1856, Ross of "52nd Street n. 9th Avenue," was awarded a diploma "for the best Banjo" exhibited at the American Institute Fair. (*American Institute Records*) A musician of the same name was listed at 268 W. 43rd Street in 1862 (*NYCD*), but their relationship is not known.

ROSS, William J.

1843	pianoforte mkr	7 Jersey

Probably the son of a cabinet maker of the same name with whom he shared his Jersey Street address. His relationship to other instrument makers of the same surname is not known.

ROTH, William

1869	see below	53 First
1870-71	not listed	
1872-78	mus instrs	"
1879	"	385 Bowery
1880	"	215 Fifth
1881-84	"	272 E. Houston
1885	see below	

Scholar Robert Eliason (PC:Eliason) places Roth at 53 First (Avenue?) as early as 1869, but he was not listed in the *NYCD* until 1872. Roth advertised as a "Manufacturer of Brass Instruments...All kinds of musical instruments will be made to order." (*CmRg* 1872:101) He was listed as a musical instrument manufacturer at 272 E. Houston in the *1885 AMD* (p.212), but his shop had apparently closed by that date. A musician of the same name was listed at 78 E. 4th Street in 1886 (*NYCD*), but their relationship is not known.

ROWELL, Warren

1837	see below	23 Chambers
1838	organ builder	Ave. 3 n. 13th
1839	see below	23 Chambers

Rowell was awarded silver medals at the 1837 American Institute Fair "for the best 8 keyed flute"; and the 1839 Fair "for the best keyed flutes." (*American Institute Records*) In both instances, his address was given as 23 Chambers Street. He was listed as an organ builder only in 1838 *NYCD*.

ROZ, Theodore (Theodule Joseph Vite)

1856-57	upright, French Piano-Forte Manuf	127 Elm
1858-61	pianos	"
1863	"	163 Sixth Ave.
1864	Victorine, lacework	"

Roz was also listed as a piano manufacturer in the *1861 AMD* (p.171). Victorine Roz, listed in 1864, might have been the maker's wife. On August 4, 1864, Roz was granted a British patent "for improvement in keyboards for piano-fortes & similar instruments," (*Great Britain Patent Office* 1871 No.1939) and an 1867 patent (No 64,371) gave Roz's address as Paris, France.

RUCK, John

1843	pianos	251 E. Broadway
1844-47	"	83 Anthony
1848-51	"	r. 114 Laurens
1852	"	63 Centre
1853	"	63 & 65 Centre
1854	piano mkr	178 E. 33rd
1856	pianos	395 First Ave.
1857	piano mkr	h. 210 E. 33rd
1858	pianos	106 E. 34th
1859	Nancy M. wid John	h. 123 E. 31st

Ruck was described as a clever inventor of piano improvements. (**Spillane** 1890:197) In 1843, with *Henry Reichard*, he entered into the short-lived piano-manufacturing partnership *Reichard & Ruck*. After its dissolution, Ruck worked alone. In 1853, he exhibited a piano at the New York Crystal Palace. (**Rimbault** 1860:402) Ruck might have been related to a Parisian piano-making family of the same name who were active c.1870-1913. (**Pierce** 1965:205) See *Reichard & Ruck*.

RUTH, Xavier

1858	organ mkr	h. 30 Ludlow
1859	not listed	
1860-61	organs	h. 28 Canal
1862-63	not listed	
1864-65	organ mkr	h. 326 Fifth

According to the *1861 AMD* (p.158), Ruth was a "Manufacturer of Organs (Hand) & Musical Clocks."

RYDER, Langford T.

1818-22	pianoforte mkrs	15 Barclay
1823	"	Varick n. Provost
1824	"	15 Barclay & 39 Barclay
1825-27	"	15 Barclay

From 1818-24, Ryder headed *Ryder & Company*. In 1821, he shared his address at 15 Barclay with the piano maker *Daniel Thomas*; and from 1825-27, he joined *John Tallman* in the piano-making firm *Ryder & Tallman*. After their partnership ended, Tallman remained at 15 Barclay Street until 1839, but Ryder's name disappeared from city records.

RYDER & COMPANY

1818-23	pianoforte mkrs	15 Barclay
1824	"	" & 39 Barclay

See above *Langford Ryder*.

RYDER & TALLMAN

1825-27	pianoforte mkrs	15 Barclay

See above *Langford Ryder*.

S

SAENGER, Jonas

1863	accordeons	h. 21 Ave. B
1864	"	h. 163 Essex
1865-68	mus instrs	165 Essex
1869-71	"	355 Bowery
1872-74	"	21 Murray & 355 Bowery
1875-79	"	106 Chambers
1880-86	"	105 Chambers
1887	"	" & 712 Eighth Ave.
1888-90+	"	5 Ave. A

In 1871, Saenger advertised himself as a "Manufacturer of Accordeons, and Importer of all kinds of Musical Instruments, 165 Essex Street. Specialty — German Accordeons, Concertinas, Bandonions, Kittlinger Method Harmonicas, Cither, Guitars, Musical Boxes, & Instruction Books." (*CmRg* 1871:128) From 1869-72, the maker's business was listed as *J. Saenger & Company*.

SAENGER, J. & COMPANY

1869-71	mus instrs	355 Bowery
1872	"	21 Murray & 355 Bowery

See above *Jonas Saenger*.

SAKMEISTER, Charles P.H.

1829	piano mkr	138 Amity
1830-31	"	51 Morton
1832	"	13th n. Ave. 6

Sakmeister was a piano designer and maker who, according to **Spillane**, furnished *R. & W. Nunns* with an innovative scale design c.1827 that was widely copied by piano manufacturers in New York and Philadelphia. Sakmeister then "drifted around the city drawing 'scales' and modelling improvements for piano-makers, who realized largely by his skill and gave him little credit. Germans were scarcely tolerated in those days, and had a hard time to get along, therefore Sakmeister . . . was kept down by force of circumstances." (**Spillane** 1890:151-52) On May 17, 1830, the maker was granted a patent for a down-striking piano action.

SAXE, George G. (Rev.)

1863	agent	61 Broad
1864	"	37 Park Row
1865	melodeons	" & 145 Nassau
1866	pianos	417 Broome
1868-85+	organs	5-9 Union Sq.

It is likely that the Reverend Saxe was only a dealer; however, in 1867 he was listed as a "Manufacturer & dealer in Pianos, Melodeons, & Cabinet Organs." (*CmRg* 1867:136) In 1866, his firm was listed as *Saxe & Company*; and after 1868, with partner James H. Robertson, he established the dealership Saxe & Robertson. According to the *1885 AMD* (p.212), the firm specialized in selling Estey organs.

SAXE & COMPANY

1866	pianos	417 Broome

See above *George Saxe*.

SCHAEFFER/SCHAFFER, William

1874	pianos	621 Tenth Ave.
1875	"	472 W. 43rd
1876	piano mkr	h. 512 W. 44th
1877-79	pianos	472 W. 43rd
1880-83	"	524 W. 43rd
1884	"	456 W. 37th

In 1875, Schaeffer advertised himself as a "Manufacturer of First Class Piano-Fortes. Upright Pianos a Specialty." (*CmRg* 1875:91) He used both spellings of his surname throughout his career.

SCHAFFER, F.G. & W.

1811	mus instr mkr	219 Greenwich

Nothing further is presently known about the Schaffers, although it is possible that one of them was the same person as the instrument maker *George Schaffer* listed below.

SCHAFFER, George

1804-06	------	438 Pearl
1807	musician	270 Pearl

Redway (1941:91) suggests Schaffer was the same person as the mariner George Schaff listed at 91 Henry Street in 1808, but this has not been established. Likewise, Schaffer's relationship to *F.G. & W. Schaffer*, see above, remains unclear.

SCHAFFER, William

See above *William Schaeffer*.

SCHATZ, Henry Anton

See *Martin & Schatz*.

SCHILBACH, Oswald Anton

Schilbach was born at Schoneck, Saxony in 1862, and trained as a violin maker by Neumarker before he immigrated to New York c.1887. He was not listed in the *NYCD* before 1891, but during the late 1880s he reportedly worked for *Herman Konig* and *Victor Flechter*. He later worked as an independent violin and bow maker until his death in the city in 1947. See: **Roda** (1959:259); **Henley** (1960:5:14).

SCHMIDT, Louis

1836	mus instrs	92 Chatham
1837-38	not listed	
1839-42	mus instrs	412 1/2 Broadway
1843-48	guitar mkr	"
1849	not listed	
1850-51	guitar mkr	388 Broadway
1852-58	guitars	"

From 1839-58, Schmidt and his partner, George Maul, headed the well-known guitar and violin-making firm *Schmidt & Maul*. Their instruments did well at American Institute Fairs: receiving a diploma for the best (rosewood) guitar exhibited at the 1841 Fair; and a diploma "for the second best specimens of Guitars" exhibited at the 1842 Fair. (*American Institute Records*)

Following the dissolution of the partnership, Schmidt might have left the city, although a piano dealer of the same name was listed at 423 Broome Street from 1859-60. Examples of *Schmidt & Maul* instruments, some of them quite innovative, are extant.

SCHMIDT, Theodore

See *Kroeger & Schmidt*.

SCHMIDT & MAUL

1839-42	mus instrs	412 1/2 Broadway
1843-48	guitar mkrs	"
1849	not listed	
1850-58	guitar mkrs	388 Broadway

See above *Louis Schmidt*.

SCHMITT, Adam

See *Schraidt, Schmitt & Company*.

SCHNABEL, Edward

1876	pianos	93 E. 4th

Schnabel was born in Zeitz, Germany on November 14, 1850, and learned piano making in his father's shop and that of the Zeitz's craftsmen Knhau, Schmitt & Bishop. He emigrated to New York in 1862, and during the next few years, as "one of the 'silent workers' in the great army of piano makers" (**Spillane** 1890:275), Schnabel found work with *Marschall & Mittauer*, *Behning*, and *Lighte & Bradbury*.

About 1875, with partners *Henry Lambert* and Adolph Hintz, the maker established *Schnabel, Hintz & Lambert* at 136 Elm Street. (This firm, however, was never listed in the *NYCD*.) In 1876, the firm was reorganized as *Schnabel, Lambert & Company*, and with Schnabel in charge of the technical aspects of production, they "made quite a name in a comparatively short period, and were in business for some years, until through financial mismanagement they dissolved, meantime honorably settling all debts." (**Spillane** 1890:272) In 1877, Schnabel was working as a journeyman in the shop of *Wheelock & Company*. The maker was rarely listed in *NYCD*, and might have lived outside Manhattan.

SCHNABEL, LAMBERT & COMPANY

1876	pianos	93 E. 4th

See above *Edward Schnabel*.

SCHNEIDER, Albert

See *Kraushaar & Company*.

SCHONEMANN, Charles J.

See *Kraushaar & Company*.

SCHONS, Bernard

1807	pianoforte mkr	88 Chatham
1808	"	267 Broadway
1809	"	403 Greenwich
1810	"	17 Chatham

Schons might have been related to the Danish piano maker T.C. Schons, who was active later in the century (see **Dolge** 1911:456), but this has not been established and nothing else is presently known about the New York maker.

SCHRAIDT, Louis

1866	piano mkr	h. 255 E. 4th
1867	pianos	86 Walker
1868	"	382 Broome & 521 5th St.
1869-72	"	719 5th St.
1873	piano mkr	h. 744 5th St.

In 1867, with *Adolph Hintz*, Schraidt formed the short-lived piano-manufacturing firm *Hintz & Schraidt*. In 1868, he joined *Adam Schmitt* in the more successful concern *Schraidt, Schmitt & Company,* which "attained some note towards 1870 as makers of instruments for the masses." (**Spillane** 1890:252)

According to the *1870 U.S. Census,* Schraidt, Schmitt & Company owned $15,000 of real capital, and employed 16 men and 2 boys at annual wages $10,000. Using only hand tools, the firm that year produced 120 piano worth $36,000. In 1872, the firm's title was changed to *Schraidt & Schmitt,* and after the firm's dissolution, Schraidt worked briefly as a journeyman before his name disappeared from city records. See *Hintz & Schraidt.*

SCHRAIDT & SCHMITT

| 1872 | pianos | 719 & 721 Fifth St. |

See above *Louis Schraidt.*

SCHRAIDT, SCHMITT & COMPANY

| 1868 | pianos | 382 Broome & 521 5th St. |
| 1869-71 | " | 719 5th St. |

See above *Louis Schraidt.*

SCHREIBER, August

1867	importer	h. 25 Essex
1868	mus instr mkr	h. 99 Mott
1869-70	"	420 Broome
1871	mus instrs	"
1873	music & importer	137 Bowery
1874	importer	------
1875-76	mus instrs	137 Bowery
1877	Amelia widow of August	"

Schreiber was a "Manufacturer of all kinds of German, French and Italian Musical Instruments." (*CmRg* 1867:112) How he managed to make foreign instruments in New York is not clear. Also uncertain is this maker's relationship to *Louis Schreiber* listed below.

SCHREIBER, Louis

1865	music	------
1867-68	manuf of instrs	21 Maiden la.
1869	intrs	363 Bowery
1870	mus instrs	321 Sixth
1872-73	"	363 Bowery
1874	importer	"
1875-76	music	23 Union Sq.
1877-79	mus instrs	"
1880-84	importer	57 E. 91st
1885-86	mus instrs	"
1887-88	------	"

Schreiber, a brass instrument designer and manufacturer, was born at Coblenz, Germany in 1827. He might have established a New York shop as early as 1858, although it was not listed in the *NYCD* before 1865. In 1866 and 1867, his teardrop-shaped brasses were granted patents in both Britain and the United States. He exhibited his wares at American Institute Fairs in 1867, 1869 and 1870. (*American Institute Records*) During this period, he was also active as a musician. (*Bio-Bibliographical Index* 1956:335)

From 1867-68, the *Schreiber Cornet Manufacturing Company* advertised that it was "Established for the purpose of manufacturing wind instruments in brass and German silver. These instruments are rendered superior to all others by various improvements which have been patented both in this country and in Europe." (*NYBD* 1867:366)

More information on this firm was included in the *Chickering Exhibition Catalogue* (1902:37): "Mr. Schreiber of New York was the inventor [of exhibited brasses], and in 1858 a company with a capital of $150,000 was formed to manufacture this style of instrument. Only a few sets were completed, as owing to delays, the great expense incident to the introduction of the instruments and in making the models, drawings, etc., the capital of the company was exhausted and manufacturing operations were suspended. These instruments were sold in sets of seven, the price being $1,000." Schreiber died on August 3, 1900 at Los Angeles, California.

SCHREIBER CORNET MANUFACTUR-ING COMPANY

| 1867-68 | manuf of brass instrs | 21 Maiden la. |

See above *Louis Schreiber*.

SCHROEDER, Luke/Richard

1833	mus instr mkr	54 Elizabeth
1834	instr mkr	191 Mulberry
1835-36	"	163 Mott
1837	"	191 Mulberry

This maker was listed as "Richard" from 1834-35, but little else is presently known about his career. He might have also been related to the Schroeder Brothers, who manufactured mathematical instruments during this period.

SCHUBERT PIANO COMPANY

1886-87	pianos	423 Ave. 11
1888	"	542 W. 40th
1889-90+	"	E. 134th n. Alexander

In 1886, mastercraftsman *Peter Duffy* changed this title of his firm to the *Schubert Piano Company*. According to **Spillane** (1890:302), "The instruments bearing this name are meritorious for their price and character." The firm continued in operation until 1937. (**Pierce** 1965) See *Peter Duffy*.

SCHUETZE, Otto

1853-54	piano mkr	63 Grand
1855	"	85 Varick
1856-57	pianos	452 Broome
1858-63	"	" & 165 Chrystie
1864-76	"	452 Broome
1877	Frederica widow of Otto	h. 128 MacDougal

Schuetze, a practical piano maker, began his career with *Charles Krall* c.1854 in the firm *Schuetze & Krall*. In 1855, with *August Luedolff*, he established the successful long-lasting partnership *Schuetze & Luedolff*.

Schuetze & Luedolff pianos were exhibited at several American Institute Fairs: receiving a silver medal in 1855; a bronze medal in 1856; and a "small

gold" medal in 1857. (*American Institute Records*) On February 20, 1866 the partners capitalized on a recent Civil War battle by patenting a "Monitor Plate Piano" (Patent No. 52,725).

According to the *1870 U.S. Census,* Schuetze & Luedolff owned $10,000 of real capital; and had $4,000 of wood and $1,000 of varnish in stock. They employed 7 men who that year produced $12,000 worth of pianos. The firm continued in operation under Luedolff's direction after Schuetze's death in 1876.

SCHUETZE & KRALL

| 1854 | piano manufs | 85 Varick |

See above *Otto Schuetze*.

SCHUETZE & LUEDOLFF

1855	piano mkrs	85 Varick
1856-57	pianos	452 Broome
1858-59	"	" & 165 Chrystie
1860-63	"	452 Broome
1864	"	" & r. 85 Mercer
1865-76	"	452 Broome

See above *Otto Schuetze*.

SCHULER, Frederick/Charles F.

1866-67	pianos	178 Prince
1868-74	"	367 Broome
1875-77	"	26 E. 14th
1878-90+	"	19 E. 14th

From 1869-70, Schuler and piano maker *Ferdinand Ludke* headed the piano-manufacturing firm *Ludke & Schuler*. Later, Schuler headed his own firm, advertising: "Patent Pianos (Patented 1872), With all modern improvements, securing the most beautiful tone, as well as cheapness." (*CmRg* 1877:52) By 1885, he had expanded and was also manufacturing organs. (*1885 AMD* p.213) See *Ludke & Schuler*.

SCHULZE, William G.

1880	mus instrs	260 Bowery
1881	"	278 Bowery
1882-83	"	261 Bowery
1884-85	"	r. 255 Bowery
1886-90+	"	359 Bowery

Schulze was a maker and importer of flutes, clarinets, oboes, and other types of woodwinds. He was a pupil of *Alfred Badger*, and had worked in New Haven for several years before coming to New York. He might have maintained his Connecticut shop even after moving to the city. See **Krivin** (1961:255); *DMC Catalog*.

SCHUSTER, William

1883-90+ music/mus instrs   1104 Second

Listed as an instrument maker only in the *1885 AMD* (p.213), in 1883 Schuster had worked with Tobias J. Marshall in the dealership Schuster & Marshall.

SCHWARTZHOLTZ, I.C.

1797	pianoforte mkr	450 Pearl
1798	"	23 Chatham

Nothing further is presently known about this maker.

SCUDDER, Egbert

See *Griffin & Scudder.*

SEABURY, Charles Saltonstall

1843-44   pianoforte mkr   r. 13 Crosby

Seabury was working in New York as a journeyman cabinet maker as early as 1824 when he joined, resigned from and rejoined several volunteer fire engine companies. (See *MCC* 1917:13:687; 15:634; 16:27; 17:35.) On May 20, 1830, the maker was granted a patent for a piano improvement (**Spillane** 1890:364); and later, from 1843-44, he joined with *William Dubois* to head the firm *Dubois & Seabury.*

Seabury was the brother-in-law of the artist William Sydney Mount who wrote on January 30, 1839: "Brother Charles Seabury is going to build a piano forte factory near where his house stands [in Stony Brook, Long Island]. To commence building it in a few days, he will put his farm on shares." (**Frankenstein** 1975:56) Nothing further is currently known about Seabury's Long Island factory, or its connection with the nearby *Nunns Brothers'* shop at Sautuket, Long Island, whose owners apparently had some business dealings with Seabury's partner Dubois. Seabury died on September 16, 1859. See *Dubois & Stodart.*

SECOR, Joseph B.

Although listed only in the 1829 *NYCD* as the partner of *Allen Jollie* in the instrument-making firm *Jollie & Secor* at 17 Stanton Street, Secor had been in the city as early as November 6, 1826 when he was appointed to a volunteer fire engine company. At that time, he was listed as a "musical instrument maker" at Wooster n. Amity Street. He resigned from the engine company on March 21, 1831. (*MCC* 1917:15:681; 19:570) See *Jollie & Secor.*

SEELE, Charles E.

1878	violins	h. 27 Cornelia
1879	music	1 Thompson
1880	instr mkr	h. 7 Sullivan
1881	cases	"
1882	"	40 Thompson
1883-85	"	58 Thompson
1886	"	h. 298 W. 112th

Seele had previously been listed as a piano case maker during the 1860s and 1870s. The *1885 AMD* (p.213) listed his trade as "Musical Instrument Manufacturing," but he had probably already returned to case making by that date.

SEIFERT, Ferdinand

See *Gerbeth & Seifert.*

SELDEN/SELDON, John

1796-97	mus instr mkr	25 Chapel
1798	not listed	
1799-1801	mus instr mkr	"
1802-06	not listed	
1807-19	mus instr mkr	41 Chapel
1820	not listed	
1821	mus instr mkr	"
1822	not listed	
1823-32	mus instr mkr	"

From 1814-19, Selden's surname consistently appeared as Seldon, but little else is presently known about his activities. Given his periodic absences from the city, it is probable that he operated one or more shops in another city.

SELLECK/SILLECK, George W.

1822-23	cabinet mkr	21 Barclay
1824	not listed	
1825-26	cabinet mkr	Raisen n. Herring
1827	"	52 Raisen
1828	"	33 Herring
1829-33	not listed	
1834	piano mkr	505 Houston
1835-36	"	123 Barrow
1837	"	116 Ave. 6
1838	"	11th n. Ave. 3
1839	not listed	
1840-41	piano mkr	188 Broome
1842	"	11th n. Ave. 3
1843	carpenter	11th bet. Ave. 2 & 3

Selleck, and his relative *Sands Selleck*, see below, worked as cabinet makers for many years. Sands began making pianos c. 1827, and following his death, c.1832, George took over the instrument-making business. There is no evidence that the two men were ever in partnership, however, **Pierce** (1965) mistakenly listed the firm "Sellick & Sands," which has caused some confusion. Both spellings of their surname were used.

SELLECK/SILLECK, Sands F.

1820	-------	69 Division
1821	-------	Division n. Allen
1822-23	cabinet mkr	21 Barclay
1824	not listed	
1825-26	cabinet mkr	Raisen n. Herring
1827	piano mkr	63 Herring
1828	"	--- Herring
1829	"	641 Greenwich
1830	"	126 Barrow
1831	"	641 Greenwich
1832	Sarah widow Sands milliner	355 1/2 Hudson

See above *George Selleck*.

SEMPF, William G.

1861	carpenter	h. 15 Delancey
1862-63	drums	64 Forsyth h. 15 Delancey
1864-66	"	209 Grand
1867-68	"	211 Grand
1869	"	209 Grand
1870	brass & snare drum	"
1871-80	drums	211 Grand
1885	------	h. 75 St. Mark's Pl.

Sempf, who began his career as a carpenter, might have been drawn into drum making through a government contract during the Civil War. From 1864-68, he and the musician *Joseph Ottes* headed the drum-making concern *Sempf & Ottes*. According to the *1870 U.S. Census*, they owned $1,0000 of capital and had in stock 10,000 feet of wood worth $200, and 1,800 skins worth $1,500. The partners employed 2 workmen—perhaps themselves?—who were paid $800 annually; and that year produced 200 drums worth $1,800. The *1885 AMD* (p.213) described Sempf as a "Manufacturer of bass and snare drums."

SEMPF & OTTES

1864-67	drums	209 Grand
1868	"	211 Grand

See above *William Sempf*.

SENIOR, Edward H.

1839	piano mkr	148 13th
1840	"	39 Burton
1841	"	67 Carmine
1842	"	75 1/2 Carmine
1843-44	late piano mkr	"
1845	"	34 Burton
1846+	undertaker	49 Bedford

Senior was probably the father of *William H. Senior*, but his relationship to *William F. Senior* has not been established. He continued to work as an undertaker and sexton through the 1850s.

SENIOR, William F.

1831	piano mkr	186 William
1832	not listed	
1833-34	accountant	167 Broadway
1835-39	not listed	
1840	piano mkr	86 Grove
1841	"	708 Greenwich
1842	not listed	
1843	piano mkr	29 Christopher
1844	pianos	152 Spring
1845	"	120 Varick
1846	"	120 Grand
1847	"	" & 38-40 W. 14th
1848	"	117 Grand & 44 W. 14th
1849-52	not listed	
1853	pianos	h. 55 King
1854-56	"	603 Broadway
1857	"	434 Broome
1858	"	r. 208 Sullivan
1859	not listed	
1860	pianos	26 Wooster

From 1846-48, Senior and *James Grovesteen* headed the piano-manufacturing firm *Senior & Grovesteen*. Their firm was awarded a silver medal for the second best piano exhibited at the 1847 American Institute Fair. (*American Institute Records*) After the dissolution of their partnership, Senior briefly joined *Robert Bennett* and *William Bennett* in the concern *Bennett, Senior & Company*; and in 1858, the maker shared his 208 Sullivan Street address with piano makers *Francis Taylor* and Joseph Rittenhaus. His relationship to other instrument makers of the same surname is not known. See *Bennett, Senior & Company*.

SENIOR, William H.

A relative of *Edward Senior*, see above, William H. was first listed as an undertaker at 31 Hammersley in 1848. During the 1860s, he occasionally worked as a journeyman piano maker. Then, in 1859, he entered a banjo in the American Institute Fair and was awarded a diploma for his "beautiful specimen of work"; his address was given as 544 Broome Street. (*American Institute Records*) The *1861 AMD* (p.85) listed Senior as a piano maker in Hudson City, New Jersey; and in the *1885 AMD*, he was listed as a piano dealer at 16 E. 13th Street.

SENIOR & GROVESTEEN

1846	see *Grovesteen & Senior*	
1847	pianos	120 Grand & 38-40 W. 14th
1848	"	117 Grand & 44 W. 14th

Established as *Grovesteen & Senior* in 1846, for unknown reasons, the names of the partners were reversed the following year. See *William F. Senior*.

SHAFF, Thomas

1829	piano mkr	Tenth c. Bowery
1830	"	364 Fifth
1831	not listed	
1832	piano mkr	189 Allen
1833	"	207 Allen
1834	"	438 Bowery
1835	not listed	
1836	piano mkr	30 Bank
1837	"	118 Bleecker c. Wooster
1838	"	50 Carmine
1839-40	not listed	
1841	pianos	386 Sixth
1842	pianofortes	"
1843	not listed	
1844	pianofortes	1 Mulberry c. Chatham

Shaff's creative drive was apparently directed at moving his shop annually. Nothing more is presently known about his career.

SHELLARD, Benjamin

| 1848 | mus instr mkr | 172 Chrystie (*NYBD*) |
| 1849 | organ builder | " |

A member of an instrument-making family from Brooklyn whose other members included Henry, see below; the organ builder Daniel S. listed at 172 Chrystie in 1850; organ builder Edward listed at 172 Chrystie in 1851; and Stephen, an organ builder listed at E. 90th Street near Ave. 4 in 1854.

SHELLARD, Henry

| 1856 | piano mkr | Franklin bet. Centre & Elm |

Shellard was also listed as a manufacturer of piano keys at 4 Cook Street, Brooklyn in the *1861 AMD* (p.166).

SHEIUBLE/SHEYBLI, John

On March 30, 1772, John Sheiuble advertised in *The New-York Gazette & Weekly Mercury*: "Organ Builder from Philadelphia, Makes and repairs all kinds of Organs, Harpsichords, Spinnets, and Piano, in the best Manner, and with the greatest Dispatch. Any Person that has any Thing to be done in the above Way, may depend on having it executed in the best Manner, and at the cheapest Rate. He is to be spoken with at Mr. Samuel Price's Cabinet Maker, at the Sign of the Chest of Drawers, in New York."

On October 10, 1774, an advertisement in the same paper listed Sheiuble at a new address, Horse and Cart Lane (now William Street), and mentioned he had for sale "one neat chamber organ, one hammer spinnet, one common spinnet." An illustration accompanying the advertisement, purporting to be of the maker's shop, shows two men at work in a small neat room.

SHEYBLI, John

See above *John Sheiuble*.

SHIELDS, Thomas

1827-28	pianoforte mkr	92 Liberty
1829-30	"	125 Orange
1831	"	109 Chrystie
1832	"	103 Chrystie

No further information about this maker is presently known.

SICKELS, Jacob

| 1832 | piano mkr | 114 Charles c. Hudson |

Nothing further about this maker is presently known.

SIEBERT, Charles

1873	Manuf of Piano-Fortes	524 Broome (*CmRg*)

Although apparently not related to *Ferdinand Seifert*, nothing else is presently known about this maker.

SIEGEL, Jacob H.

1878-79	pianos	60 E. 4th
1880-82	"	23 E. 4th
1883-84	"	37 E. 4th

Although probably more active as a dealer, Siegel was listed as a piano manufacturer at 37 E. 4th Street in the *1885 AMD* (p.213).

SIEH, Charles

1847	piano mkr	258 Stanton
1848-49	not listed	
1850	piano mkr	266 Division
1851	not listed	
1852	pianoforte mkr	267 Division
1853	"	109 Fourth
1854	"	Fourth c. Lewis
1855-56	"	709 Fourth
1857-60	pianos	"
1861	not listed	
1862	piano manuf	Fourth c. Lewis & 86 Walker
1863	pianos	86 Walker

Sieh and *Adolph Hintz* headed the piano-manufacturing firm *Sieh & Hintz* at Fourth & Lewis and 86 Walker from 1859-62. After their partnership ended, Hintz continued to work in the trade through 1872; but Sieh, after a short-lived attempt at establishing *Sieh & Company* in 1863, vanished from city records.

SIEH, CHARLES & COMPANY

1863	pianos	86 Walker

See above *Charles Sieh*.

SIEH & HINTZ

1859-60	pianos	709 Fourth
1861	not listed	
1862	piano manuf	4th & Lewis & 86 Walker

See above *Charles Sieh*.

SILLECK

See *Selleck*.

SIMON, Lewis T./Louis

1856-57	piano repairer	h. 8 Vandewater
1858	not listed	
1859	accordeons	403 Pearl
1860	fancygoods	447 Pearl
1861	music	h. 224 Division

Simon's listings in the *NYCD* suggest that he was primarily an instrument dealer and repairer, even though the 1860 *NYBD* (p.321) did list him as an instrument maker.

SIMONTON, John C.

1825	cabinet mkr	18 Thomas
1826-27	"	54 Anthony
1828	"	9 Anthony
1829-31	not listed	
1832	piano mkr	85 Sullivan
1833	not listed	
1834	cabinet mkr	"
1835-41	"	various addresses
1842	not listed	
1843	Eliza widow of John	30 First

After a short-lived attempt at piano making, Simonton returned to building cabinets in 1834. The Eliza Simonton listed in 1843 was probably the maker's widow.

SIMPSON, John Boulton, Jr.

1874-75	treasurer	5 E. 14th & 149 n. Ave. 3
1876-85	pianos	" & "
1886-90+	"/vice pres.	5 E. 14th & S. Blvd c. Lin.

Simpson was active as early as 1871 as the secretary of the *Arion Piano Company*. In 1875, Simpson took control of *Arion* and changed the firm's name to *Simpson & Company*. Robert Proddow was admitted into partnership in 1886, and the firm's title changed to *Simpson & Proddow*. In the early 1890s, the firm's name was changed again, and it became well-known as the *Estey Piano Company*. See *Arion Piano Company*.

SIMPSON & COMPANY

| 1876-80 | pianos | 5 E. 14th & 149 n. Ave. 3 |
| 1881-85 | " | 5 E. 14th & 127 E. 129th & 232 E. 40th |

See above *John Simpson.*

SIMPSON & PRODDOW

| 1886-90 + pianos | 5 E. 14th |

See above *John Simpson.*

SIVERT

See *Kroeger & Sivert.*

SLATER, Moses

1865	mus instrs	538 Broadway
1866	"	706 Broadway
1867-68	"	" & 41 Greene
1869-70	"	221 Greene
1871-74	"	36 Courtlandt
1875-88	"	42 Courtlandt
1889-90 + mus instrs/vice pres.		56 Vesey & 41 Union Sq.

Slater was born in November 1826 in England. From 1867-68, Slater joined with *Stephen Gordon* to form *Gordon & Slater*; and in 1868, with *Robert Martin*, he headed a firm that was initially titled *Martin & Slater*, but later, from 1869-71, called *Slater & Martin*.

During the 1870s, Slater headed the *Slater Musical Instrument Company*, which was managed by the respected brass-instrument designer *Henry Distin*. Distin's name appeared on all of Slater's instruments produced during this period, however, the firm itself was never listed in city records. Slater described himself in the *1885 AMD* as follows: "Manufacturer of Brass & German Silver. Rotary, Ordinary Piston Valve & Celebrated American Patent Light Piston, Valve Band Instruments. Awarded the Semi-Centennial Gold Medal at the American Institute Fair 1881. (also agent for Stewart banjos)." Slater died in New York on October 11, 1899, however, his firm continued in operation until 1920. See *New Grove* (1980:17:37); *Henry Distin*; *Martin & Slater*; *Gordon & Slater*.

SLATER & MARTIN

1868	see *Stephen Gordon*	
1869-70	mus instrs	221 Greene
1871	"	36 Courtlandt

See above *Moses Slater.*

SLATER MUSICAL INSTRUMENT COMPANY

See *Moses Slater.*

SMALL, R.E.

See *Dusinberre & Company.*

SMITH, Albert G./Albertus

1787	tuner	Golden-hill
1789-90	"	15 Golden-hill
1791-93	mus instr mkr & turner	"
1794	not listed	
1795-97	mus instr mkr & turner	86 John
1798-1815	mus instr mkr	"
1816-17	------	"
1819	turner	"

In 1835, a journeyman piano maker of the same name was listed in the *NYCD*. Redway (1941:77) assumed they were the same person, however, this remains to be confirmed. See below.

SMITH, Albert G.

1835	piano mkr	385 Broadway
1836	not listed	
1837	piano mkr	Broadway n. 18th
1838-41	"	55 Elm

See above *Albert Smith.*

SMITH, D. & T.

| 1849 | pianos | 223 12th |

See *Tunis Smith.*

SMITH, David

See *Tunis Smith.*

SMITH, Freeborn Garrettson

1872-73	pianos	427 Broome
1874	"	435 Broome
1875-79	"	14 E. 14th
1880-85	pianos & pres.	95 Ave. 5 & 176 Fulton
1886-90 +	" & "	123 Ave. 5 & 119 Ave. D

Smith learned the piano-making trade in Baltimore, and worked for Chickering in Boston before coming to New York c.1860. In 1861, he became the superintendent of the *William Bradbury* piano company. Bradbury, who had previously been a member

144

of *Lighte, Newton & Bradbury*, was a musician and entrepreneur who needed a practical maker like Smith to oversee his factory. After Bradbury's death in 1867, Smith took over the business and continued to produce Bradbury pianos for several years, before changing the firm's title to his own name c.1872. According to the *1870 U.S. Census*, Smith owned $100,000 of real capital, and had in stock $120,000 worth of goods. He employed 150 workmen at annual wages of $90,000; and that year they produced 600 pianos worth $275,000.

Smith was a clever and successful businessman, and according to **Dolge** (1911:315), was "among the first who opened warerooms in leading cities, selling his products direct to the public rather than through dealers. He is counted among the wealthiest of those men in the trade." **Spillane** (1890:249) wrote that "Smith may be credited here with the distinction of personally directing and controlling more retail branch warerooms than any other pianoman in the United States. Some individuals with ordinary heads think it difficult to manage one concern, but Mr. Smith thinks little of undertaking them per quantum." According to the *1885 AMD* (p.193) Smith's factory was located at 338 Fulton Street, Brooklyn. The maker died on October 9, 1911 at the age of 83. (**Tonk** 1926:238) See *William Bradbury*.

SMITH, Jacob

The only record of this maker appears in 1827 when Smith, a piano-maker from 26th Street, joined a volunteer fire engine company whose membership included piano makers *Seabury, Snyder, Charles Taylor, Kenard, Van Horne, Rogers,* and *Wentworth*. (**MCC** 1917:16:543) All these men might have been employed as apprentices in the same local piano shop, possibly that of *R. & W. Nunns*, which was located on Third Avenue and 26th Street.

SMITH, James T.

| 1828 | pianofortc mkr | 11th n. Ave. 3 |

There was also an umbrella maker (active c.1820), and a carpenter (active c.1825) of the same name, but their relationship with this maker is not known.

SMITH, John

| 1792 | mus instr mkr | 39 Bowery La. |
| 1793 | " | Liberty |

Possibly related to *Albert Smith*, see above, who was worked in the city from 1787-1819, but tracing

information on anyone with this name is very difficult. **Langwill** (1980:166) does list a brass trumpet maker named John Smith who worked at Wolverhampton, England from 1800-1818.

SMITH, Robert W.

1875-78	pianos	47 University Pl.
1879	"	8 W. 11th
1880-82	pres.	"

A small-time piano manufacturer who might have done subcontracting for larger firms, Smith was only listed as a piano maker in the 1875 *NYBD* (p.85).

SMITH, Rudolph

| 1866 | manuf of pianos | 424 Broome |
| 1867 | pianos | h. r. 61 Sullivan |

Smith is not traceable after 1867, and no further information about him is presently known.

SMITH, Tunis

1835-38	carpenter	112 MacDougal
1839	------	13th n. Ave. 3
1840-42	------	115 Ave. 3
1843	piano mkr	101 Ave. A
1844	not listed	
1845	piano mkr	E. 27th c. Ave. 3
1846	"	3 E. 28th
1847	policeman	h. 2 E. 28th
1848	piano mkr	h. E. 27th n. Ave. 3
1849-50	"	223 12th
1851	"	315 Rivington
1852	not listed	
1853	piano mkr	h. 3 Ave. 2
1854-55	not listed	
1856	piano actions	127 Elm
1857	pianos	"
1858	"	210 Laurens

In 1849, Smith joined *David Smith* in the firm *D. & T. Smith* at 223 12th Street. David Smith worked as a piano action maker through the 1860s, and was probably involved in the dealership Stebbins & Smith c.1854. Less is known about Tunis; a person of the same name was listed in connection with steamboats c.1863, but this might have been the other Tunis Smith, a cartman, who was also listed in the *NYCD* during this era. See *D. & T. Smith*.

SMYTH, James

See *Brumley & Smyth*.

SNEYDER, Joseph

1830	piano mkr	18th n. Ave. 10
1831-33	not listed	
1834-37	piano mkr	22nd n. Ave. 3
1838-41	not listed	
1842	piano mkr	"
1843	not listed	
1844	piano mkr	"
1845-50	"	105 13th

On March 10, 1828, Sneyder a "Cabinet Maker" of 26th Street n. 3rd Avenue, joined volunteer Fire Engine Company 46. (*MCC* 1917:17:35) He resigned from the company on May 17, 1830—and was replaced by piano maker *Charles Taylor*—but later rejoined the same company on September 20, 1830, when his occupation was listed as "pianoforte maker." (*MCC* 1917:19:37,243) It is likely that Sneyder was employed as an apprentice piano maker throughout this period.

SOEBBELER, Nicholas

1854	see *Morgenroth & Soebbeler*	228 Ave. 3
1855-56	pianos	"
1857-68	"	423 Broome
1869-71	"	101 Second
1872-80	"	103 Second
1880	Catherine widow Nicholas	"

In 1854, Soebbeler and *Gustavus Morgenroth* headed the piano-manufacturing firm *Morgenroth & Soebbeler*; and from 1856-66, with *Louis Schmidt*, he manufactured actions for grand and square pianos in the partnership *Soebbeler & Schmidt*. A relative of this maker, *William Soebbeler*, see below, was apparently also involved in this firm since he later advertised himself as "Late of Soebbeler & Schmidt." (*CmRg* 1879) See *Morgenroth & Soebbeler*.

SOEBBELER, William

1868-72	piano mkr	h. 165 Hester
1873-76	"	h. 87 St. Mark's Pl.
1878-80	"	4 St. Mark's Pl.
1880	Antoinette widow William	h. 103 Second

See above *Nicholas Soebbeler*.

SOEBBELER & SCHMIDT

1856-57	pianos	228 Ave. 3
1858-66	"	423 Broome

See above *Nicholas Soebbeler*.

SOHMER, HUGO & COMPANY

1873-82	pianos	149 E. 14th
1883-85	"	" & 143 E. 23rd
1886-90+	"	151 E. 14th

Sohmer was born at Dunningen, Würtemberg in the Black Forest Region on November 11, 1846. He was the son of a physician, and as a teenager immigrated to New York where he found work in the piano factory of *Schuetze & Luedolff*, and learned the trade. After returning to Europe for several years, Sohmer came back to New York in 1872 and, with a partner named Joseph Kuder, took control of *Marschall & Mittauer*—themselves successors to *John Bornhoeft*—later changing its title to *Sohmer & Company*.

Sohmer's new firm won awards at the 1876 Centennial Exhibition, and its business expanded rapidly. In 1883, Sohmer acquired additional factory space on 23rd Street, and c.1887, built a large new factory in Astoria, Queens. Sohmer died in October 1913 at New York City; his company continued to manufacture pianos in the city until the 1980s. For further information see **Dolge** (1911:320); **Spillane** (1890:252-57).

SONNTAG, Herman

1856-64	mus instrs	11 Maiden La.
1865-72	"	1 1/2 Maiden La.
1873-76	"	9 Park Pl.
1877	"	11 Park Pl.
1878-79	"	9 Park Pl.
1880-83	"	11 Park Pl.
1884-90+	"	12 Park Pl.

Sonntag worked primarily as an importer of musical instruments. In 1859, he was a member of the importing firm *Cargill & Sonntag*; and from 1860-66, he and Joseph P. Beggs headed the partnership *Sonntag & Beggs*. Thereafter, Sonntag operated his own firm, and in the *1885 AMD* (p.213) he advertised as both an importer and manufacturer of instruments. Although Sonntag probably stencilled many of the instruments he sold, there is little to suggest he was actually involved in instrument making. See *Cargill & Sonntag*.

SONNTAG & BEGGS

1860-64	mus instrs	11 Maiden La.
1865-66	"	1 1/2 Maiden La.

See above *Herman Sonntag*.

SPANGER, John P.

| 1860-67 | piano manuf | 173 Prince |
| 1868 | pianos | h. 173 Prince |

Spanger was a small-time piano manufacturer (*1861 AMD* p.171), whose firm was also listed in the *CmRg* during this period.

SPIESS, Charles

| 1855 | repairing all kinds of musical instruments, from the church organ to the smallest flute, also all kinds of fancy articles | 10 N. William |

Spiess was also listed as an instrument maker in the 1855 *NYBD* (p.281). In 1895, there was a Spies Piano Manufacturing Company in the Bronx (**Pierce** 1965), but the relationship between the two firms is not known.

SPRAWLL, Robert

See *Robert Sprowll*.

SPRENGER, Matthew/Mathias

| 1847-49 | instr mkr | 145 1/2 Centre |

Sprenger was apprenticed as a violin maker in Mittenwald, Germany, and worked at Carlsruhe c.1840, before settling in New York in 1846. In 1850, he was awarded a silver medal for "Excellent Violins" exhibited at that year's American Institute Fair. (*American Institute Records*) According to **Henley** (1960:5:79), his instruments appealed "to the best players in America." Sprenger was probably related to the violin maker *John Springer*, see below, and both men disappeared from city records after 1849. A keyed guitar built by this maker while he still worked in Carlsruhe in now in the collection of the Metropolitan Museum of Art, New York.

SPRINGER, John

| 1849 | violin mkr | 128 Leonard |

The 1849 *NYBD* (p.198) listed Springer's address as 138 Leonard Street. He was almost certainly related to Matthew Sprenger, see above, and the two men left the city c.1849. He was probably the same person as the Springer who during the 1890s patented the aluminum violin which is now in the collection of the Smithsonian Institution, however, his activities after leaving New York await documentation.

SPROULL, Robert

See *Robert Sprowll*.

SPROWLL/SPRAWLL/SPROULL, Robert

1810	joiner	173 Church
1811-12	cabinet mkr	55 Anthony
1813-14	"	231 Church
1815-18	organbuilder	9 Thomas
1819	"	173 Church
1820	not listed	
1821-22	------	Vandam n. Herring
1823	------	Reason n. Herring
1824	------	Arden n. Herring
1825-26	pianoforte mkr	Herring n. Jones
1827-29	"	Bowery n. Tenth
1830-33	"	Bowery n. Ninth
1834	"	443 Bowery
1835	"	r. 140 Sullivan

This maker used all three spellings of his surname throughout his career, but no further information about him is presently known.

STACKPOLE, James

1846	pianoforte mkr	202 Hudson
1847	"	108 Reade
1848-50	"	85 Cherry
1851	"	40 1/2 W. 14th
1852-53	harps	"
1854-56	"	h. 295 W. 19th
1857	"	h. 317 W. 19th
1858	harp mkr	"
1859-61	harps	"
1862-63	pianos	"
1864	------	"
1865	piano mkr	"
1866	harp mkr	"
1867-69	"	h. 457 W. 19th
1870	piano mkr	h. 244 Eighth Ave.
1871	not listed	
1872	piano mkr	"
1873	harp mkr	"
1874	mus instrs	"
1875	harp mkr	h. 303 W. 46th
1876	"	244 Eighth Ave.
1877	harps	"
1878	piano mkr	h. 311 W. 24th
1879-81	"	h. 227 Tenth
1882-83	"	h. 441 W. 27th

Stackpole's listing as a "harpmaker" in the *1861 AMD* (p.91) and the frequent listings of his home address in the *NYCD* suggests that he worked primarily as a journeyman throughout his career.

STAFFORD, Geoffrey

Stafford was a luthier from London who was transported to Boston as a felon c.1691, and later moved to the Albany frontier where he was employed as an Indian fighter. The Royal Governor of New York, Benjamin Fletcher, asked Stafford to the city, where he reportedly worked for some time as an instrument maker before being obliged to flee after murdering Fletcher's favorite body servant. Stafford was later hanged by a "Dutchman" he had tried to rob, probably in the Hudson River Valley. Information about Stafford comes exclusively from **Spillane** (1890:74-75), who also claims that the maker built several lutes and violins during his stay in New York, however, no independent documentation of Spillane's information has been located in city records.

STALDER, Constant

1882	mus instrs	260 Bowery
1883	music box repairer	764 Broadway
1884-88	mus instrs	130 Fulton
1889	music boxes	h. 221 Wooster
1890+	instr mkt	"

Stalder was apparently a maker and dealer of mechanical musical devices. In the *1885 AMD* (p.214) he was listed as "Musical boxes & Instrument Manufacturer" at 260 Broadway.

STANDFORD, David R.

1849	pianos	343 Broadway
1850-54	"	" & 15 & 21 Tenth
1855-56	"	501 Broadway, 15 Tenth & 194 W. 35th
1857-58	late pianos	501 Broadway
1859+	vice pres.	66 William

From 1852-56, Standford headed the firm *Standford & Company*, and later, in the 1870s, headed a continuation of an earlier firm established by piano maker *Adam Stodart*. **Spillane** (1890:183) wrote that "At one time the house was Stodart & Company, then Stodart & Morris, until the name went out of the trade prior to 1870, when Mr. D.R. Standford, a respected member of the trade, succeeded to the business and continued the manufacture of the Stodart piano for sometime. The Stodart piano has been out of existence for many years, Mr. Standford finding it impossible to resuscitate interest in a name,

[that] though once eminent, had gone down with time into oblivion, as far as the public was concerned."

STANDFORD & COMPANY

1852-54	pianos	343 Broadway, 15 & 21 Tenth, & 194 W. 35th
1855-56	"	501 Broadway, 194 W. 35th

See above *David Standford*.

STANDIFORD, Daniel

1834	piano mkr	Ave. 3 n. 25th
1835	not listed	
1836	piano mkr	26th n. Ave. 3
1837-40	not listed	
1841+	mahogany	12 h. 83 Ave. 3

It is likely that Standiford worked only as a journeyman. During the 1840s, he was listed as a grocer.

STARK, Christian G.

1856	mus instrs	r. 42 Delancey
1857	"	67 Chrystie
1858	"	175 Chrystie
1859-65	"	181 Chrystie
1866	importer	23 Dey
1867-70	mus instrs	10 Maiden La.
1871-72	"	89 Chambers
1873	not listed	
1874-78	mus instrs	25 Murray
1879	------	"
1880	mus instrs	"

Stark was an instrument dealer and importer who also claimed to manufacture "brass." (*1861 AMD* p.90) From 1856-58, with *John Albrecht*, he headed *Stark & Albrecht*. Then, in 1866, he joined George Kober to found *Stark & Kober*, "importers & wholesale dealers in Musical Instruments, Strings, Busson's accordeons & flutinas, German accordeons, concertinas, &c." (*NYCD* 1866:962) In the *1885 AMD* (p.214), *Stark & Company*, musical instrument importers, were belatedly listed at 25 Murray Street, however, it is likely that the firm ceased operations in 1880. Stark's relationship to *Otto Stark*, see below, is not known.

STARK, Otto

1875-79	accordeons	117 Hester
1880-85	"	96 Hester

Stark had been listed as a curtain maker before 1875. The *1885 AMD* (p.214) listed him as a "Musical Instrument Manufacturer" at 96 Hester Street. His relationship to *Christian Stark*, see above, is not known.

STARK & ALBRECHT

1856	mus instrs	r. 42 Delancey
1857	"	67 Chrystie
1858	"	175 Chrystie

See above *Christian Stark*.

STARK & COMPANY

| 1885 | mus instr importers | 25 Murray |

See above *Christian Stark*.

STARK & KOBER

| 1866 | importers & wholesale dealers in Mus Instrs, Strings, Busson's accordeons & flutinas, German accordeons, concertinas, &c. | 23 & 25 Dey |

See above *Christian Stark*.

STEALY, Jacob

1827	cabinet mkr	492 Greenwich
1828	"	32 Thompson
1829-33	not listed	
1834	piano mkr	22nd n. Ave. 3
1835	not listed	
1836+	cabinet mkr	21 Catherine

Stealy spent most of his career working as a cabinet maker. Nothing further is presently known about his activities as a piano maker.

STECK, George A.

1858	pianos	5 First Ave.
1859	"	105 12th
1860	"	79 Ave. 3
1861	"	98 Elm
1862-63	"	102 Elm
1864-65	"	26 Wooster & 113 Walker
1866-68	"	148 8th St; factory 113 & 115 Walker
1869-70	"	141 8th; 510-514 W. 34th
1871-77	"	25 E. 14 & 512 W. 34th
1878-87	"	11 E. 14 & 512 W. 34th
1888-90+	"	11 E. 14 & 520 W. 48th

Steck was born on July 19, 1829 at Hesse Cassel, Germany, and apprenticed there to the piano maker Carl Scheel. He immigrated to New York c.1853, and worked as a journeyman until 1858 when, with partner *William Grupe*, he founded the piano-manufacturing firm *Steck & Grupe*. Their partnership lasted until 1860, and then, in 1865, he established the successful firm *Steck & Company*.

By 1869, Steck & Company was the 12th largest piano firm in the nation, with gross annual sales of $145,000. (*New York Tribune*, March 15, 1869) According to the firm's advertisements, the Steck piano "Received the only gold MEDAL at the Vienna Exposition," (*CmRg* 1875:91), and the "First Medal & Highest Award at the Centennial Exhibition" (*CmRg* 1878:36). Steck was awarded several patents during his career. (**Spillane** 1890:233-36)

In 1884, "To assure for his coworkers proper compensation for faithful service, Steck incorporated his business . . . allotting shares of stock to his employees." In 1887, Steck retired to devote the last decade of his life to "his pet project of constructing a piano which could stay permanently in tune." (**Dolge** 1911:318-19) He died on March 31, 1897, apparently without fulfilling his dream. See also **Pelz** (1865).

STECK & COMPANY

1865	pianos	113 Walker
1866-68	"	141 8th; 113-115 Walker
1869-70	"	& 510-514 W. 34th
1871-77	"	25 E. 14 & 512 W. 34th
1878-87	"	11 E. 14 & 512 W. 34th
1888-90+	"	11 E. 14 & 520 W. 48th

See above *George Steck*.

STECK & GRUPE

1858	pianos	5 First Ave.
1859	"	105 E. 12th
1860	"	79 Third Ave.

See above *George Steck*.

STEEDMAN, James

1863	piano mkr	h. 23rd c. Second
1864	pianos	40 W. 18th
1865	"	108 W. 15th

1866-68	"	79 W. 14th
1869-76	"	55 W. 16th
1877	piano mkr	h. 514 W. 51st

Steedman emigrated from Britain where, on February 26, 1856, he had been granted a patent "for curved or arched bars for support of [piano] sounding board." (**Great Britain Patents** 1871:No.490) In New York, Steedman first joined *John Dingle* to establish the partnership *Dingle & Steedman* in 1864. From 1868-72, Steedman and Alexander Hollyer headed the dealership *Steedman & Hollyer*; and in 1873, he admitted into partnership William and Mark A. Steedman (his sons?), to form *Steedman & Company*. Their firm, which **Pierce** (1965) mistakenly listed as Steedman & Son, was in operation until 1876. See *Dingle & Steedman*.

STEEDMAN & COMPANY

1873-76	pianos	55 W. 16th

See above *James Steedman*.

STEEDMAN & HOLLYER

1868	pianos	79 W. 14th
1869	not listed	
1870-72	pianos	55 W. 16th

See above *James Steedman*.

STEIN, Edward

1876-81	musician	h. 43 First
1885-87	instr mkr	"
1888	not listed	
1889-90+	instr mkr	315 Bowery

The *1885 AMD* (p.214) listed Stein as a "Musical Instrument Manufacturer" at 32 First, however, he was probably more active as an instrument dealer.

STEINWAY/STEINWEG, Henry

1851-52	piano manuf	199 Hester
1853	piano mkr	85 Varick

After 1853, this maker's name was anglicized to *Steinway*. See below *Steinway & Sons*.

STEINWAY & SONS

1851-53	see *Steinway*	
1854	piano manufs, semi-grand three-string & square two-string pianos	88 Walker & n. Broadway
1855	pianos	88 Walker

1856-58	"	84 Walker, 91 Mercer, 85 Varick
1859	"	83 & 113 Walker, 91 Mercer
1860-62	"	82 Walker & Ave.4 c. E.53rd
1863	" (will remove to their new warerooms, 71 & 73 E. 14th St. about Feb. 1st, 1864)	" & "
1864-68	"	71 & 73 E.14th; Ave.4 bet. 52 & 53
1869-82	pianofortes, Steinway Hall & warerooms	109 & 111 E. 14th; fact. Ave. 4 bet. 52nd & 53rd
1883-90+	"	"; fact. L.I. City

Probably the best known of all New York piano manufacturers, Steinway & Sons was established by Heinrich Engelhard Steinweg (1797-1871), and his sons Charles (1829-65), Henry Jr. (1830-65), William (1835-96), and Albert (1840-77). The family came from Seesen, Germany, where the elder Steinway had worked as a cabinet maker and piano builder.

The Steinways arrived in New York on June 29, 1850, and found work as journeymen in local piano shops. On March 5, 1853, the family business, *Steinway & Sons*, was established in a loft at 85 Varick Street. Like many other New York shops, Steinway & Sons produced well-made pianos, but what sets them apart was their use of the latest innovations in design and instrument construction combined with their clever use of advertising and self-promotion. The firm proved extremely successful. By 1860, they expanded into a giant factory on Fourth Avenue between 52nd and 53rd Street. In 1866, they opened a combination salesroom and concert space, Steinway Hall, on 14th Street. During this period, the firm received numerous national and international awards for their instruments.

The firm suffered a major setback in 1865 when two of its founding members, William and Henry Jr., died within a few months of each other. The eldest Steinway son, C.F. Theodore, who had remained in Germany to work as a piano maker, was brought to New York to help manage the firm. During the 1870s and 1880s, the Steinways, especially Charles and Theodore, became the most prominent members of the instrument-making trade in the city. About 1881, William Steinway bought over four hundred acres of undeveloped farmland in what was to become known as the Steinway section of Queens, New York, where he attempted to establish a company town complete with company housing, churches, schools and libraries to accommodate the needs of his journeymen and their families. The company town was only a moderate success, and when Steinway discovered many of his workmen preferred to commute from the encroaching city he became an outspoken advocate for improved mass transit. Steinway & Sons is one of the only nineteenth- century New York instrument firms to remain in business in the city. For further information see: **Groce** (1982); **Theodore Steinway** (1953); **William Steinway** (1895); **Baker** (1958); **Dolge** (1911:301-13); **Hoover** (1981); **Jones** (1971:160-61).

STEVENS, John

1840	cabinet mkr	7 Doyers
1841	"	83 Bowery h. 7 Doyers
1842-48	blind manuf	various addresses
1849	thread	311 Hudson

Although never listed as an instrument maker in the *NYCD*, the 1844 *NYBD* (p.184) listed Stevens as a "Banjo Maker" at 7 Doyers Street. His relationship to the organ builder *John Stevens*, see below, is not known.

STEVENS, John R.

1825	mus instr mkr	112 Chambers
1826-27	"	148 Chambers
1828-29	"	271 Greenwich
1830	not listed	
1831	mus instr mkr	73 Hudson
1832	"	114 Warren

Steven's relationship with the banjo maker *John Stevens*, see above, is not known. He was mentioned as an organ builder by George Templeton Strong in his diary. (See **Lawrence** 1988:79.)

STODART, Adam

1822-34	see *Dubois & Stodart*	
1835	lithographer	1 Wall
1836-38	piano mkr	375 Broadway
1839-44	pianos	361 Broadway
1845-47	"	" & 87 E. 13th
1848	"	343 Broadway & 111 Ave. 4
1849-51	"	" & 15 & 21 Ave. 10

1852-54	"	325 Broadway & "
1855	"	501 Broadway & 15 Ave. 10; W. 35th bet. 8th & 9th
1856-60	"	506 Broadway & 194 W. 35th
1861-65	"	" & 322 W. 35th
1866-68	piano manuf	684 Broadway
1869	"	" & 479 Ave. 1
1870	not listed	
1871-72	------	h. 747 Lexington Ave.
1872-75	Stodart's Piano-Fortes	684 Broadway
1873	Ellen widow of Adam	747 Lexington

Stodart was either a son or nephew of the English piano maker Robert Stodart, and the grandson of one of the "12 Apostles," German craftsmen who had brought the craft of piano making to England at the close of the eighteenth century. He was probably the same person as William Stodart, a music and piano-store owner who appeared in Richmond, Virginia c.1818, and whose shop served as a retail outlet for the publications of New York's *William Dubois*. (See **Wolfe** 1980:56:224.) About 1819, Stodart moved to the city where he began selling imported instruments made by his relatives in London.

In 1822, Stodart went into partnership with William Dubois, and their firm, *Dubois & Stodart*, operated a successful music store and instrument manufactory until 1834. In 1835, Stodart joined Nathaniel Currier in the lithography business; their firm, *Stodart & Currier*, apparently specialized in producing sheet music. (Currier is best remembered for his later partnership with fellow lithographer James Ives.)

From 1836-44, Stodart, *John Dunham*, and *Horatio Worcester* headed the piano-manufacturing firm *Stodart, Worcester & Dunham*. Worcester withdrew in 1844, and the firm was reorganized as *Stodart & Dunham*. Their firm remained in business until 1849; and from 1850-55, Stodart headed his own firm, *Stodart & Company*. Then, from 1856–69, Stodart and Charles M. Morris headed *Stodart & Morris*, from which Stodart retired c.1870. The firm was later, c.1872, taken over by *David Standford*, who continued the firm as *Stodart's Piano-Forte* through 1875. (**Spillane** 1890:108) Stodart died sometime before 1873 when his widow's name appeared in the *NYCD*.

STODART & COMPANY

1850-51	pianos	343 Broadway; 15 & 21 Ave. 10
1852-54	"	325 Broadway; 15 Ave. 10; W. 35th
1855	"	501 Broadway; " & "

See above *Adam Stodart*.

STODART & CURRIER

| 1835 | lithographer | 1 Wall |

See above *Adam Stodart*.

STODART & DUNHAM

1845-47	pianos	361 Broadway & 87 E. 13th
1848	"	343 Broadway & 111 Ave. 4
1849	"	" & 15 & 21 Ave. 10

A continuation of the firm *Stodart, Worcester & Dunham*. See above *Adam Stodart*.

STODART & MORRIS

1856-59	pianos	501 Broadway & 194 W. 35th
1860	"	506 Broadway & "
1861-63	"	" & 322 W. 35th
1864-65	"	526 Broadway & 322 W. 35th
1866-68	piano manuf	684 Broadway
1869	"	" & 479 Ave. 1

See above *Adam Stodart*.

STODART, WORCESTER & DUNHAM

| 1836-38 | piano mkrs | 375 Broadway |
| 1839-44 | pianos | 361 Broadway |

See above *Adam Stodart*.

STODART'S PIANO-FORTE

| 1872-75 | pianos | 684 Broadway |

See above *Adam Stodart*; also *David Standford*.

STOESS, Ferdinand A.

1882	mus instr mkr	h. 156 Ludlow
1883	not listed	
1884	bow mkr	h. 116 E. 4th
1885	bows	"
1886	mus instrs	118 E. 4th
1887-88	bows	"

Stoess was listed as a "Manufacturer of Musical Instruments" in the *1885 AMD* (p.214). In 1892, his shop had relocated to 319 Fifth (Street?).

STONE, J.F.

| 1872 | pianos | 413 W. 42nd |

In the 1872 *CmRg* (p.123), Stone's concern was listed as "Successor of Mixsell & Co.," and "Manufacturers of 1st Class Piano-Fortes." Mixsell's firm had been in business since the 1840s. Stone repeated his advertisement in the 1873 *CmRg* (p.108), but thereafter his name disappeared from city records.

STRATTON, Eliphalet

1832	piano mkr	234 Orange
1833	"	117 Sullivan
1834	cabinet mkr	446 Broome
1835+	"	326 Bowery

Stratton probably worked as a journeyman. During the 1840s, he was employed in the hardware trade. His relationship to the brass-instrument maker *John Stratton*, see below, is not known.

STRATTON, John Franklin

1860	mus instrs	Centre c. White
1861-64	instrs	105 E. 22nd
1865	mus instrs	31 Maiden La.
1866	"	735 Broadway & 118 W. 27th
1867-69	"	63 Maiden La.
1870	mus instrs & merchant	"
1871-81	" & "	55 Maiden La.
1882-88	mus instrs	49 Maiden La.
1889-90+	"	43 Walker

Stratton was born on September 14, 1832 in West Swanzey, New Hampshire, and trained as a musician during his childhood. At the age of fourteen, he was apprenticed to a machinist in North Chelmsford, Massachusetts, but left after a few years for Hartford, Connecticut where he made a living by conducting the local brass band and operating a small music store. His business was closed by the Panic of 1857, and he resolved to try his luck in New York City.

Stratton moved to the city in 1857, and initially worked as a musician and the conductor of Stratton's Palace Garden Orchestra. About 1859, Stratton combined his knowledge of music and machining to establish a brass-instrument manufactory, which proved an immediate success. In 1865, he joined the instrument dealer *John Foote* in the firm *Stratton & Foote*. The partners advertised themselves as "Successors to Rohe & Leavitte and to John F. Stratton." (*NYCD* 1865:852) After only a year, Stratton withdrew to head *Stratton & Company* (1870-88), and in 1889, admitted his son, Frank A., to form *Stratton & Son*.

In 1866, Stratton reversed immigration patterns and established a brass-instrument factory at Markneukirchen, Saxony. In 1868, he moved his European operation to Gohlis, near Leipzig; where in 1869, he also established a violin-making factory. These shops supplied instruments to his large mail-order and retail outlets in the United States. At one point, Stratton reportedly owned a brass factory which employed 150 workmen "who were obliged to work day and night to fill orders," as well as guitar and mandolin-making shops. (**Stratton** 1885) It is likely that all his manufacturing was done in Germany since no mention of it has been found in city records. Stratton divided his time between the United States and Europe until 1883 when he sold his German shops. He died in Brooklyn on October 23, 1912. His firm continued in business until 1914, and many instruments made or stencilled by Stratton are extant. For further information see: **Stratton** (1885); **Krivin** (1961:255-56); *New Grove* (1980:18:204).

STRATTON, F. & COMPANY

1870	mus instrs & merchant	63 Maiden La.
1871-81	" & "	55 Maiden La.
1882-88	mus instrs	49 Maiden La.

See above *John Stratton*.

STRATTON & FOOTE

| 1865 | mus instrs, Successors to Rohe & Leavitte and to John F. Stratton importer & manuf of Mus Instrs; Manufactory | 31 Maiden La. 105 & 107 E. 22nd |

See above *John Stratton*.

STRATTON & SON

| 1889-90+ | mus instrs | 43 Walker |

See above *John Stratton*.

STRODL, John

1852-55	violin mkr	235 Centre
1856	mus instrs	"
1857	violins	"
1858	musician	"
1859-65	violins	"
1866	mus instrs	"
1867-69	violins	"
1870	"	198 Grand
1871	mus instrs	"
1872-78	mus instrs/violins	194 Grand
1879-80	violin mkr	"
1881	Anna widow of John	"

In the *1861 AMD* (p.91), Strodl was listed as a violin and guitar manufacturer at 100 White Street. He had been in the city as early as 1852, and in 1853, one of his violins was displayed at the New York Crystal Palace Exhibition (*Official Catalogue* 1851:95). According to **Henley** (1960:5:111), Strodl made "cheap-looking, ugly instruments varnished brown." Two of the maker's sons, John H. and Edward N., worked as instrument dealers in the 1880s. Strodl was belatedly listed as a manufacturer at 190 Grand Street in the *1885 AMD* (p.214), however, he had probably died sometime in 1880.

STROTHOFF, Christopher

See *Districhsen, Ludewig & Strothoff*.

STUEHLER, Joseph

See *Hoffman & Stuehler*.

STULTZ, Henry

1880-82	piano mkr	h. 166 Ludlow
1883-84	pianos	701 First Ave.
1885	"	340 E. 31st
1886-90+	"	338 E. 31st

In 1883, Stultz joined Frederick Bauer to form the firm *Stultz & Bauer*. Although their firm was listed as a dealership in the *1885 AMD* (p.214), they were probably manufacturing pianos since they were later asked to join the National Piano Manufacturers Association.

STULTZ & BAUER

1883-84	pianos	701 First Ave.
1885	"	340 E. 31st
1886-90+	"	338 E. 31st

See above *Henry Stultz*.

STUYVERSANT PIANO COMPANY

See *Wheelock & Company*.

SUYDAM, Israel

1824-32	cabinet mkr	various addresses
1833	plough mkr	197 Grand
1834	cabinet mkr	104 Allen
1835	piano mkr	230 Broome
1836-41	grocer	46 Ferry c. Cliff
1842-53	"	76 Cliff
1854-58	liquors	"
1860-61	"	h. 56 Clermont, Brooklyn

Involved only briefly in the piano trade, Suydam died on October 1, 1862 at the age of 65. (**Barber** 1933:39:25)

SWARTZ, Abraham S.

1849-50	melodeon mkr	6 Spring

Swartz was probably only a journeyman, however, he was listed as a "Melodeon Manufacturer" in the 1849 *NYCD* (p.199). A Samuel C. Swartz, "melodeons" was also listed at the same address.

T

TALLMAN, John

1825	cabinet mkr	15 Barclay
1826-32	pianoforte mkr	"
1833-39	piano mkr	"

A cabinet maker of the same name had been active at 77 Chapel Street during the early 1820s, but their relationship has not been established. With *Langford Ryder*, this maker headed the piano-manufacturing firm *Ryder & Tallman* from 1825-27. (Ryder had been at the 15 Barclay Street address since 1818.) **Spillane** (1890:162) wrote that "Tallman & Randal" had started as small manufacturers on White Street c.1838 and later moved to William Street, however, no record of this firm has been found, and the author seems to have confused "Randal" with Ryder. Several pianos built by Tallman are now in museum collections, including the Smithsonian Institution and the Metropolitan Museum of Art. See *Ryder & Tallman*.

TALLMAN & RANDAL

See above *John Tallman*.

TAUBALD, Edward

See *Pappenberger & Taubald*.

TAWS(E), Charles

Taws, the son of a Presbyterian minister, was born in Aberdeen, Scotland. He immigrated to New York in 1786, and in *The Daily Advertiser* of May 23, 1786 announced that: "Charles Tawse, Organ Builder, lately arrived in this City from Britain, builds and repairs finger and barrel organs. He also repairs and tunes spinnets, harpsichords, piano fortes and guitars. Orders will be received at No. 68 Fair-street." **Spillane** (1890:78) wrote that Taws also worked as teacher in a private school and gave his address as 26 Franklin Street, but this remains to be confirmed by other sources. Taws remained in New York for only a year, after which he moved to Philadelphia where he worked as an instrument maker until his death c.1833. For further information see **Mann** (1977:164-180); **Gerson** (1940:45-46).

TAYLOR, Charles

Charles Taylor, "Piano Forte Maker" living on 26th Street near 3rd Avenue, joined volunteer Fire Engine Company 46 on May 17, 1830. (*MCC* 1917:19:37) Taylor was probably an apprentice at the time, and his name does not reappear in later city records.

TAYLOR, Charles

Bagpipe maker. See *William Taylor*.

TAYLOR, Francis

1850-51	pianos	157 Franklin
1852	"	r. 208 Sullivan
1853	piano mkr	"
1854-68	pianos	"
1869-70	"	12 Carroll Pl.
1871-75	"	151 Bleecker
1876-80	"	101 Bleecker
1881	"	178 Wooster
1882	"	58 E. 13th
1883	"	39 E. 13th
1884-90 +	"	8 E. 18th

Taylor was a small-time piano maker who in 1858 shared his 208 Sullivan Street address with *William Senior*. In 1859, he entered into partnership with *Guitan Dupuy* to form *Taylor & Dupuy*. Their firm continued in operation until 1881, and according to the *1870 U.S. Census*, they owned $8,000 of real capital, and $2,000 of raw materials. They employed 8 men for eight months of work that year and paid them $7,500 in wages. In 1870, the firm produced 50 pianos worth $25,000. (This figure seems quite high and might have been an error on the part of the census taker.) After leaving Dupuy in 1882, Taylor admitted his son into partnership to form *Taylor & Son*, which continued in business past 1890.

TAYLOR, Henry S.

1854	mus instrs	16 Essex
1855-58	not listed	
1859	organs	47 Chrystie
1860-61	"	New Bowery c. Oliver
1862	mus instrs	"
1863	"	63 New Bowery
1864-65	organs	189 Chatham & 66 New Bowery
1866	"	191 Chatham & "
1867	"	181 Chatham & "
1868	"	66 New Bowery
1869-72	"	" & 189 Chatham
1873-75	"	66 New Bowery
1876-77	"	189 Chatham
1878-85	"	" & 66 New Bowery
1886-90+	"	229 Park Row

Harlow in *Old Bowery Days* (1931:452) wrote: "Taylor's hand organ factory prospered in the New Bowery until the open-air musical profession began to be monopolized by Italians who preferred imported instruments. Taylor's plant for several years found little to do but repair foreign organs and the proprietor finally committed suicide," probably c.1900.

According to the *1870 U.S. Census*, Taylor owned $2,500 of real capital; and his shop employed 4 men for eight months at wages of $3,328. That year, using $1,500 worth of raw materials, the factory produced $5,000 worth of hand organs. The shop also made cylinder pianos (*1861 AMD* p.174); and at one time, the hand-organ manufacturer *David Davies* was employed in Taylor's shop.

TAYLOR, William (Billy)

Taylor was born c.1830 in Drogheda, County Louth, Ireland, and trained by his father to be an organ and bagpipe maker. It is claimed that Taylor and his stepbrother, Charles, decided to immigrate to America due to a decline of interest in traditional pipe music in Ireland. They arrived in New York c.1872, and lived with a friend named Gaffney. William made a set of pipes for the noted piper Tom Kerrigan, and worked for about a year in a little workshop fitted up in Kerrigan's basement, corner of Eighth Street and Avenue D. Thereafter, the Taylors moved to Philadelphia where they worked until their deaths: William in 1901, and Charles c.1902. Neither man's activities can be traced in city records; for further information see **O'Neill** (1973:160-61).

TAYLOR & DUPUY

1859-68	pianos	208 Sullivan
1869-70	"	12 Carroll Pl. & 208 Sullivan
1871-75	"	151 Bleecker
1876-79	"	101 Bleecker & r. 208 Sullivan
1880	"	" & 178 Wooster
1881	"	178 Wooster

See *Francis Taylor*.

TAYLOR & SON

1882	pianos	58 E. 13th
1883	"	39 E. 13th
1884-90+	pianos	8 E. 18th

See *Francis Taylor*.

TEED, George

1860-61	turner	h. 497 E. Houston

A fretted 8-bracket banjo of the "early commercial type" made by Teed is in the collection of the Smithsonian Institution. (Catalog No. 68.6) In the 1860s, banjo making seems to have been a sideline for many craftsmen in woodworking trades.

TERHUNE, William

1885	see below	
1886	banjo mkr	h. 441 W. 38th

The *1885 AMD* (p.215) listed Terhune as a maker of "Banjos" and "Manufacturer of Musical Instruments" at 269 W. 4th Street, however, no further information about this maker is presently known.

TEUFEL, Joseph

1854	piano manuf	89 Mercer
1855-56	piano mkr	219 Mercer
1857	not listed	
1858	pianos	168 Elm
1859-64	not listed	
1865	pianos	100 Centre

A small-time piano manufacturer, in 1854, Teufel joined Henry Dierkes to form *Teufel & Dierkes*. Teufel was occasionally listed as a journeyman during the 1870s, however, no further information about him is presently known.

TEUFEL & DIERKES

1854	piano manuf	89 Mercer

See above *Joseph Teufel*.

THOMAS, Daniel

1815	cabinet mkr	Chambers c. Greenwich
1816-19	"	87 Warren
1820-21	pianoforte mkr	15 Barclay h. 87 Warren
1822-30	"	87 Warren
1831-33	"	89 Warren
1834-39	"	87 Warren
1840-41	not listed	
1842	pianoforte mkr	80 Laight
1843-44	"	31 Clarkson
1845	not listed	
1846	piano mkr	"
1847-54	"	596 Washington
1855	"	81 Greenwich Ave.
1856	"	h. 213 Varick
1859	pianos	"
1860	"	h. W. 51st n. 10th

Thomas began his career as a cabinet maker, and from 1820-21 shared his address at 15 Barclay Street with the piano maker *Langford Ryder*. Never officially listed as partners, Thomas might have been a member of the later firm *Ryder & Tallman* (1825-27).

THOMPSON, James

1844-48	piano mkr	7 Barclay
1849-51	pianos	"
1852	"	8 Barclay

A small-scale piano maker, Thompson's firm was listed as *James Thompson & Company* from 1849-51. His relationship to other makers of this name is not known.

THOMPSON, Jesse

1827-28	mus instr mkr	108 Reed
1829	grocer	41 MacDougal
1830	not listed	
1831	piano mkr	409 Broadway

Thompson was awarded a patent on August 6, 1831 for improvements he made in piano actions (**Spillane** 1890:364). No further information about his career is presently known.

THOMPSON, Zacharias

1834-35	piano mkr	Ave. 3 n. 24th
1836-37	varnisher	479 Houston
1840+	cabinet mkr	r. 105 Spring

Thompson continued to work as a cabinet maker through the 1840s. No further information about his work is available.

THOMPSON, JAMES & COMPANY

1849-51	pianos	7 Barclay

See *James Thompson*.

THORN(E), Stephen R.

1854	pianos	300 E. Broadway
1855	"	--- Second Ave.
1856-61	pianos/piano mkr	h. 83 Hester
1862-63	pianos	91 Eldridge
1864-65	"	455 Broome & r. 40 Thompson
1866	"	40 Thompson

Thorn was a small-scale piano manufacturer. It is not known if he was the same person as the cabinet maker of the same name who appeared in city records as early as 1829. (See *MCC* 1917:18:125.)

THURSTON, Jasper

1829-30	piano mkr	259 William
1831	"	120 Duane
1832	"	88 Chrystie
1833-35	"	259 William

Thurston was related to *Joshua*, *Nathaniel*, and possibly *Peter Thurson*, see below, but little else is presently known about his career. From 1836-38, a

Jasper, Jr. was also listed at the William Street address.

THURSTON, Joshua

1820-22	pianoforte mkr	Chatham c. Duane
1823	"	68 William
1824-25	"	10 Duane
1826-53	"	259 William

Thurston apparently worked as a journeyman for most of his career. He was related to the piano makers *Jasper* and *Nathaniel*, and possibly also to *Peter Thurston*.

THURSTON, Nathaniel

Nathaniel Thurston operated a music shop and also published a few pieces of sheet music from 1821-c.1830. (**Wolfe** 1980:56) During the 1830s, he worked as a clerk and secretary on Wall Street. In 1853, with the journeyman piano maker Joseph Thurston, he founded the instrument dealership J. & N. Thurston at 8 Bible House. He later operated a coal business, and in 1856, with his son Nathaniel Jr., established the piano dealership Thurston & Son. He was related to the piano makers *Jasper* and *Joshua Thurston*, and possibly also to *Peter Thurston*.

THURSTON, Peter K./R.

1827-28	pianoforte mkr	56 Sullivan
1829-30	"	60 Sullivan
1831	cabinet mkr	152 Crosby
1832	"	620 Broadway

Peter Thurston apparently worked as a journeyman piano maker. His relation to the other Thurstons in the trade has not been established.

TIETGEN, John/Hans

| 1887-90+ violins | 321 E. 9th |

Tietgen was born in 1857 at Wankendorf, Prussia, and studied violin making on his own. He immigrated to New York in 1886 and established his own shop, ultimately producing approximately 500 instruments before his death in 1929. (**Henley** 1960:5:143)

TILTON, William B.

1853	see below	65 Chatham
1854	violins & guitars	18 Beekman
1855	violins	"

1856	not listed	
1857	guitarmkr	62 White
1858	violins	"
1859	mus instrs	459 Broadway
1860	"	575 Broadway
1861	guitars	"
1862-65	mus instrs	"
1866	"	56 W. 32nd
1867	"	763 Broadway

Tilton was in business as early as 1853 when his firm, *Tilton & Company*, received a silver medal for "improvements on the Guitar & Violin" at that year's American Institute Fair. At the 1855 Fair, the maker, whose address was then listed as 101 E. Broadway, won another silver medal for improved guitars and violins, the awards committee noting that "Although we consider the 'Tilton Guitar' with the improvement to be the best, still from our examination we are convinced that Hall & Sons' Guitars with Tilton's improvements attached would be superior to all other makes." (*American Institute Records*)

Tilton's patented improvements consisted of two special features: "One was that the grain of the wood ran slantwise instead of up and down as usual. The other was a circular metal disc, attached to the sound bar at the sound hole, which bore the name Tilton." (**Ayars** 1937:274) Later in the century, after Tilton's patent had expired, his improvements were used by other makers, including the New York guitar maker *Pehr Anderberg*.

TILTON & COMPANY

1853	violins & guitars	65 Chatham
1854	"	18 Beekman
1855	violins	"

See above *William Tilton*.

TOMPKINS, William Shute

1836-37	cabinet mkr	233 Spring
1838	"	324 Bowery
1839-42	"	262 Bleecker c. Morton
1843-44	chair mkr	262 1/2 Bleecker
1845	"	77 Sullivan
1846-48	not listed	
1849-50	cabinet mkr	69 Watts

Tompkins was born in New York in 1812, and although he worked primarily as a furniture maker, he also manufactured drums. Two of his instruments, made at his 69 Watts Street address c.1849, are in the collection of the New-York Historical Society. One of these instruments has a picture of his Watts Street shop painted on its label. During the 1850s, Tompkins moved just north of the city to Yonkers, New York, and in the *1861 AMD* (p.90), he was listed as a drum manufacturer in that town. Tompkins remained in Yonkers until his death on November 28, 1882. See **NYHS Quarterly Bulletin** (1935:10:66-68).

TONK, William

1880	manager	127 E. 129th
1881-82	[piano] stools	47 Maiden La.
1883-86	mus instrs	"
1887-90 +	"	26 Warren

Tonk headed the firm *Tonk & Company* from 1881-82; and with his brother, Charles J., headed *Tonk & Brother* from 1883-90 +. He was primarily an importer of instruments and a maker of piano stools, however, the *1885 AMD* (p.215) listed Tonk & Brother as a "Jobber of Musical Instruments." The Tonks were nephews of the instrument dealer *Julius Bauer*, and after 1890, when several more brothers joined the firm, the family began to manufacture pianos. See **Tonk** (1926).

TONK & BROTHER

| 1883-86 | mus instrs | 47 Maiden La. |
| 1887-90 + | " | 26 Warren |

See above *William Tonk*.

TONK & COMPANY

| 1881-82 | [piano] stools | 47 Maiden La. |

See above *William Tonk*.

TOOMEY, (C.?)

From 1837-40, Tonk was a member of the instrument-making firm *Toomey & Hoey*. In 1838, the firm was awarded a diploma "for the second best specimen of flutes" exhibited at the year's American Institute Fair. The firm's address was given as "Spring-street," but it was never listed in the *NYCD*. (*American Institute Records*) Toomey's first name was not mentioned in New York records, however, he might have been the same person as the clarinet maker C. Toomey who worked in Georgetown, D.C. (**Langwill** 1980:178) Nothing further is known about Hoey.

TOOMEY & HOEY

See above *Toomey*.

TORP, Otto

1832-33	prof of music	87 Grand
1834	"	465 Broadway
1835-37	music store	"
1838-39	music	229 Broadway
1840	"	435 Broadway
1841	"	h. 378 Houston

Torp, a musician and music store owner, was a member of several partnerships. The first was *Torp & Viereck*, a music store at 465 Broadway; then, from 1836-37, Torp joined *James Love* in *Torp & Love*. At the 1836 American Institute Fair, the partners were awarded a gold medal for a "Horizontal grand action pianoforte highly finished in mahogany. . .ornamented by portraits of C.M. Von Weber, and Meyerbeer, music composers. Price $500." They also received a gold medal at the Institute's 1837 Fair; and in 1838, a silver medal for "the second best pianoforte." (*American Institute Records*)

In 1838, with *Ferdinand Unger*, Torp established the firm *Torp & Unger*, which lasted until 1840. An Egyptian-style square piano built by Torp & Unger is now in the collection of the Smithsonian Institution. (Catalog No.277,897) In addition to manufacturing pianos, Torp was also involved in music publishing; see **Dichter** (1977:238).

TORP & LOVE

| 1836-37 | piano mkrs | 465 Broadway |

See above *Otto Torp*.

TORP & UNGER

| 1838-39 | piano mkrs | 229 Broadway |
| 1840 | " | 327 Bowery & 435 Broadway |

See above *Otto Torp*.

TORP & VIERECK

| 1834 | music store | 465 Broadway |

See above *Otto Torp*.

TORRINS, Edward

Chickering (1902:34) claimed that Torrins was the first person in the United States to make ophicleides. Organologist Robert Eliason (PC:Eliason) noted that Torrins was listed as a musician at 98 E. Broadway in 1835, but no other record has been found to document his activities in the city.

TREMAINE, John

Tremaine was an actor, musician, conductor and stage hand with the Old American Company c.1750. On August 26, 1751, he advertised in *The New-York Gazette* that "having declined the Stage, [he] proposed to follow his Business of cabinet-making." (**Gottesman** 1938:1:119) Perhaps it was his combination of skills that led him to build a harpsichord of "a most agreeable and melodious volume and tone character," which was used at a benefit concert in 1759. (**Spillane** 1890:61-62) Tremaine was active on the New York stage through the Revolution, but there is no record that he built any more instruments.

TREMAINE, William

1861	music seller	333 Broadway
1867-68	music	481 Broadway
1869-72	pianos	435 Broome
1873-74	not listed	
1875-76	organs	14 E. 14th
1877-78	pianos	21 E. 14th & 421 E. 12th
1879-82	"	" & 124 W. 25th
1883	music	h. 144 W. 23rd

Born in 1840, Tremaine was a salesman and entrepreneur primarily involved in selling instruments. From 1869-72, with his brother Charles M., he headed the dealership *Tremaine Brothers*; and in 1875, with *Andrew Billings*, he was briefly a partner of *Billings & Tremaine*.

In 1878, Tremaine organized a company to manufacture and market an automatic organ, the "orguinette," which had been invented and developed in 1876 by Mason J. Mathews. In 1888, Tremaine acquired the patents and stock of the Automatic Music Paper Company of Boston, with the patents of instrument designer *Merritt Gally*. With these holdings, Tremaine established the well-known Aeolian Organ & Music Company. He continued to make contributions to automatic instrument manufacturing during the 1890s. See *NCAB* (XVIII:171-72); *Billings & Tremaine*.

TREMAINE, C.M. & BROTHER

1869-72	pianos	435 Broome

See above *William Tremaine*.

TRIPPELL, Jacob

Information about Trippell comes from an advertisement the maker placed on August 24, 1767 in *The New-York Gazette*: "Musical Instrument Maker from London at the House of Mr. John Ent, Watchmaker, opposite to, on the West Side of the Old Slip Market, a few Doors below Duyckinck's Corner, makes and repairs all sorts of Violins, Bass and Tenor Viols; English and Spanish Guitters [**sic**], Loutens, Mentelines, Mandores, and Welsh Harps, at reasonable Rates, as neat as in Europe, Having work't at the Business Nine Years, with the best Hands in London, since I left Germany; I shall Endeavour to Give Satisfaction to those Ladies and Gentlemen, that shall favour me with their Custom."

TRUSLOW, William

See *Grovesteen & Truslow*.

TUBBS, Edward

1879-80	mus instrs	384 Bowery
1882	bow mkr	"
1883	violins	6 Fourth Ave.
1884-90+	mus instrs	374 Broadway

Tubbs was born at London in 1837, and was probably related to the famous British bow maker James Tubbs, who was active from 1835-1921. In the *1885 AMD* (p.215), he was listed as a "Violin & Bow Manufacturer." In 1889, he was joined by John Tubbs (his son?), and continued to work in the city until his death in 1922. See **Roda** (1959:294); **Henley** (1960:5:158).

TURK, Ahashuerus, Sr.

1787-90	turner & mus instr mkr	24 Nassau
1791-93	" & "	61 Maiden La.
1794	mus instr mkr	35 Nassau
1795	turner & mus instr mkr	"
1796	ivory turner	36 c. of John & Nassau
1797-1805	turner & mus instr mkr	35 Nassau
1806	widow of Ahashuerus	"

Turk was probably the son of a cordwainer of the same name who had been listed in city records as early as 1741. The younger Turk engaged in wood and ivory-turning and musical instrument making, which suggests that he made woodwinds since similar techniques were needed for both trades. Turk must have been an important and respected member of his trade, since he was chosen to head the delegation of instrument makers who participated in the parade marking New York's ratification of the Federal Constitution in 1788. Turk was also a member of the General Society of Mechanics and Tradesmen from 1792 onwards. (**Earle** 1882:23) Turk shared his shop with his son, *Ahashuerus, Jr.*, see below, although they were never formally listed as partners. The elder Turk died on March 1, 1806 at the age of 61. (**Barber** 1933:1:66)

TURK, Ahashuerus, Jr.

| 1793 | turner & mus instr mkr | 61 Maiden La. |
| 1794 | mus instr mkr | 49 Broad |

Turk probably learned his trade from his father, see above, and worked as an instrument maker for only a few years. He was later listed as a grocer at 19 Courtlandt Street in 1819, appointed "City Weigher" in 1820, and also served as an engineer to the Fire Department, a tax assessor, and an election inspector in the 44th Ward.

TURNER, Richard

1826	pianoforte mkr	Bedford n. Burton
1827	"	57 Bedford
1828-29	"	28th n. Ave. 3
1830	not listed	
1831-33	piano mkr	142 Elm
1834-35	"	66 Sullivan
1836-40	"	41 Delancey
1841	"	22nd n. Ave. 3
1842	------	"
1843-44	not listed	
1845	piano mkr	Lexington Ave. n. 28th
1846	"	215 Ave. 3
1847-49	"	E. 27th n. Ave. 4
1850-51	"	55 E. 27th
1852	pianos	h. "
1853 +	"	h. 135 E. 25th

Turner apparently began his career as an instrument maker and later became involved in selling pianos. He continued in the trade as a dealer through the 1860s.

U

ULSHAFFER/ULSHOEFFER/
WESHAEFFER, George

1789	musician	39 William
1790-92	"	50 Nassau
1793	"	10 Nassau
1794-95	"	19 Dutch
1796	musician & grocer	102 Broad c. Pearl
1797-1800	" & "	3 John
1801-05	musician	"
1806-11	prof of music	"
1812-14	"	10 Nassau
1815-17	"	3 Cedar
1818	not listed	
1819-20	teacher of music	"
1821-24	"	2 Cedar
1825	------	459 Broadway
1826	------	22 Reede

Ulshaffer was a German-born musician who in 1785 exhibited a "patent high-strung pianoforte" he had made in the coffee-room of the City Tavern. (**Spillane** 1890:70,101) On August 8, 1786, Ulshaffer announced in the New York *Daily Advertiser*: "Musical Instruments repaired & Tuned by George Weshaeffer [sic] in William Street, No.38 . . . he understands the reparations & tunings of Harpsichords, spinnets, forte-pianos, guittars, violins, violincellos, etc." Ulshaffer probably worked primarily as a musician throughout his career. In 1795, for example, he was employed as a violinist at New York's Park Theatre. (**Sonneck** 1915:88)

UNGER, Ferdinand C.

1834	------	54 Howard
1835	prof of music	52 1/2 Howard
1836	"	65 White
1837	"	96 Grand
1838	"	229 Broadway

1839	------	"
1840	------	435 Broadway
1841-42	------	385 Broadway
1843	piano mkr	57 Amos
1844	"	32 King
1845	not listed	
1846	------	97 Bank
1847	------	141 MacDougal
1848	------	231 Fifth
1849	------	10 Hammersley

From 1838-40, Unger was the practical member of the partnership *Torp & Unger*. A piano made by this firm was awarded a silver medal at the 1838 American Institute Fair. (*American Institute Records*) After the partnership ended, Unger remained active as a maker of piano keys. (**Spillane** 1890:161) See *Torp & Unger*.

UNION PIANO-FORTE COMPANY

1870-71	The Great Union Piano-Forte Co. Chartered 1866, Samuel Fisk, president, J.P. Hale, Treasurer & Gen'l Agent	479 Tenth Ave.
1872	" Hale pres., treas. & Gen'l agent	"
1873-75	", ", "& "	W. 35th & Ave. 10

Although this firm claimed to be established in 1866, see above, it was first mentioned in the 1870 *CmRg*. Samuel Fisk, who was listed as the firm's president from 1870-71—and possibly a relative of the piano maker *Edward Fisk*—left the firm before 1872 when *Joseph Hale* took over all the company's major offices. Union might have been one of the many stenciled names used by Hale, and by 1876, the firm either went out of business or was merged with Hale's other concerns. See *Joseph Hale*.

UNITED PIANO MAKERS' (STOCK) COMPANY

1864-66	86 Walker
1868-69	103 Bleecker
1870	101 Bleecker c. Greene
1871-72	105 Bleecker
1873-79	Depot 547 B'way; Fact & Ware Williamsburg, L.I.

This firm often advertised as the *United Piano Makers' Company*, and it is likely that it produced pianos which were stencilled and sold by other firms. After 1872, it was listed only in the *CmRg*, possibly because its factory and warerooms were moved to 1st & S. 3rd in the Williamsburg section of Brooklyn.

UNITED STATES FANCY WOOD WORKING COMPANY

In the *1885 AMD* (p.215), this firm advertised as "Manufacturers of drums, Banjos, tambourines, Guitars, Zithers, & Trimmings. Factory George Street, Brooklyn, E.D. Office 502 & 504 Broadway. Orders solicited. Catalogues furnished on application." Never listed in the *NYCD*s of the period, the firm probably specialized in instruments that were stencilled and sold by other firms.

UNITED STATES PIANO COMPANY

1871-72	645 Broadway
1873-76	810 Broadway
1877	" & 163 Bleecker
1878	163 Bleecker

This firm claimed to have been founded in 1868. (NYHS Laundauer Collection 16:C:Circular) In 1879, its title was changed to the *United States Piano Forte & Organ Company*, see below, and as such, it continued in operation until 1884. The firm probably produced pianos which were stencilled and sold by others, however, it was apparently not connected with the similarly-named *United States Piano-Forte Company* which was active from 1878-90+.

UNITED STATES PIANO & ORGAN COMPANY

1879	163 Bleecker
1880-83	not traceable/ not listed
1884	130 Reade

See above *United States Piano Company*.

UNITED STATES PIANO-FORTE COMPANY

1877	1280 Broadway
1878	Ave. 11 c. W. 35th
1879-85	423 Ave. 11
1886	" & 346 E. 32nd
1887-90+	" & 443 W. 34th

According to the *1885 AMD* (p.215), this firm manufactured pianos under the direction of General Superintendent L.W. Fullam. It was apparently not connected with any of the similarly titled firms listed above, although it is likely that this concern also produced pianos intended for stencilling and sale by other firms.

UNRUH, George M.

1856	carpenter	h. 147 Essex
1857	banjos	5 1/2 Bayard
1858	mus instrs	62 Division
1859-60	"	14 Division
1861	instrs	h. 127 Seventh

Unruh was a banjo maker, and in 1858, he joined *Frederick Lohr* to establish the partnership *Lohr & Unruh*. In 1860, with *Daniel Moser*, he founded the short-lived instrument-making firm *Moser & Unruh*. See *Lorh & Unruh*; *Moser & Unruh*.

URBAN, Joseph

Urban was born at Cernuc, Bohemia in 1821 and trained as a violin maker in Homlka. He worked in Prague before immigrating to New York in 1847. It is uncertain how long Urban remained in the city—he was not listed in the *NYCD*—but by 1852 he had moved to California. After returning briefly to Prague in 1863, he settled in San Francisco where he worked as a violin and guitar maker until his death in 1893. (**Henley** 1960:5:163)

UTT, Peter N.

1795-96	mus instr mkr	Greenwich
1797	"	76 Barclay
1798	"	Chambers
1799	"	90 Chambers
1800-06	not listed	
1807-08	shipmaster	49 N. Moore
1809	tavern	18 First
1810	porterhouse	20 James
1811	------	245 Water
1812	teacher of music	506 Pearl
1813-17	not listed	
1818-20	coffee house	Washington Market
1821	------	Chapel n. Robinson
1822	------	171 Duane
1823-26	not listed	
1827-28	teacher of music	19 Warren

In addition to his many other talents, Utt was also a flutist and composer. His name often appears in city records of this period, especially the *MCC*, usually in connection with his activities as a tavern owner. See **Lawrence** (1978:147-48).

V

VALLATE/VALLOTE, L.

1816-19	mus instr mkr	135 William
1820	importer of fr. goods	"

From 1816-17, Vallate headed the instrument-making firm *Vallate & Company*. Later in 1819, he was a partner in *Vallote & Lett*. Nothing more is known about either partner except that in 1820, they listed themselves as "importers of foreign goods."

VALLATE & COMPANY

1816-17	mus instr mkr	135 William

See above *L. Vallate*.

VALLOTE & LETT/LETE

1819	mus instr mkr	135 William
1820	importer of fr.goods	"

The firm's shop served as the New York retail outlet for sheet music published by Allyn Bacon of Philadelphia. (**Wolfe** 1980:224) See above *L. Vallate*.

VANDERBECK, Abraham

1828	pianoforte mkr	48 Grand
1829	"	115 Grand

A blacksmith of the same name had been listed for several years prior to 1828 at 296 Grand Street, but their relationship is not known.

VANDERBECK, James, Jr.

1833	mus instr mkr	1 Centre
1834	"	273 1/2 Houston
1835	"	189 Mott
1836	"	193 Mott
1837-42	not listed	
1843	mus instrs	r. 1 Franklin Sq.
1844	"	h. 162 Essex

No further information about this maker or his relation to other makers of the same surname is presently known.

VANDERBECK, John V.

1832	mus instr mkr	166 Essex
1833	"	126 First
1834-35	------	282 Second
1836	not listed	
1837	mus instrs	284 Second
1838	"	113 1/2 Rivington
1839-42	"	113 1/2 Stanton
1843-44	manuf mus in-strs	"

A person of the same name was listed during the 1840s as a grain measurer at 21 Coentis Slip, but it is not known if he was the same person as this maker. This maker's relationship to the other craftsmen of the same surname has not been established.

VAN OECKELEN, Charles J. & Cornelius

| 1859 | melodeons | 618 Broadway & 172 Mercer |
| 1860 | triolodeons | 618 Broadway |

In 1859, the Van Oeckelens, who lived at 19 W. Houston Street, joined their neighbor, the grocer *Melchior Ducker* of 21 W. Houston, in the partnership *Van Oeckelen & Ducker*. The firm manufactured triolodeons, a melodeon-type keyboard instrument. At the 1859 American Institute Fair, the firm was awarded a "Large Silver Medal" for exhibiting "the Triolodeon an ingenious invention." (*American Institute Records*) Ducker apparently had more faith in the new instrument than did the Van Oeckelens, and he took over the firm when they left in 1860. See *Melchior Ducker*.

VAN OECKELEN & DUCKER

| 1859 | melodeons | 618 Broadway & 172 Mercer |
| 1860 | triolodeons | 618 Broadway |

See above *Charles J. & Cornelius Van Oeckelen*.

VAN RIPER, James

1854	piano mkr	h. 42 Sixth Ave.
1855-56	pianos	120 MacDougal
1857-64	"	178 Wooster

Van Riper was a small-scale piano manufacturer who advertised in 1857 that he "Offers to dealers and others a fine assortment of First Class Instruments of 6, 6 1/2, and 7 octaves. Warranted equal to any made for beauty of tone, workmanship, and for staying in tune in any climate." (*CmRg* 1857)

Cornelius Van Riper, a journeyman piano maker who was later associated with the action makers Stubbins & Eckert, was also listed during the 1850s and 1860s; their relationship has not been established.

VANTILBURG, Thomas L.

| 1846 | pianoforte mkr | 15 Doyers (*NYBD*) |

Listed only in the 1846 *NYBD* (p.170), Thomas shared his shop at 15 Doyers Street with the piano maker *Benjamin Browning*. The two were never listed as partners.

VAN WINKLE, Abraham I.

1843-45	pianos	r. 92 W. 16th
1846	"	r. 67 W. 15th
1847	grocer	27 Jones

Less prominent than his relatives *David* or *Cornelius Van Winkle*, see below, this maker was active for only a few years as a piano maker before changing his profession.

VAN WINKLE, Cornelius

1855	see below	
1856-58	pianos	1 Bedford
1859	"	1 Hammersley

Although not listed before 1856 in the *NYCD*, Cornelius was reported as a piano maker by the *1855 New York Census*. His address was not given, but it is probable that he worked with his relative *David Van Winkle*, see below, in the latter's shop at 1 Bedford Street.

According to the *1855 Census*, he owned no real capital, but did have $1,000 worth of tools, and that year his shop employed 12 men and a boy at average monthly wages of $45, to produce 52 pianos worth $15,700. The zealous census taker also noted that the shop contained: 20,000 feet of lumber @ $600; 100 lbs. of wire @ $122.50; 52 sets of pins @ $156; 52 yards of cloth @ $375; 52 piano plates @ $26; 60 dozen hinges @ $75; 13 dozen rods @ $14.50; 52 sets of leg plates @ $39; 6,000 (gallons?) varnish @ $600; 52 sets of petal feet @ $26; 52 sets of ivory and sharps [keys] @ $338; 239 gross of screws @ $139.50; 10 gallons of glue @ $200; 52 locks @ $20; 52 name plates @ $52; 52 gallons of varnish @ $150; and 80 buck skins @ $320.

VAN WINKLE, David I./David J.

1841-42	piano mkr	128 Hammond
1843	piano manuf	r. 92 W. 26th
1844-51	pianos	"
1852	piano manuf	" & 118 Amity
1853-54	pianoforte manuf	1 Bedford
1855	piano mkr	1 Bedford c. Hammersley
1856-59	pianos	"
1860-62	"	" & 180 W. Houston
1863	"	"c. Hammersley

Probably the most prominent member of this piano-making family, David's shop was likely the one reported under *Cornelius'* name in the *1855 New York Census*, see above. In 1849, David was awarded a gold medal for the best piano exhibited at that year's American Institute Fair (*American Institute Records*), and **Spillane** (1890:210) mentioned him as a maker of "excellent pianos." The *1861 AMD* (p.171) listed Van Winkle as a "Piano Manufacturer" at 180 West Houston. See *Cornelius Van Winkle*.

VAN WINKLE, John D.

1848	see below	92 W. 16th
1849	piano mkr	191 Prince
1850	"	17 King
1851-52	"	90 Thompson
1853	pianoforte mkr	" h. 14 Hammersley
1854	"	r. 208 Sullivan
1855	pianos	"

John Van Winkle, a member of the piano-making family listed above, was awarded a diploma for a piano he exhibited at the 1848 American Institute fair. (*American Institute Records*) From 1843-45, *Abraham Van Winkle* was also listed at 92 W. 16th Street. **Kaufman** (1976:33) lists a piano maker named John P. Van Winkle working in New Jersey in 1854 and 1860.

VARROY, Charles

1883	mus instrs	88 Charlton

Varroy probably worked only as a dealer or importer of instruments, even though the *1885 AMD* (p.215) listed him as a "Musical Instrument Manufacturer" at 297 Bowery.

VAUPEL, Adam V.

1864	pianos	101 Bleecker
1865-67	"	" & 136 Ludlow
1868	"	333 W. 36th
1869-71	"	335 W. 36th
1872-79	"	10 Union Sq. & 335 W. 36th
1880-84	"	335 W. 36th
1885-90+	"	440 Ave. 7 & 335 W. 36th

From 1864-90+, Vaupel and his partner, *Henry Calenberg*, headed the piano-manufacturing firm *Calenberg & Vaupel*. Both men were practical makers, but nothing further is presently known about Vaupel. See *Calenberg & Vaupel*.

VIENOT, Louis

1858	hosiery	191 1/2 Division
1859	not listed	
1860	pianos	Broadway c. W. 37th

Vienot was probably a piano dealer, however, the *1861 AMD* (p.171) listed him as a "Piano Manufacturer" at Broadway c. W. 37th Street.

VIERECK

See *Torp & Viereck*.

VINTON, Charles A.

1861	tuner	487 Broadway
1863	pianos	h. 50 Fourth Ave.
1864	"	E. 34th c. Ave. 3
1865-68	"	108 E. 25th
1869	not listed	
1870-74	pianos	841 Broadway

Vinton had been listed as a piano tuner at 487 Broadway before 1863. (See *1861 AMD* p.173.) In 1865, Vinton entered into a partnership with his son, Henry A. Their firm, *Vinton & Son*, was active until 1871 when another son, Frederick H., was admitted and the firm's name changed to *Vinton & Sons*.

Vinton & Son advertised as "manufacturers of Square & Upright Piano-Fortes" in the 1866 *CmRg* (p.117); and though not listed in the late 1870s, Vinton Brothers reappeared in the 1880 *NYCD* as "general agents for the standard organ manufactured by Peloubet & Co."

VINTON & SON

1865-68	pianos	108 E. 25th
1869	not listed	
1870	pianos	841 Broadway & E. 74th n. 2nd

See above *Charles Vinton*.

VINTON & SONS

1871-73	pianos	841 Broadway
1874	"	" & Fourth n. 179th

W

WAKE, John F.

1838	piano mkr	Attorney
1839-41	"	168 Fulton
1842-44	pianoforte	"
1845	not listed	
1846	pianos	297 Broadway
1847	pianos	W. 27th n. Ave. 9
1848-52	"	184 Fulton
1853-54	"	58 Barclay
1856-58	"	167 Canal & 8 Vesey
1859	not listed	
1860+	pianos	364 Broome

From 1839-42, Wake and *Robert Glenn* headed the piano-making firm *Wake & Glenn*. According to **Spillane** (1890:162), the partners "ultimately separated and were known in the trade in after years in connection with action and key-making." Wake joined piano-makers *John Myer* and *Hiram Herrick*, from 1846-47, to form *Wake, Myer & Herrick*; and then, from 1853-54, established *Wake & Company*. His partners in the latter concern might have been James A. or William Wake, journeymen piano makers who were active during this period and might have been John's relatives.

In 1850, Wake was listed as a piano manufacturer in Fort Lee, New Jersey (**Kaufman** 1976:33), and it is possible that his factory was located outside New York even during the period his name appeared in the *NYCD*s. The *1855 New York Census* reported Wake as a maker of "hardware for pianos" in the Sixth Ward, and he continued to be listed as a piano dealer through the early 1860s.

See above *Charles Vinton*.

VORWERCK, Charles W.

1851	mus instr mkr	248 Pearl (*NYBD*)

Vorwerck had been listed as early as 1836 as an importer at 272 1/2 Pearl Street; in 1843 his trade was "hardware," and in 1847, he was an "importer of german hardware, cutlery, steel, guns, pistols, and fancy goods." In 1851, he moved to 248 Pearl Street where he remained until 1853. He was listed as an instrument maker only in 1851.

WAKE & COMPANY

1853-54	pianos	58 Barclay

See above *John Wake*.

WAKE & GLENN

1839-42	pianos mkrs	168 Fulton

See above *John Wake*.

WAKE, MYER & HERRICK

1846	piano mkr	297 Broadway
1847	"	172 Fulton

See above *John Wake*.

WALE, Charles M.

1839	piano mkr	569 Greenwich
1840-41	not listed	
1842	piano mkr	"
1843	not listed	
1844	pianoforte mkr	h. 571 Greenwich
1845	"	h. 569 Greenwich
1846	not listed	
1847-49	piano mkr	"
1850+	undertaker/cof- finmaker	45 1/2 Clarkson

Probably the son of the instrument maker *William Wale*, see below, both Charles and his relative *Robert Wale* left piano making for undertaking in 1850. It is likely the all members of the Wale family worked primarily as journeymen.

WALE, Robert

1840	piano mkr	577 Greenwich
1841	"	12 1/2 Leroy
1842	, undertaker	"
1843	piano mkr	35 Burton
1844-45	"	3 Bedford
1846	"	10 Downing
1847	"	27 Morton
1848-49	"	40 Leroy
1850+	sexton & under-taker	50 Leroy

See above *Charles Wale*.

WALE, William

1806+08	carpenter	81 Murray
1809-10	not listed	
1811	cabinet mkr	r. 81 Murray
1813-14	"	83 Murray
1815	mus instr mkr	81 Murray
1816	not listed	
1817-26	mus instr mkr	83 Murray
1827-37	pianoforte mkr	569 Greenwich
1838	not listed	
1839-42	piano mkr	"
1843	not listed	
1844-47	piano mkr	"
1848	"	h. 509 Greenwich
1849	"	h. 569 Greenwich
1850	"	74 King
1851	boxmaker	"
1853	------	"
1854	Ruth widow William	"

This maker was probably the father of *Robert, Charles M.,* and *William Wale, Jr.,* piano makers active during the 1830s and 1840s. William Sr. appears to have been a journeyman. Another member of the family, John Wale, Jr., was listed as an organ builder at 569 Greenwich Street in 1828.

WALE, William, Jr.

1830	piano mkr	88 King
1831	"	Hudson c. Canal
1832	carpenter	29 Rose
1833	"	469 Washington

Probably the son of *William Wale*, see above, William left the instrument trade to work first as a carpenter and later as a tobacconist.

WALKER, Daniel

1829-42	music store	23 Maiden La.
1843	pianos	"
1844	"	19 Maiden La.
1845-46	"	44 W. 14th & 411 Broadway
1847	"	411 Broadway
1848	"	413 Broadway
1849	"	" & 325 Broadway
1850-52	"	413 Broadway
1853-54	"	535 Broadway
1855-58	"	6 Astor Pl. & 136 Eighth
1859-60	"	1 Clinton Hall & 6 Astor Pl.
1861-67	"	Clinton Hall
1868-71	"	47 E. 12th

Walker was probably born in England, and apparently immigrated to America c.1820. From 1828-43, Walker and his father-in-law, *William Geib,* headed the well-known firm *Geib & Walker.* The partners published music, imported and sold instruments, and manufactured pianos. On June 19, 1838, Walker was awarded a patent for an innovative wrest-pin design which was said to have created general interest in the trade. (**Spillane** 1890:160-61) Daniel's brother *John Walker,* see below, was also associated with the firm, although his name did not always appear in the *NYCD.*

After the dissolution of Geib & Walker, the brothers formed *J. & D. Walker,* which was active from 1845-71. Daniel died in 1870, and his brother retired from the trade shortly thereafter. The firm was reorganized and continued during the 1870s as *Walker Brothers.* Among his other activities, Walker is remembered as one of the founders of the New York Philharmonic. See *Geib & Walker, John Walker.*

WALKER, John

1841-42	piano mkr	38 W. 14th
1843-45	"	411 Broadway & 38 W. 14th
1846	not listed	
1847	pianos	411 Broadway
1848	"	413 Broadway
1849-50	"	" & 325 Broadway
1851	not listed	
1852	pianos	413 Broadway

1853	not listed	
1854	pianos	535 Broadway
1855-57	"	6 Astor Pl. & 136 Eighth
1858-67	"	1 Clinton Hall (Astor & 8th)
1868-72	"	47 E. 12th

The brother of *Daniel Walker*, see above, John was born at Wisbech, England in 1791, and emigrated to America c.1820. Before 1841, John apparently worked for his brother's firm, *Geib & Walker*, and after its dissolution, the brothers founded *J. & D. Walker*. In 1843, John was awarded a silver medal for the "2nd best Piano Forte" exhibited at that year's American Institute Fair; and in 1845, he received a gold medal from the same organization for "a semi-grand Piano Forte." (*American Institute Records*)

Daniel died in 1870, and John retired shortly thereafter. He died in New York on August 15, 1880, and his obituary noted: "He was the last representative of what may be called the old school of piano-making; he carried on business at a time when competition was not so severe, and jealousies and rivalries were not carried to such extremes." (*Musical Trade Review for the General Music Merchant*, August 20, 1880) See *Daniel Walker*.

WALKER, Joseph

| 1819 | pianoforte mkr | 19 Barclay |

Walker was apparently not related to *Daniel* or *John Walker*, see above, but nothing else about him is presently known.

WALKER, J. & D.

1832-35	see below	
1845	pianos	411 Broadway & 44 W. 14th
1846	not listed	
1847	pianos	411 Broadway
1848	"	413 Broadway
1849	"	" & 325 Broadway
1850-52	"	413 Broadway
1853-54	"	535 Broadway
1855-57	"	6 Astor Pl. & 136 Eighth
1858-67	"	1 Clinton Hall (Astor & 8)
1868-71	"	47 E. 12th

The brothers *Daniel* and *John Walker* were first listed together from 1832-35 when Daniel was still in partnership with his father-in-law *Adam Geib*. The brothers' formal partnership began in 1845. See above, *Daniel* and *John Walker*.

WALKER BROTHERS

| 1873-75 | pianos | 47 E. 12th |
| 1885 | see below | " |

This firm, which advertised as "Successors to J. & D. Walker" (*CmRg* 1873:108), was headed by William H. Walker, who was probably the son of one of the founding brothers, see above. *Walker Brothers* was not listed past 1875 in the *NYCD*, but William H. Walker "Piano Manufacturer" was listed at the same address in the *1885 AMD* (p.215). See above *J. & D. Walker*.

WALLACE, (William) Vincent

| 1857-59 | pianos | 26 Wooster |

Wallace (1812-1865) was an eminent Irish composer and pianist who, during his residence in New York, briefly headed the *Wallace Piano Forte Company*. Although Wallace was granted a patent on October 30, 1866 for an improved piano action (No. 59,295), it is unlikely that he was ever involved in actually constructing instruments. (**Spillane** 1890:366) The piano designer *Spencer Driggs* oversaw the construction of Wallace pianos, and **Rimbault** (1860:169) wrote their pianos were "highly spoken of by some of the most eminent pianoforte players, including Thalberg." See *New Grove* (1980:20:175-78); **Baker** (1958); **Flood** (1912); *Spencer Driggs*.

WALLACE PIANO FORTE COMPANY

| 1857 | | 26 Wooster |
| 1858 | | " & 467 Broome |

See *(William) Vincent Wallace*.

WALTERS, Richard M.

1881	pianos	27 E. 14 & r. 232 E. 36th
1882-88	pianos, manuf Narvesen pianos. Pianos rented, exchanged . . . sold, cash or installments	57 & 59 University Pl. fact. 230 & 232 E. 36th
		fact. 230 & 232 E. 36th
1889-90+	pianos & auctions	1370 Broadway

Walters had been active as a maker of piano actions during the 1870s. In 1880, he took over *Conrad Narvesen's* piano firm—probably *Narvesen*,

Bergman & Haugaard — "purchasing their plant and their general good-will in August of that year." (**Spillane** 1890:251) Walters continued to use Narvesen's name on his pianos, and in 1885 advertised: "R.M. Walters Pianos . . . The NARVESEN PIANO Manufactured by R.N. Narvesen is meeting with great favor from musicians and the public generally. The Board of Education of New York have awarded the contract to Mr. Walters to supply the Public Schools with these pianos." In addition to pianos, Walters also manufactured organs and sold "new & used pianos of all makes." (*CmRg* 1885:58) See *Conrad Narvesen*.

WARD & KNAPP

This firm was headed by Edward Ward and John H. Knapp. They began as members of the firm Ward, Knapp & Brown, makers of "wood, willow & case ware" in 1858. The partners were listed as "Drum Manufacturers" at 64 William Street in the *1861 AMD* (p.90). They were also involved in "toys," and might have been lured into the drum-making trade by the market for military instruments which developed during the Civil War.

WARNER, William

1819	pianoforte mkr	Grand n. Broadway
1820	"	17 Dominick
1821-26	"	489 Greenwich
1827-28	"	427 Washington
1829-30	"	18 Renwick
1831-32	"	477 Greenwich
1833	Sarah widow William piano mkr	473 Greenwich

Warner and his partner, *Hyde*, were listed as piano makers in 1819, and as carpenters from 1821-22. Nothing further is presently known about either craftsman.

WARNER & HYDE

1819	piano mkrs	Grand n. Broadway
1820	not listed	
1821-22	carpenters	51 Warren

See above *William Warner*.

WARREN, Hervey/Henry

1849	instrs	68 Fulton
1850	pianoforte mkr	289 1/2 Broadway
1851-54	pianos & piano mkr	295 Broadway
1855-57	pianos	508 Broadway

Listed as a "piano manufacturer" only in the *NYBD*s, Warren's *NYCD* listings suggest he was actually more active as a dealer.

WARRINER, Daniel C.

1848	bookkeeper	43 Grand
1849-50	pianos	315 Broadway
1851-52	"	300 Broadway
1853-55	not listed	
1856	pianos	505 Broadway
1857	accountant	"
1858	not listed	
1859	broker	33 Pine
1860	sec.	467 Broadway
1861-63	pianos	"

From 1850-52, Warriner and *William Dubois* headed the piano-manufacturing firm *Dubois & Warriner*. After the dissolution of their partnership, Warriner continued to work in the trade for another decade. Given his listings as a broker, accountant, and secretary, it is possible that he was involved in the business end of the trade. See *Dubois & Warriner*.

WATERS, Charles

1831-32	cabinet mkr	37 Sullivan
1833	not listed	
1834	piano mkr	234 Grand
1835	"	101 Allen

No further information about Waters, or his relation to the later *Horace Waters*, see below, is presently available.

WATERS, Horace

1850	pianos	447 Broadway
1851	"	447 & 333 Broadway
1852-60	" melodeons, etc.	333 Broadway
1861-64	pianos	481 Broadway
1865-75	"	" & 48 Mercer
1876-79	"	", 40 E. 14, 79 Univ Pl.
1880-82	"	826 Broadway
1883-86	"	124 Ave. 5 & 826 Broadway
1887-88	"	" & 344 E. 23rd
1889-90+	"	134 Ave. 5 & 344 E. 23rd

For many years, Waters, a music publisher, instrument shop owner and music dealer, operated the dealership Waters & Berry with his partner Thomas S. Berry. Although he sold pianos from the 1850s on, Water did not begin to manufacture his own instruments until 1880 when he left Berry to establish *H. Waters & Company*.

Spillane (1890:300-01) noted: "The name of Horace Waters has been before the musical public for over forty years in connection with music publishing and the retail pianoforte business. At present, Horace Waters & Company, of which Mr. Waters is the principal, are manufacturing pianofortes, and have been engaged in the business since 1880. Hitherto a lack of enterprise in advertising and following out progressive business methods in relation to the wholesale department has resulted to their disadvantage ... Waters, in addition to being one of the old-time men connected with the music trade, enjoys wide reputation as a temperance advocate and political reformer."

WATERS, H. & COMPANY

1880-82	pianos	826 Broadway
1883-86	"	124 Ave. 5 & 826 Broadway
1887-88	"	" & 344 E. 23rd
1889-90+	"	135 Ave. 5 & 344 E. 23rd

See above *Horace Waters*.

WATTS, Charles

1789	cabinet & mus instr mkr	29 Broad
1790-96	not listed	
1797	musician	116 Flymarket
1798	------	"

Watts immigrated to New York in the spring of 1789, on June 8th of that year, advertised in the *New-York Daily Gazette*: "C. Watts, Musical Instrument maker, at No. 29 Broad Street corner of Princess Street, Is just arrived from London, and has brought over for sale two small Forte Pianos, one of them of a new construction, with brass Dampers. Likewise makes, Tunes, and repairs all kinds of Musical Instruments. Those who please to favor him with their orders, may depend on their being punctually attended to, on the most reasonable terms. N.B. Cabinet work done in the newest fashion."

In 1790, Watts moved to Charleston, South Carolina, where he formed a partnership with the cabinet maker Thomas Wallace. On July 19, 1791,

Watts advertised in that city that, in addition to making cabinets, he also repaired harpsichords, forte pianos and spinnets. His southern furniture business was apparently successful, and in the New York *Diary* of January 28, 1797 he advertised: "Wanted from 8 to 15 Journeymen Cabinet and Chair-Makers, to go to Charleston, South Carolina where they will receive generous encouragement for further particulars." The advertisement went on to promise a 75% advance on terms of the New London book of Cabinet Prices (1793), passage money, and a salary of 3 1/2 dollars per week. (**Burton** 1955:129,131; **Bjerkoe** 1957:228-29)

Although a musician of the same name was listed from 1797- 98 in the *NYCD*, the person listed was probably Charles Watts, Jr., who remained in New York and later became a prominent merchant and lawyer. The elder Watts apparently had little connection with the instrument trade after 1790. The Watts-Jones Family Papers, now in the collection of the NYHS, contain many letters from Watts to his son, but they reveal little about him except his fondness for New York corn beef, which he frequently requests be shipped to his home in the south. Later in his career, Watts left the cabinet trade to become a mahogany merchant. His will was probated in New York on November 30, 1811; the estate consisted primarily of stocks and bonds but little real property.

WEBER, Albert

1852-54	pianos	103 W. Broadway & 28 Jones
1855-56	"	103 & 105 Broadway
1857-58	"	155 W. Broadway
1859-64	"	", factory 36 Laurens
1865	pianos	" & 41 Wooster
1866	"	429 Broome; 104 Walker & 41 Wooster
1867-68	manuf of celebrated Weber pianos	429 Broome; manuf 97 & 99 Ave. 7 & 123-127 W. 17th
1869-70	pianos	119 Ave. 7; Ave. 5 c. W. 16th
1871-83	"	108 Ave. 5 & 119 Ave. 7
1884	"	" & 121 Ave. 7
1885-88	piano manuf	708 Ave. 5 & 121 Ave. 7
1889-90+	estate of	108 Ave. 5

Weber was born July 8, 1828 in Bavaria, and immigrated to America at the age of 16. He learned piano making in the New York shop of *Charles Holder*, and later worked for one of the *Van Winkles*. **Spillane** (1890:228) claimed that Weber established his first shop on White Street, but he was first listed in the *NYCD* at 103 West Broadway. After two years, his factory burned, and he began again in a five-story marble-faced building on the corner of Broome and Crosby Streets. His firm thrived, and by 1869, when he opened a showroom at 108 Fifth Avenue, his was the sixth-largest piano-manufactory in the nation with gross annual sales of $221,444. (*New York Tribune* March 15, 1869) Weber died on June 25, 1879, and his young son, Albert, Jr. (b. New York 1858), took control of the firm. In 1903, the firm was bought by Aeolian Company which continued to produce Weber pianos into the mid-1960s. The Weber piano and the Webers themselves, were widely respected in the trade. For further information see: **Dolge** (1911:296-99); *New Grove* (1984:3:845); **Spillane** (1890:228-33); **Weber** (1897).

WEISS, George

1842	musician	45 Delancey
1843	"	26 Delancey
1844	prof of music	"
1845	"	27 Delancey
1846-52	music/musician	"
1853	fiddles	"
1854-56	music/musician	"
1857	mus instr mkr	"
1858-59	music/musician	"
1860-63	mus instrs	"
1864-65	violin mkr	"
1866	not listed	
1867-68	mus instrs	"

Weiss was also listed in the *1861 AMD* (p.91) as "Violin, Violincellos, etc. Manufactory 27 Delancey," and as an instrument maker from 1851-60 in the *NYBD*.

WEISSENBORN, Herman W.

See *Bruno, Weissenborn & Company*.

WENNERSTROM, Peter A./Andrew P.

1837-42	see *Lindell, Wennerstrom & Company*	
1843-44	pianofortes	115 Franklin
1845	"	h. 1 St. John's La.
1846	piano mkr	"
1847	not listed	

1848-49	pianos	Ave. 5 n. 10th
1850	"	40 Ave. 5

From 1837-45, Wennerstrom and *Eric Lindell* headed the firm *Lindell, Wennerstrom & Company*. Their firm shared its address at 1 St. John's Lane with the piano maker *William Nunns*. After leaving Lindell, Wennerstrom worked alone for several years, possibly as a journeyman, before joining *Gustave Bergquist* to form *Wennerstrom & Bergquist*. In 1849, the partners advertised: "Table pianofortes constantly on hand. Grands manufactured to order, & any repairs in the line neatly executed." (*CmRg* 1849:198) Bergquist remained at their 40 Fifth Avenue location when the firm dissolved in 1850; Wennerstrom briefly reappeared as a piano dealer at 80 Horatio Street in 1855. See *Lindell, Wennerstrom & Company*.

WENNERSTROM & BERGQUIST

1846	piano mkrs	1 St. John's La.
1847	not listed	
1848-49	pianos	Ave. 5 n. 10th
1850	"	40 Ave. 5

See above *Peter Wennerstrom*.

WENTWORTH, Richard H.

1831	piano mkr	115 Sullivan
1832	"	124 Walker
1833-37	"	46 Crosby
1838-39	"	118 MacDougal
1840	"	1 MacDougal

Wentworth was first listed in city records on January 11, 1830, when he joined a volunteer fire engine company. His address was given as 26th Street, and his profession listed as "pianoforte maker." (*MCC* 18:471) He was probably still an apprentice when he resigned to join another company on May 2, 1831. (*MCC* 19:688)

WERMERSKIRCH, William A.

See *Lauter & Wermerskirch*.

WESER BROTHERS (George W.; Nicholas M.; John A.; William H.)

1879	see below	
1881-90+	pianos	555 W. 30th

The Weser Brothers were "Manufacturers of Square & Upright Piano-Fortes. With all modern improvements, securing the most beautiful Tone as well as Cheapness." (*CmRg* 1882:63) John A. (d. March 19, 1918) was apparently the most prominent of the brothers, and when William Tonk visited his "small factory" in the 1880s, he expressed surprise to find Weser working "at a bench." (**Tonk** 1926:72) Both Tonk, and later Weser advertisements gave 1878 as the year of the firm's founding. The company continued in operation, at least on a limited scale, as late 1980.

WESHAEFFER, George

See *George Ulshaffer.*

WESTERN, Thomas

1794	patent pianoforte mkr	13 Wall
1795	"	14 Wall
1796	" – orders received	62 Wall
1797	"	64 Maiden La.
1798-99	pianoforte mkr	"
1800	dry goods store	60 Chatham
1801	------	55 Maiden La.
1802-03	livery stable	"
1804	------	"
1805-07	not listed	
1808	------	95 Maiden La.
1809-12	------	53 Maiden La.
1813	not listed	
1814	piano mkrs	88 Murray
1815-18	"	104 Waters
1819	------	"

Western had worked as a piano maker in London before immigrating to New York c.1794. On January 2, 1794, the maker advertised in *The Diary; or Evening Register*: "Thomas Western, from London, respectfully informs the public, that he is just arrived in this city, and intends to establish here a Manufactory of Piano Fortes, on the same extensive scale he carried it on in London. He likewise will repair regulate, tune and take old instruments in exchange. He has imported with him, a large assortment of Piano Fortes from his manufactory in London, which will be ready for inspection and sale on Monday the 23rd inst. at his house, No. 11, Great-Dock street, where he hopes to be favoured with the company of the amateurs of these instruments and doubt not they will find them of a superior quality in touch and tone, to any yet offered to the public, except as has been imported immediately from his manufactory."

The following year, on January 6, 1795, the maker advertised in the *New-York Daily Advertiser* that his shop was doing well: "The reception his piano fortes has met with from the public, merits his grateful acknowledgement, and supercedes the necessity of any encomiums on their excellence, and as they are manufactured under his immediate inspection, the most difficult parts by himself alone, he will at all times answer for their goodness." And, Western continued, he wanted "an apprentice of creditable connections . . . if he has a taste for music, he will be better approved of."

From 1800-14, Western apparently did not work as a piano maker. In 1815, he was joined by his son, Thomas, Jr., in the piano-making partnership *Western & Son*. In addition to pianos, their firm also operated a music store. In an imported barrel organ built by G. Astor & Company, London, Western inserted a paper label reading, "Thomas Western & Son, manufacturers of Patent Upright, Grand and Commode Piano-Fortes & Organ Builders. At their music store, No. 104 Waters Street. Nearly facing the Phoenix Stores." (**NYHS** Landauer Collection 16:C) A piano built by Western before he came to New York, labeled "Thomas Western/ Maker/ near Westminster Bridge/ London" is now in the collection of the Metropolitan Museum of Art (*MMA* **Catalog** No. 89.4.1855).

WESTERN, THOMAS & SON

1815-18	piano mkr	104 Waters

See above *Thomas Western.*

WESTFIELD, John

1832	piano mkr	11 Thomas

No further information is presently known about Westfield.

WHAITES, Archibald

1793	mus instr mkr	82 Queen
1794	"	382 Pearl
1795	"	Wine St. Bowery
1796	"	Winne St. Bowery
1797-1807	pianoforte mkr	19 Barclay
1808-09	"	262 Bowery
1810-11	"	Mott n. Spring
1812-15	"	262 Bowery
1816	widow of Archibald	"

Whaites was born in England, but immigrated to New York as a young man in 1784 (**Libin** 1985:163), and learned the piano trade as an apprentice to *Thomas Dodds*. A *Dodds & Claus* piano, built c.1792 and now in the collection of the *MMA*, bears a semi-legible signature on the bottom on the instrument which might be that of the apprentice Whaites.

Whaites established a shop of his own in 1793, advertising on September 22 in *The Diary; or Loudon's Register:* "Archibald Whaites, Musical Instrument Maker from London. Late apprentice to Thomas Dodds, Respectfully informs the public in general that he makes tunes and repairs all kinds of musical instruments in the best manner . . . his abilities in respect to the tuning has been well known in this city for upwards of six years . . . His place of residence at present, is No. 17 Frankfort Street."

In 1796, Whaites and the piano maker *George Charters* formed the partnership *Whaites & Charters* which manufactured and sold pianos "equal in point of tone to any that are imported and 25 per cent cheaper." (*The Diary*, January 8, 1796) Their firm continued in business until 1804, when Charters left the city for several years. Whaites continued to work as a piano maker until his death on August 14, 1815. In his obituary, he was listed as "Archibald Whaites, native England." (Evening Post [N.Y.], August 15, 1815)

After Whaites' death, his widow, Maria, came before the city's Common Council several times to request an exemption from property taxes on the grounds of poverty. Her request was ultimately denied in 1823. The Whaites were either relatives or friends of the *Neilson* family; in 1796, one of the Whaites' sons was named Saml Neilson Whaites after the piano maker, and on August 26, 1816, the Common Council appointed William Neilson "guardian of the infant children of Archibald Whaites, deceased." See *MCC* (1917); **Kelby** (NYHS:ms).

WHAITES & CHARTERS

1796-1804 pianoforte mkrs   19 Barclay

See above *Archibald Whaites*.

WHEELER, Lewis B.

1829-32	piano mkr	31 Second
1833-34	"	201 Broadway
1835	"	35 Second
1836	"	31 Second
1837	not listed	
1838	piano mkr	27 Second
1839	not listed	
1840-41	piano mkr	"
1842-49	piano tuner	"

Wheeler (b.1793, New Jersey) was listed in the city records as early as September 8, 1828 when his name appeared on property assessment records. (**MCC** 1917:17:355) He left the city in 1849, and in 1850 was listed by the *U.S. Census* as a piano maker in Hackensack, New Jersey. (**Kaufman** 1976:33)

WHEELOCK, William E.

1874-76	see *Billings & Wheelock*	
1875	organs	14 E. 14th
1876	pianos	"
1877-78	"	521 W. 24th
1879	piano manuf	218 & 220 E. 26th
1880-82	pianos	149th n. Ave. 3
1883	"	779 E. 149 & 25 E. 14th
1884-90+	"	763 E. 149th

Wheelock was born in Brooklyn c.1852, the son of A.M. Wheelock, "an eminent and highly respected citizen . . . who for years has been treasurer of city funds." (**Spillane** 1890:287) Unlike most of the masters in this study, at the age of 21, Wheelock had

Detail of a nameboard on a Whaites & Charters square piano manufactured
c. 1796-1804 at 19 Barclay Street.

enough money to buy into the large piano-manufacturing firm owned by *Andrew Billings*. Their firm, *Billings & Wheelock*, was in operation from 1874-76.

In 1880, Wheelock established *Wheelock & Company*, and since the owner was not a practical maker, the master piano maker *Charles Borst* was engaged as superintendent. The firm was a success, and Wheelock was personally respected for "traits of sterling commercial honesty and moral uprightness." (**Spillane** 1890:287-89) About 1886, the company began to market less expensive pianos under the label of the *Stuyvesant Piano Company*. Wheelock was one of the first in the trade to use modern advertising and marketing techniques. See *Billings & Wheelock*.

WHEELOCK & COMPANY

1880-82	pianos	149th n. Ave. 3
1883	"	779 E. 149th & 25 E. 14th
1884-90+	"	763 E. 149th & 25 E. 14th

See above *William Wheelock*.

WHITE, John

| 1827 | piano mkr | 92 Mott |

No further information is presently known about White.

WHITING, Luther

1822	see *Jacobus & Whiting*	
1823	pianoforte mkr	123 Elm
1824	"	133 Elm
1825	"	199 Mulberry
1826-28	"	192 Mulberry
1829	"	195 Mulberry h. 192 same
1830	"	234 North
1831	"	Bowery c. Ninth
1832-33	"	Ninth c. Broadway
1834-42	not listed	
1843-47	pianos	165 Eldridge

Whiting began his career in 1822 as the partner of *Jacobus* in the instrument-making firm *Jacobus & Whiting*. Thereafter, he worked alone for several years, left the city for several years, and later returned to work as a piano dealer. In 1846, his business was taken over by the piano dealer George A. Whiting, almost certainly a relative, who had been active since 1825 as a instrument maker in New Jersey. (See **Kaufman** 1976:33) It is possible that Whiting worked in New Jersey with his relative from 1834-42, when

his name did not appear in the *NYCD*. See *Jacobus & Whiting*.

WHITNEY, Abijah

See *William Whitney*.

WHITNEY, William Eugene

1870-71	intrs	48 Wall
1872-73	not listed	
1874-75	instrs	261 Broadway
1878	"	173 & 261 Broadway
1880-81	"	173 Broadway
1882-84	pianos & intrs	2374 Ave. 3 & 55 Liberty
1885-90+	instrs & pianos	" & 146 Broadway

In 1881, Whitney and his relative Abijah founded the firm *A. & W. Whitney*, and remained in partnership until 1884. In 1885, Whitney established his own firm, *Whitney & Company*, and although the *1885 AMD* (p.216) listed him as a piano manufacturer, it is likely that Whitney was only a dealer.

WHITNEY, A. & W.E.

| 1882-84 | pianos/instrs | 2374 Ave. 3/55 Liberty |

See above *William Whitney*.

WHITNEY & COMPANY

| 1885-90+ | instrs/pianos | 146 Broadway/2374 Ave. 3 |

See above *William Whitney*.

WILDER, Benjamin B.

See *Bennett & Wilder*.

WILKIE, Francis

1827	piano mkr	215 Mulberry
1828-29	"	73 Amos
1830	"	95 Thomas
1831-39	not listed	
1840	piano mkr	5 Essex
1841	"	79 Chrystie
1842	"	103 Bowery
1843-44	not listed	
1845-46	piano mkr	r. 36 White

No further information is presently known about this maker, however, he might have been related to a piano maker of the same name who worked in Breslau, Germany c.1835. (See **Pierce** 1965)

WILLISON, John

1825	pianoforte mkr	244 Duane
1826	not listed	
1827	pianoforte manuf	"
1828	"	42 Gold

Nothing further is presently known about Willison.

WILSON, Henry

1850	pianoforte mkr	50 Troy
1851-52	melodeons	75 E. 13th
1853-55	pianos	150 W. 27th
1856-64	piano mkr	h. 150 1/2 W. 27th

Wilson owned a small-time piano-manufacturing shop. According to the *1855 New York Census*, he employed 4 men at individual monthly wages of $50. He owned $8,000 of real capital; $2,000 worth of tools; and had in stock 3,000 feet of pine and rosewood worth $2,000. That year he produced 50 pianos worth $10,000.

During the 1860s, Wilson was only occasionally listed in the *NYCD*, and it is probable that he had already moved to 90 Pearl Street, Brooklyn, where he was listed as a piano manufacturer in the *1885 AMD* (p.194).

WINANT, Daniel D.

See *Rogers & Winant*.

WING, Luman B.

1860s	grocer & ship chandler	363 South
1869	see *Brainard, Wing & Co.*	
1870-75	pianos	423 Broome & 19 W. Houston
1876-82	"	521 W. 24th
1885-90+	"	245 Broadway & 555 W.30th

In 1869, this merchant joined *James Brainard* in the piano-manufacturing firm *Brainard, Wing & Company*; in 1870, they reorganized as *Brainard & Wing*. The following year, Wing organized his own firm, which was continued after his death in 1873 by his son, Frank L., who changed the firm's title to *Wing & Son*.

Dolge (1911:336) wrote: "This firm is probably the pioneer of the mail-order business in pianos. Building a reliable instrument, the concern has met with uninterrupted success." Little information about the firm's operation survives, but it is possible that many of their piano parts were built by sub-contractors. See *Brainard & Wing; Brainard, Wing & Company*.

WING & SON

1876-82	pianos	521 W. 24th
1883-84	"	245 Broadway
1885-90+	"	" & 555 W. 30th

See above *Luman Wing*.

WOEHR, Frederick E.

1856	mus instr mkr	127 Worth
1857	guitar mkr	"
1858-61	guitars	"
1863	drums, guitars, banjos, tambourines & ebony sharps for pianos	125 Worth
1864-65	mus instrs	h. 534 Pearl
1866	not listed	
1867+	sawing	129 Worth

Woehr advertised as a "Manufacturer of Guitars, Banjos, Tambourines, Toy, Military Brass & Bass Drums . . . Constantly on hand Guitars & Violin Cases. Ebony Sharps for Piano-Fortes." In 1868, Woehr entered into the partnership *Woehr & Miller*, which was involved in "sawing," and producing wooden piano parts. The 1868 *CmRg* (p.102) listed them as "Manufacturers of Patent Machine Piano Fortes & Billiard Table Legs, Table & Stool Pillars, Blocks for Carved Piano Legs & Lyres, Piano Forte Tops, Backs, & Lockboards, Music Desks, Guitars, Banjos, Brass & Bass Drums & Ebony Sharps, Bureau & Looking Glass Knobs & Door Stoppers." Woehr continued to manufacture these items into the 1890s.

WOEHR & MILLER

1868	sawing	129 Worth

See above *Frederick Woehr*.

WOLHAUPTER/WOOLHAUPTER, David/Gottlieb

On November 16, 1761, Gottlieb Wolhaupter, "living at the Sign of the Musical instrument-Maker" advertised a "parcel" of imported box-wood for sale in *The New-York Gazette*, adding that "he continues to make and mend, all Sorts of Musical Instruments, such as German Flutes, Hautboys, Clareonets, Flageolets, Bassoons, Fifes, and also Silver Tea-Pot Handles." In 1770, advertising as David Wolhaupter, the maker informed the public in *The New-York Gazette and Weekly Mercury* (June 18, 1770) that his shop had moved "to the house where Mr. Muller, leather breeches maker, formerly lived, nearly opposite the Flattenbarrack-Hill, in the Broadway." To his earlier list of instruments, he added that he also made bagpipes, and mended mathematical instruments.

The maker's last notice appeared on June 8, 1775 in *The New-York Journal; or the General Advertiser*: "In Fair Street, opposite St. Paul's Church [Wolhaupter] Makes and sells all sorts of Drums and Fifes. Drums are made of Mahogany, curled maple, and Beech wood, in the best and neatest manner." He also mentioned his ability to make German and common flues, hautboys, clarinets, "and all sorts of Instruments."

WOOD, George

1830	carpenter	151 Spring
1831-32	piano mkr	22 Fifth
1833	not listed	
1834	piano mkr	14th n. Ave. 6

Wood had worked as a carpenter before becoming a piano maker in 1831. His relation to other dealers and makers of this surname is not known.

WOOD, Robert

1834	piano mkr	199 Hester
1835-36	"	112 Orange

No further information about this maker is presently known.

WOOLHAUPTER, David

See *David Wolhaupter*.

WORCESTER, Horatio E.

1834	piano mkr	8 Warren
1835-37	"	6th n. Ave. 2
1838	"	375 Broadway
1839-42	"	361 Broadway
1843-44	pianos	"
1845-46	piano manuf	139 Ave. 3
1847-49	"	137 Ave. 3
1850-52	pianos	E. 14th c. Ave. 3
1853-54	piano manuf	137 E. 17th
1855	pianos	137 Ave. 3
1856-69	"	117 Ave. 3
1870-72	------	h. 39 Irving Pl.

From 1836-44, Worcester was a member of the prominent piano-manufacturing firm *Stodart, Worcester & Dunham*. He had come to the city from the Albany area, where he had reportedly worked as a carpenter and possibly as a journeyman in *John Osborn's* piano shop. It is not known if Worcester followed Osborn to New York, but he was also apparently a skilled craftsman and the "ruling spirit" behind Stodart, Worcester & Dunham. In 1845, he began to manufacture his own pianos; by 1858, his shop was producing 8 pianos per week. Although was somewhat overshadowed in his later years by younger and more innovative makers, he continued to work as a respected member of the trade until his death c.1890. See **Spillane** (1890:180); *Stodart, Worcester & Dunham*.

Y

YOUNG, Emma A.

1885-87	pianos	82 E. 9th

Young, and her firm *Young & Son*, were listed as "Piano Manufacturer" at 171-175 Lewis Street in the *1885 AMD* (p.217). It is unlikely that Young actually built instruments herself.

YOUNG, John

1832	piano mkr	326 Bowery

No further information about this maker is presently known.

YOUNG & SON

See *Emma Young*.

Z

ZIEGLER, Andrew

1872	pianos	110 Bleecker
1873	"	169 Bleecker
1874	"	178 Wooster
1875-79	"	73 Christopher
1880	"	147 W. 18th
1882	"	147 E. 22nd

Although Ziegler's listings suggest that he was merely a piano dealer, **Spillane** (1890:252) wrote that Ziegler & Co. [sic] were "among the other piano-making firms that had attained some note towards 1870 as makers of instruments for the masses." The firm was listed as a manufacturer only in the 1874 *CmRg* (p.105).

ZOEBISCH, CHARLES A. & SONS

1848	mus instrs & mus inst mkrs	171 & 189 Mott
1849-53	" & "	179 Mott
1854-65	" & "	163 William
1866-90+	" & "	46 Maiden La.

Charles Zoebisch and his sons, Charles A. Jr., Gustav, and Herman E., began their firm in Lancaster, Pennsylvania, sometime before 1846. The family seems to have been associated with the Moravian community in Lancaster (PC:Eliason), and might have originally come from Neukirchen, Germany. (See **Langwill** 1980:195.)

C.A. Zoebisch & Sons were primarily importers and dealers, though they did manufacture some of their own brass instruments. They received an award for brasses at the 1847 American Institute Fair (*American Institute Records*); and at the 1853 New York Crystal Palace, they exhibited "Musical Instruments of German silver & brass, with rotary valves; guitars." (*Official Catalogue* 1853:94)

In 1861, Zoebisch & Sons advertised as "Manufacturers & Importers of all kinds of Musical Instruments, Strings & Trimmings. All the newest styles of Brass & German Silver Instruments for Bands, with or without Rotary Valves, either over the shoulder or upright, constantly on hand or made to order." Probably because *Christian F. Martin* knew the Zoebisches as neighbors in Pennsylvania, their

New York store served as the "Wholesale Depot of C.F. Martin celebrated Guitars."

According to the *1870 U.S. Census*, Zoebisch & Sons owned $30,000 of real capital, and had $10,000 of raw material in stock. Their shop employed 8 men at annual wages of $9,000, who that year produced $30,000 worth of instruments. In the *1885 AMD* (p.217), the firm was listed as an instrument importer. The firm was a large one, and many instruments bearing the Zoebisch label are extant.

ZOGBAUM, Ferdinand

1854	mus instrs	99 Maiden La.
1855-56	"	97 Maiden La.
1857-58	"	10 Maiden La.
1859-69	importer	"
1870	importer & manuf of mus instrs	"
1871-75	mus instrs	89 Chambers & 71 Reade
1876	"	21 Park Pl.
1877-79	not listed	
1880+	pres./broker	RR Ave. n. 167th

Zogbaum had previously been active as an instrument dealer in Charleston, South Carolina c.1852 (PC:Eliason). Arriving in New York c.1854, he established *Zogbaum & Company*, which became *Zogbaum & Fairchild* in 1858 when Rufus Fairchild was admitted into partnership. In 1859, they advertised in the *NYCD* (p.1164): "Zogbaum & Fairchild beg the attention of the trade to our extensive stock of Musical Instruments and Strings of our own manufacture and direct importation. Our agents on the Continent of Europe are directed to purchase mostly for Cash, and to send all novelties, either in Musical Instruments or articles appertaining there to. Our particular attention is given to the manufacture of Guitars, Saxhorns, Cornets, Flutes, Clarinets, Banjos, Drums, etc. . . . which are manufactured at our factory here & immediately under our own supervision—none but the most experienced workmen being engaged and the best material used."

According to the *1861 AMD* (p.41), the firm then specialized in making and importing violins, guitars, flutes, accordeons, concertinas, flutinas, drums, banjos tambourines, brass instruments, clarionets, and the Tilton celebrated patent guitar. Zogbaum left the partnership c.1875, but apparently continued to work in the trade as an executive for an uptown factory. A Rufus Zogbaum—probably Ferdinand's son named after his former partner—was active in the instrument trade during the 1870s.

ZOGBAUM & COMPANY

1854	mus instrs	99 Maiden La.
1855-56	"	97 Maiden La.
1857	"	10 Maiden La.

See above *Ferdinand Zogbaum.*

ZOGBAUM & FAIRCHILD

1858	mus instrs	10 Maiden La.
1859-69	importers	"
1870	importers & mus instr manufs	"
1871-75	mus instrs	"

See above *Ferdinand Zogbaum.*

ZWAHLEN, Lewis

1831	mus instr mkr	250 William
1832-33	"	15 Rose
1834	"	43 Ann
1835-36	surgical pumpmaker	"
1837-39	not listed	
1840	turner	70 Mott
1841	not listed	
1842	surgical pumpmaker	57 Gold
1843	not listed	
1844	filterer	123 Warren

Zwahlen was granted a patent on May 5, 1832 for a "Seraphina or hamonicon organ." Zwahlen's patent predated the patenting of John Green's better

remembered seraphine by a year. (See **Gellerman** 1976:7.) The maker's later work with surgical and filter pumps probably also involved the designing of air bellows. Zwahlen was probably related to *Rudolph Zwahlen,* see below.

ZWAHLEN, Rudolph

1838	cabinet mkr	189 Reade
1839	"	35 Rose
1842	piano mkr	189 Reade
1843	"	193 West
1844	"	94 James
1846	cabinet mkr	6 E. Clinton Pl.
1848-52	pianos	2 E. Clinton Pl.
1855	piano mkr	h. 96 Ave. A
1857	"	h. 143 Orchard
1859-60	"	h. 66 Ave. D
1862	Elsa widow Rudolph	h. 43 Sixth

Zwahlen probably worked as a journeyman for most of his career. His relation to *Lewis Zwahlen* is not known.

ZWECK, CHARLES & COMPANY

| 1849 | mus strings | 169 Ludlow |

The "& Company" was probably *Daniel Zweck,* see below.

ZWECK/ZWICK, Daniel

| 1850-55 | music strings | 169 Ludlow |
| 1856-63 | brewer | " |

Although listed as an instrument maker in *CmRg*s of the period, it is likely that Zweck was primarily a dealer. He was probably the partner of *Charles Zweck,* see above, in the firm *Zweck & Company.*

William Shute Tomkins' workshop at 69 Watts Street.

CHECK LIST OF MUSICAL INSTRUMENT MAKERS BY TYPES OF INSTRUMENTS PRODUCED

In this Appendix, the musical instrument makers are cross-listed by the type of instruments they manufactured. Makers who listed themselves only as "musical instrument makers" without specifying any particular type, will be listed as such. When a maker is known to have specialized, the type of instrument will follow immediately after the artisan's name. This does not mean, however that the maker did not also produce other types of instruments.

ACCORDIONS & CONCERTINAS

Adler, Albert C.
Ahlers, William
Busch, Frederick
Carles, Severin
Chesky, Abraham
Christman, Charles G.
Gamble, James E.
Goetze, Frederick
Hess, Daniel
Jacobs
Kallenberg, Henry
Ludwig, Francis
Rasenberger, Carl
Rewald, Justus H.
Saenger, Jonas
Simon, Lewis T.
Stark, Otto

BAGPIPES

Carolan, Michael
Egan, Michael
Taylor, Charles
Taylor, William

BELLS

Pugh, William

CONCERTINAS

see accordions

GLASS HARMONICAS

Cogner, Alexander

HAND ORGANS

Davis, David
Ginocchio, Antonio
Ginocchio, John
Hicks, George
Ruth, Xavier
Taylor, Henry S.

HARMONICAS

Busch, Frederick
Christman, Charles G.
Hess, Daniel

HARPS

Browne, John F.
Browne, Edgar J.
Buckwell, George H.
Delveau
Hanley, James
Hawley, James
Jones, Daniel L.
Lewis, Laban
Lewis, Reese
O'Neill, Patrick C.
Pitt, John B.
Stackpole, James

JEW'S HARPS

Andrews, John

MUSICAL INSTRUMENTS

Adams, Nathan
Adler, Albert C.
Ahlers, William
Albrecht, John B.
Aleithe, Ernst
Allen, Joseph L.
Andrews, John
Averell, W.H. & E.D.

Baack, Edward
Baldwin
Ball, William H.
Barber, Thomas
Beames, Jonathan
Beggs, Joseph P.
Bender, John J.
Bernard, Frederick
Berndardt, Louis
Bernhadt, Edward
Bertau, Ferdinand
Berteling, Theodore
Bogert, David
Bolen, John
Boyde, George
Brand, Thomas
Bruggmann, William
Bruno, Charles
Buchan, James
Buckbee, John H.
Buckin(g), James
Busch, Frederick
Butler, John
Canschat, Michael
Cargill
Carles, Severin
Carter, Alden J.
Chanschet, Michael
Charters, George
Child(s), William
Cohen, Jacob
Cook, John J.
Cuff, John
Dale, Benjamin B.
Darling, David
Davis, Francis
De Jannon, Charles
Dodds, Thomas
Dodge, Samuel
Dubois, William H.
Duparge, Luther
Ebner, August
Eisenbrand, Henry
Exner, Sebastian
Fairchild, Rufus
Ferris, Benjamin
Foote, John H.
Frost, John
Furguson, Peter
Gallan, Joel
Gamble, James E.
Garvie, George D.
Gerbeth, August F.

Gervais
Gever, Adam
Giffin, Simon M.
Gillespie
Gleitz, August
Glor, Peter P.
Gondone, Gasper
Goetting, A.H.
Goetze, Frederick
Goodman
Griffin, Charles
Gutwennyer, Peter
Hall, William
Halliday, Thomas
Hamm, John
Hartmann, Alfred
Hartmann, Rudolph
Hatton, Paul
Hatton, William
Hawes, George
Hegarty, Michael
Hess, Daniel
Hill, Warren
Hingston, John
Hintz, Adolphus
Hooper
Horn, Charles E.
Horne, Robert
Howe, William
Jacobs
Joerdons, John F.M.
Johnston, Robert
Jollie, Allen R.
Jollie, Edward Jr.
Jones, Luther
Kaempf, Reinhardt A.
Kallenberg, Henry
Kelly, Josph E.
King, Matthew
King, Peter
Kober, George
Koch, John J.
Konig, Herman
Kubin, Joseph
Kuypers, Henry
Lacombe, Hypolite
Lamson, Paul
Landres, Michael W.
Lauter, Franz E.
Leavitte
Lete
Lucas, John
Malley, Francis D.

Meisenharter, Charles
Merrill, James F.
Millet, William E.
Monniot
Montgomery, John C.
Morris, Richard M.
Ochsner, Sebastian
Oehrlein, Gustave
Olier, T.
Overin, John
Page, John H.
Paulus, William
Pfaff Brothers
Pike
Pond, Sylvanus B.
Pond, William A.
Priest, John C.F.
Pullis, Conrad
Reinhard, Frederick
Rewald, Justus H.
Robinson, William, Jr.
Schaffer, F.G. & W.
Schaffer, George
Schreiber, August
Schroeder, Luke
Schuster, William
Secor, Jospeh B.
Seifert, Ferdinand
Selden, John
Simon, Lewis T.
Smith, Albert G.
Smith, John
Sonntag, Herman
Spiess, Charles
Stalder, Constant
Stark, Charles G.
Stein, Edward
Stevens, John R.
Thurston, Nathaniel
Tonk, William
Trippell, William
Turk, Ahasuerus, Jr.
Turk, Ahasuerus, Sr.
United States Fancy Wood Working Company
Utt, Peter N.
Vallate, L.
Varroy, Charles
Vorwerck, Charles W.
Watts, Charles
Weissenborn, Herman V.
Wermerskirch, William
Woehr, Frederick E.
Wolhaupter, David

Zoebisch, Charles A.
Zogbaum, Ferdinand
Zwahlen, Lewis

PERCUSSION

Bertau, Ferdinand
Brouwer, Samuel S.
Cohen, Jacob
Harlass, Frederick W.
Huzza, George
Jones, Luther
Kell, Charles
Knapp, John H.
Kompff, Philip H.
Meins, Richard
Oldendorf, Henry
Ottes, Joseph
Pelton, Daniel
Pelton, Philip
Sempf, William G.
Tompkins, William S.
Ward

PIANOS & KEYBOARDS

Abbott, John
Abbott, Nathaniel B.
Abbott, William
Ackerly, Henry S.
Albro, William
Aleithe, Ernst
Allovon, Jean D.
Altenburgh, Frederick
Altenburgh, Otto
Ambler, Samuel M.
Anderson, Andrew
Arion Piano-Forte Co.
Bach, Jacques
Bacon, Francis
Bacon, George
Baird, Lyman
Baker, Samuel
Ball, Sheldon X.
Barberie, Andrew V.T.
Barmore, Garrit
Barmore, Harvey
Barnes, J.C.
Bassford, Abraham
Bauer, Frederick
Bauer, Julius
Baus, Augustus
Beames, James F.
Beck, Gottlieb
Bedell, Joseph L.

Behning, Henry
Behr, Henry
Bender, John J.
Benjamin, Joel
Bennet, Isaiah
Bennett, Sullivan E.
Bennett, William W.
Bent, Richard M.
Berge, Louis
Bergin, Rudolph
Bergman, John
Bergquist, Gustave
Betts, Charles J.
Billings, Andrews
Bjur, William L.
Black, Frederick C.
Bloomfield, Edward
Blount, George
Boedicker, John D.
Bogardus, Henry S.
Bollermann Brothers
Bornhoeft, John
Borst, Charles
Boston, Bartholomew
Boston, James B.
Bowden, William H.
Bradbury, William B.
Brainard, James E.
Brambach, Stephen
Brand, John
Brand, Thomas
Braumuller, Otto L.
Brautigam, Adam
Brennison, William
Bridgland, James M.
Briggs, Gilbert V.
Bristow, George
Britton, Jacob
Brooks, Alanson E.
Brown, John W.
Brown, Thomas B.
Browning, Thomas C., Jr.
Browning, Thomas C., Sr.
Brumley, Augustus
Bull, Francis I.
Buttikofer, John
Cable, Robert
Calenberg, Henry S.
Callaway, Thomas C.
Cammeyer, John C.
Canfield, Ardon V.
Canschat
Carhart, Jeremiah

Cary, William
Casing, John
Central Piano-Forte Co.
Chambers, Thomas H.
Charters, George
Chatain, Amand
Chevalier, Louis Antoine
Choplain, Anthony
Christie, Jacob J.
Christopher, William H.
Clark, John
Clark, Joseph S.
Clause, Christian
Combes, Henry
Compton, William
Connor, Francis
Conover Brothers
Cook, John J.
Cook, Sebastian
Coquillat, Emanuel
Corbett, William
Costello, Patrick
Cregier, Michael V.
Cross, John W.
Cruse, Francis
Cummings, Laurence P.
Davies, Edward J.
Davies, Julian G.
Davis, Jesse J.
Davis, Morgan
Davis, William
Day, Charles M.
Day, Jacob
De Baum, Peter
Decker, Davis & John
Decker, Myron A.
Dederer, Levi
De Hoog, Peter
Denobriga, Augustus
Denobriga, Louis
Dent, James
Diehl, Justus
Dierkes, Henry D.
Diertichsen, William
Dingle, John W.
Disbrow, William
Dixson, Horatio
Dixson, John
Doane, Richard
Dodds, Thomas
Doll, Jacob
Dowling
Doyle, Thomas J.

Driggs, Spencer B.
Drucker, Sigmund
Dubois, William H.
Dubreuil
Ducker, Melchoir
Duffy, Peter
Dunham, John B.
Dupuy, Guitan B.
Dusinberre, Theodore
Dwyer, James
Eggleso, Arthur
Ehrlich, Edward
Empire City Piano-Forte Company
Ernst, Louis
Estey Piano Company
Evans, John
Falker
Farrand, Daniel M.
Fischer, Charles S.
Fischer, John U.
Fisk, Edward
Fleming, Joseph A.
Foster, Caleb T.
Foster, David
Foster, Edward
Fox, John C.
Fox, Joseph
Fritz, John
Fuller, John I.
Gabler, Emil
Gabler, Ernest
Gale, Adam H.
Gally, Merritt
Gassin, Andrew
Geib
Gibson, Thomas
Glenn, Robert
Gleitz, August
Godfrey, Cornelius
Godone, Gasper
Gordon, James
Gordon, Stephen T.
Gorton, Cephas
Grim, Davis
Grovesteen, James H.
Grow, Wales F.
Gruss, Francis
Guck, Paulus
Guttwaldh, Joseph
Haines, Francis W.
Haines, Napoleon J.
Hale, Jospeh P.
Hamm, Tobias

Hammond, Achiloe
Hanset, Henry P.M.
Hardman, Hugh
Harper, John
Harper, Robert
Harrington, Elbridge
Harrison, Frederick V.
Hasting, A.H.
Haugaard
Haugh, Casper
Hausmann, Christian
Hawkey, Henry
Hazelton, Henry
Hazelton, Frederick
Hearne, Edward
Heers
Henderson, John
Herrick, Hiram
Heyer, Frederick
Hoffman, Charles E.F.
Hoffman, Theodore
Hoger, George W.
Holder, Charles J.
Hollyer, Alexander
Holmes, George F.
Holstrom, Andres
Horne, Robert
Housman, Abraham
Howe, William
Huner, John F.
Hyde
Hyslop, Samuel C.
Ihlseng, Lars C.
Ihne, John
Ilsley, Ferdinand I.
Jackson, James, Jr.
Jacob Brothers
Jacob, Christian J.
Jacobus
James, Amos C.
Jardine, John
Jennys, John L.R.
Johnson, William
Karr, William H.
Kearsing, John
Kearsing, George W.
Kearsing, Thomas
Kearsing, William
Kenard, Isaac
Kern
Kernan, Richard
Kindt, Louis
Kindstrom, Gustave W.

Kinkeldey, Carl
Klix, Albrecht
Knauf(f), Frederick
Kohnle, Joseph
Kompff, Philip H.
Krakauer Brothers
Krall, Charles
Kranich, Hellmuth
Kraushaar, Anthony
Kroeger, Bernard
Kroeger, Henry C.
Kuder, Joseph
Kuhner, Leopold
Lambert, Henry
Laukota, Jean
Lenden, William
Lesieur, John D.
Leuchte, Ferdinand C.
Lewis, Henry
Lick, James
Lighte, Ferdinand C.
Lindell, Eric J.
Lindeman, William
Linden, William
Linsted(t), J.E.L.
Loomis, William J.
Loud, Thomas, Sr.
Love, James H.
Ludewig, Herman
Ludke, Ferdinand
Luedolff, Augustus
Luther, John F.
Lynch, Patrick
McDonald, James & John
Mahon, John
Malthaner, John C.
Manhattan Piano Company
Manner, Goerge C.
Manz, George M.
Marchal, James C.
Marschall, Theodore
Martins, Martin
Mathushek, Frederick M.
Maxwell, Charles M.
Maxwell, Samuel
Medcalf, Charles E.
Meeks, Henry S.
Mehlin, Paul G.
Mein, Robert
Meister
Miller, William
Mills, James B.
Mittauer, George

Mixsell, Aaron
Mixsell, Peter
Monroe, Peter
Moran, Edward G.
Morgenroth, Christopher
Morgenroth, Gustavus A.
Morris, Charles A.
Morse, E.L.
Mundy, Edward N.
Munroe, Thaddeus
Myer, John
Narvesen, Conrad
Nash, Issac
Nash, Thomas
Needham, Elias P.
Neilson, James
Neilson, Jason
Neilson, John
Neilson, Samuel
Neuhardt, Julius
New York Piano-Forte Company
New York Pianoforte Manufacturing Company
Newby, Alfred J.
Newman, Edward G.
Newton, Henry J.
Nitschke, Frederick W.
Nugent, James B.
Nunns, Robert
Nunns, William
O'Brien, John
Ogden, Cornelius G.
Osborne, John
Otis, Dwight P.
Ouvrier, Peter
Palmer, H.
Pappenberger, Andrew
Parmelee, Spencer
Pease, Chauncey D.
Peck, Leopold
Peek, David C.
Peek, David T.
Pemberton, Jacob
Perrin, David
Perry, Richard
Peterson, Garret
Pethick, John
Pethick, William
Phyfe, Isaac M.
Pirsson, Alexander T.
Pirsson, James
Pirsson, Talbot
Pleslin, William
Plowman, John

Poyner, Joseph
Proddow, Robert
Provost, Peter
Randell, John
Randle, Adonijah
Randle, Culver
Randle, Jesse
Ratz, Gothold
Raven, Richard M.
Reichard, Henry
Reid, William T.
Richardson, Thomas
Richmond
Riedel
Robb, Alickham T.
Robertson, William
Rogers, Able
Rogers, Charles H.
Rogers, George
Ross, John J.
Ross, William J.
Rowell, Warren
Roz, Theodore
Ruck, John
Ryder, Langford T.
Sakmeister, Charles P.H.
Saxe, George C., Rev.
Schaeffer, William
Schmidt, Theodore
Schmitt, Adam
Schnabel, Edward
Schneider, Albert
Schonemann
Schons, Bernard
Schraidt, Louis
Schubert Piano Company
Schuetze, Otto
Schuler, Frederick C.
Schwartzholtz, I.C.
Seabury, Charles S.
Selleck, George W.
Selleck, Sands F.
Senior, Edward H.
Senior, William F.
Shaff, Thomas
Shellard, Benjamin
Shellard, Henry
Sheiuble, John
Shields, Thomas
Sickels, John
Siebert, Charles
Siegel, Jacob H.
Sieh, Charles

Simonton, John C.
Simpson, John B.
Sivert
Small, R.E.
Smith, Albert G.
Smith, David
Smith, Freeborn, G.
Smith, Jacob
Smith, James T.
Smith, Robert W.
Smith, Tunis
Smyth, James
Sneyder, Joseph
Soebbeler, Nicholas
Sohmer, Hugo
Spanger, John P.
Sprawll, Robert
Sprenger, Matthew
Springer, John
Sprowll
Stackpole, James
Standford, David R.
Standiford, Daniel
Stealy, Jacob
Steck, George A.
Steedman, James
Steinway
Stodart, Adam
Stone, J.F.
Stratton, Eliphalet
Strothoff, Christopher
Stuehler, Joseph
Stultz, Henry
Stuyversant Piano Company
Suydam, Israel
Swartz, Abraham S.
Tallman, John
Taubald, Edward
Taws(e), Charles
Taylor, Charles
Taylor, Francis
Teufel, Joseph
Thomas, Daniel
Thompson, James
Thompson, Jesse
Thompson, Zacharias
Thorne, Stephen R.
Thurston, Jasper
Thurston, Joshua
Thurston, Peter K.
Torp, Otto
Tremaine, C.M.
Tremaine, John

Tremaine, William
Turner, Richard
Ulshaffer, George
Unger, Fredinand C.
Union Piano-Forte Company
United Piano Makers' Stock Company
United States Piano Company
United States Piano & Organ Company
United States Piano-Forte Company
Vanderbeck, Abraham
Vanderbeck, James, Jr.
Vanderbeck, John V.
Van Oeckelen, Charles
Van Oeckelen, Cornelius
Van Riper, James
Vantilburg, Thomas L.
Van Winkle, Abraham I.
Van Winkle, Cornelius
Van Winkle, David I.
Van Winkle, John D.
Vaupel, Adam V.
Vienot, Louis
Viereck
Vinton, Charles A.
Wake, John P.
Wale, Charles M.
Wale, Robert
Wale, William
Wale, William, Jr.
Walker, Daniel
Walker, John
Walker, Joseph
Wallace, Vincent W.
Walters, Richard M.
Warner, William
Warren, Hervey
Warriner, Daniel C.
Waters, Charles
Waters, Horace
Watts, Charles
Weber, Albert
Wennerstrom, Peter A.
Wentworth, Richard M.
Weser Brothers
Western, Thomas
Westfield, John
Whaites, Archibald
Wheeler, Lewis B.
Wheeler, William E.
White, John
Whiting, Luther
Whitney, William E.
Wilder, Benjamin B.

Wilkie, Francis
Willison, John
Wilson, Henry
Winant, Daniel D.
Wing, Luman B.
Wood, George
Wood, Robert
Worchester, Horatio E.
Young, Emma A.
Young, John
Ziegler, Andrew
Zwahlen, Lewis
Zwahlen, Rudolph

STRINGS

Albert, Charles F. (violins)
Albert, John (violins)
Anderberg, Pehr A. (guitars)
Baack, Edward (violins & guitars)
Bausch, Ludwig (violins)
Bogan, John J. (banjos)
Buckbee, John H. (banjos)
Busch, Frederick
Childs, Richard (violins)
Christman, Charles G. (guitars)
Clarke, James A. (banjos)
Clause, Christain (guitars)
Cohen, Jacob (banjos)
Coupa, John B.
Dobson, Charles E. (banjos)
Dobson, Edward C. (banjos)
Dobson, Franklin P. (banjos)
Dobson, George C. (banjos)
Dobson, Henry Clay (banjos)
Ebner, August (violins)
Flechter, Victor S. (violins)
Friedrich, John (violins)
Friedrich, William (violins)
Gemunder, August Martin (violins)
Gemunder, George (violins)
Glasel, August (violins)
Gould, Napoleon W. (guitars)
Guetter, Moritz
Halles, William (banjos)
Hamming, E. (banjos)
Harlass, Frederick W. (banjos)
Horne, Robert
Jacobs (banjos)
Kell, Charles (banjos)
Knopf, Henry R. (violins)
Kompff, Philip H. (banjos)
Konig, Herman (violins)
Konig, Herman, Jr. (violins)

Kreutzer, Carl (violins)
Kriner, Alois L. (violins)
Kyes, Charles H. (banjos)
Lanzer, Charles (violins)
Lauter, Edward A.
Lauter, Franz E.
Lohr, Frederick (banjos)
Lohr, Theodore (banjos)
Lowendall, Lewis (violins)
Martin, Christian F. (violins & guitars)
Maul, George (guitars)
Mercier, Charles (violins & guitars)
Miremont, C. Augustin (violins)
Morrell, Charles, Sr. (banjos)
Morrison, James (banjos)
Moser, Daniel (banjos)
Patent Violin Company
Ray, J.S. (banjos)
Remy, John
Richter, Adam (banjos)
Ross, William H. (banjos)
Schatz, Henry Anton
Schilbach, Oswald A. (violins)
Schmidt, Louis (violins & guitars)
Seele, Charles E. (violins)
Stafford, Geoffrey
Stevens, John (banjos)
Stoess, Ferdinand A. (bows)
Strodl, John
Teed, George (banjos)
Terhune, William
Tietgen, John (violins)
Tilton, William B. (violins & guitars)
Trippell, Jacob
Tubbs, Edward
Unruh, George M. (banjos)
Urban, Joseph (violins)
Weiss, George
Woehr, Frederick E.
Zweck, Charles
Zweck, Daniel

WINDS

Adams, Nathan (brass)
Albrecht, John B. (flutes & clarinets)
Allen, Joseph L. (brass)
Baack, Edward (flutes, clarinets & brass)
Badger, Alfred G. (flutes)
Ball, William H. (flutes)
Bauer, Julius
Berteling, Theodore (flutes, clarinets & oboes)
Bonnet, Carl

Busch, Frederick (brass)
Cerveny, Franz V. (brass)
Christman, Charles G.
Clearman, James (woodwinds)
Clearman, John
Cottier, Hugh (flutes)
Czerweny, Franz V. (brass)
Dash, John B. (horns)
Davis, W.J. (flutes)
Distin, Henry (brass)
Dodworth (brass)
Ebner, August (flutes)
Firth, John (woodwinds)
Hefely(e), Frederick (brass)
Hatton, Paul (woodwinds)
Hawes, George (flutes)
Hooey, James (woodwinds)
Horne, Robert
Ives, Seth (fifes)
Jollie, Allen R.
Kerrison, Robert (brass)
Lacombe, Hypolite (brass)
Larrabee, James D. (flutes)
Lauter, Franz E.
Lecocq, Jules (brass)
Longhurst, Thomas (flutes)
Martin, Gotfried R. (brass)
Meinell, William R. (flutes)
Mitchell, William (flutes)
Moennig, Henry W. (brass)
Monzani, Theobald P. (flutes)
Peloubet, Louis A. (woodwinds)
Peloubet, "Chabrier" (woodwinds)
Penzel, Gustave L.
Pollmann, Henry A.
Riley, Edward, Sr. (woodwinds)
Riley, Edward C. (woodwinds)
Riley, Frederick (woodwinds)
Riley, Henry (woodwinds)
Rohe, Joseph Anton
Ronnberg, William (flutes & clarinets)
Rosenbeck, John C. (brass)
Roth, William (brass)
Rowell, Warren (flutes)
Schreiber, Louis (brass)
Schulze, William G. (woodwinds)
Slater, Moses (brass)
Stratton, John F. (brass)
Toomey, (C.?) (flutes)
Torrins, Edward (brass)
Wolhaupter, David

SELECTED BIBLIOGRAPHY

BOOKS, ARTICLES, and MANUSCRIPTS

Albion, Robert Greenhalgh. *The Rise of New York Port* (1815-1860). New York: Charles Scribner's Sons, 1939.

American Advertising Directory, for Manufacturers and Dealers in American Goods. For the Year 1831. New York: Jocelyn, Darling & Co., 1831.

American Antiquarian Society., comp. "Index of Marriages and Deaths in *New York Weekly Magazine* 1788- 1817." [Worcester, Mass.], 1952. (Typewritten.)

American Institute of the City of New York. Papers and Manuscripts. New-York Historical Society Library, New York City.

American Musical Directory, 1861. New York: Thomas Hutchinson, 1861.

American Musical Directory of the United States and Provinces 1885. Compiled by Central City Publishing House. Syracuse, N.Y.: Central City Publishing House, 1885.

Anderson, Alexander. Diary. New-York Historical Society Library, New York City.

Arion Piano-forte Company. *Illustrated Catalogue of the Arion Piano-forte Company with a Description of the Different Styles of Pianos Manufactured, Their Peculiarities and Patented Improvements.* New York: Munroe & Metz, 1875.

Ayars, Christine Merrick. *Contributions to the Art of Music in America by the Music Industries of Boston, 1640- 1936.* New York: H.W. Wilson Co., 1937.

Badger, Alfred G. *An Illustrated History of the Flute & Sketch of the Successive Improvements Made in the Flute & A Statement of the Principles Upon Which Flutes Are Constructed, by A.G. Badger, Manufacturer of First Quality Flutes.* New York: Firth, Pond & Co., 1853.

Baker's Biographical Dictionary of Musicians. 5th ed. Revised by Nicolas Slonimsky. New York: G. Schirmer, 1958.

Barber, Gertrude A. "Abstracts of Wills from New York County 1850-1856." 7 vols. New York, 1951-54. (Typewritten.)

_____ . "Deaths Taken from the *New York Evening Post* 1801-1890." 54 vols. New York, 1933-47. (Typewritten.)

_____ . "Marriages Taken for the *New York Evening Post* 1801-1890." 23 vols. New York, 1933-48. (Typewritten.)

Bill, Edward Lyman., ed. *General History of the Music Trades of America.* New York: Bill & Bill Publishers, 1891.

Bio-Bibliographical Index of Musicians in the United States of America Since Colonial Times. Music Division. D.C. Historical Survey. 2nd ed. Washington, D.C.: Pan American Union, 1956; reprint ed., New York: Da Capo Press, 1971.

Bishop, John Leander. *A History of American Manufacturers, from 1608 to 1860: Exhibiting the Origin and Growth of the Principal Mechanic Arts and Manufacturers, from the Earliest Colonial Period to the Adoption of the Constitution.* 3 vols. 3rd ed. Philadelphia: Edward Young & Co., 1868.

Bjerkoe, Ethel Hall. *The Cabinetmakers of America.* Garden City, N.Y.: Doubleday & Co., 1957.

Boalch, Donald Howard. *Makers of the Harpsichord and Clavichord, 1440 to 1840.* 2nd ed. Oxford: Clarendon Press, 1974.

Boston, Noel and Langwill, Lyndesay G. *Church and Chamber Barrel-Organs; Their Origin, Makers, Music and Location: A Chapter in English Church Music.* Edinburgh: L.G. Langwill, 1967.

Bowers, Q. David. *Encyclopedia of Automatic Musical Instruments*. Vestal, N.Y.: Vestal Press, 1972.

———. *Put Another Nickel In: A History of Coin Operated Pianos and Orchestrions*. New York: Bonanza Books, 1966.

Boyer, Carl. *Ship Passenger Lists: New York & New Jersey, 1600-1825*. 3rd ed. Newhall, California: By the Author, 1978.

Bridenbaugh, Carl. *The Colonial Craftsman*. New York: New York University Press, 1950.

Brody, David. "Labor History in the 1970s: Towards a History of the American Worker." In *The Past Before Us: Contemporary Historical Writing in the United States*, pp. 252- 69. Edited by Michael Kammen. Ithaca, N.Y.: Cornell University Press, 1980.

Brown, Henry Collins. *Book of Old New-York*. New York: Lent & Graff Co., 1913.

Burton, E. Milby. *Charleston Furniture, 1700- 1825*. Charleston, S.C.: Charleston Museum, 1955.

Cammeron, Peter T. "A Chronology of the Organ Builders Working in New York City; From the Mid-Eighteenth Century to the Early Twentieth Century." In *The Bicentennial Tracker*, pp. 81-99. Edited by Albert F. Robinson. Wilmington, Ohio: The Organ Historical Society, 1976.

Catalano, Kathleen M. "Cabinetmaking in Philadelphia, 1820-1840: Transition from Craft to Industry." In *American Furniture and Its Makers*, pp. 81-138. Edited by Ian M.G. Quimby. Winterthur Portfolio, no. 13. Chicago: University of Chicago Press for the Henry Francis du Pont Winterthur Museum, 1979.

Chase, Gilbert. *America's Music From the Pilgrims to the Present*. 2nd ed. New York: McGraw-Hill Book Co., 1966.

Chickering & Sons. *Historical Musical Exhibition: Catalogue of the Exhibition*. Boston: Barta Press, 1902.

Clark, Victor Seldon. *History of Manufacturers in the United States*. 2 vols. Washington, D.C.: Carnegie Institution, 1916-28. Cole, Arthur H. *American Wool Manufacturers*. 2 vols. Cambridge, Mass.: Harvard University Press, 1926.

Commons, John Rogers; Saposs, David J.; Somner, Helen L.; Mittleman, E.B.; Hoagland, H.E.; Andrews, John B.; Perlman, Selig. *History of Labour in the United States*. 4 vols. New York: Macmillan Co., 1918-35.

Cornelius, Charles Over. *Furniture Masterpieces of Duncan Phyfe*. Garden City, N.Y.: Doubleday, Page & Co., for the Metropolitan Museum of Art, 1922.

Coxe, Tench. *A Statement of the Arts and Manufacturers of the United States of America for the Year 1810*. Philadelphia: A. Cornman, 1814.

———. *A View of the United States of America, In a Series of Papers Written at Various Times Between the Years 1787 and 1794*. Philadelphia: William Hall, 1794.

The Crystal Palace and Its Contents; Being an Illustrated Cyclopedia of the Great Exhibition of the Industry of All Nations, 1851. London: Bradbury & Evans, 1852.

Curti, Merle. "America at World Fairs, 1851- 1893." *American Historical Review* 55 (July 1950): 833-56.

Darling Foundation. *New York State Silversmiths*. Eggertsville, N.Y.: Darling Foundation of New York State and Early American Silver-Smiths and Silver, 1964.

Decatur, Stephen. *The Private Affairs of George Washington, from the Records and Accounts of Tobias Lear, Esquire, his Secretary*. Boston: Houghton Mifflin Co., 1933.

Depew, Chauncey M., ed. *One Hundred Years of American Commerce 1795-1895*. 2 vols. New York: D.O. Haynes & Co., 1895.

De Rozario, Pedro., comp. "Cabinet Makers and Chairmakers of New York." New York, 1940. (Typewritten.)

Deyrup, Felicia Johnson. *Arms Makers of the Connecticut Valley: A Regional Study of the Economic Development of the Small Arms Industry, 1798-1870*. Northampton, Mass.: Smith College, 1948.

Dichter, Harry and Shapiro, Elliott. *Handbook of Early American Sheet Music, 1768-1889*. New York: R.R. Bowker Co., 1941; reprint ed., New York: Dover Publications, Inc., 1977.

Dictionary of American Biography. 25 vols. New York: C. Scribner's Sons, 1928-53.

Dodworth, Allen. *Dodworth's Brass Band School.* New York: H.B. Dodworth & Co., 1855.

Dolge, Alfred. *Pianos and Their Makers; A Comprehensive History of the Development of the Piano from the Monochord to the Concert Grand Player Piano.* Corvina, California: Corvina Publishing Co., 1911.

Earl, Polly Anne. "Craftsmen and Machines: The Nineteenth-Century Furniture Industry." In *Technological Innovation and the Decorative Arts*, pp. 307-29. Edited by Ian M.G. Quimby and Polly Anne Earl. Winterthur Conference Report, 1973. Charlottesville: University of Virginia Press for the Henry Francis du Pont Winterthur Museum, 1974.

Earle, Thomas and Congdon, Charles T. *Annals of the General Society of Mechanics and Tradesmen of the City of New-York.* New York: Published by Order of the Society, 1882.

Ehrlich, Cyril. *The Piano: A History.* London: J.M. Dent & Sons, 1976.

Eliason, Robert E. *Early American Brass Makers.* Brass Research Series, no. 10. Nashville, Tenn.: The Brass Press, 1979.

_____. "Early American Valves for Brass Instruments." *Galpin Society Journal* 23 (1970): 86-96.

_____. *Keyed Bugles in the United States.* Washington, D.C.: Smithsonian Institution Press, 1972.

Ernst, Robert. *Immigrant Life in New York City, 1825-1863.* New York: King's Crown Press, 1949.

Fisher, William Arms. *Notes on Music in Old Boston.* Boston: Oliver Ditson Co., 1918.

Flick, Alexander Claspence., ed. *History of the State of New York.* 10 vols. New York: Columbia University Press, 1933-37.

Flood, William Henry Grattan. *William Vincent Wallace: A Memoir.* Waterford, Ireland: Office of the Waterford News, 1902.

Francis, John W. *Old New York, or Reminiscences of the Past Sixty Years.* New York: W.J. Widdleton, 1866.

Frankenstein, Alfred V. *William Sidney Mount.* New York: Harry N. Abrams, Inc., 1975.

Gellerman, Robert F. *The American Reed Organ: Its History; How It Works; How to Rebuild It.* Vestal, N.Y.: Vestal Press, 1976.

Gemunder, George. *George Gemunder's Progress in Violin Making, with Interesting Facts Concerning the Art and Its Critics in General.* Astoria, N.Y.: By the Author, 1881.

Gerry, Roger G. "Some Early Pianos in Philadelphia." *Chronicle of Early American Industries Association* 6 (July 1953): 25-28.

Gerson, Robert A. *Music in Philadelphia; A List of Philadelphia Music, A Summary of Its Current State, and a Comprehensive Index Dictionary.* Philadelphia: Theodore Presser Co., 1940.

Gibb, George Sweet. *The Saco-Lowell Shops; Textile Machinery Building in New England, 1813-1949.* Cambridge, Mass.: Harvard University Press, 1950.

Gildersleeve, Alger C. *John Geib and His Seven Children.* New York: By the Author, 1945.

Gottesman, Rita Susswein. *The Arts and Crafts in New York, 1726-1804.* 3 vols. New York: New-York Historical Society, 1938-65.

Grafing, Keith. "Alpheus Babcock: American Pianoforte Maker (1785-1842), His Life, Instruments, and Patents." Ph.D. dissertation, University of Missouri, Kansas City, 1972.

Great Britain Patent Office. Patents for Inventions. *Abridgements of Specification Relating to Music and Musical Instruments, A.D. 1694-1866.* 2nd ed. London: Spottiswoode, 1871.

Greeley, Horace, ed. *The Great Industries of the United States: Being an Historical Summary of the Origin, Growth and Perfection of the Chief Industrial Arts of this Country.* Hartford, Conn.: J.B. Burr & Hyde, 1872.

Greve, Charles Theodore. *Centennial History of Cincinnati and Representative Citizens.* 2 vols. Chicago: Biographical Publishing Co., 1904.

Gutman, Herbert. "Work, Culture and Society in Industrializing America, 1815-1919." In *Work, Culture and Society in Industrializing America: Essays in American Working- Class and Social History*, pp. 3-78. Edited by Herbert Gutman. New York: Alfred A, Knopf, 1976.

Harding, Rosamond E.M. *The Piano-Forte; Its History Traced to the Great Exhibition of 1851*. Cambridge, England: University Press, 1933.

Harlow, Alive Fay. *Old Bowery Days; The Chronicles of a Famous Street*. New York: D. Appleton & Co., 1931.

Harris, William Laurel. "Musical Instruments as an Indication of Refinement and Culture: The Unfortunate Story of Piano Legs." *Good Furniture* 9 (1917):44-52.

Hart, G. "H.C. Eisenbrandt in Baltimore." *Das Musikinstrument* [Frankfurt] 13 (February 1974): 276.

Hartmann Brothers & Reinhard. *Illustrated Catalogue and Price List*. New York: Charles H. Ludwig, 1893.

Haswell, Charles H. *Reminiscences of an Octogenarian of the City of New York (1816 to 1860)*. New York: Harper & Brothers, 1897.

Hazard, Blanche Evans. *The Organization of the Boot and Shoe Industry in Massachusetts Before 1875*. Cambridge, Mass.: Harvard University Press, 1921.

Heatherington, Avis. "The American Piano 1800-1840; A Reflection of Taste and Style." *The Decorator* 27 (Spring 1973): 3-24.

Hemstreet, Charles. *Nooks & Corners of Old New York*. New York: Scribner's Sons, 1899.

Henley, William. *Universal Dictionary of Violin and Bow Makers*. 5 vols. Brighton, Sussex: Amati Publishing, Ltd., 1959-60.

Hershkowitz, Leo. *Tweed's New York: Another Look*. Garden City, N.Y.: Anchor Press/Doubleday, 1977.

Hirsch, Susan E. *Roots of the American Working Class: The Industrialization of Crafts in Newark, 1800-1860*. Philadelphia: University of Pennsylvania Press, 1978.

Hitchcock, Wiley. *Music in the United States; A Historical Introduction*. 2nd ed. Englewood Cliffs, N.J.: Prentice-Hall, Inc., 1974.

Hoover, Cynthia Adams. *Music Machines -- American Style: A Catalog of the Exhibition*. Washington, D.C.: Smithsonian Institution Press, 1971.

_____. "The Steinways and Their Pianos in the Nineteenth Century." *Journal of the American Musical Instrument Society* 7 (1981): 47-89.

Horlick, Allan Stanley. *Country Boys and Merchant Prices: The Social Control of Young Men in New York*. Lewisburg, Pa.: Bucknell University Press, 1975.

Howard, Norman. "The Banjo and Its Players; Collected from Various Sources." New York, 1959. (Typewritten.) New York Public Library.

_____. "A History of the Banjo." New York, 1957. (Typewritten.) New York Public Library.

Howe, Mabel Amy, comp. "Music Publishers in New York City Before 1850; A Directory." *Bulletin of the New York Public Library* 21 (Sept. 1917): 589-604.

Huether, Charles. "The Great Piano Bonfire." *New Jersey Music & Arts* 30 (Sept. 1974): 31.

Humphries, Charles and Smith, William C. *Music Publishing in the British Isles, from the Beginning until the Middle of the Nineteenth Century; A Dictionary of Engravers, Printers, Publishers and Music Sellers, with a Historical Introduction*. 2nd ed. with supplement. New York: Barnes & Noble, 1970.

James, Philip B. *Early Keyboard Instruments from Their Beginnings to the Year 1820*. London: P.Davies, Ltd., 1930; reprint ed., London:Holland Press, 1960.

Johnson, Harold Earl. *Musical Interludes in Boston, 1795-1830*. New York: Columbia University Press, 1943.

Jones, Alice Hanson. *Wealth of a Nation To Be: The American Colonies on the Eve of the Revolution*. New York: Columbia University Press, 1980.

Jones, F.O., ed. *A Handbook of American Music and Musicians, Containing Biographies of American Musicians and Histories of the Principal Musical Institutions, Firms and Societies.* Canaseraga, N.Y.: By the Author, 1886; reprint ed., New York: Da Capo Press, 1971.

Journeymen Piano-forte Makers' Society. *The New York Book of Prices for the Manufacturing of Piano-Fortes.* New York: For the Society, 1835.

Kammen, Michael. *Colonial New York - A History.* New York: Charles Scribner's Sons, 1975.

Kass, Philip. "Exhibition of Pre-1900 American Stringed Instruments." *Journal of the Violin Society of America* 2 (Fall 1976): 70-83.

Kasson, John F. *Civilizing the Machine; Technology and Republican Values in America, 1776-1900.* New York: Grossman Publishers, 1976.

Kaufman, Charles H. "Musical-Instrument Makers in New Jersey 1796-1860." *Journal of the American Musical Instrument Society* 2 (1976): 5-33.

Kelby, J.S., comp. Notes on Trinity Church Yard. New-York Historical Society, New York City. (MS Files.)

Kirkland, Edward C. *Industry Comes of Age: Business, Labor and Public Policy 1860-1897.* New York: Holt, Rinehart and Winston, 1961.

Krivin, Marvin. "A Century of Wind Instrument Manufacturing in the United States: 1860-1960." Ph.D. dissertation, State University of Iowa, 1961.

Lancour [Adlore] Harold., comp. *A Bibliography of Ship Passenger Lists, 1538-1825; Being a Guide to Published Lists of Early Immigrants to North America.* 3rd ed. Revised and enlarged by Richard J. Wolfe. New York: New York Public Library, 1963.

Langwill, Lyndesay G. *An Index of Musical Wind-Instrument Makers.* 6th ed. Edinburgh: Lindsay & Co., Ltd., 1980.

Laurie, Bruce. "Nothing on Impulse: Life Styles of Philadelphia Artisans, 1820-1850." *Labor History* 15 (1974): 337-66.

Lawrence, Vera Brodsky. "Micah Hawkins, the Pied Piper of Catherine Slip." *New-York Historical Society Quarterly* 62 (April 1978): 138-65.

_____. *Strong on Music: The New York Music Scene in the Days of George Templeton Strong, 1836-1875.* Vol I, *Resonances.* New York: Oxford University Press, 1988.

Libin, Laurence. *American Musical Instruments in The Metropolitan Museum of Art.* New York: W.W. Norton & Company, 1985.

Loesser, Arthur. *Men, Women and Pianos; A Social History.* New York: Simon and Schuster, 1954.

Lohr, Steve. "The Steinway Tradition." *New York Times* August 24, 1980.

Longworth, Mike. *Martin Guitars: A History.* Cedar Knolls, N.J.: Colonial Press, 1975.

MacBean, William M., comp. Notes of the St. Andrews Society. New-York Historical Society, New York City. (MSS)

McKee, Samuel. *Labor in Colonial New York, 1664-1776.* New York: Columbia University Press, 1935.

Mangler, Joyce Ellen. *Rhode Island Music and Musicians, 1733-1850.* Detroit Studies in Music Bibliography, no. 7. Detroit: Detroit Information Services, 1965.

Mann, Walter Edward. "Piano Making in Philadelphia Before 1825." Ph.D. dissertation, University of Iowa, 1977.

Marcuse, Sibyl. *A Survey of Musical Instruments.* New York: Harper & Row, 1975.

Massachusetts Charitable Mechanic Association. *Exhibition & Fair.* Boston: Dutton & Wentworth, 1837-50.

Mates, Julian. *The American Musical Stage Before 1800.* New Brunswick, N.J.: Rutgers University Press, 1962.

Mathews, William S.B., ed. *A Hundred Years of Music in America, An Account of Musical Effort in American During the Past Century, including Popular Music and Singing Schools, Church Music, Musical Conventions and Festivals, Orchestral, Operatic and Oratorio Music; Improvements in Musical Instruments; Popular and Higher Musical Education; Creative Activities, and the Beginning of a National School of Music Composition.* Chicago: G.L. Howe, 1889; reprint ed., New York: AMS Press, 1970.

Matteson, David Maydole. *Minutes of the Common Council of the City of New York, 1784-1831: Analytical Index*. 2 vols. New York: Published for the City of New York, 1930.

Michel, Norman E. *Historical Pianos, Harpsichords & Clavichords*. Pico Rivera, California: By the Author, 1970.

Miller, Nathan. *The Enterprise of a Free People: Aspects of Economic Development in New York State During the Canal Period, 1792-1838*. Ithaca, N.Y: Cornell University Press for the American Historical Association, 1962.

Minor, Andrew C. "Piano Concerts in New York City, 1849-1865." Ph.D. dissertation, University of Michigan, 1947.

Minutes of the Common Council of the City of New York, 1675-1776. 8 vols. New York: Dodds, Mead and Co., 1905

Minutes of the Common Council of the City of New York, 1784-1831. 19 vols. New York: The City of New York, 1917.

Montgomery, Charles F. *American Furniture, The Federal Period, 1788-1825 in the Henry Francis du Pont Winterthur Museum*. New York: Viking Press, 1966.

Mott, Frank Luther. *American Journalism; A History of Newspapers in the United States Through 260 Years: 1690 To 1950*. New York: Macmillan Co., 1950.

National Industrial Conference Board. *A Graphic Analysis of the Census of Manufacturers of the United States 1849 to 1919*. New York: National Industrial Conference Board, 1923.

National Cyclopaedia of American Biography; Being the History of the United States As Illustrated in the Lives of the Founders, Builders, and Defenders of the Republic, and of the Men and Women Who Are Doing the Work and Moulding the Thought of the Present Time. 59 vols. New York: James T. White & Co., 1893- 1980.

National Piano Manufacturers Association of America. *The Stencilling of Pianos*. New York: Caslon Press, 1899.

New Grove Dictionary of Music and Musicians. 20 vols. Edited by Stanley Sadie. London: Macmillan, 1980.

New Grove Dictionary of Musical Instruments. 3 vols. Edited by Stanley Sadie. London: Macmillan, 1984.

New York City Wholesale Business Directory for 1875; for the Use of Wholesale Buyers Throughout the United States and Territories. New York: Smythe & Wilcox, 1875.

New-York Historical Society. "Abstracts of Unrecorded Wills Prior to 1790 on File in the Surrogate's Office, City of New York." *Collections of the New-York Historical Society* 11 (1902).

_____. "Abstracts of Wills." *Collections of the New-York Historical Society* 1-10, 12-17 (1892-1908).

_____. "Revolutionary Muster Rolls 1775- 1783." *Collections of the New-York Historical Society* 2 (1915).

_____. "Drums Made in New York by William Shute Tompkins." *New-York Historical Society Quarterly Bulletin*. 19 (Oct. 1935): 66-68.

New York State. Secretary of State. *Census for the State of New York, for 1835; Containing an Enumeration of the Inhabitants of the State with Other Statistical Information*. Albany: Croswell, Van Benthuysen & Burt, 1836.

_____. *Census of the State of New York, for 1845; Containing an Enumeration of the Inhabitants of the State, with Other Statistical Information*. Albany: Carroll & Cook, 1846.

_____. *Census of the State of New York for 1855; Prepared from the Original Returns, Under the Direction of the Hon. Joel T. Headley, Secretary of State, by Franklin B. Hough*. Albany: Charles Van Benthuysen, 1857.

_____. *Census of the State of New York for 1865; Prepared from the Original Returns, Under the Direction of the Hon. Joel T. Headley, Secretary of State, by Franklin B. Hough*. Albany: Charles Van Benthuysen, 1867.

_____. *Census of the State of New York for 1875; Compiled from Original Returns, Under the Direction of the Secretary of State, by C.W. Seaton*. Albany: Weed, Parsons & Co., 1877.

_____. Manufacturing Schedules of the 1855 State Census. Office of the County Clerk for New York County, New York City. (MS)

New York State. *Journals; Senate and Assembly of New York, Eleventh Session, January-March, 1788.* Pourkeepsie, N.Y.: Samuel & John Loudon, 1788.

Ochse, Orpha. *The History of the Organ in the United States.* Bloomington: Indiana University Press, 1975.

Official Catalogue of the New-York Exhibition of the Industry of All Nations. New York: George P. Putnam & Co., 1853.

Ogasapian, John. *Organ Building in New York City: 1700-1900.* Braintree, Mass.: The Organ Literature Foundation, 1977.

O'Neill, Francis. *Irish Minstrels and Musicians, with Numerous Dissertations on Related Subjects.* New introduction by Barry O'Neill. Chicago: Regan Printing House, 1913; reprint ed., Darby, Pennsylvania: Norwood Editions, 1973.

Ord-Hume, Arthur W.J.G. *Clockwork Music: An Illustrated History of Mechanical Musical Instruments from the Musical Box to the Pianola from Automaton Lady Virginal Players to Orchestrion.* New York: Crown Publishers, Inc., 1973.

Pelz, Edward. *On Piano-Forte Manufacture, Especially in America.* Leipzig & New York: J. Schuberth & Co., 1865.

Pierce, William R. [Bob]. *Pierce Piano Atlas: Successor to "The Original Michel's"* 6th ed. Long Beach, California: By the Author, 1965.

Pole, William. *Musical Instruments in the Great Industrial Exhibition of 1851.* London: R. Folkard, 1851.

Post, C. "The Origin & Growth of the Guitar, Mandolin & Banjo Industry in America." *Musical Trades* 26 (Dec. 1903):77.

Prime, Alfred Coxe. *The Arts and Crafts in Philadelphia, Maryland and South Carolina, 1721-1785: Gleanings from Newspapers.* 2 vols. Topsfield, Mass.: The Walpole Society, 1929-32.

Redway, Virginia Larkin. *Music Directories of Early New York City; A File of Musicians, Music Publishers and Musical Instrument-makers Listed in New York City Directories from 1786 through 1835, Together with the Most Important New York Music Publishers from 1836 through 1875.* New York: New York Public Library, 1941.

_____. "Notices, Announcements, Etc., on Music from the *Commercial Advertiser*, 1838." New York: [1941]. (Typewritten.)

Rensch, Roslyn. *The Harp: Its History, Techniques and Repertoire.* London: Gerald Duckworth & Co., 1969.

Rimbault, Edward F. *The Pianoforte, Its Origin, Progress, and Construction.* London: Robert Cocks & Co., 1860.

Ritter, Frederick Louis. *Music in America.* New York: C. Scribner's Sons, 1890.

Roberts, Kenneth D. and Roberts, Jane W. *Planemakers and Other Edge Tool Enterprises in New York State in the Nineteenth Century.* Cooperstown, N.Y.: New York State Historical Association and Early American Industries Association, 1971.

Rock, Howard B. "The American Revolution and the Mechanics of New York City: One Generation Later." *New York History* 57 (July 1976): 367-94.

_____. *Artisans of the New Republic; The Tradesmen of New York City in the Age of Jefferson.* New York: New York University Press, 1979.

_____. "The Delicate Balance: The Mechanic and the City in the Age of Jefferson." *New-York Historical Society Quarterly* 63 (April 1979): 93-114.

Roda, Joseph. *Bows for Musical Instruments of the Violin Family.* Chicago: William Lewis & Son, 1959.

Schulz, Russell Eugene. "The Reed Organ in Nineteenth-Century America." Ph.D. dissertation, University of Texas at Austin, 1974.

Scott, Kenneth. "Nineteenth Century Apprenticeship Registers, N.Y.C." *New York Genealogical and Biographical Record* 115 (Jan 1984).

Scoville, Joseph A. [Walter Barret]. *The Old Merchants of New York City.* 5 vols. New York: Carleton, 1863-70.

Seybolt, Robert Francis. *Apprenticeship and Apprenticeship Education in Colonial New England and New York.* Contributions to Education, no. 85. New York: Teachers College, Columbia University, 1917.

Silverman, Kenneth. *A Cultural History of the American Revolution; Painting, Music, Literature and the Theatre in the Colonies and the United States from the Treaty of Paris to the Inauguration of George Washington, 1763-1789.* New York: Thomas Y. Crowell Co., 1976.

Simpson, Mary Jean. "Alfred G. Badger (1815-1892), Nineteenth-Century Flutemaker: His Art, Innovations, and Influence on Flute Construction, Performance, and Composition, 1845- 1895." D.M.A. dissertation, University of Maryland, 1982.

Singer, Aaron. "Labor-Management Relations at Steinway & Sons, 1853-1896." Ph.D. dissertation, Columbia University, 1977.

Siracusa, Carl. *A Mechanical People; Perceptions of the Industrial Order in Massachusetts, 1815-1880.* Middletown, Conn.: Wesleyan University Press, 1979.

Smith, Adam. *An Inquiry Into the Nature and Cause of the Wealth of Nations.* 1776; reprint ed., New York: Random House, Inc., 1937.

Smith, Merritt Roe. "From Craftsman to Mechanic: The Harpers Ferry Experience, 1798-1854." In *Technological Innovations and the Decorative Arts*, pp. 103-39. Edited by Ian M.G. Quimby and Polly Anne Earl. Winterthur Conference Report, 1973. Charlottesville: University of Virginia Press for the Henry Francis du Pont Winterthur Museum, 1974.

Smith, Nancy A. "Pianoforte Manufacturing in Nineteenth-Century Boston." *Old-Time New England* 69 (Summer-Fall 1978):37-47.

Smith, Thomas R. *The Cotton Textile Industry of Fall River, Massachusetts: A Study of Industrial Localization.* New York: Columbia University Press, 1944.

Sohmer Piano Company. Advertising Flyer. New York, [modern].

Sonneck, Oscar. *Early Concert-Life in America (1731- 1800).* Leipzig: Breitkopf & Hartel, 1907; reprint ed., New York: Da Capo Press, 1978.

Spillane, Daniel. *History of the American Pianoforte; Its Technical Development and the Trade.* New York: D. Spillane, 1890.

Steffen, Charles G. "Changes in the Organization of Artisan Production in Baltimore, 1790-1820." *William and Mary Quarterly* 26 (Jan. 1979): 101-17.

Steinert, Morris. *Reminiscences of Morris Steinert.* Comp. and arr. by Jane Marlin. New York: G.P. Putnam's Sons, 1900.

Steinway, Theodore E. *People and Pianos, A Century of Service to Music.* New York: Steinway & Sons, 1953.

Steinway, William. "American Musical Instruments." In *One Hundred Years of American Commerce 1795-1895*, pp. 509-15. Edited by Chauncey M. Depew. 2 vols. New York: D.O. Haynes & Co., 1895.

Steinway & Sons. Personnel Book. (MS)

Stieff, Frederick Phillip. "Baltimore's Contributions to the Development of the Pianoforte." In *Musical Instruments and Their Portrayal in Art*, pp. 25-30. Baltimore: Baltimore Museum of Art, 1946.

Stokes, Isaac Newton Phelps. *The Iconography of Manhattan Island, 1498-1909.* 6 vols. New York: Robert H. Dodds, 1915-28.

Stoutamire, Albert. *Music of the Old South: Colony to Confederacy.* Rutherford, N.J.: Fairleigh Dickerson University Press, 1972.

Stratton, John F. "Revised Private and Confidential Price List for the Jobbing Trade." New York, [189?]. New York Public Library.

Stratton & Son. *1885 Catalog.* New York: Stratton & Son, 1885.

Strong, George Templeton. *Diary.* 4 vols. Edited by Allan Nevins and Milton H. Thomas. New York: Macmillan, 1952.

Teahan, John. "A List of Irish Instrument Makers." *Galpin Society Journal* 16 (May 1963): 28-32.

Tonk, William. *Memoirs of a Manufacturer.* New York: Presto Publishing Co., 1926.

U.S. Office of the Census. Eighth Census, 1860. *Manufacturers in the United States in 1860; Compiled from Original Returns.* Washington, D.C.: Government Printing Office, 1865.

_____. *Preliminary Report on the Eighth Census, 1860,* by Joseph C.G. Kennedy. Washington, D.C.: Government Printing Office, 1862.

_____. Ninth Census, 1870. *Census Reports, Compiled from the Original Returns of the Ninth Census, 1870, under the direction of the Secretary of the Interior.* 3 vols. Washington, D.C.: Government Printing Office, 1872.

_____. Tenth Census, 1880. *Census Reports, Compiled from the Original Returns of the Tenth Census, 1880, under the direction of the Secretary of the Interior.* 22 vols. Washington, D.C.: Government Printing Office, 1883-88.

_____. *Report on Manufacturers in the United States at the Eleventh Census, 1890.* Vol. 1, *Total for States and Industries.* Vol. 2, *Statistics of Cities.* Washington, D.C.: Government Printing Office, 1895.

Valentine's Manual of New York. 12 vols. Edited by Henry Collins Brown. New Series. New York: Valentine's Manual, inc., 1916-28.

Vallance, Aymer. "The Decoration of the Grand Piano." *The Magazine of Art* 25 (1901): 201-10.

_____. "The Decoration of the Upright Piano." *The Magazine of Art* 25 (1901): 544-50.

Vanderbilt, Gertrude Lefferts. *The Social History of Flatbush, and Manners and Customs of the Dutch Settlers in Kings County.* New York: D. Appleton & Co., 1882.

Van Der Zee, Henri and Van Der Zee, Barbara. *A Sweet and Alien Land; The Story of Dutch New York.* New York: Viking Press, 1978.

von Khrum, Paul. *Silversmiths of New York City, 1684-1850.* New York: Paul von Khrum, 1978.

Ware, Norman. *The Industrial Worker 1840-1860: The Reaction of American Industrial Society to the Advance of the Industrial Revolution.* Boston: Houghton Mifflin Co., 1924.

[Weber & Company]. *Progress of Time.* New York: Weber Piano Co., 1897.

Weeks, Joseph D. *Report on the Statistics of Wages in Manufacturing Industries, with Supplementary Reports on the Average Retail Prices of Necessaries of Life & on Trades, Societies, & Strikes & Lockouts.* Tenth Census. Vol. 20. Washington, D.C.: Government Printing Office, 1886.

Weil, Martin Eli. "A Cabinetmaker's Price Book." In *American Furniture and Its Makers,* pp. 174-79. Winterthur Portfolio, no. 13. Edited by Ian M.G. Quimby. Chicago: University of Chicago Press for the Henry Francis du Pont Winterthur Museum, 1979.

Weiss, Henry B. *American Baby Rattles from Colonial Times to the Present.* Trenton, N.J.: By the Author, [1941].

Wile, Frederick William, ed. *A Century of Industrial Progress.* Forward by Herbert Hoover. Garden City, N.Y.: Published for the American Institute of the City of New York by Doubleday, Doran & Co., 1928.

Wolfe, Richard J. *Early American Music Engraving and Printing; A History of Music Publishing in American from 1787 to 1825 with Commentary on Earlier and Later Practices.* Urbana: University of Illinois Press, in cooperation with the Bibliographical Society of America, 1980.

Zankovich, Paul. "The Craftsmen of Colonial New York." Ph.D. dissertation, New York University, 1956.

INSTRUMENT COLLECTIONS AND CATALOGS

Bate Collection of Historical Wind Instruments. *Catalogue of the Instruments.* Oxford: University of Oxford Press, 1976.

Densmore, Frances. *Handbook of the Collection of Musical Instruments in the United States Museum.* Bulletin, no. 136. Washington, D.C.: U.S. National Museum, 1927.

Gai, Vinicio. *Gli Strumenti Musicali Della Corte Medices e il Museo del Conservatorio Luigi Cherubini di Firenze".* Florence: Licosa, 1969.

Larson, Andre Pierre. "Catalog of the Nineteenth-Century British Brass Instruments in the Arne B. Larson Collection of Musical Instruments." Ph.D. dissertation, University of West Virginia, 1974.

Metropolitan Museum of Art. *Catalogue of the Crosby Brown Collection of Musical Instruments of All Nations.* 6 vols. New York: Metropolitan Museum of Art, 1901-07.

————. Department of Musical Instruments. *A Checklist of European Harps.* New York: Metropolitan Museum of Art, 1979.

————. Department of Musical Instruments. *A Checklist of Western European Fifes, Piccolos and Transverse Flutes.* New York: Metropolitan Museum of Art, 1977.

————. Department of Musical Instruments. *A Checklist of Western European Flageolets, Recorders and Tabor Pipes.* New York: Metropolitan Museum of Art, 1976.

Miller, Dayton C. *The Bibliography of the Flute.* Cleveland, Ohio: By the Author, 1935.

Dayton C. Miller Flute Collection: A Checklist of the Instruments. Compiled by Laura E. Gilliam and William Lichtenwanger. Washington, D.C.: Library of Congress, 1961.

Shrine to Music Museum. *Catalog of the Collections.* Vermillion, S.D.: University of South Dakota, 1980. Vol 1: *Keyed Brass Instruments*, by Gary Stewart.

Smithsonian Institution. Division of Musical Instruments. "A Checklist of Banjos." Compiled by Scott Odell. (Typewritten.)

————. Division of Musical Instruments. *A Checklist of Keyboard Instruments at the Smithsonian Institution.* 2nd ed. Washington, D.C.: Smithsonian Press, 1975.

Skinner, William., comp. *The Belle Skinner Collection of Old Musical Instruments: A Descriptive Catalogue.* Holyoke, Mass.: By the Author, 1933.

Smith, Bruce M. "Two-Hundred Forty-One European Chordophones in the Stearns Collection of Musical Instruments." 3 vols. Ph.D. dissertation, University of Michigan, 1977.

Stanley, Albert A. *Catalogue of the Stearns Collection of Musical Instruments.* Ann Arbor: University of Michigan, 1918.

Victoria & Albert Museum. *Catalogue of Musical Instruments.* 2 vols. London: Her Majesty's Stationery Office, 1968. Vol. 1: *Keyboard Instruments*, by Raymond Russell. Vol. 2: *Non-Keyboard Instruments*, by Anthony Baines.

————. *Eighteenth Century Musical Instruments: England and France.* Prepared by G. Thibault, Hean Jenkins and Josiane Bran-Ricci. London: Thanet Press, 1973.

Yale Collection of Musical Instruments. *Checklist.* New Haven, Conn.: Yale University, 1968.

CITY DIRECTORIES

1786. *The New-York Directory.* By David Franks. New York: Shepard Kollock, 1786; reprint ed. New York: John Doggett, Jr., 1851.

1787. ————. By David Franks. New York: Shepard Kollock, 1787.

1788. No directory published for 1788.

1789. *The New-York Directory, and Register, For the Year 1789.* New York: Hodge, Allen, and Campbell, 1789.

1790. ————. By William Duncan. New York: T. & J. Swords, 1791.

1791. ————. By William Duncan. 1792.

1793. ————. By William Duncan. 1793.

1794. ————. By William Duncan. 1794

1795. ————. By William Duncan. 1795

1796. ————. By John Low. New York: John Buel & John Bull, 1796.

1796. *The American Almanack, New-York Register, and City Directory, For the Twenty-first Year of American Independence.* By David Longworth. New York: T. & J.. Swords, 1796.

1797. *Longworth's American Almanack, New-York Register, and City Directory, For the Twenty-second Year of American Independence.* New York: T. & J. Swords, 1797.

1798. ————. 1798.

1799. ————. 1799.

1800. ————. New York: D. Longworth, 1800.

1801. ————. 1801

1802. ————. 1802

1803. _____. 1803

1804. _____. 1804.

1805. _____. 1805.

1806. _____. 1806.

1807. _____. 1807.

1808. _____. 1808

1809. _____. 1809.

1810. _____. 1810.

1811. _____. 1811.

1812. *Elliot's Improved New-York Double Directory.* New York: William Elliot, 1812.

1812. *Longworth's American Almanack, New-York Register, and City Directory.* By David Longworth. New York: D. Longworth, 1812.

1813. _____. 1813.

1814. _____. 1814.

1815. _____. 1815.

1816. _____. 1816.

1817. _____. 1817.

1818. _____. New York: Thomas Longworth, 1818.

1819. _____. New York: Jona Olmstead, 1819.

1820. _____. New York: Thomas Longworth, 1820.

1821. _____. 1821.

1822. _____. 1822.

1823. _____. 1823.

1824. _____. 1824.

1825. _____. 1825.

1826. _____. 1826.

1827. _____. 1827.

1828. _____. 1828.

1829. _____. 1829.

1830. _____. 1830.

1831. _____. 1831.

1832. _____. 1832.

1833. _____. 1833.

1834. _____. 1834.

1835. _____. 1835.

1836. _____. 1836.

1837. *The Classified Mercantile Directory, for the Cities of New-York and Brooklyn.* New York: J. Disturnell, 1837.

1837. *Longworth's American Almanack, New-York Register, and City Directory, For the Sixty-second Year of American Independence.* By Thomas Longworth. New York: Thomas Longworth, 1837.

1838. _____. 1838.

1839. _____. 1839.

1840. _____. 1840.

1841. _____. 1841.

1842. _____. New York: T. Longworth & Son, 1842.

1842. *[Doggett's] New York City Directory for 1842 and 1843.* New York: John Doggett, Jr., 1842.

1843. *The New-York City and Co-Partnership Directory for 1843 and 1844.* New York: John Doggett, Jr., 1843.

1844. *The New-York City Directory for 1844 and 1845.* New York: John Doggett, Jr., 1844.

1844. *The New-York Business Directory for 1844 and 1845.* New York: John Doggett, Jr., 1844.

1845. *Doggett's New-York City Directory for 1845 and 1846.* New York: John Doggett, Jr., 1845.

1846. _____. 1846.

1847. _____. 1847.

1848. _____. 1848.

1849. _____. New York: John Doggett, Jr., & Co., 1849.

1850. _____. New York: John Doggett, Jr., 1850.

1851. *The New York City Directory for 1851-1852.* New York: Doggett & Rode, 1851.

1852. _____. New York: Charles R. Rode (Late Doggett & Rode), 1852.

1852. *The Directory of the City of New York for 1852-53.* Comp. by Henry Wilson. New York: John F. Trow, 1852.

1853. *Trow's New-York City Directory for 1853-54.* Comp. by H. Wilson. New York: John F. Trow, 1853.

1853. *The New York City Directory for 1854-1855.* New York: Charles R. Rode, 1853.

1854. *Trow's New-York City Directory for 1854- 1855.* Comp. by H. Wilson. New York: John F. Trow, 1854.

1855. *Trow's New-York City Directory for the Year Ending May 1, 1856.* Comp. by H. Wilson. New York: John F. Trow, 1855.

1856. *Trow's New-York City Directory for the Year Ending May 1, 1857; [with] Wilson's New-York Commercial Register to Accompany Trow's New-York City Directory for the Year Ending May 1, 1857.* New York: John F. Trow, 1856.

1857. _____. 1857.

1858. _____. 1858.

1859. _____. 1859.

1860. _____. 1860.

1861. _____. 1861.

1862. _____. 1862.

1863. _____. 1863.

1864. *Trow's New York City Directory for the Year Ending May 1, 1865; [and] New York City Commercial Register, Containing the Cards of the Principal Merchants, Manufacturers, & c., in the City and Vicinity Classified According to the Business forming a Business Directory of Reliable Parties in all the Various Branches.* Comp. by H. Wilson. New York: John F. Trow, 1864.

1865. _____. 1865.

1866. _____. 1866.

1867. _____. 1867.

1868. _____. 1868.

1869. _____. 1869.

1870. _____. 1870.

1871. _____. 1871.

1872. _____. New York: The Trow City Directory Co., 1872.

1873. _____. 1873.

1874. _____. 1874.

1875. _____. 1875.

1876. _____. 1876.

1877. *Goulding's New York City Directory for 1876-1877.* New York: Lawrence G. Gouldings, 1877.

1877. *Trow's New York City Directory for the Year Ending May 1, 1878; [and] New York City Commercial Register.* New York: The Trow City Directory Co., 1877.

1878. _____. 1878.

1879. _____. 1879.

1880. _____. 1880.

1881. _____. 1881.

1882. _____. 1882.

1883. _____. 1883.

1884. _____. 1884.

1885. _____. 1885.

1886. _____. 1886.

1887. _____. 1887.

1888. _____. 1888.

1889. _____. 1889.

1890. _____. 1890.

1891. _____. 1891.

MAGAZINES, JOURNALS AND PERIODICALS

American Historical Review, 1950.

American Musical Journal, 1834-35.

Bicentennial Tracker, 1976.

Chronicle of Early American Industries, 1953.

Das Musikinstrument (Frankfurt), 1974.

Decorator, The, 1973.

Galpin Society Journal, 1963, 1970.

Good Furniture, 1917.

Journal of the American Institute of the City of New York, 1835-39.

Journal of the American Musical Instrument Society, 1976-87.

Journal of the Violin Society of America, 1976.

Labor History, 1974.

Leslie's Illustrated Weekly Newspaper, 1860, 1864.

Magazine of Art, The, 1901.

Mechanics' Magazine and Register of Inventions and Improvements, 1833.

Music Trade Indicator, 1885-90.

Music Trade Review for the General Music Merchant, 1880-90.

Musical and Dramatic Times and The Music Trade Review, 1875-79.

Musical Trades, 1903.

New York History, 1976.

New-York Historical Society Quarterly, 1935, 1978- 79.

Piano and Organ Purchaser's Guide, 1880-90.

Old Time New England, 1978.

William and Mary Quarterly, 1979.

NEWSPAPERS

Albion [N.Y.], 1850.

American Citizen and General Advertiser [N.Y.], 1800-1802.

The Argus [N.Y.], 1795-1800.

Argus & Greenleaf's New Daily Advertiser [N.Y.], 1795-1800.

Commercial Advertiser [N.Y.], 1838.

Daily Advertiser [N.Y.], 1788-97.

Diary [N.Y.], 1797.

Diary; or Evening Register [N.Y.], 1794.

Diary; or Loudon's Register [N.Y.], 1797.

Evening Post [N.Y.], 1801-35.

Independent Journal; or, the General Advertiser [N.Y.], 1785.

Mercantile Advertiser [N.Y.], 1801.

Morning Chronicle [N.Y.], 1803.

New-York Daily Advertiser, 1795.

New-York Daily Gazette, 1761.

New-York Gazette and General Advertiser, 1799.

New-York Gazette, and the Weekly Mercury, 1770- 74.

New-York Gazette, or the Weekly Post Boy, 1768.

New York Herald, 1853-73.

New-York Journal; or General Advertiser, 1775.

New York Mercury, 1756, 1767.

New York Packet, 1787.

New York Tribune, 1854-69.

New York Spectator, 1856.

New York Times, 1875-90.

Rivington's New-York Gazette, 1773.

Spectator [N.Y.], 1800.

The Sun [N.Y.], 1894.